# Dachau and the SS

## *A Schooling in Violence*

CHRISTOPHER DILLON

**OXFORD**
UNIVERSITY PRESS

# OXFORD
UNIVERSITY PRESS

Great Clarendon Street, Oxford, OX2 6DP,
United Kingdom

Oxford University Press is a department of the University of Oxford.
It furthers the University's objective of excellence in research, scholarship,
and education by publishing worldwide. Oxford is a registered trade mark of
Oxford University Press in the UK and in certain other countries

First published 2015
First published in paperback 2016

Published in the United States of America by Oxford University Press
198 Madison Avenue, New York, NY 10016, United States of America

British Library Cataloguing in Publication Data
Data available

Library of Congress Cataloging in Publication Data
Data available

ISBN 978–0–19–965652–3 (Hbk.)
ISBN 978–0–19–879452–3 (Pbk.)

# Acknowledgements

It is a rare pleasure, given the dispiriting topic, to be able to thank all those who have contributed to this book. It began life in a collaborative research project 'Before the Holocaust: Concentration Camps in Nazi Germany, 1933–1939', generously funded by the Arts and Humanities Research Council and directed by my esteemed doctoral supervisor at Birkbeck College, Professor Nikolaus Wachsmann. Whatever merits it possesses have been immeasurably enhanced by this experience of collegiate research and intellectual collaboration. My debt to my fellow research students on the project, Julia Hörath, Paul Moore, and Kim Wünschmann, for eight years of unflagging support and debate is incalculable. My profound thanks also to the project's postdoctoral researcher, Dr Christian Goeschel, for his personal encouragement and unfailingly acute and constructive criticism.

I am very grateful to my doctoral thesis examiners, Professors Jane Caplan and Richard Overy, for an unyielding, stimulating, and highly productive viva which has driven the direction of the monograph ever since. Back in the earliest stages of my development as a historian, Andrew Thorpe at Exeter and Rod Kedward at Sussex were inspiring and indefatigable mentors. Sean Brady, Robert Dale, Maria Fritsche, Julia Hörath, Mark Jones, Clare Makepeace, Paul Moore, Esther von Richthofen, and Kim Wünschmann have all offered insightful and constructive feedback at various stages of the book's development. I am also grateful here to the anonymous readers for Oxford University Press, all of whom helped greatly to improve its structure and precision.

The ideas in the book have benefitted from discussion at academic seminars and conferences too numerous to list, but I would particularly like to thank the convenors and audiences at the Modern German History Seminar at the London Institute for Historical Research, the Eleventh Biennial Lessons and Legacies Conference on the Holocaust, and the 15th Workshop zur Geschichte der nationalsozialistischen Konzentrationslager. The German History Society generously provided research funding at a critical point in 2011.

During the writing of the book, I have received help and guidance from many libraries in Germany and Britain. The German Historical Institute in London has afforded me the opportunity to present my work at many workshops and conferences, while its library and unfailingly helpful staff have been a constant in the development of the project. I would also like to record my particular gratitude to the staff of the Bundesarchiv in Berlin, the Staatsarchiv and Hauptstaatsarchiv in Munich, and the Memorial site archive at Dachau. I must single out Albert Knoll at Dachau, and Robert Bierschneider at the Staatsarchiv, in recognition of their forensic expertise and seemingly inexhaustible patience.

It is also a great pleasure to thank my students at various University of London colleges for countless hours of discussion and debate which have done much to shape my thinking about modern German and European history. Finally, to my family and friends—who do not, mercifully, share my preoccupation with this history—countless thanks for your patience and forebearance.

C. D.

# Contents

# List of Figures

# List of Tables

# List of Abbreviations

| | |
|---|---|
| BAB | Bundesarchiv, Berlin |
| BayHSta | Bayerisches Hauptstaatsarchiv |
| BDC | Berlin Document Center |
| BVP | Bayerische Volkspartei (Bavarian Peoples' Party) |
| DaA | Archiv der KZ-Gedenkstätte Dachau |
| Gestapo | Geheime Staatspolizei (lit. State Secret Police) |
| IfZ | Institut für Zeitgeschichte, Munich |
| IKL | Inspektion der Konzentrationslager (Concentration Camp Inspectorate) |
| IMT | International Military Tribunal, Nuremberg |
| KPD | Kommunistische Partei Deutschlands (German Communist Party) |
| NSDAP | Nationalsozialistische Deutsche Arbeiterpartei (National Socialist German Workers' Party) |
| RuSHA | Rasse- und Siedlungshauptamt (Race and Settlement Main Office) |
| POW | Prisoner of War |
| RSHA | Reichssicherheitshauptamt (Reich Security Main Office) |
| SA | Sturmabteilung (Storm Troopers) |
| SAM | Staatsarchiv Munich |
| SD | Sicherheitsdienst (Security Service) |
| SOPADE | Deutschland-Berichte der Sozialdemokratischen Partei Deutschlands |
| SPD | Sozialdemokratische Partei Deutschlands (German Social Democratic Party) |
| SPE | Stanford Prison Experiment |
| SS | Schutzstaffel (lit. Protection Squad) |
| USPD | Unabhängige Sozialdemokratische Partei Deutschlands (Independent German Social Democratic Party) |
| WL | Wiener Library, London |

# Introduction

'*I went to Dachau*'. When Rudolf Höβ wrote these words in a Kraków prison cell in 1947 he knew that he would hang.[1] The former commandant of Auschwitz had been captured by the British Military Police and handed over to the Polish authorities for trial. He blamed his decision to volunteer for the guard units at Dachau in 1934 for setting him on an 'intricate course' of 'destiny' which led him to become one of the great mass murderers in history.[2] This was untrue. But Höβ was certainly only one of many senior concentration camp officials to have learned his craft in pre-war Dachau. Dachau had been the most important of the early concentration camps, a bastion of the Nazi revolution and the sole bridge between this early violence and the vast citadels of terror constructed in the late 1930s. It was the training ground and forge of the concentration camp SS, an academy of violence where guards were schooled in steely resolution and the techniques of terror. An international symbol of Nazi depredation, Dachau was the cradle of a new and terrible spirit of destruction.

This book offers the first systematic study of the pre-war Dachau SS. It is not a narrow organizational history and seeks to contextualize the 'Dachau School' by approaching it from a variety of perspectives. It charts the depths of individual and collective conduct in an institutional setting while encouraging the reader to suspend comforting preconceptions that violent behaviours are simply products of pathological personalities and beliefs. Without losing sight of the specificities of Dachau, it claims a significance even beyond the thousands of SS guards trained there: for the pre-history of the Holocaust, and for the social and institutional organization of violence more broadly. Contrary to an ongoing tendency to mystify the Nazi concentration camps and to sequester them from broader historical processes, Dachau was the product of human interaction and its guards amenable to analysis as social phenomena.[3]

---

[1] Rudolf Höβ, *Commandant of Auschwitz: The Autobiography of Rudolf Hoess*, trans. Constantine FitzGibbon (London, 2000 [1959]), p. 65. Emphasis in original.

[2] Höβ, *Commandant*, p. 64.

[3] For the international context, see the recent succinct analysis by Richard Overy, 'Das Konzentrationslager: Eine internationale Perspektive', *Mittelweg*, Vol. 36, No. 4 (2011), pp. 40–5. Available in English translation at <http://www.eurozine.com/articles/2011-08-25-overy-en.html> (accessed 14 February 2014). For the social dimension, see the discussion of literature below, especially Wolfgang Sofsky, *The Order of Terror: The Concentration Camp* (Princeton, 1997), pp. 3–15.

The book brings together two streams of research into the history of National Socialism which have moved towards the centre of the historiographical agenda in recent years. The first is research into the history of the pre-war concentration camps. Surprisingly, there is still no comprehensive monograph on Dachau. Like the other pre-war camps, its history has been written instead by former German and Austrian political prisoners and is commemorative, rather than analytical, in intent. Quite understandably, these authors (and their readers) were concerned with documenting and memorializing the suffering of their comrades in the camps rather than with analytical reflection on their historical context. If they wrote about the guards at all, it was as either atavistic brutes or epiphenomenal figures, secondary expressions of an underlying 'fascist' ideology.[4]

During the 1980s impulses to fresh research beyond the canonized texts of former inmates came from the German 'history workshop' movement. Younger research-ers, often affiliated with concentration camp memorial sites, gathered documents and oral histories from the localities of concentration camps. These have greatly enriched our understanding of their social context. They also began the process of rendering visible the experiences of non-political inmate groups hitherto marginal-ized in 'anti-fascist' literature. And in the last decade or so a range of empirical stud-ies on the domestic concentration camps, coordinated by the memorial sites and their heads (frequently trained historians themselves), has picked up the baton from the history workshop movement. A range of encyclopaedic treatments of individual camps is now available in German, along with a massive encyclopaedia in English published recently by the United States Holocaust Memorial Museum.[5] Yet it is striking how rarely the SS personnel are discrete topics even in this literature, falling as they do beyond what remains a largely commemorative exercise.

The second stream of research is the burgeoning historiography of those who have become known as National Socialist 'perpetrators' (*Täter*), the agents of per-secution and violence who enacted the policies of the regime at ground level. These men and women were long marginalized by a universalizing historiographical dis-course which, since the 1960s, had privileged the role of supra-personal structures in the criminality of the Third Reich.[6] Höß played something of a posthumous role here as the pioneering text was Martin Broszat's introduction to the German

[4] The most recent contribution to this distinguished line of writing on Dachau is Stanislav Zámečník, *That Was Dachau: 1933–1945* (Paris, 2004). Although the book is described in the blurb as a 'complete, scholarly presentation of the history of the Dachau concentration camp' it has very little to say about the SS. Similar caveats apply to Hans-Günter Richardi, *Schule der Gewalt: Das Konzentrationslager Dachau 1933–1934* (Munich, 1933), a well-researched yet commemorative com-pendium of prisoner memoirs.

[5] Wolfgang Benz and Barbara Distel (eds), *Der Ort des Terrors: Geschichte der nationalsozialistischen Konzentrationslager* (8 vols, Munich, 2005–2009); *The United States Holocaust Memorial Museum Encyclopaedia of Camps and Ghettos, 1933–1945* (2 vols, Washington, DC, 2009–2012).

[6] A. D. Moses, 'Structure and Agency in the Holocaust: Daniel J. Goldhagen and his Critics', *History and Theory*, Vol. 37, No. 2 (May, 1998), pp. 194–219. Moses uses the ancient philosophical binary of the particular and universal to code, respectively, dispositional/ideological and situational/social readings of perpetrators. This taxonomy will also be used throughout the present study. For a penetrating bibliographical essay on *Tätergeschichte*, see also Gerhard Paul, 'Von Psychopathen, Technokraten des Terrors und "ganz gewöhnlichen" Deutschen. Die Täter der Shoah im Spiegel

edition of his memoirs in 1958. Broszat depicted Höß as a 'normal petit-bourgeois type' who 'always did his duty' to 'whichever authority' he recognized at the time.[7] This concept of the SS perpetrator's normality, a reaction in part to the immediate post-war tendency to demonize him, would guide scholarship for decades. Hannah Arendt offered a very similar reading in her account of the Israeli trial of Adolf Eichmann in 1961. Like Broszat, Arendt could find no 'demonic profundity', little evidence even of antisemitism, in the accused whom she presented instead as an unremarkable German bureaucrat: ambitious, anomic, unreflective, a lesson in the 'banality of evil'.[8] Arendt's intellectual prestige and sparkling, authoritative prose contributed to the fertile reception of *Eichmann in Jerusalem* but her conclusions echoed those of a then lesser-known German émigré. Raul Hilberg's monumental *The Destruction of the European Jews* likewise offered a universalist reading of the Nazi perpetrator as a detached, coldly careerist Everyman.[9] Values and ideology featured in this universe less as motivation than cynical rationalization. In Hilberg's guiding metaphor, the Holocaust was the culmination of an unbound, self-propelled 'machinery of destruction' requiring no great personal malice from most participants: 'all necessary operations were accomplished with whatever personnel were at hand'.[10]

In the resurgent field of social psychology, too, consensus formed on the universal human readiness to inflict suffering. In the early 1960s Stanley Milgram carried out a series of laboratory experiments on the evolutionary tendency towards 'obedience to authority'. His hypothesis that cruelty was a social phenomenon driven by situational power relationships seemed confirmed when two-thirds of his ordinary American volunteers administered what they believed were electric shocks of up to 450 volts on his accomplice learner, despite his screams of pain and complaint of a heart condition.[11] The analogies to concentration camp personnel were evident and Milgram did not refrain from ambitious extrapolations from his laboratory. The Holocaust, he proposed, was 'the most extreme instance of abhorrent immoral acts carried out by thousands of people in the name of obedience'.[12] He later added that if a system of concentration camps were set up in the United States, sufficient personnel to staff them could be found 'in any medium-sized American town'.[13]

der Forschung', in Paul (ed.), *Die Täter der Shoah: Fanatische Nationalsozialisten oder ganz normale Deutsche?* (Göttingen, 2002), pp. 13–90. Specifically on the SS, see the literature review by Jan Erik Schulte, 'Zur Geschichte der SS: Erzähltraditionen und Forschungsstand', in Schulte (ed.), *Die SS, Himmler und die Wewelsburg* (Paderborn, 2009), pp. xi–xxxv.

[7] Martin Broszat, 'Einleitung', in Broszat (ed.), *Rudolf Höß: Kommandant in Auschwitz. Autobiografische Aufzeichnungen* (Munich, 1963 [1958]), s. 11.
[8] Hannah Arendt, *Eichmann in Jerusalem: A Report into the Banality of Evil* (New York, 1994 [1963]), p. 287.
[9] Raul Hilberg, *The Destruction of the European Jews* (London, 1983). Hilberg's book was first published in 1961.
[10] Hilberg, *Destruction*, p. 649.
[11] Stanley Milgram, *Obedience to Authority* (London, 2005 [1974]), pp. 33–56.
[12] Milgram, *Obedience*, p. 4.
[13] In Thomas Blass, *Obedience to Authority. Current Perspectives on the Milgram Paradigm* (New Jersey, 1985), pp. 35–6.

Similarly unequivocal conclusions were reached by his colleague, Philip Zimbardo, in the Stanford Prison Experiment of 1971.[14] We will return to the details and implications of these experiments later in the book; for now it is sufficient to note that their explicit linkage to the Holocaust and to Arendt's work in particular helped to create a universal interpretive paradigm of Nazi perpetrators which, according to David Cesarani's biography of Eichmann, 'straitjacketed research into Nazi Germany and the persecution of the Jews for two decades'.[15] Cesarani debits Milgram personally with the interpretation of the Holocaust as 'the zenith of modern bureaucracy, rather than a throwback to barbarism' but this is reductive.[16] The pre-eminence of the abstract bureaucratic trope in this period also reflected the talents of a cohort of young structuralist historians at the Munich Institute for Contemporary History. They produced what remains one of the finest analyses of the SS and concentration camp system, *Anatomy of the SS State*, as expert consultants to the Frankfurt trial of Auschwitz personnel in 1963. A masterly and judicious reconstruction of the bureaucratic chain of command in the SS, this was nonetheless a distinctly arid and impersonal history.[17]

A number of important later works also stand in this universalist tradition. Zygmunt Bauman's *Modernity and the Holocaust* casts Nazi perpetrators as 'men in uniforms, obedient and disciplined, following the rules and meticulous about the spirit and letter of their briefing'.[18] Calls for a more dispositional, ideological reading are accused of seeking a 'metaphysical prop', where '[d]iscussion of guilt masquerades as the analysis of causes'.[19] Wolfgang Sofsky, in a bold and compelling sociology of the concentration camps, concurred. 'Institutional terror', he concluded, 'produces perpetrators who do without reasons for their actions . . . the identity of the victim was totally immaterial'.[20] There is a lot at stake in this debate and the heavy burden of explanation generates partisan positions framed in aggrieved moral vocabulary. Historians too often adopt a posture of embattled empiricism when dealing with situational theorists like Bauman and Sofsky, as isolated voices of sensitivity amid a deluge of relativizing social science.[21] Seldom do they trouble to engage with the broader argument about the contribution of social

[14] Philip Zimbardo, *The Lucifer Effect: How Good People Turn Evil* (London, 2007).
[15] David Cesarani, *Eichmann: His Life and Crimes* (London, 2004), p. 15.
[16] Cesarani, *Eichmann*, p. 15.
[17] Helmut Krausnick et al., *Anatomy of the SS State*, trans. Richard Barry et al. (London, 1968). A lively, morally aggrieved critique of this type of 'structural' literature is offered by Nicolas Berg, *Der Holocaust und die westdeutschen Historiker: Erfahrung und Erinnerung* (Göttingen, 2004).
[18] Zygmunt Bauman, *Modernity and the Holocaust* (Cambridge, 2000 [1989]), p. 151.
[19] Bauman, *Modernity*, pp. xi, 168.   [20] Sofsky, *Order*, p. 229.
[21] In addition to Cesarani, see Michael Burleigh and Wolfgang Wippermann, *The Racial State: Germany 1933–1945* (Cambridge, 1991), p. 2 and passim; Karin Orth and Michael Wildt, 'Die Ordnung der Lager: Über offene Fragen und frühe Antworten in der Forschung zu Konzentrationslager', *Werkstatt-Geschichte*, Band 12 (1995), pp. 51–6; Andrea Riedle, *Die Angehörigen des Kommandanturstabs im KZ Sachsenhausen: Sozialstruktur, Dienstwege und biografischen Studien* (Berlin, 2011), p. 19; Karin Orth, *Die Konzentrationslager SS: Sozialstrukturelle Analysen und biographische Studien* (Munich, 2004), p. 11, 297; Falk Pingel, 'Social Life in an Unsocial Environment: The Inmates' Struggle for Survival', in Jane Caplan and Nikolaus Wachsmann (eds), *Concentration Camps in Nazi Germany: The New Histories* (London and New York, 2010), pp. 58–81, here p. 59; Omer Bartov, *Germany's War and the Holocaust. Disputed Histories* (USA, 2003), pp. 99–111. As the fiery

factors to Nazi violence. Yet as the recent scholarship of James Waller and Harald Welzer makes clear, registering these phenomena is essential to any convincing account of perpetrator behaviour.[22] Both, like Milgram, stress the fundamental importance of the perpetrators' situation but also of how they construe this situation in the first place: an important moderation of extreme role-based accounts. Both also stress the complex and reciprocal relationship between thought and deed which will be seen throughout this book.

The most powerful case study in Welzer's comparative analysis is of the police battalions (units of the Order Police) seconded to the SS in occupied Poland.[23] Their murderous conduct during the Holocaust had already generated the best-known controversy in perpetrator historiography. Christopher Browning's *Ordinary Men*, a microstudy of one such unit of unremarkable middle-aged policemen, was published in 1992 and documented the role of peer pressure and group psychology in their conduct.[24] While some aspects of his analysis—the fact that these subjects were policemen, and the fact that they were men—are clearly underplayed, *Ordinary Men* is a classic of interpretive historical narration. The same could not be said of its antagonist, Daniel Goldhagen's *Hitler's Willing Executioners*.[25] Warming up the self-righteous, exoticist tenets of Allied wartime propaganda, Goldhagen argued that German society harboured proto-genocidal intent long before Hitler. Nazi perpetrators did not need to be induced to kill: they murdered Jews because they were 'Germans first, and SS men, policemen, or camp guards second'.[26] Goldhagen regards more universalist readings of the perpetrators as morally compromised in diminishing their personal responsibility and relativizing the singular horror of the Final Solution. He was quite right to demand greater focus on the Jewish identity of its victims. Yet among its many shortcomings, Goldhagen's book offers no explanation for the avid involvement of tens of thousands of non-Germans in the Holocaust, nor for the abrupt disappearance of the German tradition of murderous antisemitism after 1945. The latter he attributes, in a pair of footnotes,[27] to an efficacious post-war Allied re-education programme, whilst disregarding the possible impact of propaganda and schooling by the Nazis during the Third Reich.[28]

introductions to *Modernity and the Holocaust* and *The Order of Terror* show, this sense of grievance is mirrored on the other side of the disciplinary divide.

[22] James Waller, *Becoming Evil: How Ordinary People Commit Genocide and Mass Killing* (2007); Harald Welzer, *Täter: wie aus ganz normalen Menschen Massenmörder werden* (Frankfurt am Main, 2005) and, to a lesser extent, Sönke Neitzel and Harald Welzer, *Soldaten: On Fighting, Killing, and Dying* (London, 2012). I am not persuaded that the tapped and boastful conversations between these personnel offer as robust a basis for social psychological analysis (Welzer's contribution to the book) as the much broader fabric of sources and case studies in *Täter*.

[23] On the Order Police, see the dependable, if diffident, monograph by Edward B. Westermann, *Hitler's Police Battalions: Enforcing Racial War in the East* (Kansas, 2005).

[24] Christopher R. Browning, *Ordinary Men: Reserve Police Battalion 101 and the Final Solution in Poland* (London, 2001 [1992]).

[25] Daniel Jonah Goldhagen, *Hitler's Willing Executioners: Ordinary Germans and the Holocaust* (London, 1997).

[26] Goldhagen, *Executioners*, p. 7.

[27] Goldhagen, *Executioners*, p. 594, fn 38; p. 605, fn 53.

[28] See Browning's demolition of Goldhagen's argument in *Ordinary Men*, pp. 193–212.

Goldhagen was clearly wrong about 'the Germans', but might his arguments still apply to the SS? Contrary to his historiographical caricatures, a number of important works had already flagged the importance of ideological and dispositional factors. Tom Segev's pioneering group biography of concentration camp commandants stressed their fervent commitment to the Nazi cause and gradual inurement to atrocity through a 'process of inner hardening'.[29] Segev emphasized the personal leadership of Theodor Eicke, Dachau's second commandant and subsequently head of the camp network, as the driving force in the pre-war camps and father of the Dachau School. Most commandants had joined the National Socialist movement at a young age and Segev, an Israeli, encountered little contrition in his discussions with surviving perpetrators and their families.[30] Bernd Wegner's monograph on the Waffen SS, published in 1983, also located ideology in the perpetrators' foreground.[31] One of these SS combat formations, the Death's Head Division, was commanded by Eicke and formed around a core of sentries from the pre-war concentration camps. Wegner focused on the distinctive and unstable admixture of the modern and anti-modern in SS ideology. The SS man envisaged himself as a 'political soldier' primed to forge the Nazi new order with ruthless and steely ideological commitment: mere 'banal' obedience in his universe was inadequate.[32] Charles Sydnor's compelling monograph on the Death's Head Division took a similar line.[33] In Sydnor's narrative the men of the division, much like the commandants investigated by Segev, were ideological warriors brutalized by service in the camps whose trail of racial murder throughout Europe is inexplicable in universal, situational terms.

Historical research into concentration camp personnel has been rejuvenated in the last decade by Karin Orth's study of its leadership corps. The book emerged under the auspices of a project on generation and ideology which has generated some outstanding scholarship on the SS.[34] The 200 senior camp officials analysed by Orth saw themselves as heroic figures battling at an 'inner front'.[35] While their inner camp world reflected the group dynamics explored by universalist literature, Orth also contributes to the process of ideologizing the perpetrators. This was a group of lower-middle class men deeply imprinted with the social and economic crises of the Weimar Republic. They had committed early to the Nazi movement and their murderous tenure in the camps reflected political conviction as much as brutalization and environment.[36] Four recent German monographs, building

---

[29] Tom Segev, *Soldiers of Evil: The Commandants of the Nazi Concentration Camps* (Glasgow, 2000), p. 272.

[30] Segev, *Soldiers*, p. 7.

[31] Bernd Wegner, *The Waffen SS: Organisation, Ideology and Function* (Oxford, 1990 [1983]).

[32] Wegner, *Waffen SS*, pp. 27–33.

[33] Charles W. Sydnor, *Soldiers of Destruction: The SS Death's Head Division 1933–1945* (Princeton, 1990 [1977]).

[34] Ulrich Herbert, *Best: Studien über Radikalismus, Weltanschauung und Vernunft 1903–1989* (Bonn, 1996); Isabel Heinemann, '*Rasse, Siedlung, deutsches Blut'. Das Rasse- und Siedlungshauptamt der SS und die rassenpolitische Neuordnung Europas* (Göttingen, 2003); Orth, *Konzentrationslager SS*; Michael Wildt, *An Unconditional Generation: The Nazi Leadership of the Reich Security Main Office* (Wisconsin, 2009).

[35] Orth, *Konzentrationslager SS*, p. 11.      [36] Orth, *Konzentrationslager SS*, p. 88–9.

on Orth's work and taking different approaches, have explored the perpetrators of individual camps. Hans-Peter Klausch chronicles the commandants of the early SS camps in the Emsland in five richly detailed biographies.[37] Although stronger on biographical minutiae than explanation, Klausch makes a convincing case for the centrality of visceral anticommunism, rather than Nazi eugenic and racial precepts, to the self-understanding and motivation of these men.[38] A biographical approach also guides Andrea Riedle's immaculately researched monograph on the commandant staff personnel of Sachsenhausen. The great merit of the book is its rigorous and detailed quantitative analysis of their backgrounds as well as the patterns of promotion to the officer corps.[39] Yet Riedle has little to say on the social and cultural factors shaping the collective ethos at Sachsenhausen. These aspects are explored in detail by Elissa Mailänder Koslov's acclaimed study of the female guard personnel at Majdanek concentration camp.[40] Drawing primarily on postwar judicial proceedings, Koslov focuses on the entwined contributions of gender, power, and performance to the terror in Majdanek. Women were not admitted as members to the masculine SS but many of Koslov's subjects were not outshone in violence and terror by their male counterparts.[41] Marc Buggeln's equally impressive monograph on the wartime satellite camps of Neuengamme is also informed by a social and cultural methodology.[42] Buggeln stresses the importance of universalist factors such as role and situation in the perpetrators' propensity for violence. But, drawing on Pierre Bourdieu's work, he also shows that role and situation are dynamic rather than static, constantly constructed and constituted by their protagonists.[43]

The present book also supports an 'interactionist' analysis, the proposition that culture, cognition, and situation interact in perpetrator behaviour.[44] Like the monographs discussed above, it is somewhat constrained by the available source material. The concentration camp SS were careful to destroy most of their files towards the end of the war with the approach of the Allied armies.[45] The Dachau SS seem to have been particularly diligent in this regard and very few commandant

---

[37] Hans-Peter Klausch, *Tätergeschichten: Die SS Kommandanten der frühen Konzentrationslager im Emsland* (Bremen, 2005).
[38] Klausch, *Tätergeschichten*, pp. 265–78.   [39] Riedle, *Angehörigen*, pp. 67–129.
[40] Elissa Mailänder Koslov, *Gewalt im Dienstalltag: Die SS-Aufseherinnen des Konzentrations- und Vernichtungslagers Majdanek* (Hamburg, 2009).
[41] On female guards, see also the absorbing collection of essays edited by Simone Eberle. Simone Eberle (ed.), *Im Gefolge der SS: Aufseherinnen des Frauen-KZ Ravensbrück* (Berlin, 2007).
[42] Marc Buggeln, *Arbeit und Gewalt: Das Außenlagersystem des KZ Neuengamme* (Göttingen, 2009).
[43] Buggeln, *Arbeit*, pp. 19–21.
[44] Interactionism is associated above all with the social psychologist Thomas Blass. See for example Thomas Blass, 'Understanding Behavior in the Milgram Obedience Experiment: The Role of Personality, Situations, and their Interactions', *Journal of Personality and Social Psychology*, Vol. 60 (1991), pp. 398–413; Thomas Blass, 'Psychological Perspectives on the Perpetrators of the Holocaust: The Role of Situational Pressures, Personal Dispositions, and their Interactions', *Holocaust and Genocide Studies*, Vol. 7, No. 1 (1993), pp. 30–50. See also the judicious comments in Robert J. Lifton, *The Nazi Doctors: Medical Killing and the Psychology of Genocide* (New York, 1986), p. 468.
[45] Johannes Tuchel, *Konzentrationslager: Organisationsgeschichte und Funktion der 'Inspektion der Konzentrationslager 1934–1938* (Boppard, 1991), p. 27. Tuchel's monograph offers an excellent organizational history of Eicke's Concentration Camp Inspectorate.

staff circulars (*Kommandanturbefehle*), for example, a source compiled into an invaluable documentary collection for Auschwitz, survive from Dachau.[46] 'Ego documents' by concentration camp personnel, such as Höß's memoirs, are also few and far between. Other sources, fortunately, are relatively abundant. Although the judicial testimony of former camp guards is frequently sullen and mendacious, it can sometimes prove very illuminating. For Dachau the historian has cause to thank the conspicuous purpose and tenacity of the post-war investigation led by the Munich coroner Dr Nikolaus Naaff. His team focused primarily on the early years of the camp, picking up documentary threads left by their thwarted judicial predecessors in 1934. This resource, comprising some 140 criminal investigations, has barely been used by historians.[47] The US-led Dachau Trials, too, although restricted juridically to crimes committed against Allied personnel after 1941, gathered testimony from pre-war guards and inmates.

Published prisoner memoirs from the period of the Dachau School are also plentiful as the majority of its inmates were political prisoners, the group most likely to record its experiences in the camp. To these can be added hundreds of unpublished testimonies held in the Dachau memorial site archive, the Munich Staatsarchiv, the Institute for Contemporary History, and the Wiener Library. The great majority were written shortly after the liberation of the camp and as such are less subject to the intrusion of extraneous and collective memory into the material. Of the memoirists who will accompany us throughout this book, special mention should be made of Paul Martin Neurath, Ludwig Schecher, Alfred Hübsch, Karl Röder, Hugo Burkhard, Hans Schwarz, and Alfred Laurence.[48] Their unfailing acuity and stubborn humanity has made its writing a good deal easier. Another illuminating and largely untapped source are SS personnel records held in the former Berlin Document Center collection at the Bundesarchiv. SS personnel files, although uneven in content, offer some intriguing case studies as well as the basis for quantitative analysis of guard personnel. The documentary record of the broader SS, including the evidence gathered for the Nuremberg Trials, is also extensive.

One thing most historians and former prisoners agree on is that concentration camp guards, contrary to popular assumptions, were seldom psychopaths:

[46] Norbert Frei et al. (eds), *Standort und Kommandanturbefehle des Konzentrationslagers Auschwitz 1940–1945* (Munich, 2000). Only for Stutthof are these orders available in comparable fullness.

[47] A recent exception is Rolf Seubert's combative essay on the early months in Dachau. Rolf Seubert, '"Mein lumpiges Vierteljahr Haft . . ." Alfred Anderschs KZ-Haft und die ersten Morde von Dachau: Versuch einer historiografischen Rekonstruktion', in Jörg Dörig and Markus Joch (eds), *Alfred Andersch 'Revisited': Werkbiographische Studien im Zeichen der Sebald-Debatte* (Berlin, 2011), pp. 47–146.

[48] Paul Martin Neurath, *The Society of Terror: Inside the Dachau and Buchenwald Concentration Camps* (Colorado, 2005); Dachau Gedenkstätte (DaA), A1603, Karl Ludwig Schecher, 'Rückblick auf Dachau'; DaA, A1436, Alfred Hübsch, 'Die Insel des Standrechts'; DaA, A1960 Hans Schwarz, 'Wir Haben es nicht Gewusst. Erlebnisse, Erfahrung und Erkenntnisse aus dem Konzentrationslager Dachau'; Karl Röder, *Nachtwache: 10 Jahre KZ Dachau und Flossenbürg* (Wien, 1985); Hugo Burkhard, *Tanz Mal Jude! Von Dachau bis Shanghai. Meine Erlebnisse in den Konzentrationslagern Dachau—Buchenwald—Getto Shanghai 1933–1948* (Nuremberg, 1967); DaA Alfred Laurence, 'Dachau Overcome: The Story of a Concentration Camp Survivor'.

individuals with clinical, medical disorders. Psychopaths there doubtless were among these perpetrators but most memoir literature places them as a tiny minority of the personnel, no more than 5 to 10 per cent.[49] Individuals with clinical personality disorders are not easily deployed in military and paramilitary organizations, particularly in so confined an institution as a concentration camp. They do not follow routines or develop the requisite comradely values.[50] Instead, violent behaviours at Dachau were variously encouraged, instilled, and excavated from a heterogeneous body of mostly very young males. As Neurath puts it, the 'conditions under which these SS men were trained made the system independent of the available supply of psychopaths'.[51] This dispiriting and disarming truth informs the book to follow.

[49] See the insightful discussion in Tzvetan Todorov, *Facing the Extremes: Moral Life in the Concentration Camps* (1999), pp. 121–4. As Todorov observes, 'we cannot understand the evils of the concentration camps in terms of abnormality unless we define abnormality, tautologically, as the behavior in question'.
[50] Waller, *Becoming Evil*, pp. 73–5.      [51] Neurath, *Society*, p. 71.

# 1

# 'We'll Meet Again in Dachau': The Early Dachau SS

Erwin Kahn was certain there had been a mistake. A Jewish businessman from Munich, he was one of Dachau's first prisoners, taken into protective custody on the street by an SA man a few days previously and brought to the new concentration camp via Stadelheim prison. On 23 March 1933 he wrote a letter to his wife, Evi.[1] The camp was under the stewardship of the Bavarian State Police (*Landespolizei*) and he assured her she need not be unduly concerned; he was not a member of the German Communist Party (KPD) and was confident the misunderstanding would be cleared up when he was interrogated. The treatment and food were 'very good' and his cellmates 'mostly good sorts', some 'very pleasant'. Kahn was curious to see 'how long this business goes on' but also bored of waiting around and anxious to get back to his work. He asked Evi to send cigarettes, matches, and a newspaper with her next letter, along with some thick socks as the floor of his cell was cold. One week later Kahn wrote to her again. He was now, to his relief, working for six hours every day in the camp and determined to 'keep his chin up'. The detainees were now allowed to receive inspected parcels and he asked for toothpaste, butter, marmalade, *Streichwurst* (meat paste), plums, cake, hard-boiled eggs, and his pipe, the latter in view of rumours that the camp ban on smoking was to be lifted. His next letter, dated 5 April, remained guardedly optimistic that everything would be resolved as soon as the police got round to interrogating him. Evi's letters were a consolation amidst uncertainty and 'on the whole', he concluded, 'I can't really complain'.[2]

Twelve days later Erwin Kahn was dead, shot five times at point-blank range in woods near the camp on the mendacious grounds that he had been 'trying to escape'. He lay in Schwabing hospital for five days before succumbing to his wounds. Kahn was one of twelve protective custody prisoners murdered by the Dachau SS in just two months, under the very noses of the Bavarian State Police.

---

[1] Following from Staatsarchiv Munich (SAM), Staatsanwaltschaft (StA) 34479/2, Beglaubigte Abschrift Briefe Erwin Kahn, 16 February 1953. These files very seldom have page numbers, comprising instead brief paper transcripts of interrogations filed in date order: accordingly date only will be cited throughout.

[2] SAM, StA 34479/2, Beglaubigte Abschrift Briefe Erwin Kahn, 16 February 1953.

At least ten more met violent deaths by the end of 1933, confirming Dachau as the most lethal and feared concentration camp in the nascent Third Reich.[3] The SS, like the much larger SA, had been involved in the establishment of a still-unknown number of loci of extra-judicial confinement in the early weeks of the new regime.[4] Here, foes of National Socialism were kidnapped, terrorized, and beaten up, as its paramilitary formations used the advent of the Hitler government to settle local scores. On 27 February the torching of the Reichstag by a Dutch anarchist was seized on by the Nazis and conservatives in the Cabinet as an opportunity to launch a long dreamed of, more systematic crackdown on the political Left. The following day the regime promulgated a Decree for the Protection of People and State, whose suspension of personal liberties became the foundation of protective custody and, indeed, 'the constitutional charter of the Third Reich'.[5] Concentration camps soon sprang up throughout Germany to detain tens of thousands of political opponents: real and, as with Erwin Kahn, wholly imagined. Kahn was an early and poignant adherent to the 'fallacy of innocence' among Nazism's victims, one to be rehearsed untold times in the twelve years ahead.[6] On one level he may have been the victim of mistaken identity; on another, as a Bavarian Jew, he was laden, as will be seen, with historical perfidy in the eyes of the Dachau concentration camp SS.

Dachau, which lay 18 km to the north-west of Munich, was the most enduring and important of the early Nazi camps. It was the first state camp run solely by the SS, announced at a press conference by acting Munich Police President and *Reichsführer* of the SS Heinrich Himmler.[7] It was a prototype for subsequent concentration camps, a national school of violence for camp personnel, and a linguistic shorthand for the nameless horrors waiting beyond barbed wire throughout the Third Reich. A cautionary verse was soon in popular circulation:

> Please oh Lord, make me dumb
> So I won't to Dachau come.[8]

For Himmler and the SS, left largely empty handed in the wake of the 'seizure of power', Dachau was a laboratory of terror and an opportunity to prove its

---

[3] Slightly different figures appear in the literature in Dachau, and reflect the difficulty in some cases of ascertaining whether an inmate died in the camp, or on transports to and from it.

[4] Nikolaus Wachsmann, 'The Dynamics of Destruction: The Development of the Concentration Camps, 1933–1945', in Caplan and Wachsmann (eds), *Concentration Camps in Nazi Germany: The New Histories* (London and New York, 2010), pp. 18–20.

[5] Ernst Fränkel, *The Dual State: A Contribution to the Theory of Dictatorship* (New York, 1941), p. 3.

[6] George M. Kren and Leon Rappaport, *The Holocaust and the Crisis of Human Behaviour* (New York, 1980). As the authors argue, '[i]f individuals or groups cast in the role of victim are aware of being innocent—that is, that there is no rational basis for their status as victims—there follows an almost inevitable and fallacious conclusion. They can only assume that their oppression proceeds from a mistaken judgment or momentary lapse of rationality by their oppressor . . . It then follows that if this cause or fault in the oppressor can be understood ("Why do you mistake me for something I am not"?) it can be corrected, or at least moderated' (p. 74).

[7] For a taxonomy of the early camp types, see Tuchel, *Konzentrationslager: Organisationsgeschichte und Funktion der 'Inspektion der Konzentrationslager' 1934–1938* (Boppard, 1991), pp. 38–44.

[8] Sybille Steinbacher, *Dachau—Die Stadt und das Konzentrationslager in der NS-Zeit* (Frankfurt, 1993), p. 151.

credentials as the staunchest servant of the National Socialist state. The SS later went to considerable lengths to export what was known admiringly in its circles as the 'Dachau spirit' (*Dachauer Geist*) to other concentration camps.[9] Alumni of the early Dachau SS—defined here as those stationed at the camp at the time of its final handover from the State Police on 30 May 1933—were to rise far and wide in the SS camp network. Among the rank-and-file personnel of the early Dachau SS were three future concentration camp commandants: Richard Baer (Auschwitz), Max Koegel (Ravensbrück, Majdanek, and Flossenbürg), and Martin Weiß (Neuengamme, Majdanek, and Dachau), as well as six future heads of prisoner compounds (*Lagerführer*); Friedrich Ruppert (Dachau), Anton Thumann (Gross-Rosen and Neuengamme), Wolfgang Seuss (Natzweiler), and Franz Hössler, Vincenz Schöttl, and Johann Schwarzhuber (all Auschwitz). The remainder of the early Dachau SS were not to achieve such infamy, but comprised a professional corps of camp staff and aspirant political soldiers, many of whom exported techniques developed in Dachau throughout the Reich, and later occupied Europe.

The provenance of these first Dachau guards has not hitherto been explored by historians, although it has sometimes been claimed that a particularly brutal local Dachau *Sturm* (platoon) had already made a name for itself in the street-fighting years of the late Weimar Republic.[10] This is fiction; with just twenty members as late as 1932, Dachau's local SS was tiny and even the local NSDAP was very much a fringe player before 1933.[11] The source base for such matters is generally meagre as personnel files in Dachau and the Concentration Camp Inspectorate in Oranienburg were burned with the approach of the Allied armies in April 1945. Preserved in the records of the Bavarian State Police, however, is a largely intact list of the early Dachau SS personnel drawn up by the police as part of the handover documentation.[12] These 192 names offer a robust sample of the 264 men guarding 1,763 prisoners at this point (see Figure 1.1).[13] They were drawn almost entirely from *Standarten* of Group South of the Bavarian SS. A *Standarte*—the term derived from the Roman Standard, reflecting the influence of Italian fascism—denoted a paramilitary unit of up to 2,000 SS men linked to one of eighty regional headquarters.[14] Of these 192 men, seventy-five were drawn from *Standarte* Munich, sixty from *Standarte* Augsburg, the populous industrial city to Dachau's north-west, twenty-nine from Greater Munich, twenty-three from Landshut to the north-east,

[9] Carina Baganz, 'Dachau als Historischer Ort im System des Nationalsozialismus', in Wolfgang Benz and Angelika Königseder (eds), *Das Konzentrationslager Dachau: Geschichte und Wirkung Nationalsozialistischer Repression* (Berlin, 2008), pp. 31–42; Orth, *Konzentrationslager SS*, pp. 127–52. For greater detail see Chapters 2 and 3 of the present book.

[10] Shlomo Aronson, *The Beginnings of the Gestapo System: The Bavarian Model in 1933* (Jerusalem, 1969), pp. 20–1; Martin Gilbert, *The Holocaust: The Jewish Tragedy* (London, 1987), pp. 32–3.

[11] Steinbacher, *Dachau*, pp. 67–84.

[12] DaA, A 4118, Übergabe-Prokoll, 30 May 1933.

[13] Total SS and prisoner numbers from Klaus Drobisch and Günter Wieland, *System der NS-Konzentrationslager 1933–1939* (Berlin, 1993), pp. 51–2.

[14] Robert Koehl, *The Black Corps: The Structure and Power Struggles of the Nazi SS* (Winsconsin, 1983), p. 10.

**Figure 1.1** Early Dachau SS sentries, May 1933. Bundesarchiv, image 152-01-22.

with a handful of representatives from Nuremberg, Kolberg, Linz, and Vienna. Their occupations as noted by the police are largely lower-middle class, with sixty traditional working-class roles in heavy industry and unskilled agriculture, and the remainder in food production, sales, engineering, and artisanal codes.[15] Whilst the early SS was far from lacking in the rowdy, beery element associated with the more proletarian SA, a disciplined self-image and the occupational background of its personnel lent it a more bourgeois character.[16] Even if some of the early Dachau SS overstated their jobs, or gave learned rather than actual occupations, this is a measure of their social aspiration.

Their average age at the handover was 25.7. In contrast to the later, more youthful, profile of the SS in Dachau, these men are overwhelmingly within range of the 'war youth' generation of National Socialist perpetrators.[17] This subcohort of

[15] This accords with Detlef Mühlberger's analysis of the rank-and-file Bavarian SS between 1929 and 1933, which identifies a 'lower class' percentile of 41 per cent (Mühlberger includes certain crafts in this figure), a middle class of 39 per cent, with the balance comprising students and well-heeled members: Detlev Mühlberger, *Hitler's Followers: Studies in the Sociology of the Nazi Movement* (London, 1991), p. 188.

[16] Mühlberger, *Hitler's Followers* (London, 1991), pp. 162–80.

[17] A conceptual model of generation was developed in the 1920s by the sociologist Karl Mannheim, at a time when a rich body of literature was asserting the existence of a German 'Front Generation' forged in the trenches of the First World War. Mannheim concluded that 'individual members of a generation become conscious of their common situation and make this consciousness the basis of their group solidarity' and it is the integrative dynamic of a perceived shared identity, as much as any experiential homogeneity, which guides the numerous books to emerge from Herbert's 'Ideology and

middle-class males, born between 1900 and 1910, was deeply marked by Germany's experience between 1914 and 1933. Too young to have seen action in the First World War, they imbibed a rich German tradition of chauvinistic nationalism consolidated on the jingoistic home front, where school drills and a diet of mendacious news reports depicted the trenches as a gallant, masculine adventure.[18] For these children, Germany's unexpected defeat, revolution, and the Bolshevik terror in Russia marked a definitive rupture in their socialization, soon compounded by political chaos, a humiliating peace, then hyperinflation and foreign occupation in the early 1920s.[19] These attracted a significant number of future perpetrators to the radicalized student movement, exposure to *völkisch* racism, and ultimately the NSDAP in the final crisis of the Weimar Republic from 1929.

While historians have focused on the SS intellectuals from this cohort who later staffed its various departments and think tanks, the 'war youth' Bavarians of the early Dachau SS were also enmeshed in this generational narrative. Indeed, the experience of defeat and revolution had taken a particularly traumatic course in Bavaria. Munich, cradle of National Socialism, was the primary referent for its hardy myth of 1918, in which a German army poised for victory had been 'stabbed in the back' by foreign, revolutionary, and Jewish elements on the home front.[20] It is worth recalling these events in some detail as their impact on the Bavarian political consciousness, as the historian Ian Kershaw writes, 'would be hard to exaggerate',[21] and they would remain key points of reference in 1933, both inside and outside the camp.

## A BAVARIAN REVOLUTION

Although Bavaria had been among the last and most reluctant states to join Bismarck's Reich, it went to war in 1914—on the whole—in good spirits, buoyed

---

Dictatorship' project (books listed in introduction, footnote 32). An early reflection on the 1900–1910 generation was offered by Sebastian Haffner, *Germany: Jekyll and Hyde. An Eyewitness Account of Nazi Germany* (London, 2005 [1940]), pp. 49–64. More broadly on generation, see the excellent conceptual evaluation by Ulrike Jureit and Michael Wildt (eds), *Generationen: Zur Relevanz eines wissenschaftlichen Grundbegriffs* (Hamburg, 2005) and Mark Roseman, *Generations in Conflict. Youth Revolt and Generation Formation in Germany 1770 to 1968* (Cambridge, 1995). For a critical reflection on generation, ideology, and dictatorship, see Bernd Weisbrod, 'The Hidden Transcript: The Deformation of the Self in Germany's Dictatorial Regimes', *German Historical Institute London Bulletin*, Vol. 34, No. 2 (Nov., 2012), pp. 61–72.

[18] Wildt, *An Unconditional Generation: The Nazi Leadership of the Reich Security Main Office* (Wisconsin, 2009), pp. 21–4. See also Haffner's memoirs *Defying Hitler: A Memoir* (New York, 2002), pp. 14–18.

[19] On the interplay between generation and rupture or 'historical transition', see also Mary Fulbrook, *Dissonant Lives: Generations and Violence Through the German Dictatorships* (Oxford, 2011).

[20] See especially Tim Mason, 'The Legacy of 1918 for National Socialism', in Anthony Nicholls and Erich Matthias (eds), *German Democracy and the Triumph of Hitler: Essays in Recent German History* (London, 1971), pp. 215–39. A weighty monograph on the genesis of the stab in the back mythologies is Boris Barth, *Dolchstoßlegenden und politischen Desintegration: Das Trauma der deutschen Niederlage im Ersten Weltkrieg 1914–1933* (Düsseldorf, 2003).

[21] Ian Kershaw, *Hitler. 1988–1936: Hubris* (London, 1998), p. 114. On the brutalizing memory of the revolutionary interlude in Munich, see especially Martin Geyer, *Verkehrte Welt: Revolution, Inflation, und Moderne. München 1914–1924* (Göttingen, 1998), pp. 278–318.

by the prospect of annexations from a defeated France and Belgium.[22] A photograph capturing jubilant scenes on Munich's Odeonsplatz after the declaration of war on Russia later became famous when a euphoric, 25-year-old Adolf Hitler was identified in the crowd.[23] Hitler was among 1.43 million men to serve in the Bavarian army, around 20 per cent of the state's population.[24] Mounting casualties in Flanders soon dented public enthusiasm and rekindled ancestral anti-Prussian sentiment and bitterness at Bavarian 'cannon fodder for Berlin'.[25] Each year the Bavarian army lost a third of its men through death, injury, or illness. By the end of the war it had suffered 345,000 wounded and 200,000 killed in action, with almost half the latter coming from the nineteen to twenty-four age group.[26] On the home front spiralling inflation, acute food shortages caused by the Allied blockade, falling crop yields, and a command agricultural economy brought further disillusionment and widespread malnutrition.[27] For the war youth generation, material want was compounded by the absence of male relatives and teachers at the front, each of which found expression in elevated delinquency, theft, and a good deal of bureaucratic hand-wringing about the 'demoralization' and 'brutalization' of young males at home.[28] Perceived inequalities in the social distribution of privation, as elsewhere in Germany, ratcheted up class tensions barely submerged by the 'civil truce' (*Burgfrieden*) of 1914.[29]

Munich soon became the focus of politicized war weariness and discontent. Hitler returned on leave in 1916 to a Bavarian capital where, he recalled in *Mein Kampf*, the public mood was 'much much worse' even than in restive Berlin: 'to be a slacker passed almost as a sign of higher wisdom, while loyal steadfastness was considered a symptom of inner weakness and narrow-mindedness'.[30] Behind this, of course, he detected the machinations of Jews seeking to camouflage their parasitic and revolutionary activities with anti-Prussian propaganda. As so often in his autobiography, Hitler was claiming a prescience in reality born of the German

[22] Geyer, *Verkehrte Welt*, pp. 28–9; MacGregor Knox, *To The Threshold of Power, 1922/33: Origins and Dynamics of the Fascist and National Socialist Dictatorships* (Cambridge, 2007), pp. 148–50; Robert S. Garnett, *Lion, Eagle, and Swastika: Bavarian Monarchism in Weimar Germany, 1918–1933* (New York and London, 1991), p. 21.

[23] Kershaw, *Hitler, 1889–1936*, p. 89.

[24] Benjamin Ziemann, *War Experiences in Rural Germany 1914–1923* (Oxford, 2007), p. 30.

[25] Michaela Karl, *Die Münchner Räterepublik: Porträts einer Revolution* (Düsseldorf, 2008), p. 8. These complaints extended to widespread bitterness about the declining quality of beer, widely pinned on Berlin's requisitioning of Bavarian hops. As Ernst Toller put it in his memoirs, 'Just because the Prussian swine didn't mind bad beer, the Bavarian also had to swallow dishwater'. Ernst Toller, *Eine Jugend in Deutschland* (Hamburg, 1963), p. 132. The food situation was in fact a good deal worse in northern Germany, particularly after 1916.

[26] Ziemann, *War Experiences*, p. 32.

[27] Geyer, *Verkehrte Welt*, pp. 40–7; Ziemann, *War Experiences*, pp. 166–73.

[28] Richard Bessel, *Germany after the First World War* (Oxford, 1993), pp. 23–4, 239–52; Andrew Donson, *Youth in the Fatherless Land: War Pedagogy, Nationalism and Authority in Germany 1914–1918* (London, 2010).

[29] David Clay Large, *Where Ghosts Walked: Munich's Road to the Third Reich* (London & New York, 1997), pp. 57–65. A thematic analysis of rural unrest is offered by Robert Moeller, 'Dimensions of Social Conflict in the Great War: The View from the German Countryside', *Central European History*, Vol. 14 (1981), pp. 142–69.

[30] Hitler, *Mein Kampf*, trans. Ralph Manheim (London, 1972 [1926]), p. 175.

Right's subsequent 'lessons' of defeat. In January 1918 a wave of industrial strikes was organised in Munich by Kurt Eisner, stellar propagandist of the anti-war Independent German Social Democratic Party (USPD). Eisner, although born himself in Berlin, undoubtedly mobilized anti-Prussian sentiment in his agitation. He was also, as one historian puts it, 'a caricaturist's dream'.[31] A bohemian Jewish journalist and theatre critic, Eisner was a denizen of arty Munich Schwabing: pale and balding with a luxurious beard, hat, and pince nez. Convicted of treason, he was imprisoned for nine months in Stadelheim prison before being released in a general amnesty in October. Eisner was to be at the forefront of the November revolution in Bavaria, a state previously noted for conservatism and stability but the only one in which the declaration of a republic preceded the German armistice, thus enabling the Right most fully to misrepresent cause for effect. In Munich, too, the revolutionary interval lasted the longest of all German cities, leaving a commensurate scar on the Bavarian political consciousness.

Eisner, however, had minimal control over fast-moving events. The capitulation of Austria–Hungary on 3 November 1918 exposed Bavaria to the prospect of Entente invasion through Bohemia and the Tyrol, while a simultaneous American breakthrough at Verdun presaged the collapse of German resistance on the Western Front.[32] The example of the German Baltic fleet, which mutinied at orders to engage the British in a final act of operatic defiance, proved instructive. Munich, like other German cities, was soon awash with rifles brought home or discarded by demobilized and, frequently, deserting soldiers.[33] Revolutionary soldiers' and workers' councils on the Russian model filled the space vacated by a crumbling monarchy.[34] From these Eisner secured authorization to proclaim a republican government, and led crowds in occupying barracks and military installations. His regime proved more radical than its Prussian counterpart, reflecting the relative weakness of moderate, and moderating, Social Democracy in Bavaria. It lost little time in alienating mainstream opinion. On 25 November 1918, Eisner published a collection of 'Documents on the Origins of the War', confidential papers from the Foreign Ministry highlighting Germany's role in Austria–Hungary's unyielding ultimatum to Serbia in 1914. Coming at a time when Allied deliberations over the peace treaty had barely begun, this was considered scandalously unpatriotic and irresponsible even on the Left.[35] For the German Right it was high treason and eloquent confirmation of treacherous socialist and Jewish attitudes to

[31] Large, *Where Ghosts Walked*, p. 48. Another vivid portrait of Eisner is given in Richard M. Watt, *The Kings Depart: The German Revolution and the Treaty of Versailles 1918–1919* (London, 1973 [1968]), pp. 312–30. A more conventional and detailed biography is offered by Bernhard Grau, *Kurt Eisner 1867–1919* (Munich, 2001).

[32] Alarm at this saw the best-equipped and most reliable Bavarian units in Munich deployed on the Tyrolean border immediately after the Habsburg collapse, greatly easing the revolutionaries' takeover of the city in the following weeks: Garnett, *Lion*, p. 23.

[33] Large, *Where Ghosts Walked*, pp. 241–2.

[34] On the councils' movement and (far from homogeneous) ideologies, see especially Eberhard Kolb, *Die Arbeiterräte in der deutschen Innenpolitik 1918–1919* (Düsseldorf, 1962).

[35] Allan Mitchell, *Revolution in Bavaria 1918–1919: The Eisner Regime and the Soviet Republic* (Princeton, 1965), p. 256.

the war effort. Eisner's *nostra culpa* contributed to his assassination by an aristocratic Munich student, Count Anton von Arco-Valley, on 21 February 1919. This proved the opening salvo in a bitter 'mini-civil war' and enduring brutalization of Bavarian politics.[36] Mass protest demonstrations marked the funeral of the hitherto unloved Eisner and weapons were distributed to the soldiers' and workers' councils. A would-be assassin from the latter stormed the Bavarian *Landtag* (state parliament) and shot the SPD leader Erhard Auer during his eulogy for Eisner, while another deputy and a porter were gunned down during his escape.[37]

After a chaotic struggle with a successor SPD government under the reformist Johannes Hoffmann, power in Munich passed briefly to a pseudo-soviet republic dominated by another picturesque figure, the young Jewish playwright Ernst Toller. Toller had been radicalized by his spell on the Western Front with the Bavarian army and had played a leading role in the Munich munitions workers' strike.[38] Upon Eisner's assassination he assumed reluctant leadership of the Bavarian USPD and of political radicalism in Munich. The latter was given a considerable fillip on 22 March with news that the Hungarian Communist Béla Kun—another Jewish revolutionary for reactionary discourses—had established a soviet regime in Budapest. Back in Munich, on 6 April, Toller joined a group of anarchists and eccentrics in the occupation of the iconic Wittelsbach Palace, where they declared a People's Republic.[39]

The memory of Toller's eclectic regime was to prove more significant than its material impact. Wholly lacking either Communist or popular backing, the 'Schwabing Soviet' managed nonetheless to alarm the Bavarian middle classes with wordy proclamations for socializing mines, banks and the press, and for the promulgation of world revolution in permanence.[40] Dislodged in a bungled coup d'état sponsored by Hoffmann, it was succeeded instead by a *Räterepublik* (councils' republic) under Communist leadership. The prospect of a chain of revolutionary republics linking Munich, Vienna, and Budapest to Russia greatly excited the newly founded Communist International, and the expectation of proletarian victory in Germany saw it adopt German, rather than Russian, as its official language.[41] Lenin, from Moscow, cabled the *Räterepublik* to urge the mass kidnapping of hostages from the bourgeoisie.[42] The Munich police were disarmed and a Red Army of Communists, demobilized soldiers, and prisoners of war raised, equipped, and paid for in part through extortion and plundering of the city's wealthier quarters. In poorer districts posters were put up inviting inhabitants to seize the flats of the well-to-do, while *Räterepublik* chief Eugene Leviné, a veteran of the 1905 revolution in Russia, contemplated starving bourgeois children

---

[36] Kershaw, *Hubris*, p. 112.     [37] Large, *Where Ghosts Walked*, pp. 91–2.
[38] Toller, *Jugend*, pp. 59–95.     [39] Toller, *Jugend*, pp. 146–7.
[40] Mitchell, *Revolution*, pp. 307–12. For an effervescent account of the interdependence of political and cultural modernity in pre-revolutionary Schwabing, see Large, *Where Ghosts Walked*, pp. 3–42.
[41] Eric Hobsbawm, *Age of Extremes: The Short Twentieth Century 1914–1991* (London, 1994), p. 376.
[42] Knox, *Threshold*, pp. 244–5.

who otherwise would 'grow into enemies of the proletariat'.[43] Many of the senior figures in this altogether more brutal regime were both Russian and Jewish. They were highly congenial to right-wing demonology, able to build here on the contemporary propaganda work of Hoffmann's exiled administration in Bamberg. Hoffmann's regime flooded Bavaria with leaflets condemning the 'Russian terror' in Munich and spread hysterical rumours through the conservative and observant countryside of murdered priests, plundered monasteries, and bloody requisitioning on the Russian model.[44] Contemporary events in Russia were indeed offering an object lesson in Bolshevism at civil war. Mass terror, hostage slaying, and concentration camps were central to what was being billed there by November 1918 as the 'extermination of the bourgeoisie as a class'.[45] In Munich, a noisy community of refugees from the Bolshevik revolution, among them the future Nazi ideologue Alfred Rosenberg, kept these developments firmly in the political consciousness.

The town of Dachau itself entered national discourse as a site of civil war in mid-April 1919. The Hoffmann government attempted to crush the *Räterepublik* by force but its advance troops were routed at Dachau by an improvised Red Army under Toller's command.[46] Whilst this rare military victory for the Left was undoubtedly milked by the Munich regime for propaganda purposes, Dachau was a site of strategic importance. It contained both the functioning munitions factory and a large paper mill used to print money to pay *Räterepublik* troops.[47] The town was also located on the Munich–Ingolstadt rail link, a vital transport and supply artery for the increasingly besieged Bavarian capital. Several participants in what was soon elevated to 'The Battle of Dachau' asserted that workers—male and female—from the munitions factory intervened decisively on the side of the Red troops.[48] For some two weeks the town was under martial law and played host to stirring scenes of proletarian victory, as worker soldiers supped at field kitchens and prepared to roll Hoffmann's troops back over the Danube.[49] Red soldiers freely billeted themselves in the prevailingly bourgeois local homes, insensitive to the fears of their owners for the family silver.[50] Twice daily Dachau residents were treated to solemn parades in the market square advertising the resolve of the thousand-strong 'Army Group Dachau', which included a brigade of Russian prisoners of war.[51] Military forms of locution were frowned upon as 'Ludendorffism' and a voluntaristic take on following 'orders' saw the Red Guards pass the time in their quarters

---

[43] Large, *Where Ghosts Walked*, pp. 114–16.

[44] Hans Beyer, *Von der Novemberrevolution zur Räterepublik in München* (Berlin, 1957), p. 115; Toller, *Jugend*, pp. 182–3.

[45] In Geoffrey Hosking, *A History of the Soviet Union* (London, 1990), p. 70.

[46] Mitchell, *Revolution*, pp. 310–25; Toller, *Jugend*, pp. 103–7.

[47] Robert G. L. Waite, *Vanguard of Nazism: The Free Corps Movement in Postwar Germany, 1919–1923* (Cambridge, MA, 1970), pp. 84–5.

[48] Gerhard Schmolze (ed.), *Revolution und Räterepublik in München 1918–1919 in Augenzeugenberichten* (Munich, 1969), pp. 314–20; Toller, *Jugend*, pp. 175–6.

[49] Schmolze, *Revolution*, p. 328; Heinrich Hillmayr, 'Rätezeit und Rote Armee in Dachau', *Amperland*, No. 3 (1960), pp. 74–80.

[50] Erich Wollenberg, *Als Rotarmist vor München* (Hamburg, 1972), p. 41.

[51] Wollenberg, *Rotarmist*, p. 42.

and in local taverns. A 7.5-kilometre-wide front stretched to nearby Schleissheim, militarily crucial due to its airfield, and saw recurrent skirmishes with bands of counter-revolutionaries who offered no quarter to captured Red Army troops.[52]

The indignity of Dachau 1919 remained a wounding, mobilizing topos on the Bavarian Right. The rowdy behaviour of the Red Guards—from requisitioning food to fishing with hand grenades—was generally restrained by the standards of the time but this did not impede the gathering propaganda narrative.[53] In the recollection of a photographic compendium published by Nazi court photographer Heinrich Hoffmann, Dachau locals had 'suffered greatly from the drunkenness of the Red Guards' and 'breathed a sigh of relief' when liberated from their 'Red Terror'.[54] This liberation, the compendium fails to mention, was accompanied by the murder of eight unarmed Red Guards and up to twenty medical orderlies.[55] For by now the Bamberg regime had engaged the services of around 35,000 paramilitary volunteer *Freikorps* troops, including a Bavarian contingent under the command of Franz Ritter von Epp. Already a lionized figure in nationalist circles, von Epp had proven his aptitude for civilian butchery in the massacre of the Herero in German Southwest Africa during the 'war' of 1904–1907.[56] Several *Freikorps* formations sported the Death's Head (*Totenkopf*) insignia later adopted by the SS and after which its concentration camp guards would be named.[57] A further provocation to such troops was the murder on 30 April by a marooned Red Army unit, probably in retaliation for the execution of the captured soldiers at Dachau, of ten affluent hostages, including six members of the *völkisch* Thule Society, in Munich's Luitpold-Gymnasium. Many of the bodies were gruesomely mutilated, a crime which introduced the term *Rotmord* (Red murder) to Bavarian political discourse.[58] Particularly heinous to the assembling forces of armed reaction, one of the victims was female and, indeed, a minor Bavarian countess.[59] The bloody sacking of the Munich commune was overdetermined. On 4 May, Major Schulz of the Lützow *Freikorps* prepared his men with a motivational address whose refrain would resound once more fourteen years later:

---

[52] Wollenberg, *Rotarmist*, pp. 110–36.

[53] Hillmayr, 'Rätezeit und Rote Armee in Dachau', *Amperland*, No. 3 (1960), pp. 89–91.

[54] Heinrich Hoffmann, *Ein Jahr Bayrische Revolution im Bild* (Munich, 1937), pp. 33–4. The first edition of the book sold out in late 1919.

[55] Large, *Where Ghosts Walked*, pp. 118–20.

[56] These *Freikorps* units comprised 19,000 Bavarians, 12,000 Prussians and other North Germans, and 3,000 Württemberger. See David Clay Large, 'The Politics of Law and Order: A History of the Bavarian Einwohnerwehr, 1918–1921', *Transactions of the American Philosophical Society*, Vol. 70, No. 2 (1980), pp. 1–87, here p. 16. On the genocide of the Herero, see especially Gesine Krüger, *Kriegsbewältigung und Geschichtsbewusstsein: Realität, Deutung und Verarbeitung des deutschen Kolonialkrieges in Namibia 1904 bis 1907* (Göttingen, 1999) and Isabella Hull, *Absolute Destruction: Military Culture and Practices of War in Imperial Germany* (Ithaca and London, 2005).

[57] Beyer, *Novemberrevolution*, p. 133.

[58] The 'Red Terror' in Munich is explored in loving detail by many Nazi-era publications. The most detailed are Rudolf Schricker, *Rotmord über München* (Berlin, 1934) and Adolf Ehrt/Hans Roden, *Terror: Die Blutchronik des Marxismus in Deutschland* (Berlin, 1934), pp. 10–29.

[59] A fact recalled with particular outrage by one Dachau SS guard in his post-war judicial apologia: SAM, StA 34479/2, Vernehmungsniederschrift Hans Steinbrenner, 3 January 1953. On the

Gentlemen! Anyone who doesn't now understand that there is a lot of hard work to be done here or whose conscience bothers him had better get out. It is a lot better to kill a few innocent people than to let one guilty person escape . . . You know how to handle it . . . shoot them and report that they attacked you or tried to escape.[60]

That very afternoon twelve Social Democratic workers were denounced in Perlach, brought to the Munich Hofbräuhaus, and summarily executed. Fifty three Russian prisoners of war were led to a quarry and massacred, while twenty-one Catholic workers assembled to discuss a theatre production were slain as 'Communist terrorists'.[61] Tanks, aircraft, and heavy artillery were deployed against the *Räterepublik's* disintegrating 20,000-strong Red Army. The aggregate death toll among soldiers and civilians is unclear and the Bavarian authorities' figure of slightly over 600 was without doubt deeply conservative. It excluded, for example, the arbitrary murder of countless alleged ringleaders of the Left; many, on the pretext suggested by Major Schulz and later institutionalized in the Nazi concentration camps, that they had tried to escape. 'We even shoot the wounded', one *Freikorps* volunteer wrote to his wife, '[a]ll who fall into our hands get the rifle butt and then are dispatched with a shot . . . We were much more humane against the French in the war'.[62] The devastated city's health authorities were unable to cope with the decaying corpses in the streets; the *Freikorps* simply piled them into unmarked shallow graves.[63]

With the military defeat of the *Räterepublik* Munich citizens who had cowered in their flats during the fighting emerged to denounce and round up Communists, and localized atrocities continued for weeks to come.[64] Numerous Red Guards met terrible deaths in Stadelheim prison, whose gates, according to Toller, were adorned with a placard reading 'Leberwurst from Spartacist blood made here. Reds executed free of charge'.[65] The most odious violence in this brief civil war was perpetrated by the Right, but this was overlooked in Bavarian public memory of the *Räterepublik*.[66] An association between communism and atrocity was seared into the political consciousness, nourishing a sense of legitimacy for the use of extreme counter-revolutionary violence against the Left in times of crisis. The range of future Nazi leaders present in Munich during the revolutionary interlude is striking and includes Hitler, Himmler, Rosenberg, Rudolf Heß, Ernst Röhm,

---

Thule Society, which included a number of later prominent Nazis, see Hermann Gilbhard, *Die Thule Gesellschaft: vom okkulten Mummenschanz zum Hakenkreuz* (Munich, 1994) and, a good deal more succinct, Reginald H. Phelps, '"Before Hitler Came": Thule Society and Germanen Ordnen', *Journal of Modern History*, Vol. 35 (1963), pp. 245–61.

[60] Cited in Waite, *Vanguard*, p. 89.

[61] Detailed eyewitness accounts in Schmolze, *Revolution*, pp. 349–98; Mitchell, *Revolution*, pp. 299–311: as Kershaw points out, there are many discrepancies in the historical record concerning dates and casualties in this period: Kershaw, *Hubris*, p. 114, p. 640 fn 16.

[62] In Scott Stephenson, *The Final Battle: Soldiers of the Western Front and the German Revolution of 1918* (Cambridge, 2009), p. 312.

[63] Waite, *Vanguard*, p. 90.          [64] Large, *Where Ghosts Walked*, p. 121.

[65] Ernst Toller, *Briefe aus dem Gefängnis* (Amsterdam, 1935), p. 27.

[66] For an early, popular regional text, see Josef Karl Fischer, *Die Schreckensherrschaft in München und Spartakus im bayerischen Oberland. Tagebuchblätter und Ereignisse aus der Zeit der 'bayrischen Räterepublik' und der Münchner Kommune im Frühjahr 1919* (Munich, 1919). See also the equally vehement Rudolph Kanzler, *Bayerns Kampf gegen den Bolshevismus* (Munich, 1931).

Hans Frank, Wilhelm Frick, Heinrich Müller, and Gregor and Otto Strasser. The narrative and topoi of Bavaria's civil war would be exhumed by the Bavarian Right in 1933.

Counter-revolution largely restored a traditional Bavarian conservatism founded on agrarian and Catholic interests, yet also brought a reactionary swing in political culture. In the early 1920s the state presented itself as a 'nucleus of order' (*Ordnungszelle*) and offered juridical sanctuary to nationalist plotters, terrorists, and assassins opposed to the 'Marxist' SPD regime in Berlin.[67] The Bavarian judiciary approached the revolutionary period with a partisan fervour which ensured that, if anything, popular memory was polarized and radicalized. Leviné was tried for high treason in June 1919 and briskly condemned to death by firing squad, a sentence carried out two days later. Toller, facing the same charge, owed his more modest prison sentence of five years to an international campaign for clemency.[68] Sixteen former Red Guards were tried for the Gymnasium hostage murders, six of whom were sentenced to death and seven to lifelong imprisonment. Sensationalist newspaper coverage of the trial surmised that the murderers had hacked off the deceased's genitalia and thrown them into rubbish bins, and the connotations of *Rotmord* grew more lurid by the day.[69] In all, over 2,200 defendants were sentenced for involvement in the Munich *Räterepublik*.[70] In 1922 Felix Fechenbach, Eisner's private secretary, was also belatedly tried for high treason for his role in the publication of the foreign policy documents. The defendant, Jewish, was sentenced to eleven years' imprisonment.

Proceedings for excesses committed in the name of counter-revolution were equally partisan and only a handful of *Freikorps* personnel were brought before the courts. During the trial of Arco-Valley in 1920, the public prosecutor drew attention to the assassin's 'glowing' patriotic spirit and, to widespread jubilation, the mandatory death sentence was immediately commuted by the Bavarian Cabinet to a custodial term. Arco used the closing words afforded by a smitten court to confirm his love of Bavaria and monarch, and his hatred of Bolshevism and Jews.[71] The poster boy of Bavarian reaction was released in 1924, having been little more inconvenienced by his time in Landsberg prison than was the man who moved into his vacated quarters, one Adolf Hitler. For the NSDAP was another beneficiary of the paranoidly anti-Marxist and anti-Republican climate of post-war

[67] Anthony Nicholls, 'Hitler and the Bavarian Background to National Socialism', in Nicholls and Matthias, *German Democracy the Triumph of Hitler: Essays in Recent German History*, pp. 101–4; detailed narrative account provided by Wilhelm Hoegner, *Die verratene Republik: Geschichte der deutschen Gegenrevolution* (Munich, 1979 [1958]), pp. 109–32.

[68] Karl, *Räterepublik*, pp. 202–5; Richard Dove, *He Was a German: A Biography of Ernst Toller* (London, 1990), pp. 88–93. Toller only narrowly avoided being murdered by soldiers in Stadelheim Prison, the scene of many illicit executions in 1919 (and, again, in 1933/4). More broadly on the divisive commemoration of 1918–1919 in Munich, see Gavriel D. Rosenfeld, 'Monuments and the Politics of Memory: Commemorating Kurt Eisner and the Bavarian Revolutions of 1918–1919 in Postwar Munich', *Central European History*, Vol. 30, No. 2 (1997), pp. 221–51.

[69] Large, *Where Ghosts Walked*, p. 119.    [70] Beyer, *Novemberrevolution*, p. 137.

[71] *New York Times*, 19 January 1920 [State Prosecutor: 'If the whole of German youth were imbued with such a glowing enthusiasm we could face the future with confidence'].

Munich. At the trial for the attempted *Putsch* of November 1923, an indulgent judiciary allowed Hitler to turn the court into a propaganda event and also passed up on the opportunity to deport him back to Austria under Protection of the Republic Act.[72] The court held that these perpetrators, too, had been motivated by 'pure patriotic spirit and the most noble will', against which the deaths of four policemen in the episode was evidently of subordinate import.[73] Nonetheless, for all its celebrity, during the remainder of the 1920s the NSDAP was to play a marginal role in Bavarian high politics, as steady national economic and diplomatic progress chipped away at the market for extremist, violent politics of both Left and Right. The KPD likewise found itself a revolutionary body in a non-revolutionary situation, reduced to optimistic diagnoses of the imminent collapse of the capitalist system under the pressure of its internal contradictions.[74]

## SA AND SS

The extreme Bavarian Left and Right remained, however, in a state of 'latent' civil war.[75] It was in the nurturing environment of Bavaria that Nazi paramilitarism emerged and flourished before dispersing along with the NSDAP throughout Weimar Germany in the later 1920s. Nazi paramilitarism was a 'synthesis of violence and politics' structured and organized on military lines.[76] Its imagery and self-conception drew on the ideals of 1918/19 and a mythologized trench experience: youthful vigour and commitment, masculine camaraderie, a rough primitivism, and Manichaean thinking. The streets of Germany stood in for the fields of Flanders, with the steely but selfless patriotism of the *Freikorps* a discursive precedent.[77] Politics in this environment was 'increasingly viewed as a battle which must end in the enemy's unconditional surrender'.[78]

The genesis of the SA lay back in the infancy of the Nazi Party, when strong-arm security squads were recruited to protect meetings and, increasingly, to disrupt those of rivals.[79] In 1921 they were rebranded as the *Sturmabteilung* (Storm Division) and furnished with weapons and training by Röhm, a charismatic and well-connected member of the early Nazi Party and former adjutant of the *Freikorps* von Epp. The SA promoted and boosted the visibility of the NSDAP while keeping an independence from Hitler commensurate with his need not to become judicially accountable for its violence. Here lie the roots of the principle of

[72] Kershaw, *Hubris*, pp. 215–17.   [73] Evans, *Coming*, p. 196.
[74] Eve Rosenhaft, *Beating the Fascists? The German Communists and Political Violence 1929–1933* (Cambridge, 1983), pp. 70–81.
[75] James M. Diehl, *Paramilitary Politics in Weimar Germany* (Bloomington and London, 1977), p. 137.
[76] Knox, *Threshold*, p. 254   [77] Diehl, *Paramilitary Politics*, p. 285.
[78] George L. Mosse, *Fallen Soldiers: Reshaping the Memory of the World Wars* (Oxford, 1990), pp. 159–81.
[79] Until very recently, the historiography of the SA has been far more impressive and analytical than that on the SS. The best of these are Conan Fischer, *Stormtroopers: A Social, Economic and Ideological*

'working towards the Führer' which would play such a fateful radicalizing role in the Nazi state.[80] Much of its inspiration came from the Italian Blackshirts, fascist thugs loosely aligned to Mussolini who fought the Italian Left during his ascent to power in the early 1920s. The rationale of *squadrismo* and Nazi paramilitarism was identical; to provoke disorder and then stand as protector of order. Paramilitary armies were a potent means of exercising extra-Parliamentary pressure on the state and the SA sustained the NSDAP's self-conception as a 'movement' rather than a 'party' complicit in the hated Weimar 'system'.[81] The debacle of the Munich *Putsch*, however, had shown that conspiratorial paramilitarism alone held little prospect for achieving power in Germany without the blessing of the police, army, and patrician elites. In *Mein Kampf*, composed during his confinement in Landsberg, Hitler now envisaged the role of the SA in more propagandistic terms:

> What we needed and still need were and are not a hundred or two hundred reckless conspirators, but a hundred thousand and a second hundred thousand fighters for our philosophy of life. We should not work in secret conventicles, but in mighty mass demonstrations, and it is not by the dagger and poison or pistol that the road can be cleared for the movement, but by the conquest of the streets. We must teach the Marxists that the future master of the streets is National Socialism, just as it will some day be master of the state.[82]

Hitler was being coy about the personalized violence of the SA, which remained endemic and meted out with knuckledusters, truncheons, and beer glasses as well as daggers and pistols, and played out in a seedy context of localized rivalries, extortion, and vendetta. Tension was immanent to the notion of the SA 'political soldier'. While Hitler sought to accentuate the 'political' dimension, the 'soldiers' of the SA often had only the most fleeting familiarity with the NSDAP programme and electoral strategies. It was in the space ceded by this incompatibility that the SS emerged, and it would be the SS that resolved it forcibly with murder in the SA purge of 1934.

If the emphasis in the SA was on provoking disorder, the SS sought to convey discipline and order. Its own roots stretched back to 1923 with the creation of a dedicated bodyguard unit for Hitler, the 'staff guard' (*Stabswache*), soon renamed the Adolf Hitler 'assault troops' (*Stosstruppe*).[83] With the reconstitution of the Nazi movement after the *Putsch* in April 1925 it was rebranded once again, as the *Schutzstaffel* (Protection Squad). Little more initially than a devoted band of

---

*Analysis* (London, 1983); Richard Bessel, *Political Violence and the Rise of Nazism: The Storm Troopers in Eastern Germany 1925–1934* (Yale, 1984); and Peter Longerich, *Die braunen Bataillone: Geschichte der SA* (Munich, 1989). An outstanding work both on SA violence and its Italian inspiration is Sven Reichardt, *Faschistische Kampfbünde: Gewalt und Gemeinschaft im italienischen Squadrismus und in der deutschen SA* (Cologne, 2002).

[80] Kershaw, *Hubris*, pp. 529–91. For an interesting account of the attendant Weimar judicial contortions, see Bejamin Carter Hett, *Crossing Hitler: The Man Who Put the Nazis on the Witness Stand* (Oxford, 2008), pp. 65–154.

[81] The best overall account of the early SA is still Longerich, *Geschichte der SA*, pp. 9–52.

[82] Hitler, *Mein Kampf*, p. 494.

[83] Koehl, *Black Corps*, p. 18ff.

personal chauffeurs and dogsbodies, in 1926 it was entrusted with the hallowed and bloodied Nazi flag from the *Putsch*. The elite pretensions of the unit were clear from its name; in military parlance the term 'squadron' denoted specialized cavalry, motorized, and air units.[84] 'Elite', of course, is a relative term. The most detailed analysis of officers from this 'infancy period' of the SS identifies a motley brigade of ill-educated, heavy-drinking, and maladjusted men with colourful criminal records.[85] In September 1927 Himmler was appointed deputy SS commander and resolved to forge the SS into a racial aristocracy in line with his *völkisch* 'blood and soil' enthusiasms. The size of the task ahead is evident from his introductory guidelines, which were concerned with remedying undignified scenes at the previous month's Nuremberg Rally, where Lederhosen and multi-coloured sports attire had clashed with black SS caps and breeches.[86] A minimum height criterion of 170 cm for entry into the SS was introduced in March 1928, although this was waived for candidates with experience at the front. The SS remained, numerically at least, a tiny formation united by a sense of 'hard bitten vigour' until Himmler's promotion to commander, or *Reichsführer*, in January 1929.[87] At this point SS legend held that membership had been just 280 men. The Bavarian Political Police, contrarily, put the total at over 1,200, with 154 in Munich alone.[88] Nevertheless, expansion was certainly rapid under Himmler, with 15,000 members by the end of 1931 and 52,000 by the 'seizure of power'.[89]

The basis for the expansion of the SS in these twilight years of the Weimar Republic was the SA Basic Order VII of 12 April 1929. This instructed local SA commanders to select five to ten men to form a *Schutzstaffel* to guard senior NSDAP speakers.[90] Piecemeal emancipation from the SA began in 1930 when Hitler, against the wishes of the SA leadership, removed the latter's control over SS promotions and recognized it as a discrete formation with a new, distinctive, black uniform. The latter was knowingly distant from the SA; an SS man sported a black cap, black tie, black breeches, and a black-bordered swastika armband. A black stripe two inches above the cuff contained the number of his SS *Sturm* in Arabic script.[91] To promote the sense of a select, Himmler decreed that SS men should pay higher membership dues than the SA, and they were required to find the 40 Reichsmark for their black boots and uniforms themselves, substantially more expensive than SA kit. The SS also took a less understanding position on unemployed members lacking proper uniform than the SA.[92] The Munich police

[84] Koehl, *Black Corps*, p. 21.

[85] Gunnar Charles Boehnert, 'A Sociography of the SS Officer Corps 1925–1939' (PhD Dissertation, University of London, 1977), pp. 48–57.

[86] Koehl, *Black Corps*, p. 29.          [87] Koehl, *Black Corps*, p. 30.

[88] Michael H. Kater, 'Zum gegenseitigen Verhältnis von SA und SS in der Sozialgeschichte des Nationalsozialismus von 1925 bis 1939', *Vierteljahrsschrift für Sozial- und Wirtschaftsgeschichte* 62 (1975), p. 349.

[89] Koehl, *Black Corps*, p. 53. The SA, in contrast, had 60,000 members in November 1930, 290,000 in January 1932, and around 450,000 by 30 January 1933.

[90] Koehl, *Black Corps*, p. 33.

[91] Heinz Höhne, *The Order of the Death's Head: The Story of Hitler's SS* (London, 1980), p. 58.

[92] Kater, 'Verhältnis', pp. 360–1.

noted the strict discipline expected of SS men, especially when it came to matters of uniform and public conduct.[93] In his early years as *Reichsführer*, Himmler apparently vetted membership applications personally, paying close attention to the accompanying photograph to exclude those he identified as bearing elements of 'foreign blood'.[94] After 1931, SS men were also required to secure permission from the organization to marry, a conscious imitation of the elitist principles of the Imperial army to be discussed in detail later on (Chapter 5).

In the course of internal crises in the Nazi movement in Berlin during 1930 and 1931, the SS began to acquire its independent function as an internal police force. The eastern German SA commander Walther Stennes, an adherent of its quasi-socialist revolutionary wing, revolted against the strategy of gaining power by constitutional means.[95] The SS later claimed that its steadfast opposition to these revolts had been recognized by Hitler's fashioning of a new motto for them: 'My honour means loyalty' (*Meine Ehre heißt Treue*).[96] Whatever the provenance of the aphorism, it was soon ubiquitous in the SS, emblazoned in Gothic script on stationery, signs, ceremonial daggers, and rings as well as in membership oaths, motivational exhortations, and, later, as a spurious defence strategy in post-war trials. Its adoption implicitly cast into question the 'loyalty' of the SA. Great efforts were made by the SS to market its separation from the unreliable brownshirts as the movement's sentinel against 'brown Bolshevism'.[97] The SS man was supposed to keep a mysterious, Olympian distance from the SA:

> SS men and SS commanders are strictly forbidden to converse with SA men and commanders or with civilian members of the party other than as necessary for the purposes of duty. Should criticism be voiced in a small gathering, members of the SS will immediately and silently leave the room with the curt comment that the SS carries out Adolf Hitler's orders.[98]

Himmler told his senior commanders that the SS did not expect to be liked so much as recognized by the Nazi leadership for singular loyalty and reliability.[99] These self-conceptions did not make the SS popular with the mass of SA men who were, for example, liable to be frisked by the SS for firearms at Party meetings.[100] The Munich police picked up on the rapidly deteriorating personal relations between the SA and SS even in 1930.[101] SA commanders particularly resented the SS seeking to poach their men. This was, complained one,

> creating the impression that the SS is a privileged organisation and the SA a repository for second class elements. As soon as I develop men of a decent background and outlook along comes the SS and tries to lure them away.[102]

---

[93] Bernard Bahro, *Der SS-Sport: Organisation—Funktion—Bedeutung* (Paderborn, 2013), pp. 51–4.

[94] Longerich, *Himmler*, p. 126.   [95] Kershaw, *Hubris*, pp. 347–50.

[96] As Longerich points out, it is frequently difficult to penetrate beneath the self-regarding myths favoured by the SS in this period. Longerich, *Himmler*, p. 118. For detail, see also Bastian Hein, *Elite für Volk und Führer: Die Allgemeine SS und ihre Mitglieder 1925–1945* (Munich, 2012), pp. 77–82.

[97] Kater, 'Verhältnis', p. 348.   [98] Höhne, *Order*, p. 69.

[99] Longerich, *Himmler*, p. 124.   [100] Koehl, *Black Corps*, p. 47.

[101] Bahro, *Der SS-Sport*, p. 57.   [102] In Kater, 'Verhältnis', pp. 363–4.

Resentful of SS arrogance, local SA commanders retorted by trying to restrict the SS to demeaning activities like leafleting, collecting donations, and canvassing for subscriptions to the *Völkischer Beobachter*.[103]

It was during these unglamorous years that the majority of the early Dachau SS volunteered to join the organization. Due to the patchy nature of early personnel files, precise dates of joining are available for just forty.[104] On average, these men signed up on 21 February 1932, giving around thirteen to fifteen months of service in the organization prior to their deployment to Dachau. The actual mean length of service was probably longer. Since detailed data on rank-and-file SS men is generally only available from marriage applications, a policy introduced at the end of 1931, the sample of forty is skewed towards younger men with equivalently shorter lengths of service. The years immediately prior to the 'seizure' of power have been described as the 'formative period' of the SS.[105] The marriage regulations flagged an aspiration as a racial elite and the suppression of insurgent elements in the SA that of a Praetorian guard to Hitler. The absences of Himmler at the Reichstag in Berlin after the elections of September 1930 also ceded space to his principal subordinates in Munich, Reinhard Heydrich and Sepp Dietrich, to fine-tune the practicalities of the SS in Bavaria.[106] From Heydrich emerged a distinctive, glacially 'objective' outlook and tenor, while Dietrich's earthy charisma furnished the Bavarian SS with a more emotional, masculine allure.

Judging from the better-documented early Dachau SS, motivations for joining the SS rather than SA could be idiosyncratic. Franz Hofmann worked in his father's pub in Hof, a favoured hangout for local SS. When his brother Rudolf was expelled from the SS for financial irregularities, Hofmann joined the Bayreuth SS not least because he could wear Rudolf's discarded uniform.[107] Karl Stölzle switched from Fürstenfeldbrück SA to SS on the advice of a friend.[108] Richard Baer recalled being transfixed by the 'soldierly discipline' exhibited on parade by the Weiden SS, and the fact that it was a small, elite formation of just a dozen men.[109] He signed up alongside his friends Franz and Max Liebwein, both of whom also went on to become Dachau guards. Already a member of this small formation was the future Dachau commandant Martin Weiß. These young men met once per week, somewhat incongruously, in a church hall, to drill and play sports. Increasingly, at weekends, they stood on uniformed 'speaker protection' at public meetings where Nazi politicians and local leaders were speaking. These were often held in unsympathetic areas to ensure a charged atmosphere through the presence of local Communists.[110]

---

[103] Reichardt, *Faschistische Kampfbünde*, p. 129.

[104] Files for early SS members in the BDC collection are generally rarer than for their successors.

[105] Boehnert, 'Sociography', pp. 29–30.

[106] Koehl, *Black Corps*, pp. 44–5. Himmler remained a Reichstag Deputy until 1945 but invested little energy in the role and never got round to making his maiden speech. See Longerich, *Himmler*, p. 116.

[107] SAM, StA 34590/1, Vernehmungsprotokoll Franz Hofmann, 22 April 1959.

[108] SAM, StA 34462/1, Beschuldigtenvernehmung Karl Stözle, 7 December 1949.

[109] *Auschwitz Prozess* (CD-Rom Fritz Bauer Institut, 2004), Staatsanwaltschaftliche Vernehmung des Angeklagten Richard Baer, 29 December 1960.

[110] Reichardt, *Kampfbünde*, p. 100–10.

This shared activity and comradeship were important horizontal binding mechanisms in the Nazi paramilitary formations (see Chapter 5). Their contribution was accentuated by the other key shared attribute of the early Dachau SS: that they were unemployed or barely employed when deployed by their Bavarian *Standarten* to Dachau in spring 1933. Many early Nazi paramilitaries offered unemployment as their motive for volunteering for the movement. For such men, the dynamism and constant activism of the SA and SS offered a substitute for gainful employment, a comradely recognition. In a society where status was strongly tied to job held, political violence displaced the emasculation of unemployment and helped to assuage self-respect.[111] One careful analysis of the motivations of the SA, drawing mainly on contemporary statements to the American sociologist Theodore Abel, concludes that unemployment 'seems to have provided the decisive impetus which led them into paramilitary politics and the SA'.[112] Many activists seem to have believed that the advent of a Nazi government would bring them paid employment as officers and NCOs in an expanded military.[113] In this unemployed milieu, the decision to join the SS rather than SA was significant. For the SS offered a far less developed welfare apparatus of hostels and soup kitchens than the SA; indeed, as has been seen, it was a considerable net drawer of scarce resources from members. Volunteering for the SS, then, implied a particularly strong investment in the entangled mass of ideals and narratives which made up its 'world view' (*Weltanschauung*).

The biggest events in the paramilitary calendar were propaganda spectacles. Here Nazi paramilitaries staged public processions, occupying public space to boost the visibility of the NSDAP and to provoke rival paramilitary formations in line with Goebbels' maxim that 'he who conquers the streets can also conquer the masses'.[114] The space in question, usually a town or village, was occupied by the SA and SS for a few hours. They would hold parades, speeches, marches through the town centre, and mawkish libations to the 'fallen' at war memorials, all intended to signify Nazism as heir to the spirit of the front soldier. There were sporting events, concerts by an SA orchestra, and torchlit evening parades.[115] The musical litany came from the war and from traditional workers' songs, whose lyrics were replaced with an aggressive nationalist message to provoke local socialists.[116] The edges of the ubiquitous marching columns were manned by the so-called 'padding' (*Watte*), usually strong SA men in civilian attire or, increasingly, members of the SS. According to one participant's memoir, these were 'men of iron and steel, uniquely unflinching' who watched out for trouble and were invariably first into combat.[117] SS motorized formations also often accompanied smaller-scale SA demonstrations.[118] While, in later years, the SS tended to exaggerate its contribution in the 'time of struggle'

---

[111] Reichardt, *Kampfbünde*, p. 338.     [112] Fischer, *Stormtroopers*, p. 83.
[113] Fischer, *Stormtroopers*, p. 85.     [114] In Reichardt, *Kampfbünde*, p. 140.
[115] Reichardt, *Kampfbünde*, p. 104. See also William Sheridan Allen, *The Nazi Seizure of Power: The Experience of a Single German Town* (New York, 1973), pp. 89–93.
[116] Reichardt, *Kampfbünde*, p. 119.
[117] Reichardt, *Kampfbünde*, pp. 117–18; Longerich, *Geschichte der SA*, p. 118.
[118] Koehl, *Black Corps*, p. 56.

(*Kampfzeit*), it does seem that it was often chosen for dangerous assignments and sustained a fatality rate 41 per cent higher than the SA, with an injury rate 66 per cent higher.[119] As in the SA, rural *Stürme* had significantly fewer opportunities for political altercation than those based in towns and cities.[120] The incidence and intensity of violence and propaganda alike was closely bound to the fraught German electoral cycle, with local and above all Reichstag elections requiring heavy mobilization of paramilitaries for rallies and the disruption of those of opponents.

It was in this environment that the men who later made up the early Dachau SS were acculturated into violence. Paramilitary street violence represented a ritualization of insoluble political conflict from the post-war era, of the enduring narrative of civil war.[121] Whilst the SPD's de facto paramilitary *Reichsbanner* and the monarchist war veterans' *Stahlhelm* tended to become involved in ad hoc, localized confrontations, those of the Nazis and Communists were targeted and premeditated.[122] The paramilitary Right favoured the use of truncheons (*Gummiknüppel*) to convey discipline and legitimacy as an agent of order against lawless, criminalized communism.[123] National Socialist paramilitarism placed particular emphasis on framing its activities and identity in the imagery of soldiering. Police observers reported on amateurish 'soldier games' at weekends, involving field exercises and marches where participants sometimes got lost in forests and had to be rescued.[124] As the historian Daniel Siemens notes, street-fighting itself was conducted in a vocabulary of military operations exciting to 'war youth' fantasies: 'fanning out, advancing in skirmish lines, even the cordoning-off of entire towns'.[125]

Paramilitaries of all sides used the language of self-defence, of heroic courage and sacrifice in the face of perfidious attack.[126] Street violence was fuelled by reciprocal grievance and the thirst for revenge as much as linear, ideological motivations. Even before the onset of the Great Depression in 1929, the Reich Minister of the Interior fretted that '[h]ardly a day goes by in which somewhere in Germany, usually in many places, political opponents are not shot at, beaten, or stabbed'.[127] The ever-worsening economic crisis fuelled a perfect storm of paramilitary violence. In 1931, the Bavarian police recorded 509 large-scale armed altercations, 297 of which were attributed primarily to the Nazis. The total incidence of disturbances

[119] Kater, 'Verhältnis', p. 347.     [120] Hein, *Elite*, pp. 59–60.
[121] Reichardt, *Kampfbünde*, p. 98.
[122] Reichardt, *Kampfbünde*, p. 68. On the *Reichsbanner*, see Karl Rohe, *Das Reichsbanner Schwarz Rot Gold: Ein Beitrag zur Geschichte und Struktur der politischen Kampfverbände zur Zeit der Weimarer Republik* (Düsseldorf, 1966) and Benjamin Ziemann, 'Republikanische Kriegserinnerung in einer polarisierten Öffentlichkeit: Das Reichsbanner Schwarz-Rot-Gold als Veteranenverband der sozialistischen Arbeiterschaft', *Historische Zeitschrift*, Vol. 267, No. 2 (Oct., 1998), pp. 357–98.
[123] Reichardt, *Kampfbünde*, p. 84.     [124] Hein, *Elite*, p. 49.
[125] Daniel Siemens, *The Making of a Nazi Hero: The Murder and Myth of Horst Wessel* (London, 2013), p. 67.
[126] Ute Frevert, *A Nation in Barracks: Modern Germany, Military Conscription and Civil Society* (Oxford and New York, 2004), p. 246; Rosenhaft, *Beating*, pp. 128–45; on the Nazi use of martyrs and sacrifice, see Sabine Behrenbeck, *Der Kult um die toten Helden: Nationalsozialistische Mythen, Riten und Symbole 1923 bis 1945* (Vierow bei Greifswald, 1996); for the KPD paramilitaries Kurt Schuster, *Der Rote Frontkämpferbund 1924–1929* (Düsseldorf, 1975).
[127] Diehl, *Paramilitary Politics*, p. 196.

was undoubtedly far higher; the Augsburg police alone logged 440 demonstrations and fights during 1931 and 1932.[128] Nationally, the Nazis claimed to have suffered 143 deaths and 18,500 wounded in street violence with the KPD between 1930 and 1932. The Communist Red Aid reported 171 fatalities between 1930 and mid-1932, and over 18,000 injuries in 1931 and 1932.[129] Violent confrontations with Leftist paramilitaries gave a biographical character to the latent civil war, fostering the kinds of local feuds and grudges which were to be settled violently in the early months of the Nazi regime. Collective political violence helped to cement group cohesion and identity. It fostered group complicities, a routinization of violence, codes of honour, and an esprit de corps drawing on narratives and legends of victories and heroes. In all of this the role of visible affiliation was key: it was indeed with 'good reason' that the authorities sought to contain political street violence in December 1931 by banning paramilitary uniforms.[130]

## THE CIVIL WAR NARRATIVE

The particular hatred and violence of the Nazi paramilitaries towards Communists in 1932 and early 1933, however, is not explicable solely in terms of local feuds and diametrically opposed ideologies. Its intensity also reflected anxiety; anxiety that the National Socialist tide was retreating, while the Communist movement was in headlong advance as it had seemed to be in 1918. The KPD was the largest Communist party outside the USSR. It was also a party of German youth, a demographic to which the Nazis liked to assert a proprietorial claim. A sense of vulnerability, of the possibility of sinking beneath the waves, haunted the National Socialist world view in a manner wholly absent from communism, whose doctrines of historical inevitability countenanced no defeat. By late 1932 the Nazi movement was visibly flagging. Morale reports from the SA complained of problems with recruitment, retention, and most especially finances.[131] This crisis in the Nazi paramilitary movement predated, and complemented, the NSDAP's well-documented reverse at the Reichstag elections of November 1932.[132]

The perception of a Nazi movement emasculated by internal crises and dwindling returns at the ballot box played a key role in the ensuing miscalculation by anti-democratic elites that they would be able to contain Hitler as Chancellor. So too did the argument that the Communist menace was growing and had to be

---

[128] Michael Cramer-Fürtig and Bernhard Gotto (eds), *'Machtergreifung' in Augsburg: Anfänge der NS-Diktatur* (Augsburg, 2008), pp. 292–8.

[129] Rosenhaft, *Beating*, pp. 5–6.

[130] Dirk Schumann, *Political Violence in the Weimar Republic 1918–1933: Fight for the Streets and Fear of Civil War* (New York and Oxford, 2009), p. 254.

[131] Thomas D. Grant, *Stormtroopers and Crisis in the Nazi Movement: Activism, Ideology and Dissolution* (London and New York, 2004), pp. 107–47.

[132] Of the many synoptic accounts of this period the most penetrating are Kershaw, *Hubris*, pp. 318–427 and Hans Mommsen, *The Rise and Fall of Weimar Democracy*, trans. Elborg Forster and Larry Eugene Jones (Chapel Hill, 1996). See too the classic 'totalitarian' analysis by Karl Dietrich Bracher,

crushed to avoid an outright civil war which the denuded Reichswehr would be unable to contain.[133] The prospects for the new coalition government, however, were uncertain. Its predecessors had proven short-lived and futile, the commitment of President Hindenburg and the military was doubtful, the collective potential of the Left to respond as it had in 1920 to forestall the *Freikorps'* Kapp *Putsch* genuinely feared. These factors are obscured by the recent tendency to emphasize the consensual, populist dynamic of the nascent dictatorship, a narrative which leaves little scope for political instability, real or perceived.[134] The Left insurrection, it transpired, was a paper tiger. Yet it was not merely an opportunistic construct and there is no doubt that it made many Germans indulgent to the exceptional measures taken by the new coalition.[135]

Nazi activists, schooled in a paranoid world view transfixed by the 'lessons' of 1918/19, subscribed to the narrative of civil war. Having spent the previous decade invoking the Communists as an apocalyptic menace to the German nation, many were nonplussed by the absence of concerted opposition to the new Hitler government. For its part, convinced that the revolutionary hour had come, the KPD leadership openly urged local organizations not to provoke the regime into banning it by acts of individual violence, in favour of an imminent 'mass terror' action through workers radicalized by the final unmasking of German capital.[136] Neither of these totalitarian creeds had any truck with the vocabulary of moderation: each invoked and awaited the day of epochal reckoning.

The historian Hans Mommsen offers a vivid account of the resultant atmosphere of paranoia and tension in the regime's handling of the Reichstag fire of 27 February 1933.[137] In Berlin, vindication mixed with hysteria in the Nazi leadership's response to news that the arsonist Marinus van der Lubbe had Communist ties. While Goebbels and Göring competed to forge the most lurid and diabolical plot, Hitler ranted to Gestapo chief Rudolf Diels that the fire was the signal for the Communists' 'loudly-heralded mass action'.[138] As Mommsen shows, the Nazis' overreaction to the fire—from issuing orders to secure key installations militarily

---

*Die Auflösung der Weimarer Republik: Eine Studie zum Problem des Machtverfalls in der Demokratie,* 3rd Edition (Villingen, 1960 [1955]).

[133] Kershaw, *Hubris,* pp. 416–27. The best account of the machinations of the patrician elites remains Henry Ashby Turner, *Hitler's Thirty Days to Power: January 1933* (London, 1996). On the Reichswehr's position, see Michael Geyer, *Aufrüstung oder Sicherheit: Die Reichswehr in der Krise der Machtpolitik 1924–1936* (Wiesbaden, 1980).

[134] Evans, R. J., 'Coercion and Consent in Nazi Germany', *Proceedings of the British Academy* 151 (2007), pp. 53–81.

[135] A fine recent monograph on this topic is Schumann, *Political Violence.* For a less balanced account presenting nonetheless a range of interesting primary material on narratives of civil war, see Dirk Blasius, *Weimars Ende: Bürgerkrieg und Politik* (Göttingen, 2005).

[136] Rosenhaft, *Beating,* p. 81; Siegfried Bahne, 'Die Kommunistische Partei Deutschlands', in Erich Matthias and Rudolf Morsley (eds), *Das Ende der Parteien 1933: Darstellungen und Dokumente* (Düsseldorf, 1960), pp. 655–739, passim, here p. 690. See also the memoirs of Rudolf Diels, *Lucifer ante Portas: Es spricht der erste Chef der Gestapo* (Stuttgart, 1950), pp. 185–90. Diels' memoirs are far from reliable but demonstrate, at the very least, the referents used to emplot the narrative of civil war.

[137] Hans Mommsen, 'The Reichstag Fire and its Political Consequences', in Hajo Holborn (ed.), *Republic to Reich: The Making of the Nazi Revolution* (New York, 1973), pp. 129–222.

[138] Mommsen, 'The Reichstag Fire', p. 167.

through to instigating a public trial of KPD figures which was to prove highly embarrassing—suggests the sincerity of their paranoia.[139] When Diels visited Göring in his offices, the new Prussian Minister of the Interior gave picturesque vent to characteristic Nazi revenge fantasies:

> In bloodthirsty outbursts he railed against the Commune. He offered visions of fighting at the barricades, bloodily suppressed uprisings, of fluttering flags and heroic deeds on the battlefield. He wanted war. He believed that the communist 'foe' would soon reveal himself. Every report suggesting the Communists were preparing to launch civil war fired his excitement.[140]

Whilst it is impossible to disentangle the respective contributions of cynicism and paranoid excitement in Göring's rant, his complacent performance at the Reichstag Fire trial indicates that the Nazis had indeed worked themselves into a genuine and self-righteous paranoia by spring 1933.[141] The German police, with an extensive history of armed altercation with the KPD, had done much to fan it. Although not yet officially 'coordinated', the police had a vested interest in advertising the scale of the Communist threat and, in turn, the decisive importance of their work. In Diels' recollection, the torching of the Reichstag had 'fitted' rather than created the atmosphere of early 1933.[142] National Socialist activists were depicted as the primary target for the Red counter-strike (*Gegenschlag*). The murder by Communists of the young stormtrooper Hans Maikowski on 31 January 1933, was pumped up by what one diarist dubbed 'carcass propaganda' into an exemplar of this annihilatory intent, with the SA man accorded the first state funeral of the National Socialist regime, broadcast live on national radio from Berlin Cathedral.[143] A memorandum by the Nazi Minister of the Interior, Wilhelm Frick, to all German states announced that a nationwide plot had been uncovered in Berlin in which SA and SS men were to 'ruthlessly neutralized' by armed groups of Communists.[144] Another, summarizing

---

[139] Mommsen, 'The Reichstag Fire', pp. 70–2. The question of the authorship of the Reichstag Fire continues to stimulate debate. The initial consensus, based largely on the principle of *cui bono*, held that the Nazis had burned the Reichstag down to provide the pretext for enacting extant plans to destroy the organized Left. Reviewing the evidence in the 1960s Mommsen presented a now widely accepted case that van der Lubbe was, after all, a 'lone shooter'. Although by no means uncontested (see for example Klaus Fischer, *Nazi Germany: A New History* (London, 1995), p. 252) the interpretation that the Nazis were indeed surprised (although not unpleasantly so) remains dominant and the most persuasive. As Mommsen notes, for propaganda purposes it would have sufficed for the Nazis to declare that German Communists had assisted van der Lubbe 'behind the scenes': instead they pressed ahead with a trial to determine that he had on-site accomplices, in line with the initial conclusion drawn by Goering and Reichstag officials at the scene that the other arsonists had escaped down a tunnel housing the Reichstag water pipes. This was a conclusion echoed in the initial police investigation of the incident, who seem likewise to have sincerely believed in a communist conspiracy and 'signal': Mommsen, 'Reichstag Fire', pp. 137–41.
[140] Diels, *Lucifer*, p. 176.     [141] Mommsen, 'Reichstag Fire', pp. 90–1.
[142] Diels, *Lucifer*, pp. 171–93; quote p. 191. Writing in 1950, Diels compared the anti-Communist paranoia of 1933 to contemporary McCathyism in the USA, a nation obsessed and menaced by a comparatively meek Communist party. Although patently self-serving, the comparison is not necessarily invalid.
[143] Count Harry Kessler, *The Diaries of a Cosmopolitan, 1918–1937* (London, 2000 [1971]), p. 444; Reichardt, *Faschistische Kampfbünde*, p. 494.
[144] Bayerisches Hauptstaatsarchiv (BayHStA), StK 6312, Reichsministerium des Innern an die Landesregierungen, 1 March 1933, s. 106. See also Mommsen, 'Reichstag Fire', pp. 175–7.

KPD activity in the winter of 1932–1933, warned that the party had vast stock-piles of arms secreted throughout the Reich and was in the final stages of prepara-tion for confronting the army and Nazi paramilitaries in an armed takeover on the Bolshevik model.[145]

In Bavaria such material was assured an indulgent hearing, for here too a com-paratively weak KPD was deemed menacing. Bavarian KPD membership quin-tupled between 1928 and 1932, and at the Reichstag election in November 1932 its poll reached 330,000: over 10 per cent of the popular vote.[146] Communist support was overwhelmingly focused in the cities of Munich, Augsburg, and Nuremberg: headquarters of the *Standarten* from which the early Dachau SS came. The charged and expectant atmosphere in Berlin was replicated in Munich, with Bavarian points of reference. On 12 February, in a moment of sickening irony, Hans Beimler, Reichstag deputy and leader of the KPD's South Bavarian district, ended a defiant and widely publicized speech to a rally at Munich's Zirkus Krone by invoking the memory of 1919. 'If they want war', he intoned, 'we are ready for them. We have the example of the Bavarian *Räterepublik*. We'll meet again in Dachau!'[147] On 9 March the national wave of 'coordination' reached Bavaria, the last-remaining German state with an independent federal govern-ment. SA and SS men mobbed the Marienplatz, singing the Horst Wessel song and hoisting the swastika flag on its famous town hall.[148] Bavarian Prime Minister Heinrich Held was forced by Frick to resign. In his place an iconic civil warrior from 1919 re-entered the scene; for Ritter von Epp, hero of the *Freikorps*' blood-bath in Munich, was now appointed Reich Commissioner for Bavaria. Having failed to capitalize on the interval between its de facto banning after the Reichstag fire and 9 March, the KPD contrived to be caught off guard by the ensuing perse-cution as leaders and functionaries were taken into protective custody throughout Bavaria.[149] On 20 March the Left's redemptive imagery of Dachau 1919, too, was assaulted, when Himmler announced the opening of the new concentration camp at a press conference.[150] The Nazis finally caught up with Beimler on 9 April. In the police headquarters on the Ettstraße, triumphant SA and SS auxiliary police (*Hilfspolizei*) grasped the irony, whooping 'We've got Beimler. "We'll meet again in Dachau!"'. Beimler, a veteran of the Baltic Fleet mutiny and the *Räterepublik*

---

[145] BayHStA, StK 6312, Denkschrift über die kommunistische Wühlarbeit im Winter 1932/33, ss. 87–9.

[146] Harmut Mehringer, 'Die KPD in Bayern 1919–1945', in Martin Broszat and Harmut Mehringer (eds), *Bayern in der NS Zeit V. Die Parteien KPD, SPD, BVP in Verfolgung und Widerstand* (Munich, 1983), pp. 27–33.

[147] Heike Breitschneider, *Der Widerstand gegen den Nationalsozialismus in München 1933 bis 1945* (Munich, 1968), p. 25; see also Centa Herker-Beimler, *Erinnerung einer Münchner Antifaschistin* (Augsburg, 1999), p. 15.

[148] Emil Schuler, *Die Bayerische Landespolizei 1919–1935* (Munich, 1964), p. 40. On the course of the *Machtergreifung* in Bavaria, a useful recent edited volume is Andreas Wirsching (ed.), *Das Jahr 1933: Die nationalsozialistischen Machtoberung und die deutsche Gesellschaft* (Göttingen, 2009).

[149] Mehringer, 'KPD', pp. 70–5.

[150] The press conference and opening of the camp was reported extensively (and excitedly) in the local papers on 21 March including the *Münchner Neueste Nachrichten*, *Amper Bote*, *Dachauer Zeitung*, *Neue Augsburger Zeitung*, and the *Völkischer Beobachter*.

Red Army, was cast as the personification of Communist insurrection. One early Dachau SS man seems even to have believed that Beimler, rather than Toller, had led the victorious Red Army at Dachau in 1919.[151] Beimler recalled his captors' frustration that no extermination lists or maps of concealed weapons were hidden in his clothing.[152]

It was as members of the Bavarian auxiliary police that the early Dachau SS were first stationed in the camp. They would remain as such, on special assignment from SS Group South, until 9 March 1934 when they were formally recognized as a discrete formation.[153] Service in the auxiliary police represents the final common stage in the collective pre-camp biography of the early Dachau SS. Auxiliary policemen were first levied by Göring in Prussia on 22 February 1933, conferring the power of the state onto Nazi and allied paramilitary formations to bear arms and hunt down activists of the Left. They were sworn in on a ratio of 5:3:1 from the SA, SS, and Stahlhelm respectively: a huge over-representation for the SS reflecting its self-conception as a disciplined and reliable agent of violence. The SS was primarily envisaged as back-up for the political police, the SA and Stahlhelm for the regular police.[154] Auxiliary police were formed in Bavaria on 9 March when Himmler, hitherto unrewarded by the seizure of power, was appointed acting Police President in Munich. He announced that all double police posts were to be augmented with an SA or SS man who was to be armed by the police with a pistol.[155] Once again, the post-war revolutionary experience in Bavaria provided a legitimatory precedent. After the destruction of the *Räterepublik*, a civilian militia of some 400,000 men, the Civil Guard (*Einwohnerwehr*), was organized to protect the conservative restoration in Munich.[156] It was formally dissolved, under Allied pressure, in June 1921 not having been called upon to suppress an embittered Left. For most Dachau SS auxiliary police, insofar as any testimony was taken, their experience was likewise uneventful. Baer reports signing up to the Weiden auxiliary police along with eight other SS men, where they were given white armbands and paced the streets in the company of regular policemen.[157] Franz Hofmann patrolled the gasworks in Hof with a local constable.[158] Heinrich Strauss and Max von Dall-Armi, more senior SS men, were stationed as sentries outside the Wittelsbach Palace, now the offices of the Nazi Bavarian Minister of the Interior Adolf Wagner.[159]

[151] SAM, StA 34479/1, Erweiterer Lebenslauf des Hans Steinbrenner, 3 January 1953.
[152] Hans Beimler, *Four Weeks in the Hands of Hitler's Hell Hounds* (New York, 1933), pp. 11–12.
[153] See Chapter 2 for more detail on this process.
[154] Tuchel, *Konzentrationslager*, p. 74.
[155] Cramer-Fürtig and Gotto, *Machtergreifung*, p. 307.
[156] On the *Einwohnerwehr*, see David Clay Large, 'The Politics of Law and Order' and a well-researched doctoral thesis by Roy G. Koepp, 'Conservative Radicals: The *Einwohnerwehr, Bund Bayern und Reich*, and the Limits of Paramilitary Politics in Bavaria, 1918–1928' (PhD Dissertation, University of Nebraska, submitted 2010). A fascinating account of the expansive political ambitions of the *Einwohnerwehr* is provided by Diehl, *Paramilitary Politics*, pp. 55–67.
[157] *Auschwitz Prozess* (CD-Rom) Staatsanwaltschaftliche Vernehmung des Angeklagten Richard Baer, 29 December 1960.
[158] SAM, StA 34590, Vernehmungsprotokoll Franz Hofmann, 22 April 1959.
[159] SAM, StA 34460, Beschuldigtenvernehmungsprotokoll Heinrich Strauss, 30 May 1950.

Yet all this was a heady improvement in status for hitherto unemployed young men, a taste of power which no doubt eased and shaped their deployment to Dachau in the ensuing weeks and months. Their post-war accounts of this process are studiedly vague, but the general pattern obtains that all were unemployed and sent, mostly in extant *Stürme*, to the camp. Strauss claimed to have been lured on the pretext of receiving advanced military training.[160] Kurt Mayr recalled that twelve members of his Memmingen *Sturm* volunteered for what was billed as six weeks' intensive police schooling in Munich.[161] Anton Hoffmann claimed that all unemployed members of his *Sturm* were 'assigned' to duty at Dachau.[162] Dall-Armi's entire *Sturm* was transferred from guard duty at the Ministry of the Interior to Dachau.[163] Some early Dachau SS men arrived together in omnibuses, others, like Paul Szustak, came on their own, at the recommendation of superiors.[164] Most claim not to have known that they would be guarding protective custody prisoners, some never to have heard of Dachau. This is particularly dubious in view of the media commotion attending the opening of the camp, as well as Dachau's symbolism in the Bavarian political consciousness. Many newspapers, inevitably, linked the two. The *Dachauer Zeitung* was not alone in delighting at the irony when it led, even before Beimler's arrest, with an article entitled 'We'll meet again in Dachau!'. After reminding readers that Dachau was 'the well-known base of the Red Guards in the calamitous year of 1919', it crowed:

> [Beimler] was right—but in a completely different way . . . Dachau *was* once again to become the base for every Red cell bent on transforming our German Fatherland into a communist 'paradise'. Now these gentlemen are indeed together again in scenic Dachau—in the concentration camp at the German Works site. But instead of ruling, they are to perform honest work.
>
> 'We'll meet again in Dachau' . . . proving that world history is God's court![165]

There is nothing to suggest that Dachau's place in Left mythology had any role in the decision to site Munich's concentration camp there; the decisive factor was the vacant factory premises.[166] But, as has been seen, the symbolism appealed to reactionary spirits. For a Nazi world view fuelled by vengeful narratives it was especially resonant. The remainder of this chapter will show that a narrative of civil war informed by the post-war violence in Munich provided the founding, legitimatory script of the early Dachau SS. A narrative in this context is a cognitive map, a means of locating and framing the present. The historian Saul Friedländer has argued that National Socialism was a creed structured to an unusual degree by such narratives, narratives of perdition and redemption.[167] *Mein Kampf*, its guiding

---

[160] SAM, StA 34460, Beschuldigtenvernehmungsprotokoll Heinrich Strauss, 30 May 1950.

[161] SAM, StA 34465, Zeugenvernehmungsprotokoll Kurt Mayr, 20 January 1953.

[162] SAM, StA 34461/3, Zeugenvernehmungsprotokoll Anton Hofmann, 12 January 1951.

[163] SAM, StA 34461/3, Zeugenvernehmungsprotokoll Max v Dall-Armi, 12 January 1951.

[164] SAM, StA 34491/1, Vernehmungsniederschrift Paul Szustak, 12 November 1952.

[165] *Dachauer Zeitung*, 23 March 1933; *Dachauer Volksblatt*, 27 April 1933. Emphasis added.

[166] Richardi, H. G., *Schule der Gewalt: Das Konzentrationslager Dachau 1933–1934* (Munich, 1983), pp. 41–5.

[167] Saul Friedländer, *Nazi Germany and the Jews: Volume 1: The Years of Persecution, 1933–1939* (New York, 1997), pp. 73–112.

ideological text, was after all less a policy document than a personal and generational journey, at whose end lay either salvation or annihilation. To be sure, in time, these narratives would be draped in 'objective' and 'scientific' clothing, with the *Schutzstaffel* to the forefront of the exercise. But narratives they remained; biblical, almost, in their cycles of prelapsarian innocence, fall, and salvation.

## THE EARLY DACHAU SS LEADERSHIP

Dachau's first commandant was *Oberführer* Hilmar Wäckerle. Born in 1899 in Upper Franconia, Wäckerle was educated at the prestigious and profoundly conservative officers' school of the Bavarian Army and served on the Western Front in 1918. After demobilization, he studied agronomy at the Technical University in Munich and beheld the revolutionary interlude with bourgeois dismay.[168] He soon joined the *Freikorps* Wilhelm, then the *Freikorps* Oberland, where he saw action in the crushing of the Munich *Räterepublik*. He was also involved in the Oberland's campaigns of resistance and assassination in the Ruhr. Wäckerle was a very early member of the NSDAP. Having first joined in 1922 he held the Blood Order badge bestowed for membership prior to the Munich *Putsch*, an example of National Socialism's solemn reverence for its own Bavarian past. Wäckerle was the founder of SS *Standarte* Augsburg's Kempten *Sturm* and led street battles with the Bavarian Left, with scars to prove it.[169] He came to Dachau as leader of the Kempten auxiliary police and was probably appointed commandant as the highest-ranking SS man in the camp.[170] He took a close interest in all KPD functionaries, and particularly in Beimler. According to one of his subordinates, Wäckerle had a collection of photographs of murdered hostages from the Luitpold-Gymnasium, with evidence of gruesome mutilation. Wäckerle averred that Beimler was responsible for the crime and announced that he intended to shoot him himself.[171] For Wäckerle, it seems, a unilateral declaration of revolutionary martial law in the camp legitimated summary execution; this view was not shared, as will be seen, by the Munich judiciary. His 'special regulations' for Dachau included provisions for a 'camp court' empowered to sentence inmates to death, possibly inspired by the rolling courts martial (*Feldgericht*) used in the counter-revolutionary terror of 1919.[172] Wäckerle told his men that they should act as his Cheka, the Soviet Union's merciless secret police.

Second in command was Robert Erspenmüller, the commander of the guard troops. Born in Nuremberg in 1903, Erspenmüller was another Blood Order

---

[168] Segev, *Soldiers*, p. 87. For other aspects of Wäckerle's tenure in Dachau, see Chapter 3.

[169] SAM, StA 34462/4, Zeugenvernehmungsprotokoll Rudolf Wiblishauser, 9 February 1950.

[170] Same conclusion drawn by Johannes Tuchel, 'Die Kommandanten des Konzentrationslagers Dachau', in Wolfgang Benz and Angelika Königseder (eds), *Das Konzentrationslager Dachau: Geschichte und Wirkung nationalsozialistischer Repression* (Berlin, 2008), pp. 329–349, here p. 332.

[171] SAM, StA 34479/1, Vernehmungsniederschrift Hans Steinbrenner, 3 January 1953.

[172] IMT, Vol. XXXVI, Dokument 922-D, Sonderbestimmungen, May 1933. On the *Feldgerichte* in Munich in May 1919 see Waite, *Vanguard*, 90–3.

36        *Dachau and the SS: A Schooling in Violence*

bearer and fought alongside Wäckerle as a very youthful member of the *Freikorps* Oberland.[173] The son of a civil servant, like Wäckerle his social and educational background were rather comfortable: as seen above, by no means a disadvantage in the SS. A member of the restricted German army until 1923, he then signed up with the Rosenheim State Police, a position he was obliged to forfeit in 1925 due to political activism for the NSDAP, the kind of early sacrifice for the 'movement' so cherished in the Third Reich. With this, *Freikorps* activity, and a low SS membership number, Erspenmüller was everything that was prized in that organization. The one blemish on his CV was a minor corruption scandal in 1931, in which he was accused of pilfering from the proceeds of a fund-raising initiative and which led to a temporary expulsion from the SS. His subsequent reinstatement offered Himmler an interpersonal leverage characteristic of the *Reichsführer's* strategy to keep subordinates personally dependent on his goodwill.[174]

The most feared and violent man in the early Dachau SS, however, arrived in the camp without rank. He was posted in its protective custody compound for just five months, but established a tone and modus operandi to SS–prisoner relations which made him a negative legend for years to come. His biography offers a compelling case study of a Bavarian 'war youth' generation. Born in Frankfurt-am-Main in 1905, Hans Steinbrenner moved to Munich in 1910, where his father bought a gun shop. According to his own detailed account,[175] the young Steinbrenner experienced the revolutionary regimes in Munich not merely as an appalled observer, but 'personally'. His father's business was plundered for arms by both the Eisner and *Räte* regimes and the premises 'senselessly destroyed'. A brief moment of cheer came to the household with the 'hero' Arco's assassination of Eisner. Steinbrenner, however, was gravely unwell at the time, suffering delirium and fever due to an abscess on his left leg. The store's accounts and the key to its safe were secreted in his bandages. His father was taken hostage by Red Guards before being liberated by *Freikorps* troops. Hans Steinbrenner 'never forgot' the cacophony of artillery, machine gun, and rifle fire in his fevered state. After his convalescence, he and his father volunteered for the Civil Guard. Steinbrenner followed the brutal exploits of the *Freikorps* in the Baltic and the Ruhr reported in the press with excitement. He worked in his father's shop, which became a talking house for counter-revolutionary notables; among the customers were von Epp and Röhm. Steinbrenner also recalled the excitement of the *Putsch* in 1923 and claimed to have been arrested and beaten by the police at a public demonstration in the same year.

It is difficult not to question the teleology of Steinbrenner's Bavarian odyssey; in particular, the topos of a fevered young man's political awakening seems to owe something to Hitler's Pasewalk nirvana in *Mein Kampf.*[176] Its essentials nonetheless

---

[173] BAB, BDC SSO Erspenmüller, Lebenslauf, n.d. A more detailed account of Erspenmüller's tenure is contained in Chapter 2.
[174] Longerich, *Himmler*, p. 153.
[175] The following from SAM, StA 34479/1, Erweiterer Lebenslauf des Hans Steinbrenner, 3 January 1953.
[176] Hitler, *Mein Kampf*, pp. 185–6.

were repeated by his mother under questioning.[177] Certainly Steinbrenner, through-out the 1920s, remained in the company of reactionary paramilitaries including the war veterans' *Stahlhelm* and nascent SA and SS. Even these violent custom-ers, however, were not sufficient to keep the store afloat after his father's death in 1929. In 1932 he was approached by the SS to train its men on the shop's shoot-ing range, which evidently appealed to his frustrated 'war youth' militarism. In February 1933 he joined the 1st motorized *Sturm* of the Munich *Standarte*. After what he refers to as the 'subversion in Bavaria' on 9 March, Steinbrenner enlisted with the auxiliary police, where he paced Munich's Holzstraße in the company of a regular policeman: 'tedious and thankless', he recalled.[178] On the evening of 23 March Steinbrenner was on his way to clock-in as usual, when he was hailed by Erspenmüller, who informed him that all available members of *Standarte* Munich were required to embark on a grey omnibus. Wholly unprepared—Steinbrenner claimed to have had to return home in the early hours of the following morning to collect spare clothes and kit—and with no knowledge of their destination, the occupants were driven to the site of the new concentration camp at Dachau.[179]

On arrival, the early Dachau SS men received a motivational address from their aristocratic *Standarte* commander, Johann Erasmus Freiherr von Malsen-Ponickau. The *Oberführer*, himself a veteran of the *Freikorps* von Epp, used the imagery of civil war as he set out frankly the treatment the prisoners could expect:

> Now we've got the power. If these swine had taken over, they'd have made sure our heads rolled in the dust. So we too know no sentimentality. Any man in our ranks who can't stand the sight of blood doesn't belong here, he should get out.[180]

Steinbrenner's conduct in Dachau was very much in this spirit; he later recalled that the speech had been 'extremely important' and made a great impression on the men.[181] Naaff's team gathered statements from 601 witnesses attesting to Steinbrenner's five-month reign of arbitrary terror and relentless, hideous violence. Prisoner memoirs too uniformly refer to him as 'the camp horror', 'murder-bren-ner' (*Mordbrenner*), or simply 'the sadist'. An entrepreneur and catalyst of vio-lence, we will never know entirely where Steinbrenner's rage in Dachau came from: clearly, however, his biography, generational architecture, and sense of redemptive mission would be central to any explanation.

Steinbrenner was the leading figure among a handful of early Dachau SS men selected for de facto NCO roles by Wäckerle and Erspenmüller. A key criterion seems to have been prior familiarity with weapons while the remaining SS men were drilled by the State Police. Accommodated in a single-story building just

---

[177] SAM, StA 34462/4, Fortsetztes Zeugenvernehmungsprotokoll Henrietta Steinbrenner, 27 July 1950.

[178] SAM, StA 34462/7, Beschuldigtenvernehmungsprotokoll Hans Steinbrenner, 13 June 1951.

[179] SAM, StA 34479/1, Erweiterer Lebenslauf des Hans Steinbrenner, 3 January 1953.

[180] In Sofsky, *Order*, pp. 2–3. The phraseology was recorded by Martin Grünwiedl, *Dachauer Gefangene erzählen* (Munich, 1934), p. 3.

[181] SAM, StA 34462/7, Fortsetzung der Beschuldigtenvernehmung Hans Steinbrenner, 25 June 1951. On the importance of oratory in this milieu see Chapter 2.

outside the prisoner compound, they were the antecedent to the system of commandant's staff fine-tuned by Wäckerle's better-known successor Eicke. One of their functions was to carry out the so-called 'welcome beating' accorded to prominent newcomers. All prisoner memoirs note the SS feeding frenzy that attended the arrival of a fresh prisoner transport: 'woe betide', as one recalled, 'the prisoner an SS man recognised from his home town'.[182] This reflected the kinds of civil hatreds and feuds which had built up over previous years. Steinbrenner even suggested that his colleagues had shown commendable restraint under the circumstances, since they could remember 'only too well and painfully' the injuries they had sustained from paramilitary formations of the Bavarian Left.[183] The arrival of the more prominent foes was cabled in advance to the camp by Party Headquarters at Brown House on the Briennerstraße.[184] A new transport in the early days was invariably greeted by Wäckerle and camp administrator Vogel; those prisoners flagged for 'special treatment' were separated from the group and led off to their fate in the *Bunker*, as the camp lockup was known.

Like Wäckerle and Erspenmüller, Anton Vogel was a hardy and long-standing Nazi, having joined the party and SA in 1922. He appears to have taken part in the Munich *Putsch*.[185] Born in 1893, the oldest of the group, Vogel actively solicited a role in the new camp; once there his priority seems to have been extracting information from the prisoners on plots and concealed weapons. One witness reports the revealing remark: 'don't believe you can lie to us, we too are old revolutionaries'.[186] Another stalwart of the movement was Heinrich Strauss, supervisor of the notorious heavy roller work brigade for 'Jews and bigshots'. Born in 1901, Strauss joined the NSDAP in 1921, the SA in 1923, and took part in the *Putsch*. He then became a member of the *Stosstruppe* Hitler, the forerunner to the SS, and about whose personnel and exploits Himmler expected SS men to be reverentially aware. Joseph Berchtold described Strauss as 'one of my finest and most reliable men . . . a daredevil fighter who once saved my life'.[187] Strauss was also a Bavarian civil warrior from the low-budget era, with a lengthy police and prison record for violence, robbery, and gambling.[188] His post-war interrogations teem with references to prisoners he had fought personally during Weimar and with whom he used his post in Dachau to settle old grudges.[189] But despite a background impeccable by SS standards of the time, Strauss was overshadowed in Dachau by the ambitious Steinbrenner and left the camp amidst some rancour after just a month.

[182] Fritz Ecker, 'Die Hölle Dachau', in *Konzentrationslager: Ein Appell an der Gewissen der Welt* (Karlsbad, 1934), p. 25.

[183] DaA, 19.862, Hans Steinbrenner, 'Hinter den Kulissen von Dachau', 31 January 1962.

[184] Richardi, *Schule*, p. 94.

[185] SAM, StA 34420, Vernehmungsniederschrift Anton Vogel, 31 January 1949. SS men frequently inflated their contribution to the *Kampfzeit* on their CVs during the Third Reich, but since Vogel also claimed to have participated in the *Putsch* in his post-war interrogations (where this might be construed as Nazi ardour) it is highly probable he was involved in some way.

[186] SAM, StA 34420, Vernehmungsniederschrift Kasimir Dittenheber, 9 February 1949.

[187] BAB, BDC SSO Strauss, Berchtold to Gauleitung Munich, 22 August 1933.

[188] BAB, BDC SSO Strauss, Strafliste Munich 21 April 1937.

[189] SAM, StA 34460, Beschuldigtenvernehmungsprotokoll Heinrich Strauss, 30 May 1950.

Of similar hue and likewise brought into the inner fold were two restless demobilized soldiers of the SA genre, violent thrillseekers. Born in 1900, Johann Unterhuber, like Wäckerle, had featured briefly on the Western Front in 1918. Upon demobilization and return to Munich, he enlisted with the *Freikorps* von Epp and was involved in its bloody terror of April 1919.[190] Seemingly unable to adjust to civilian life, he joined the French Foreign Legion in 1920 and served in Africa until 1926. In 1929 he found a new theatre of war by joining the Pasing SA, immersing himself in the street brawling culture of the times. Unterhuber was among the audience for Malsen-Ponickau's speech, and he too claimed to have been hauled without warning into Erspenmüller's grey omnibus. In addition to eager participation in set-piece beatings and drunken night-time chicanery, Unterhuber honed his criminality in the *Bunker*. There he worked closely with Johannes Kantschuster. It is most regrettable that Kantschuster was never captured after the war, for his was the only conduct to approach Steinbrenner's in infamy. Like Unterhuber, he was a rootless aspirant soldier and had also seen action with the French Foreign Legion. He joined the violent Pasing SA in 1928, transferring to its SS in 1932.[191] Kantschuster came to Dachau in April 1933 and soon became notorious among the prisoners for wanton violence. He was the murderer of Alfred Strauss, a Munich lawyer 'shot while trying to escape' on 24 May 1933. He and Unterhuber were the only members of the inner group to survive the transition to Eicke and went on to develop the *Bunker* as a place of raw and personalized terror: in their own gruesome nod to the Bavarian past its resident attack dog was named Arco.[192]

Karl Ehmann was another, older, member of the group with a political soldier's CV.[193] Born in 1896, Ehmann served on the Eastern Front in the First World War. In 1923 he moved to Augsburg, married, and worked as an oil and fat salesman before losing his job with the crash in 1929. In 1928 he joined the Augsburg NSDAP and SS, and his activities there offer an insight into the grubby street wars of its *Standarte* which, as has been seen, provided a sizeable proportion of the early Dachau SS. Already notorious in the city for binge-drinking and wife-beating, Ehmann apparently had his motorbike emblazoned with a swastika and as a member of 'Terror Group Augsburg' devoted his time to violent altercation with the local KPD, an idealism he was able to combine with an extensive range of gangster-like extortions.[194] Ehmann's repertoire of bar brawls and stabbings took a fateful turn in August 1932. Drunk, he paid a post-pub visit to the home of local KPD functionary, Josef Goss, and fired shots through the bedroom window, seriously injuring Goss' wife in the neck. Ehmann's long-suffering wife denounced him and Augsburg KPD councillor Leonard Hausmann distributed

[190] DaA, A3856, Urteil in der Strafsache gegen Johann Unterhuber, 10 March 1952.

[191] SAM, StA 34832/3, Zeugenvernehmungsprotokoll Johann Unterhuber, 16 January 1951.

[192] DaA, A1960 Hans Schwarz, 'Wir Haben es nicht Gewusst. Erlebnisse, Erfahrung und Erkenntnisse aus dem Konzentrationslager Dachau', p. 88.

[193] SAM, StA 34462/1, Einvernahme Karl Ehmann, 8 September 1948.

[194] SAM, StA 34462/4, Zeugenvernehmungsprotokoll Karl Ziegler, 20 March 1950.

his picture to local Party members. Unfortunately for Hausmann, the KPD seem not to have caught up with Ehmann, and when, as a Communist, he was taken into protective custody in Dachau, Ehmann was among his captors. On 17 May 1933, Ehmann led Hausmann out to the woods near the camp and shot him at point blank range 'trying to escape'. He was later overheard boasting of the deed in an Augsburg pub.[195]

A final, and altogether different, member of the inner circle was Karl Wicklmayr. Wicklmayr, born in 1909, came to Nazism and the SS in 1931 via the students' movement at Munich University where he was reading philosophy.[196] A war of the totalitarian doctrines seems to have played out in his own mind: in the late 1920s he evinced a passionate commitment to Leninist communism and would harangue classmates on the need for 'heads to roll' to change the world. Then, influenced it seems by Nietzsche, he switched allegiance to the far Right and immersed himself in local beer hall politics. Prisoners are united in the judgement that Wicklmayr was an oddball (*Sonderling*). In the toxic environment of Dachau he became a murderer also; shooting Josef Goetz, KPD organizational leader for South Bavaria, in his cell on 8 May 1933.[197]

## THE EARLY VIOLENCE IN DACHAU

As this brief survey of its leadership corps makes clear, the early Dachau SS did not come to the concentration camp as the 'ordinary' men discussed by universalist perpetrator literature. They were deeply imprinted with a Bavarian narrative which embraced, and served to politicize, innumerable localized grievances and vendettas. It is not, perhaps, all that surprising that early concentration camp personnel felt empowered to murder under the rubric of revolutionary justice. For on 18 March, just a few days prior to the opening of Dachau, the SA perpetrators of a particularly brutal and notorious murder in the Upper Silesian village of Potempa had been pardoned in a national blaze of publicity. In common with many of the murders committed by the early Dachau SS, the Potempa murder had combined ideological enmity with squalid personal grievances; revolutionary patriotism disguised and indemnified base vendetta.[198] The judicial value of human life, cheapened already by successive amnesties for political murder during the Weimar Republic, was drained further.

A number of the deaths in early Dachau stood squarely in the tradition of Weimar political murder. Major Herbert Hunglinger of the SA and Sebastian Nefzger of the SS met horrific ends in the *Bunker* on suspicion of having betrayed the Nazi cause in Munich. Such killings had a rich heritage in right-wing German

[195] SAM, StA 34462/4, Zeugenvernehmungsprotokoll Therese Kraft, 21 March 1950.
[196] SAM, StA 34461/2, Zeugenvernehmungsprotokoll Otto Seemüller, 17 July 1950.
[197] SAM, StA 34461/2, Zeugenvernehmungsprotokoll Otto Seemüller, 17 July 1950.
[198] Richard Bessel, 'The Potempa Murder', *Central European History*, Vol. 10, No. 3 (Sep., 1977), pp. 241–54.

paramilitarism.[199] Höß, to take a well-documented example, was imprisoned during the Weimar Republic for the slaying of a purported turncoat and embezzler in the *Freikorps* Rossbach. In May 1923, he and some comrades had dragged Walter Kadow into woods near Parchim in Mecklenburg, beaten him unconscious, cut his throat with a knife, and finally shot him twice.[200] In his autobiography, Höß looked back on the incident with evident pride:

> The Freikorps and their successor organisations administered justice themselves, after the ancient German pattern of the *Vehmgericht* [secret court of honour, CD] of olden times. Treachery was punished with death, and there were many traitors so executed.[201]

Steeped in the mythology of the *Freikorps*, here too the early Dachau SS rehearsed their behaviour. Hunglinger was brought to Dachau in the same transport as Beimler along with six other SA men designated as traitors to the cause. The excitement among the SS at their arrival had been 'electric', Steinbrenner recalled.[202] All the prisoners were severely beaten and the brown uniforms of the SA were soon in shreds.[203] Hunglinger was afforded special treatment. After shrieks of 'you traitor, you sow, you skunk', the SS dragged him to arrest cell 1 of the *Bunker*. According to Beimler, Hunglinger confided to him that he had joined the NSDAP in 1920 and helped to run a school for Nazi leaders in Munich.[204] When the Nazis gained control of the records of the Bavarian Political Police (BPP) in 1933, however, these revealed that he had been an informant. After several days and nights of torture and violence, Hunglinger hanged himself in his cell.

The fate of traitors from the hallowed ranks of the SS could be grimmer still. Nefzger, an amputee who had lost a leg in the First World War, endured a characteristic *Feme* execution. A salaried member on the staff of *Standarte* Munich, BPP records revealed that he, too, had been passing sensitive *Standarte* information onto both the police and his brother, a member of the KPD.[205] Steinbrenner, who from his post-war prison cell took to sending helpful letters to Naaff on the crimes of the early Dachau SS, suggested that Gauleiter Wagner had played a role in arranging Nefzger's murder.[206] On 25 May two guards, Szustak and Walter Kaune, came to visit Nefzger in his cell. The details of the ensuing murder are not entirely clear, for the two displayed little comradeship in their post-war interrogations, accusing one another of sole perpetration. Undoubtedly, however, it was of a nature grotesque even by Dachau standards. According to Kaune, Szustak beckoned Nefzger, already savagely beaten, towards him.[207] As Nefzger hopped forward, supporting himself with his hand on the wall, Szustak knocked him over, removed a length

---

[199] On *Feme* murders in Bavaria, see the monograph by Ulrike Claudia Hofmann, *'Verräter verfallen der Feme!': Fememorde in Bayern in den zwanziger Jahren* (Cologne, 2000), esp. pp. 50–171.
[200] In Orth, *Konzentrationslager SS*, pp. 110–12.
[201] Höß, *Commandant*, p. 43.
[202] SAM, StA 34479/1, Erweiterer Lebenslauf des Hans Steinbrenner, 3 January 1953.
[203] Hans Beimler, *Four Weeks*, p. 21.     [204] Hans Beimler, *Four Weeks*, pp. 23–5.
[205] SAM, StA 34479/2, Zeugenvernehmungsprotokoll Steinbrenner Hans, 9 December 1951.
[206] SAM, StA 34479/2, Steinbrenner to Untersuchungsrichter, 14 February 1953.
[207] SAM, StA 34479/2, Zeugenvernehmungsprotokoll Walter Kaune, 12 November 1952.

of cord from his pocket and wrapped it around his neck. Either Szustak or Kaune then slashed Nefzger's left wrist three times with a table knife and, finally, hanged him via his prosthetic leg. The autopsy revealed the cuts had been bone deep, and it was unclear whether Nefzger had died from strangulation or bleeding.[208] Violence and murder against internal traitors is a common mechanism of cohesion and radicalization in group dynamics. Carried out internally, the murder of purported traitors highlights the value placed on loyalty in the collective, and signals the consequences of betrayal to the remainder. The same principle would operate during the 'Night of the Long Knives' in June 1934, when senior SA officers were executed by the SS in Dachau for their involvement in the supposed 'Röhm conspiracy' (see Chapter 2). These murders both punished the internal dissidents and advertised the unflinching loyalty of the perpetrators on both an individual and collective level.

The early violence in Dachau, then, was deeply inflected by its cultural and historical context. Each of the initial murders was premeditated and not, as such, a form of the everyday violence understood by universalist literature as a manifestation, above all, of a toxic environment. The latter in these cases was permissive, rather than prescriptive. It is also striking, to say the least, that fourteen of the twenty-two murder victims in Dachau in 1933 were Jewish, whereas Jews comprised less than 10 per cent of the prisoners.[209] Although not imprisoned *qua* Jews, being Jewish rendered Communist inmates highly vulnerable to lethal violence in the camp in part because they were held to unify the lessons of 1918/19. Jewish Communist prisoners, in this sense, represented a validation of the Nazi world view. It was from this matrix of localized racism and vendetta, framed still in the imagery of civil war and revolutionary justice, that the very first and definitive murders by the early Dachau SS stemmed and a Rubicon was crossed. On 12 April, just two days after the SS takeover of the protective custody compound, Erwin Kahn and three other Jewish prisoners, Ernst Goldmann, Rudolf Benario, and Arthur Kahn, were shot in woods near the camp allegedly 'trying to escape'.

Vogel later testified that he was approached in the afternoon of 12 April by a group of four or five armed SS men bearing a slip of paper with the names of four inmates. He was told that these prisoners were to be assigned to 'punishment labour' (*Strafarbeit*).[210] The prisoners were then set to work shovelling earth under the personal supervision of Steinbrenner, who led them back to the compound in the evening. The subsequent course of their murder is difficult to reconstruct due to the prevalence of hearsay and speculation in prisoner testimony, and evasion in that of former SS men. It seems that Steinbrenner handed the prisoners over to Erspenmüller and two comrades from his Munich *Sturm*, who led them out

---

[208] DaA, 8.834, Lagerarzt to Amtsgericht, 27 May 1933.

[209] DaA Häftlingsliste Statistiken. Todesfällen im KL Dachau 1933-17.02.1940; Richardi, *Schule*, p. 88. On Jewish prisoners in Dachau, see the comprehensive and definitive study by Kim Wünschmann, 'Jewish Prisoners in Nazi Concentration Camps 1933–1939' (PhD thesis, University of London, 2012), passim.

[210] SAM, StA 34461/3, Zeugenvernehmungsprotokoll Anton Vogel, 12 January 1951.

to the woods by the camp from whence up to twenty shots were soon heard.[211] Erwin Kahn, nevertheless, survived and was taken to Schwabing hospital, where he told medical staff about the incident before succumbing to his wounds. One of the more perplexing and grotesque aspects to these murders is why the SS would attempt to murder a prisoner and then send him to a hospital for treatment, even though he was now a 'bearer of secrets' (*Geheimnisträger*) who had witnessed the premeditated slaughter of three fellow prisoners. The answer is contained in Naaff's post-war interrogations of the State Police.

Police Lieutenant Schuler, the ranking police trainer for the SS troops in Dachau, was shaving in his office when he heard pistol shots.[212] He rushed outside with his revolver in the direction of the nearby woods. There he encountered Erspenmüller who, in a military fashion he was not required to adopt to Schuler, announced that four prisoners had been 'shot while trying to escape'. The scene was gruesome. Two prisoners lay motionless, while a third was seriously wounded, crying in agony and begging to be 'finished off'. This Erspenmüller proposed to do until Schuler warned it would be murder. Schuler ran off to fetch the police doctor but another shot soon rang out and he returned to find this third man now dead, shot in the back. Further moaning then alerted Schuler to the fact that the fourth prisoner, lying deeper in the woods, had also survived. This man, too, Erspenmüller proposed to 'finish off', but Schuler's ongoing presence prevented him on this occasion.

Evi Kahn saw her husband once in Schwabing hospital before he died.[213] His room was guarded by two SA men. He told her that on the evening of the shootings, he had been gathering roofing paper with Benario, Goldman, and Arthur Kahn. An SS man approached him and Benario and asked whether the load was heavy. With a polite smile, Kahn replied that it was not. The SS man commented 'we'll soon wipe that filthy smile off your face' before shooting Benario at point-blank range. Kahn, who had covered his face with his hands in horror, remembered nothing else before falling unconscious. He had been shot twice in the head. Kahn's death in the hospital some days later is more than suspicious, for its staff initially believed he was recovering: one historian argues plausibly that he was murdered by the guards posted at his bedside to prevent him being interrogated by the judiciary.[214]

The murder of these four Jewish prisoners was of incalculable importance to the institutional psychology at Dachau. A set-piece of centripetal group complicity, it was decisive in framing Dachau concentration camp as a 'murder camp', as the title of Beimler's memoir put it.[215] Yet the immediate, biographical, motivation for

[211]  Richardi, *Schule*, pp. 88–90.

[212]  SAM, StA 34465, Zeugenvernehmungsprotokoll Schuler Emil, 29 March 1951.

[213]  SAM, StA 34465, Aussage Euphrosina Ehlers, 4 February 1953.

[214]  Seubert, R., "'Mein lumpiges Vierteljahr Haft . . .'" Alfred Anderschs KZ-Haft und die ersten Morde von Dachau: Versuch einer historiografischen Rekonstruktion', in Jörg Dörig and Markus Joch (eds), *Alfred Andersch 'Revisited': Werkbiographische Studien im Zeichen der Sebald-Debatte* (Berlin, 2011), pp. 47–146, here, pp. 91–2. The official cause of death was meningitis.

[215]  Hans Beimler, *Four Weeks*.

the murders remains unclear. None of the four men were headline Communists like Beimler, although Benario and Goldman were members of the KPD.[216] Their racial status undoubtedly inflated their resonance as enemies of Nazism at a time when antisemitic passions were running particularly high in the movement after the economic boycott earlier in the month.[217] Lieutenant Schuler recalled that Wäckerle had been particularly jumpy on the day of these murders, and speculated that 'in his rage and fear of a communist revolt' he had ordered the murder of the four Jewish activists.[218] The timing of the murders, the day after the SS had taken control of the protective custody compound, suggests that the intent was exemplary, an opportunity to demonstrate the sincerity of the declaration of martial law in the camp.[219] It would not, of course, have been a great surprise to activists of the Left that Nazi paramilitaries would resort to murder; the precedents of 1919 and the violence towards the end of the Weimar Republic were eloquent enough. But in street brawls and assassinations there had always been at least an occasion, a suggestion of proportionality, absent in these four murders. They also introduced the prisoners to the fictive official explanation which would be given for their deaths and become an internal camp SS euphemism—'trying to escape'. Vogel apparently lectured the inmates that the alleged attempted escapes merely confirmed the cowardice of the leaders of the labour movement, so many of whom had already fled Germany.[220]

Steinbrenner later wrote that Erspenmüller had previously bragged about an imminent 'trial of strength' (*Machtprobe*) for the SS.[221] If true, it seems likely that the guard troop commander had the Bavarian police, as much as the prisoners, in mind. The scene in the woods brings the relationship between the SS and the police into stark focus. It is worth reiterating that Kahn was one of twelve prisoners murdered before the camp was handed over fully to the SS on 30 May 1933. To what extent were the State Police complicit in this criminality? The post-war testimony of police personnel is unanimous in averring that they treated the prisoners with courtesy, as equals, and sought to protect them from the predations of the SS.[222] Many prisoner memoirs concur: others, however, contend that some policemen partook in beatings and chicanery.[223] Relations between Communists and the Weimar police had been dire: unlike the Nazis, who postured as agents of order, Communist paramilitaries were often involved in violent altercation with the police. Nor is there any doubt that the Bavarian State Police, brought into being during the post-war revolutionary firmament, were fully paid-up members of the

[216] Excellent biographies of these men provided by Seubert, 'Vierteljahr Haft', pp. 81–92.

[217] Wünschmann, 'Jewish Prisoners', pp. 79–81.

[218] SAM, StA 34465, Zeugenvernehmungsprotokoll Schuler Emil, 29 March 1951.

[219] Erklärung Kasimir Dittenheber, Munich 1 November 1947, cited in Seubert, 'Vierteljahr Haft', p. 103.

[220] Grünwiedl, *Dachauer Gefangene erzählen*, pp. 5–6.

[221] DaA 19.862, Hans Steinbrenner, Hinter den Kulissen von Dachau, s. 2.

[222] SAM, StA 34465, passim. See also Richardi, *Schule*, pp. 48–57.

[223] *Nazi-Bastille Dachau: Schicksal und Heldentum deutscher Freiheitskämpfer* (Paris, 1938), pp. 24–8; SAM, StA 34461/3, Vernehmung Oberbürgermeister Michael Poeschke, 23 July 1948; SAM, StA 34462/7, Zeugenvernehmungsprotokoll Josef Gabriel Weilheim, 19 July 1951.

great antisocialist consensus in Bavaria. Decades later, Schuler himself penned a potted history of the organization making clear that it saw itself very much as the successor to the forces of counter-revolution in 1919:

> Civil war raged in Munich until the 'Freikorps' Epp and other formations moved in on the city and restored orderly relations . . . These units, who were able to quell the chaos reigning in Germany were not, however, suitable to guarantee peace and order throughout the land on a permanent basis . . . Thus did the governments in the individual states turn their minds to the creation of an organisation able permanently to preserve peace and order.[224]

The very insignia of the Bavarian State Police, a panther, symbolized this proactive, martial heritage. And unlike in Prussia, it had not been subject to the processes of purge and reform associated with extended state governance by the SPD: the Bavarian police were very much products of the 'nucleus of order'.[225] Many of its officers came from the army, another hotbed of reactionary and punitive opinion. It is also noteworthy how many future luminaries of the Bavarian SS have spells in the State Police on their CVs. They include Dietrich, Hermann Fegelein, Carl Demmelhuber (commander of SS *Standarte* 'Germania'), and Dachau's final commandant Eduard Weiter. The first two commanders of the Dachau guard units, Erspenmüller and Michael Lippert, were graduates of the Bavarian State Police. At least one police officer in early Dachau, Sebastian Wimmer, went on to become a commander in the Dachau guard formations, while Höß's memoirs suggest there were others besides.[226]

Even the more critical prisoner testimony does not suggest that the behaviour of the police in Dachau was comparable to the early Dachau SS. Yet their presence in the camp failed to hinder a developing murderous habitus at a time when the power of the SS was far from unbound. Indeed, Captain Winkler offered unflinching support to Ehmann in his deposition to the judiciary over Hausmann's murder. Ehmann claimed that he had been minding Hausmann as he unearthed saplings near the camp when the prisoner suddenly bolted into the undergrowth.[227] Numerous injunctions to return being unheeded, Ehmann continued, he had been forced to fire in Hausmann's direction from a distance of ten to twelve metres. The post-mortem quickly ascertained that the shots had been fired from a distance of less than a foot. Yet Winkler commended the thuggish, boozy Ehmann as a 'calm and sober man' and declared himself 'fully convinced of the truthfulness of Ehmann's account'.[228] This solidarity on the part of the ranking police officer in the camp borders, to say the least, on situative complicity.

---

[224] Schuler, *Landespolizei*, p. 5.
[225] The best general account of the Weimar Bavarian Police remains Johannes Schwarz, *Die bayerische Polizei und ihre historische Funktion bei der Aufrechterhaltung der öffentlichen Sicherheit in Bayern von 1919 bis 1933* (Munich, 1977).
[226] Höß, *Commandant*, p. 236.
[227] IMT Prozesse gegen die Hauptverbrecher, Vol. XXVI, Document 641-PS, pp. 172–3.
[228] DaA, 8.883, Zeugenvernehmung Hauptmann Winkler, 18 May 1933.

The State Police seem to have been less impressed with the early Dachau SS as a military phenomenon. Kasimir Dittenheber, one of the camp's first prisoners, noted one policeman's patronizing verdict on the SS trainees: asking with understandable concern whether the rumours of a full handover to the SS were true, he was told that for all their swaggering talk in the camp canteen, the Dachau SS could 'barely hold their guns'.[229] The SS themselves appear to have been conscious of their limitations in the event of a Communist counter-strike. There are indications of a defensive, even siege, mentality which seem inexplicable save in terms of an investment in the civil war narrative. Schuler, for example, testified that Wäckerle

> who was not a courageous man, lived in perpetual fear of an assault by communists and repeatedly came to me for advice as to what he should do in such an eventuality. After all, at this time my police trainers were the only line of defence, as the SS men did not yet know how to shoot.[230]

Prisons, as symbols of injustice and repression, had certainly been a historic focus of insurrection. In 1918, the historian Nikolaus Wachsmann notes, 'German penal institutions were in the thick of the revolution', as crowds led by armed soldiers sought to spring free political prisoners.[231] Dachau concentration camp, soon known by exile groups as the 'Nazi Bastille', would have made a prime target. The local political topography would not have assuaged such concerns. Dachau had suffered severe economic contraction in the post-war era and by 1929 had the highest level of unemployment in Weimar Germany.[232] The political beneficiaries were the SPD and, increasingly, KPD, both of whom developed a commensurate paramilitary presence.[233] In the November 1932 Reichstag election the NSDAP polled just 12.4 per cent in Dachau compared to a Bavarian average of 30.5 per cent, whereas the KPD vote of 20.5 per cent was twice the state mean. The local middle classes remained staunchly loyal to the Catholic Bavarian People's Party (BVP), with whom Nazi relations were largely rancorous and not improved by Frick's forcible dissolution of Held's venerable BVP state government. The early Dachau SS, then, was not in friendly territory. With this in mind, Wagner had ordered a round-up of seventy local Communists on the eve of the camp's opening.[234] Even the prisoners pinned some hope on a Communist uprising sponsored, perhaps, by the Soviet Union. As one memoirist recalls, 'this help, it was said, was closer than you think'.[235]

Dachau's first set of guard regulations seem to register such concerns. They include contingent defence plans for attacks from the woods to the north-west

[229] DaA, Deutsche Häftling-Bericht: Kasimir Dittenheber, 'Ich war Hitlers Gefangener', p. 3.
[230] SAM, StA 34465, Zeugenvernehmungsprotokoll Emil Schuler, 29 March 1951.
[231] Nikolaus Wachsmann, *Hitler's Prisons: Legal Terror in Nazi Germany* (New Haven, 2004), p. 36.
[232] Steinbacher, *Dachau*, p. 227.
[233] Steinbacher, *Dachau*, pp. 58–60. A speech by Rudolf Hess in the Hoerhammer pub was cut short in February 1933 in a rare moment of 'iron front' cooperation between Reichsbanner and Red Front paramilitaries.
[234] Steinbacher, *Dachau*, p. 189.
[235] Walter Hornung, *Dachau: Eine Chronik* (Zurich, 1936), p. 75.

of the camp, or from the south-west where barracks inhabited by former munitions factory workers afforded cover. The early recognition of an assault is ranked
first in the list of guards' responsibilities.[236] A reflection of, and contributor to,
this apprehensive mentality was Beimler's escape from the camp on 9 May, spar-
ing himself certain death. He was able to unscrew the wooden board over his cell
window and crawl through it, force a gap in the electrified barbed wire, and egress
using the insulation provided by the board. He then crept undetected to the 2 m
high perimeter wall of the camp and climbed out without being noticed by the SS
sentries. Beimler's escape was undoubtedly bold and ingenious, but greatly abetted
by the fact that the camp's defensive installations and, it would seem, perimeter
guards, were mainly directed outwards: focused on deterrence rather than contain-
ment. He never revealed its full details for fear of endangering his accomplices.[237]

The humiliation for the early Dachau SS was complete when Beimler, from
the relative safety of the Soviet Union, published an international account of his
nightmarish experience called *Four Weeks in the Hands of Hitler's Hell Hounds*.
Steinbrenner, catapulted to international infamy by the text, was shown a copy
in 1951 by the Munich prosecutors. He remarked sniffily that it was 'hateful
and extremely tendentious'.[238] *Four Weeks* was indeed conceived as Communist
propaganda, but its atmospheric depiction of early Dachau, and of Steinbrenner
in particular, is amply supported by other sources: this SS man merited his life
imprisonment. The escape also furthered an increasingly unhinged turn in camp
discourse. Steinbrenner recalled the wild imagery Wäckerle had invoked in ordering him to murder KPD functionary Karl Lehrburger two weeks later:

> The day before Ascension in 1933 commandant Wäckerle gave me the order to shoot
> Lehrburger. He explained that Lehrburger was a Soviet agent, trained by the Cheka in
> bacterial warfare. It was assumed that a further agent was at large who would be tipped
> off were a trial held. In order not to alarm the local populace, the captured agent had
> to be shot immediately.[239]

This was good enough for Steinbrenner, who shot Lehrburger in his cell the following day. The murderous conduct of the early Dachau SS, however, had by
now attracted the attention of conscientious individuals in the local state prosecutor's office. Deputy Prosecutor Josef Hartinger was a regular visitor to the
camp. Wäckerle, with his ever-present and menacing dog, he found obstructive
and sinister. Wilhelm Birzle, on the other hand, a guard whom he visited in
the SS infirmary for questioning, was astonished at his presumption. He accused
Hartinger of being 'an agent of the Commune' and conveyed his 'outrage' that he,
Birzle, who was fighting the critical battle with the Communists, should be called
to account.[240] Hartinger's complaint to the commandant's staff met with a volley
of invective. A wave of five feebly disguised murders in two chaotic weeks after

[236] DaA, A4118, Übergabe-Protokoll, 30 May 1933.   [237] Richardi, *Schule*, pp. 12–15.
[238] SAM, StA 34462/7, Beschuldigtenvernehmungsprotokoll Hans Steinbrenner, 13 June 1951.
[239] DaA, A3856, Vernehmungsniederschrift Hans Steinbrenner, 19 August 1948, s. 7.
[240] DaA, A3194, Zeugenvernehmungsprotokoll Josef Michael Hartinger, 27 March 1951, s. 59.

Beimler's escape sealed Wäckerle's fate: Himmler was forced to remove him from his post at the end of June. Among the Bavarian officials ranged against him was the Minister of Justice Hans Frank, evincing a punctiliousness for which he was not noted later in his career. But both Frank and German political culture had far to travel, and the SS and its *Reichsführer* were still small fish in a complex poly-cratic pond. Fundamentally, the unilateral declaration of martial law in Dachau had no validity: murder remained illegal and the camp's obstructive attitude to the judiciary had alienated powerful interests. Wäckerle had to go.[241]

Under his successor, Eicke, the majority of the early Dachau SS NCOs were also gradually moved on. By now the Nazi regime was established, the organizations of the Left had been brutally routed.[242] According to its historical schema, accounts with these particular villains of 1918 had been settled. On 6 July 1933 Hitler averred that the revolutionary impetus of the Nazi movement should henceforth 'be channelled into the secure bed of evolution'.[243] The summary execution of leading Communists in Dachau, a rehearsal of *Freikorps* behaviour from 1919, was incongruous in a stabilized post-revolutionary state. For years to come, KPD pris-oners were bullied and beaten to find out where Beimler was, where the weapons and death lists were hidden.[244] The discourse and memory of 1919 were kept alive by the presence of figures from the Bavarian revolutionary era as prisoners on the heavy roller work brigade, while the Munich authorities dedicated a procession of streets and monuments to the Bavarian *Freikorps*.[245] The Bavarian past provided a rhetorical resource and rationale for Dachau's distinctive and self-important cul-ture of nightmare order and proactive, gleeful guards. Although the undisguised executions abated, the early Dachau SS established a tone to SS–prisoner relations from which the camp never emerged. Years later, Höß recalled of his transfer to Sachsenhausen in 1938 that here 'there was not the same atmosphere of hatred as existed in Dachau'.[246] Many prisoners unfortunate enough to offer a comparative perspective of camps concur.[247] For the next six years, guards and functionaries were schooled in Dachau and dispatched to other concentration camps in the expectation that they would export with them the 'Dachau spirit'. Steinbrenner, purportedly disillusioned with one-sided violence in Dachau, had left the camp in August 1933 to take up a post guarding the Ministry of the Interior in Munich. The role of auxiliary policeman, however, was still not to his taste. In a matter of months the primary entrepreneur and protagonist of the 'Dachau spirit' was back at the camp, instilling it into the next cohort of sentries as an SS drill instructor in the Dachau School.

---

[241] Detailed account in Tuchel, *Konzentrationslager*, pp. 121–41.
[242] For recent scholarship on the camps and the Left in 1933, see Nikolaus Wachsmann and Sybille Steinbacher (eds), *Die Linke im Visier: Zur Errichtung der Konzentrationslager 1933* (Munich, 2014).
[243] In Jeremy Noakes and Guy Pridham (eds), *Nazism: 1939–1945*, Vol. 1 (Exeter, 1997), p. 171.
[244] Examples in *Nazi-Bastille Dachau*, pp. 21–30.
[245] Hornung, *Dachau*, p. 155; Rosenfeld, 'Monuments', pp. 231–3.
[246] Höß, *Commandant*, p. 82.
[247] Detailed memoirs include Bruno Heilig, *Men Crucified* (London, 1941), pp. 154–278, esp. 211; Laurence, 'Dachau Overcome', pp. 9–22; Neurath, *Society*, passim.

# 2

# The Dachau Guard Troops

The guard troops (*Wachtruppe*) were the sentries of the concentration camps. They guarded the perimeters against external threat, manned the guard towers and their machine guns, accompanied prisoner work details to and from their sites of toil, and stood watch over them during the day. The composition, organization, and outlook of the Dachau guard personnel changed considerably during the era of the Dachau School. Initially, all 250 members of the early Dachau SS not appointed to Wäckerle's prototype command staff partook in sentry duty with daily rotation for weapons training under the Bavarian State Police. Guns and ammunition were in short supply, accommodation was crude, and the longevity of both camp and the employment it provided were unclear. By the eve of the war the Dachau guard units, rebranded the SS Death's Head 'Upper Bavaria', comprised some 3,200 men who usually spent one week in the month on rotating guard detail and their remaining time on military training and exercises consonant with the Third Reich's bellicose foreign policy at the vast adjacent SS *Übungslager* (training complex). The unemployed Party activists had become, SS documentation suggests, elite professional soldiers, holding the line against the enemy within and posed for deployment against foes without. Detailed regulations governed their every action, and military discipline had replaced the chaotic violence of the camp's first years. The Death's Head guards were forbidden both to enter the prisoner compound and to interact with the prisoners, still less to abuse them. 'The Führer alone decides over the life and death of an enemy of the state' ran one of the many sworn statements signed by Dachau guards, and 'no National Socialist is entitled to lay a hand on him'.[1] The reality, of course, was quite different. The Death's Head troops enjoyed only modest prestige, even within the SS. Many of the principles, techniques, and narratives of the early Dachau SS endured; arbitrary violence remained the order of the day. Prisoners lived in daily fear of the disposition and competitive chicanery of guard units and individuals. They dropped off to sleep hoping above all, as one put it, for 'halfway decent sentries' on their work detail the next day.[2] Often, they were to be disappointed. Many sentries undoubtedly did have very little direct contact with prisoners, and did not avail themselves of the ample opportunity

[1] BAB, BDC RS B223, Ehrenwörtliche Verpflichtung, 7 September 1938.
[2] Schecher, 'Rückblick', p. 15.

to lord it over them which existed beneath the regulations. For others, abusing inmates was an escape from the tedium of sentry duty, as well as a well-trodden path to recruitment to the commandant staff. A key function of the guard troops was to provide a manpower reservoir for the latter, and transfers between the two areas were frequent. Indeed, many command staff personnel, as will be seen, had extensive prior experience in the Dachau guard units. This chapter will focus on the latter's composition, self-conception, command culture, and training, and consider which factors most shaped the behaviour of Dachau sentries. It will explore the important processes of militarization and the activities of the guard battalions as 'political soldiers' beyond the watchtowers. Before this, however, it will address the key topic of recruitment and the guiding role played here by Theodor Eicke, Wäckerle's successor as Dachau commandant.

## VOLUNTEERS

Theodor Eicke (Figure 2.1) will feature prominently throughout this study. Born in a small village in Alsace in 1892, he was the eleventh son of an austere, devout, and patriotic station master.[3] Eicke studied at his village school for eleven years with modest success before joining the Imperial Army as a paymaster at the age of seventeen. From here on his biography was contested, for Eicke was a much mythologized figure in the SS. Höß, for example, recounts him as follows:

> Eicke came from the Rhineland and during the First World War fought on every front and was many times wounded and decorated. When the Rhineland was occupied he took a leading part in the resistance movement against the French. He was sentenced to death in his absence by a French military tribunal and remained in Italy until 1928.[4]

The first five words aside, it is doubtful whether any of this is true. Eicke's war record is elusive, and the role of paymaster less front-line and heroic than SS hagiographies imply. He claimed to have chosen to leave the army after the war, but was probably discharged. Eicke then took a course in police administration attracted, no doubt, by the continuities of uniform, discipline, authority, and prestige.[5] His passion was not requited. Eicke failed to hold down three successive jobs with the police, fostering the kind of embittered loathing and self-pity which would characterize his later world view. He claimed to have been released from his final post as a consequence of 'Red terror' in the force, but most likely it was a lack of educational attainment and social nous which held him back. The tale of heroic struggle against the French occupation of the Rhineland is cut entirely from cloth. Eicke certainly lived in the Rhineland at this time, for in 1923 he found employment as a salesman and then

---

[3] Of the many detailed biographies of Eicke in secondary literature the most rigorous is Tuchel, *Konzentrationslager*, pp. 128–40. See also the more ambitious, if speculative, profile in Segev, *Soldiers*, pp. 137–55.

[4] Höß, *Commandant*, p. 235.

[5] Such is also the assumption in Tuchel, *Konzentrationslager*, p. 129.

**Figure 2.1** Theodore Eicke, Dachau's second commandant and subsequently head of the Concentration Camp Inspectorate. Here displaying his medals for service with the Death's Head Division, in 1942 or 1943. Bundesarchiv, image 146-1974-160-13A.

security officer in the I.G. Farben plant in Ludwigshafen. There is no evidence, however, of any partisan resistance to the French and it seems likely that Eicke later peddled an early biography inspired by proto-Nazi martyrs such as Leo Schlageter, who had indeed been sentenced to death by a French military tribunal. A memorial to Schlageter was built in Dachau during Eicke's tenure as commandant and beatings of inmates were known as 'Schlageter parties' (*Schlageterfeier*), a pun on the German verb *schlagen*, to beat.[6] Eicke remained undisturbed at I.G. Farben, rather than in Italian exile, until 1932. On 1 December 1928 he joined the NSDAP and the Ludwigshafen SA, transferring to its SS in July 1930. In October of the same year Himmler promoted him to officer rank and charged him with building up the local SS. So successful was Eicke in this regard that he was promoted to *Standartenführer* in October 1931. It is illustrative of the cheapness of rank in the early SS that within fifteen months of joining the organization, Eicke had risen to a position purportedly commensurate to colonel in the Reichswehr.[7]

[6] SAM, StA 34462/7, Zeugenvernehmungsprotokoll Karl Lindner, 24 October 1950.
[7] Charles Sydnor, 'Theodor Eicke: Organisator der Konzentrationslager', in Ronald Smelser (ed.), *Die SS: Elite unter dem Totenkopf. 30 Lebensläufe* (Paderborn, 2000), p. 150.

In summer 1931 Eicke was tasked by the Palatinate Gauleiter, Joseph Bürckel, with carrying out a terrorist campaign in Bavaria for the Nazis. He was arrested in March 1932 for possession of high explosives and sentenced to two years in penitentiary, a misfortune he attributed to treachery by Bürckel. Thanks to a judiciary still robustly partisan in favour of the Right, Eicke was able to secure a stay of sentence of six weeks due to ill-health during which, at Himmler's instructions, he did now flee to Italy. Promoted yet again to *Oberführer*, Eicke was put in charge of a Nazi refugee camp at Malcesine near Lake Garda. On 16 February 1933, now the beneficiary of an amnesty, Eicke returned to Germany to participate in the seizure of power. His first priority, characteristically, was vendetta. Eicke launched a clumsy armed *Putsch* against Bürckel but the latter, now a powerful Nazi potentate, was soon rescued by the police and had Eicke arrested. Eicke retorted with a two-day hunger strike, which saw him committed to a psychiatric clinic in Würzburg with Himmler's approval. This interlude did not feature in SS biographies. He was found sane by the institution's staff and passed the time writing lengthy petitions for release to Himmler. The latter was convinced that Eicke still had something to offer the SS and, after being forced to dismiss Wäckerle as Dachau commandant, it was to Eicke he turned.

Eicke arrived at Dachau directly from the Würzburg clinic. He was evidently resolved to redeem himself in Himmler's eyes, to replicate the heady days of his meteoric rise through the ranks on the strength of an undoubted organizational talent. Eicke was by now in his forties and Dachau offered him the opportunity finally to make something of his life. A keen sense of theatre, characteristic of Nazi paramilitary *Führer*, was to the fore. Max von Dall-Armi, Eicke's 'work service leader' (*Arbeitsdienstführer*) in Dachau, later penned an account of Eicke's first weeks in the camp:

> When Eicke arrived at the camp in June 1933 everything at first carried on as before. Eicke often walked around the camp on his own, asking questions and making notes. One day he summoned the whole camp SS and introduced himself as the new commandant . . . The state police gradually disappeared . . . New positions were created. Now Eicke is in his element. He works day and night at the reorganisation of the camp. He sleeps in the camp by his office (his flat was not yet built and his family joined him later). He is the first at work in the morning, and the light in his office is on late into the night. New camp regulations are drawn up and he issues directives and orders on all matters. The troops adore him and he knows how to treat them. The name 'Papa Eicke' was coined even then. He is an excellent orator . . . He is tough on the rank and file, but stricter still against officers. He hates his enemies behind the barbed wire . . . He speaks of their destruction and annihilation. He instils this hatred into the SS through speeches and conversations. Eicke is a fanatical SS officer and ardent National Socialist for who there is no compromise . . . 'SS men must hate . . . the heart in their breasts must be turned to stone.'[8]

    [8] SAM, StA 34461/4, Max von Dall-Armi, Bilder und Skizzen aus dem Konzentrationslager, 13 April 1951.

In a typically self-celebrating letter to Himmler in 1936, Eicke claimed that on appointment as Dachau commandant he had inherited a 'corrupt guard troop' of just under 120 men.[9] SS Group South, he claimed, had until then used employment in the camp as a sinecure for unwanted personnel. Dachau's sentries lived in 'draughty factory buildings', and were stricken by 'poverty and hardship'. Eicke depicted his stewardship as one of uninterrupted progress. Fortified by the 'ideals of loyalty, courage, and fulfilment of duty', his sentry units expanded and professionalized 'in the quiet of the concentration camps'. By October 1933 there were nearly 400 guards in Dachau, 764 in June 1935, and over 1,000 by the beginning of 1936. With the outbreak of war in September 1939, SS personnel records registered no fewer than 3,179 guards posted at the camp.[10] In numerical terms, Dachau's sentry formations had certainly come far from their modest beginnings: who were these SS guards, and how did Eicke and the 'Death's Head' units recruit them?

The first point to emphasize is that the SS was a volunteer formation. This was fundamental to its collective psychology, patterns of authority, and sense of historic mission. Voluntarism and idealism, highly prized concepts in the Third Reich, reached discursive apotheosis in its ranks. The SS located itself in a heroic European ancestry of soldier volunteers stretching back through Garibaldi and Lord Byron to the Wars of Liberation.[11] In this nationalist tradition, the volunteer was associated with earnest patriotism, with disdain for material gain, and with an almost biblical willingness for sacrifice.[12] Most proximate of all in the German consciousness were the volunteers of August 1914. The mythology of 1914's 'civil truce', of German youth of all classes rallying to the colours, was a primary referent for the People's Community and the volunteer was a hallowed figure in Nazi discourse. In *Mein Kampf*, guiding text of the Third Reich and the staple of SS ideological instruction, Hitler dwelt on him at length:

> the amount of irreplaceable German heroes' blood that was shed in those four and a half years was enormous. Just sum up all the hundreds of thousands of individual cases in which again and again the watchword was: *volunteers* to the front, *volunteer* patrols, *volunteer* dispatch carriers, *volunteers* for telephone squads, *volunteers* for bridge crossings, *volunteers* for U-boats, *volunteers* for airplanes, *volunteers* for storm battalions etc.—again and again through four and a half years, on thousands of occasions, volunteers and more volunteers—and always you see the same result: the beardless youth or the mature man, both filled with fervent love of their fatherland, with great personal courage or the highest consciousness of duty, *they* stepped forward.[13]

---

[9] Letter printed in Christian Goeschel and Nikolaus Wachsmann (eds), *The Nazi Concentration Camps: A Documentary Reader* (Lincoln and London, 2012), pp. 157–9, here p. 157.

[10] BAB, NSD 41/37, Statistische Jahrbücher der Schutzstaffel der NSDAP 1937 and 1938.

[11] A narrative sketched in great detail by one SS luminary: Felix Steiner, *Die Freiwilligen der Waffen-SS: Idee und Opfergang* (Oldendorf, 1958), pp. 13–40. For a typically stylish overview of war volunteering in Europe see Mosse, *Fallen Soldiers*, passim.

[12] Mosse, *Fallen Soldiers*, pp. 15–33.

[13] Hitler, *Mein Kampf*, p. 473 (emphasis in original). SS men were presented with a wood-bound copy of *Mein Kampf* at their marriage ceremonies.

It was no accident that Hitler prefaced his 'final testament' of 29 April 1945 with the observation that he had been a volunteer in 1914. The author Ernst Jünger, an icon of interwar German militarism (see Chapter 5), was also one of *them*. He pointedly contrasted the commitment of volunteers like him in the trenches with that of conscripted men.[14] Conscripts were indeed somewhat suspect to conservatives and nationalists, associated with desertion and the treacherous soldiers' councils of 1918, while Jünger and his peers cast volunteers as Nietzschean supermen, escaping the shackles of mediocrity in committing every fibre of their being to the cause.[15] The 'assault squads' of the Western Front were volunteers, the *Freikorps* were volunteers, the Reichswehr were volunteers: this was an ancestry the SS was anxious to claim and mobilize.

In 1938, a consortium of Party and business organizations inaugurated an annual 'Langemarck Studies' educational programme for German youth to explore and replicate the idealism of 1914. The SS urged talented young recruits to apply.[16] The Battle of Langemarck, near Ypres, was the centrepiece of the romantic cult of 1914. The cream of German youth, volunteers one and all, fired by pure idealism, were said to have charged the British lines with patriotic songs at their lips.[17] Perhaps 145,000 German soldiers fell in what was in reality a reckless and futile offensive, but in nationalist mythology it became a distillation of the fervent patriotism of the German Youth Movement, and of how German youth still one day might be. The poignant vocabulary of 'irreplaceability' abounded in talk of the 1914 volunteers, and it was one Nazism and the SS sought to refute with a renaissance through German youth.[18]

Recruits to the Dachau School were frequently reminded of the sacrifices of this earlier generation of volunteers. In June 1937, Eicke was moved to poetics by the trope in his orders of the month:

> Officers and NCOs should always bear in mind that our men have volunteered to come to us in good faith, in the first flush of youth, and with great excitement. With bright eyes they see their new surroundings, trusting deeply in SS officers and NCOs who enjoy great social prestige. These young men willingly subordinate themselves and enter full of expectations into the school of obedience. These men are not called up by conscription law, they come voluntarily to serve the Führer; following their inner yearning, they forego their parents' house to allow themselves to be sculpted in body and mind by the SS. This free will counts for more than law, it should be

[14] Ernst Jünger, *The Storm of Steel* (London, 1975), p. 8.

[15] Mosse, *Fallen Soldiers*, p. 211; Hans Buchheim, 'Command and Compliance', in Buchheim et al., *Anatomy*, pp. 308–20; on conscripts, see Himmler's speech to the Wehrmacht in January 1937, discussed in detail below. IMT, Vol. XXIX, 1992 (A)-PS, Himmler to National-Political Course of the Wehrmacht, 15 to 23 January 1937, here s. 209.

[16] IfZ, MA 847, SS Hauptamt Langemarckstudium 5 March 1939, s. 2958662

[17] Mosse, *Fallen Soldiers*, pp. 70–3; Eksteins, *Rites of Spring*, pp. 310–11. On the Langemarck Myth in Nazi Germany, see especially Bernd Hüppauf, 'Langemarck, Verdun and the Myth of a *New Man* in Germany after the First World War', *War and Society*, Vol. 6, No. 2 (Sep., 1988), pp. 70–103. The topos of the Verdun soldier is explored in Chapter 5 of the present book.

[18] Richard Bessel, 'The "Front Generation" and the Politics of Weimar Germany', in Roseman, *Generations*, pp. 121–8.

gratefully recognised and carefully nurtured, for out of it come the finest deeds and performance. Without this free will, there can be no obedience, no loyalty, no honour, and no sense of duty.[19]

Eicke's saccharine vocabulary clearly draws on romantic mythologies of the volunteer embedded in German nationalist discourse: 'with bright eyes' (*mit hellen Augen*) is particularly lyrical formulation. The volunteer principle lent added resonance to soldierly ideals of comradeship and youthful masculinity (see Chapter 5). It also aligned with notions of self-abnegation and disdain for material gain very useful in Eicke's under-resourced Death's Head troops. Another of his monthly orders from 1937 was sharply critical of guards who were apparently tempted to apply to join the German police for the better pay and pensions on offer there.[20] Eicke contrasted this materialism with the countless sacrifices old fighters such as him had willingly made in the 'time of struggle'. He claimed that he had never bothered to check what he would receive on retirement and opined that 'young people who have the great privilege to fight for their country under the Führer's flag do not even have to give a passing thought to so marginal a question'. The doctrine of personal sacrifice to the greater cause drew on the principle of voluntary allegiance to the SS and was part of a broader sacralization of the Great War experience on the nationalist Right.[21] 'A soldier does not expect thanks and recognition', wrote future Dachau commandant Hans Loritz in 1934: implying, of course, that both would be merited.[22]

Closely linked to the imagery of the selfless 'bright eyed' volunteer was the youthful profile of recruits to the concentration camp guard formations. National Socialism had elbowed its way into German politics in part by its gospel of youthful redemption: 'Make way you old ones', as Gregor Strasser's famous slogan had put it.[23] The 'seizure of power' was depicted as a victory of a young and vibrant Germany over the gerontocracy of the Weimar establishment, and the SS saw itself very much as young Germany's avant garde. Within it, the Death's Head were the most youthful formations, and their ranks became progressively younger during the pre-war, Dachau School, era. In August 1936 their average age was 23.2, in September 1937 22.9, and by December 1939 just 20.7. This compared with an average age at the latter date elsewhere in the SS of 28.7.[24] The youthful profile of the Death's Head personnel delighted Himmler. He enthused to an audience of SS Group Leaders in November 1938 that younger guards offered a balance of malleability and resilience ideal for carrying out such a demanding role.[25] From time to time, he confided, SS officers came to him with concerns about the potentially

[19] IfZ, MA 293, IKL Befehlsblatt 1 July 1937, s. 2550154.
[20] IfZ, MA 293, IKL Befehlsblatt 1 March 1937, s. 2550207.
[21] Mosse, *Fallen Soldiers*.
[22] BAB, BDC SSO Loritz, Loritz to Himmler, 9 January 1934.
[23] Peter D. Stachura, *The German Youth Movement 1900–1945: An Interpretive & Documentary History* (London, 1981), p. 113.
[24] BAB, NSD 41/37, Statistische Jahrbücher der Schutzstaffel der NSDAP 1937 and 1938.
[25] IfZ, MA 312, Rede der RFSS bei der Gruppenführer-Besprechung in München, 8 November 1938, s. 2012547.

corrupting influence on young SS men of daily exposure to the criminal elements held in the camps. He, however, saw their youth as an advantage. The SS had seen the problems which arose from deploying older personnel as camp guards in the first years of the Third Reich: either they became sadistic, corrupted by their power, or they turned into 'a kind of faith healer, forever sympathising with the prisoners'. Himmler believed that young SS guards were better able to avoid these twin pitfalls. Moreover, as a reserve force to defend the Reich in the event of war, it was vital that they acclimatize young to demanding tasks; youngsters should be capable, even when they were seventeen or eighteen, of guarding dangerous elements during peacetime. Eicke fully shared this enthusiasm for what were referred to in SS discourse as *blutjung* recruits. *Blutjung* means something like 'in the first flush of youth', and this in Eicke's view was no older than twenty-one.[26] Even a 16-year-old with a well-developed frame should be admitted without reservation; those older than twenty-one were merely a 'burden' for the Death's Head troops whose training programme should be bestowed only on the finest racial material. German law, not coincidentally, regarded a young male as a minor until he reached the age of twenty-one; another salient facet to the paternalist construct of 'Papa Eicke' and 'Eicke's boys'.

To an extent Himmler and Eicke were making a virtue out of a necessity. Rank-and-file sentry service in the camps was modestly remunerated, of dubious prestige, and entailed a life spent away from family and friends in the SS barracks. The two were also obliged to source new recruits in an increasingly competitive manpower environment, as the rearmament-fuelled economic recovery soaked up male labour from the market. A circular from the mid-1930s noted that the total SS complement of 300,000 men already required an intake of 30,000 new volunteers per year simply to replace those stepping down from active service.[27] Given an annual cohort in Germany of some 300,000 to 500,000 young men reaching serviceable age, the SS needed to secure between 7 and 10 per cent of these simply to replenish its ranks. Its ambition to build up the Death's Head and its sister SS Verfügungstruppe ('Special Purpose Troops') to substantial military resources notched up these demanding minima higher still.

The prized reservoir of young males for the many military institutions in Nazi Germany was the Hitler Youth, the NSDAP organization for boys aged fourteen to eighteen. This comprised some 55,000 boys in late 1932, 568,000 at the end of 1933, 1.17 million at the end of 1936, and 1.67 million by the end of 1938. In March 1939 membership was finally made compulsory for 'Aryan' children.[28] The Hitler Youth was Nazism's main tool for indoctrinating German youth, and the SS regarded it as invaluable preparation for service in its own ranks. Like the SS, the Hitler Youth stressed physical conditioning, Darwinian competition, toughness, will, loyalty, and all-round 'character'. It was suffused with military practices and ideals: even the Social Democratic underground conceded that many

---

[26] IfZ, MA 293, IKL Befehlsblatt 1 May 1937, s. 2550182.
[27] BAB, NS19/1457, 'Der Weg des SS-Mannes', n.d., s. 10.
[28] Figures in Noakes and Pridham, *Nazism*, Vol. 2, p. 421.

young Germans revelled in 'the novelty, the drill, the uniform, the camp life'.[29] The American journalist William Shirer recalled his weekend picnics around Berlin constantly interrupted by Hitler Youths 'scrambling over the woods or over heath, rifles at the ready and heavy army packs on their backs'.[30] Nurtured on militarism, anticlericalism, and racial vigilance, the most committed of these young males were highly compatible with the SS.

Systematic recruitment from the Hitler Youth seems not to have been discussed until 1935, but at the end of 1936 Himmler boasted to his Group Leaders that he had given more speeches that year to the Hitler Youth than to internal audiences.[31] At the institutional level Hitler Youth and SS officers were enjoined to establish a 'permanent comradely relationship'.[32] They were to organize joint camps and schooling sessions, and to participate jointly in cultural events. SS formations were to teach the Hitler Youth about their historic tasks and world view, while in return the Hitler Youth would pass on 'new music and songs crafted by the younger generation'. Solemn torchlit festivals provided opportunities to draw Hitler Youth into the woodsy aspects of SS culture. One such event was the summer solstice festival near Dachau on 21 June 1938. A torchlit parade of the men of the Death's Head troops and flag-bearing local Hitler Youth was set to music by an SS band. The participants heard speeches by officers from both organizations and sang 'Flame rise up' as the Hitler Youth passed a burning torch to Max Simon, commander of the Dachau guard units.[33]

No systematic data exists for the number of Dachau guards who were recruited directly from the Hitler Youth, but it can be assumed that most young recruits by the mid-1930s had served some kind of apprenticeship in this antechamber to paramilitarism. In April 1936, Eicke wrote to Himmler that the current near doubling of the national Death's Head ranks comprised the finest boys from the Hitler Youth, who were volunteering 'with enthusiasm'.[34] There is evidence, however, that some young men 'volunteered' for SS service at NSDAP and Hitler Youth offices under considerable pressure, in which reluctance to do so was depicted as a symptom of ideological and patriotic insincerity.[35] When ideological exhortation failed, recruiters linked service in the SS to future career prospects in Hitler's Germany. SS 'mustering commissions' roamed the Reich and, despite a ban on recruiting 17-year-olds, conducted 'quiet observations' at Hitler Youth events and Labour Service camps.[36] The General SS was exhorted to track down recruits for the Death's Head units and in November 1936 every SS Group set up a dedicated recruitment office. According to SS statistics, in 1937 some 6,000 volunteers

[29] Noakes and Pridham, *Nazism*, Vol. 2, p. 427.
[30] William L. Shirer, *The Rise and Fall of the Third Reich* (London, 1991), p. 254.
[31] Gerhard Rempel, *Hitler's Children: The Hitler Youth and the SS* (North Carolina, 1989), p. 24.
[32] Karl Heinz Jahnke and Michael Buddrus, *Deutsche Jugend 1933–1945: Eine Dokumentation* (Hamburg, 1989), pp. 124–5.
[33] BAB, NS19/530, Sommersonnwendfeier Dachau, 5 July 1938.
[34] BAB, NS19/1925, Eicke to Himmler, 10 August 1936, s. 3.
[35] Wegner, *Waffen SS*, p. 306. For pragmatic recruitment practices, see also Hein, *Elite*, pp. 136–9.
[36] Rempel, *Hitler's Children*, p. 30.

from the General SS applied to join either the Death's Head or Verfügungstruppe, of whom 1,400 were accepted.[37] One recruit from this era was Heinrich S., an 18-year-old volunteer from Worms. In June 1936 he was told to report to Dachau for a medical examination and prepared for the day with a detailed list of instructions.[38] He was provided with a discounted rail ticket and warned that non-appearance would result in being struck from the list of candidates. He should bring a letter of consent from his father or guardian. If accepted, he would need to register with the local police, and provide a certificate of cancelled registration (*Abmeldebescheinung*) from his previous residence. Heinrich S. was also told to bring a washing and sewing kit, undergarments, and slippers. Many such recruits barely trouble the historical record; as will be seen, service in the Death's Head formations was often an intermediate stage between the Hitler Youth and an early grave in France or Russia. Henrich S., however, survived the early campaigns and returned to Dachau as a guard after being wounded in 1943.

As he built up the Death's Head formations, Eicke also increasingly sought personnel with military experience and training, especially those who had completed compulsory service with the Wehrmacht. The military expansion of the SS, given Hitler's explicit endorsement in August 1938, forced the latter to adopt a less obstructive posture towards such recruitment.[39] General Jodl accordingly agreed with Himmler that three months prior to the conclusion of their service, soldiers would be made aware by their commanding officer of the opportunity to join the Death's Head troops.[40] Eicke also sent 'headhunters' equipped with SS propaganda and recruitment literature to army bases, often to the chagrin of garrison commanders. Ultimately, Eicke enjoined his headhunters to use their initiative:

> Bring them from bars, bring them from sports clubs, bring them from the barber. As far as I'm concerned you can bring them from brothels. Bring them from everywhere you meet them.[41]

Such remarks lay bare the tension between the Death's Head formations' proclaimed eliteness and their ravenous appetite for recruits. In truth, the SS commitment to recruiting the racial cream of German youth had been abandoned by the late 1930s. Although Himmler bragged to Wehrmacht officers in 1937 that only 10–15 per cent of applicants were accepted into the SS, local statistics suggest that the figure was much higher; around 75–80 per cent in Region (*Oberabschnitt*) Elbe, for example.[42]

Nevertheless, the SS remained a volunteer formation throughout the pre-war period of the Dachau School and, in theory at least, throughout its existence.[43]

[37] BAB, NSD 41/37, Statistisches Jahrbuch der SS 1937, s. 42. On recruitment via the General SS, see also Hein, *Elite*, pp. 258–61.
[38] BAB, BDC RS F5393, RuSHA to Heinrich S., 4 June 1936.
[39] For detail, see below and Wegner, *Waffen SS*, pp. 112–21.
[40] IfZ, Fa 127/1, Jodl to Himmler, 2 September 1938, s. 116.
[41] Segev, *Soldiers*, p. 131.        [42] Longerich, *Himmler*, p. 303.
[43] Above all, as Longerich points out, the 'voluntary' enlistment of so-called *Volksdeutsche* (ethnic Germans) into the Waffen SS was often 'a farce'. Longerich, *Himmler*, p. 612.

This self-selection indelibly shaped its patterns of authority and compliance, and its approach to discipline and personnel retention. Self-selection is an important variable in scholarship on perpetrators. Social psychology has long identified volunteering as a salient factor in subject behaviour. Milgram and Zimbardo, for example, both advertised for volunteers to participate: this self-selection accentuated their initial identification with and commitment to the experiments.[44] Perpetrators volunteering for a task, then, should be deemed more attuned to its requirements than those merely 'at hand', to use the historian Raul Hilberg's phrase.[45] Individuals frequently take decisions to place themselves in, or to avoid, certain situations and environments in the first place.[46]

Two potential decisions need to be addressed here: volunteering for the SS, and deployment at Dachau. By the later 1930s the two in practice were normally coeval, as recruits volunteered directly to serve in the Death's Head units. In many ways, the early Dachau SS was the least-selected cohort of sentries. Largely unemployed activists from the part-time Bavarian SS, they were deployed at Dachau not because their *Standarten* believed they would be the best guards for a concentration camp—whatever that might mean at this time—but because they were unemployed and available. And yet these men founded the murderous 'spirit' of Dachau and did much to establish the behavioural norms of the SS concentration camp guard. But a good deal of self-selection, of course, had been involved in joining the SS in the first place. SS activism before 1933 brought financial, social, and legal complications: membership required substantial personal investment. After 1933 many of these drawbacks were reversed and it was socially beneficial, if not universally prestigious, to be an SS man. The SS was now also able to pay salaries to some members from Party funds, courtesy of the German taxpayer. Hence the reverence in SS circles for veterans from the 'time of struggle'. Older men joining after 1933 were disdained as 'March violets', as potential opportunists signing up only after the Enabling Law signified a certain permanence to Hitler's regime.[47]

The principal recruitment channel prior to the period of direct enlistment remained the part-time General SS. In stark contrast to the contemporary SS emphasis on voluntarism, guards from this era who were interviewed by post-war prosecutors almost always used the passive voice when recounting their deployment to Dachau. The characteristic phraseology is of being 'called up' (*eingezogen*), 'posted' (*abkommandiert*), 'transferred' (*versetzt*), 'enlisted' (*herangezogen*),

---

[44] See the discussion of both experiments in Zimbardo, *Lucifer*, pp. 267–76. According to Milgram, '[i]n the case of voluntary allegiance to a legitimate authority, the principle sanctions for disobedience come from within the person. They are not dependent on coercion, but stem from the individual's sense of commitment to his role. In this sense, there is an internalized basis for his obedience, not merely an external one'. Milgram, *Obedience*, p. 142.

[45] Hilberg, *Destruction*, p. 649.

[46] There is a useful summary of issues and specialist literature in Thomas Carnahan and Sam McFarland, 'Revisiting the Stanford Prison Experiment: Could Participant Self-Selection Have Led to the Cruelty?', *Personal and Social Psychology Bulletin*, Vol. 33, No. 5 (May, 2007), pp. 603–14.

[47] Höhne, *Order*, p. 134. The literal translation of the German *Märzgefallene* is 'March fallen', an allusion to the casualties of the 1848 revolutions in Vienna and Berlin.

'assigned' (*zugeteilt, abgestellt*), even 'conscripted' (*einberufen*).[48] This of course reflected judicial calculation as much as the personnel policies of the SS. The more forthcoming testimony by recruits from this era suggests a kaleidoscope of paths to the camp. Josef D. had been forced to give up his university studies due to lack of funds, and 'heard' that volunteers were being sought for the camp.[49] Steinbrenner, too, had financial problems and went to see Eicke to offer his services anew for the guard detail.[50] Other guards, like Ottmar H., came via friends and comrades already in the guard troops.[51] Alfred Ernst transferred to the camp at the suggestion of his home SS Standarte.[52] Many others claimed to have requested transfer from part-time to active SS service solely due to unemployment.[53] There is no evidence here of violation of the voluntary principle in deployment to Dachau.

The prospect of paid employment in these early years of economic distress was clearly an important extrinsic motivation for guard service. When Dachau guards offered employment as the primary reason for signing up to Dachau—rather than to the unsalaried General SS—they were not necessarily being disingenuous.[54] The initial pay for the early Dachau SS was certainly far from munificent and, according to Steinbrenner, even the 1 Reichsmark per day they earned as auxiliary policemen was often not forthcoming and had to be begged or borrowed from various sources in Munich.[55] Yet the remuneration soon switched to a monthly pay scale financed by the Bavarian state.[56] The rank and file guard earned 115 Reichsmark per month gross, netting to 67 Reichsmark after deductions for insurance, Labour Service contributions, taxes, and meals. For married guards the respective figures were 130 and 82 Reichsmark. These men received an additional 2 Reichsmark as compensation for living away from their families and 6.25 Reichsmark per month per child. Every sentry received free accommodation and uniform, and a loyalty scheme was devised to pay a lump sum of 1,800 Reichsmark to any guard who left service in the camp after serving at least five years.

[48] For example, SAM, StA 34832/3 Zeugenvernehmungsprotokolle Ernst Angerer, 30 August 1951; SAM, StA 34462/4 Vernehmungsprotokoll Otto Franck, 28 December 1949; SAM, StA 34405 Beschuldigten-Vernehmung Erwin Busta, 12 July 1962; SAM, StA 34402 Vernehmung Maximilian Seefried, 21 May 1947; SAM, StA 34462/1 Beschuldigtenvernehmung Karl Stoelzle, 7 December 1949; SAM, StA 34764 Vernehmungsniederschrift Karl Minderlein, 20 February 1970; SAM, StA 34668 Vernehmungsprotokoll Josef D., 10 September 1965. See also Gabrielle Hammermann, 'Verteidigungsstrategien der Beschuldigten in den Dachauer Prozessen und im Internierungslager Dachau', in Ludwig Eiber and Robert Sigel (eds), *Dachauer Prozesse: NS-Verbrechen vor amerikanischen Militärgerichten in Dachau 1945–1948* (Göttingen, 2007), pp. 86–108, here p. 91.
[49] SAM, StA 34668, Vernehmungsprotokoll Josef D., 10 September 1965.
[50] SAM, StA 34462/7, Beschuldigtenvernehmungsprotokoll Hans Steinbrenner, 13 June 1951.
[51] SAM, StA 4132, Vernehmungsprotokoll Ottmar H., 8 August 1938.
[52] BAB, BDC RS B223, Verpflichtung, 6 November 1933.
[53] E.g. SAM, StA 34452/2 Urteil Spruchgerichtsverfahren gegen Josef Blank 6 January 1949; SAM StA 34479/2 Zeugenvernehmungsprotokoll August Ludwig Seyler, 28 May 1953.
[54] Buggeln, *Arbeit*, p. 390; Koslov, *Gewalt*, p. 133 Riedle, *Angehörigen* also stresses these material, extrinsic inducements.
[55] DaA, 19.862, Steinbrenner, 'Hinter den Kulissen', s. 4.
[56] DaA, 6.698, Besoldung, n.d. (1933), s. 1. More generally on the complex early financing arrangements for Dachau, see Drobisch and Wieland, *System*, pp. 86–7.

Table 2.1 Pay scale for Death's Head units, July 1937.

| Rank | Single | | Married | |
|---|---|---|---|---|
| | RM per month | Annualized | RM per month | Annualized |
| SS Mann (first year) | 65.00 | 780.00 | | |
| SS Mann (second year) | 77.00 | 924.00 | | |
| SS Sturmmann | 95.00 | 1,140.00 | | |
| SS Rottenführer | 105.00 | 1,260.00 | 127.80 | 1,533.60 |
| SS Unterscharführer | 118.70 | 1,424.40 | 153.85 | 1,846.20 |
| SS Scharführer | 158.53 | 1,902.36 | 193.03 | 2,316.36 |
| SS Oberscharführer | 181.84 | 2,182.08 | 228.93 | 2,747.16 |
| SS Hauptscharführer | 186.50 | 2,238.00 | 233.59 | 2,803.08 |

In 1935 Hitler agreed that, as of the following April, the sentry units would be financed from the Reich budget, with the other camp running costs met by the individual states. Candidates could now apply to join the Death's Head units directly, and pay for entry-level personnel was much the same as before at 65 Reichsmark per month. Substantial pay rises, however, were now available on promotion (see Table 2.1).

To place these figures in context, in 1936 the average monthly income of male German blue collar workers was 147 Reichsmark and 250 Reichsmark for male white collar workers.[57] Almost two thirds of German taxpayers reported monthly incomes of under 125 Reichsmark. Remuneration in the Death's Head formations lagged behind the police and army, but considering the subsidized food and accommodation, recruits attaining the non-commissioned rank of *Unterscharführer* would be doing well for often unskilled young men. The generous pay increments available on promotion were a powerful material incentive and binding mechanism. Kurt-Fritz Mayr was a guard in the early Dachau SS. He had joined the SS in February 1932 and came to the camp as SS-*Mann*. Yet he was promoted to *Sturmmann* in September 1933, *Rottenführer* in January 1934, *Unterscharführer* in June 1934, *Oberscharführer* in November 1934, and *Hauptscharführer* in July 1935, putting him at the top of the NCO pay scale when the above levels were introduced. By the time he headed off to the field with the Death's Head Division in 1939, he was drawing an *Obersturmführer* salary of 312 Reichsmark per month: double the average pay of a male German manual worker.[58]

With this in mind, it is striking that recruitment posters for the Death's Head formations appeal almost solely to extrinsic, rather than intrinsic (role-related), motivations. They stipulate that volunteers should be 'morally, mentally and racially pure, ideologically committed to National Socialism, [with] hunger and

---

[57] Adam Tooze, *The Wages of Destruction: The Making and Breaking of the Nazi Economy* (London, 2007), pp. 141–2.
[58] BAB, BDC, RS D5301, s. 1147; BDC, SSO Mayr.

devotion for SS service'.[59] The height and age criteria are set out, while wearers of glasses and those with criminal convictions since the Weimar era are excluded. Yet beyond this the inducements are material rather than ideological. Volunteers are promised accommodation, uniform and standard troop provision, and the opportunity to progress to officer rank. The standard period of enlistment is four years, with six and twelve years optional. Those serving the latter are guaranteed a post in the police at its conclusion, standard practice in the German Reichswehr.[60] The Dachau guard who attributed his decision to join the Death's Head troops after military service to his need for additional years to qualify for the civil service career track was presumably not alone.[61]

The Death's Head recruitment pitch, then, was framed in terms of economic benefits and social mobility. Concentration camps and prisoners are nowhere to be found in this material. This is an important point. For had the SS believed that these intrinsic aspects of the job would appeal to potential volunteers, that many young men would find the prospect of guarding inmates enticing ideologically, they would surely feature somewhere in the material. To be sure, military recruitment posters throughout history have seldom offered an accurate or comprehensive depiction of military life.[62] Their objective is to get recruits through the door after which they can be resocialized into the values and behaviours of the service. But the material and military inducements in the Death's Head recruitment literature clearly counsel against mono-motivational, dispositional hypotheses for concentration camp guard conduct. Naturally, applicants would have been well aware of the connection between the Death's Head units and the concentration camps, although even here it is important to remember that this meant something quite different in 1937 than in 1944.

For the majority of recruits coming directly from the Hitler Youth, ideological sympathy and the prospect of joining a familiar organization and self-styled, smartly uniformed elite were clearly important factors.[63] Some no doubt were attracted by the idea of military life and comradeship, others to independence from parents or to the prospects for promotion not available to those from non-privileged backgrounds in the Wehrmacht. The ideological and the material are difficult to disentangle in the Third Reich and the scattered post-war testimony of rank-and-file Dachau sentries is not detailed enough to do this. What can be said for certain is that no Death's Head volunteer had reservations over life as a concentration camp guard strong enough to offset whatever positive investment he made in signing up.

---

[59] IfZ, Fa 127/1, Merkblatt für Einstellung in die SSTV (Ausgabe Juli 37), s. 1.

[60] IfZ, Fa 127/1, Merkblatt für Einstellung in die SSTV (Ausgabe Juli 37), s. 4.

[61] SAM, StA 34462/1 Vernehmungsniederschrift Simon Meier, 2 February 1948.

[62] On this, see the monograph on US military recruitment by Melissa T. Brown, *Enlisting Masculinity: The Construction of Gender in US Military Recruiting Advertising during the All-Volunteer Force* (Oxford, 2012).

[63] These functionalist factors are (predictably) privileged by Sofsky in SS recruitment: Sofsky, *Order*, p. 99.

## COMMAND AND COMPLIANCE

The passive vocabulary and military terminology later used by ex-guards to account for their deployment in Dachau was intended to suggest that they had no real choice in the matter. Whereas the voluntarist diction of the SS implied ideological assent and enthusiasm, their vocabulary connoted soldierly compliance: that the guards had, in a well-worn phrase, merely 'followed orders' like soldiers in the Wehrmacht. This was untrue. For whereas Wehrmacht personnel did indeed have a legal duty to the state to obey orders insofar as they complied with the law, SS men had simply sworn voluntary political allegiance to Hitler.[64] They may have pledged 'obedience unto death to you and those you appoint' but this was a paramilitary oath and had no legal status. From this perspective they were perfectly entitled simply to leave the SS should they not wish to comply with assignments or instructions. Himmler came close to acknowledging this during his speech to the Wehrmacht. He observed that SS discipline during the Weimar era had depended on consent because, as he put it, an SS man could just say 'I quit, I want no more of this'.[65] Yet the legal situation during the Third Reich was little different and the implication, tailored here to the audience, that discipline in the SS was no longer a voluntary matter, was disingenuous. Although the juridical status of the armed SS formations was increasingly blurred, in June 1936 the SS Main Office confirmed that desertions from the Death's Head or Verfügungstruppe would not legally be recognized as such, unlike in the Wehrmacht.[66] Not until October 1939 was the SS permitted to set up an independent judicial system with a military penal code to oversee its armed units.[67] Throughout the era of the (pre-war) Dachau School, then, the SS had no legal sanction against non-compliance by guard personnel.

Himmler told his Wehrmacht audience that rigorous processes of racial selection had staffed the ranks of the SS with men who understood obedience as a moral virtue rather than legal requirement. As he put it elsewhere, SS obedience was the product of honour and loyalty, 'a matter of the heart' rather than rational calculation.[68] The decisive commitment in matters of compliance was joining the SS in the first place, as in Eicke's comments on the voluntary entry of guards into his 'school of obedience'. Yet this commitment was not irrevocable on either side and release (*Entlassung*), both elective and involuntary, was quite frequent from the SS. Involuntary release could be imposed by the *Standartenführer* of the man concerned

[64] Buchheim, 'Command and Compliance'. Like most German historians of his generation, Buchheim tends to present a rather optimistic picture of a 'clean' Wehrmacht, but the underlying legal and organizational arguments are sound.

[65] IMT, Vol. XXIX, 1992 (A)-PS, Himmler to National-Political Course of the Wehrmacht, 15 to 23 January 1937, s. 209.

[66] IfZ, Fa 127, Heissmeyer Memorandum, 4 June 1936, s. 408.

[67] Bianca Vieregge, *Die Gerichtsbarkeit einer 'Elite': Nationalsozialistische Rechtsprechung am Beispiel der SS- und Polizeigerichtsbarkeit* (Baden-Baden and Berlin, 2002), pp. 6–12. Vieregge argues against the assumption that the introduction of SS jusrisdictional autonomy was a response to the criminal activities of SS units in Poland and stresses the pre-war planning and antecedents. One of the punishments handed out by SS courts was hard penal labour in the 'SS and Police Penal Camp' at Dachau.

[68] Himmler, *Schutzstaffel*, p. 13. See also Hein, *Elite*, pp. 93–5.

for reasons such as physical deterioration, 'lack of interest', or unexplained absences from service.[69] Elective release was equally common. An SS man whose choice of bride was rejected by the RuSHA, for example, was entitled to leave in order to pursue the marriage. Josef D., a Dachau SS NCO and veteran of the *Freikorps* von Epp did just this in August 1937.[70] That year, according to the SS annual statistics, 7,960 men were released from the organization: 146 came from the Death's Head troops, eighty-one at their own request.[71] Requests for release were often made on professional grounds and, if not granted in good spirit, were at least tolerated, as the following order to the Sachsen guard detail in the mid-1930s suggests:

> Requests for release are continually being received from sons of farmers on the grounds that they are suddenly desirous of taking over their family farm. Such men are of no interest to the guard unit, the duties of which they have clearly failed to grasp. All such requests for release will be forwarded to higher headquarters with a recommendation for acceptance.[72]

Eicke's addresses to the Death's Head troops are peppered with such rhetorical invitations for the uncommitted to leave guard service. The guard battalions, he wrote, did not demand 'enforced loyalty' and any man who was not up to the job 'could walk away from us in peace'.[73] In a speech at Dachau, he invited 'weaklings' to 'withdraw to a monastery as quickly as possible'.[74] In orders of the month for March 1937, he commented that personnel were entitled to grouse about orders provided that they carried them out loyally and immediately. Whether a particular command was 'suitable' or 'military' was no business of the recipient to evaluate and 'whoever does not happily and willingly obey orders is no SS man, but rather a calculating man (*Zweck-Mann*); there can be no greater pleasure for us than to be rid of him'.[75] This is not to say that the process was as smooth and painless as Eicke implied or that some personnel might have feared retribution afterwards. After deserting from the early Dachau SS in May 1933, Karl Wicklmayr claimed to have spent nine months lying low as a farm labourer in Landshut in fear of being 'finished off' by Himmler.[76] Even if true, however, this had more to do with Wicklmayr's fragile mental condition than with any objective danger.

Indeed, the disciplinary sanctions available against SS men were rather limited even when they were on site and committed to the 'school of obedience'. The principal quotidian punishments, or 'means of education for SS men schooled as soldiers', as Eicke put it, were formal warnings and brief periods of arrest.[77] His

---

[69] For example, SAM, NSDAP 750, Gruppenbefehl Nr 5, 27 October 1933. On release and other sanctions in the General SS, see also Hein, *Elite*, pp. 191–200.

[70] BAB, BDC RS B32 Josef D. Entlassungsgesuch aus den SS-TV Dachau, 2 August 1937.

[71] Buchheim, 'Command and Compliance', p. 392; IfZ, MA 293, IKL Befehlsblatt, 1 May 1937, s. 2550182.

[72] Cited in Buchheim, 'Command and Compliance', p. 393.

[73] BAB, NS 31/372, Eicke Circular, 2 December 1935, s. 4.

[74] Höß, *Commandant*, p. 68.

[75] IfZ, MA 293, IKL Befehlsblatt, 1 April 1937, s. 2550196.

[76] SAM, StA, 34461/1, Vernehmungsniederschrift Karl Wicklmayr, 10 September 1948; SAM, StA, 34461/2, Claus Bastian to Munich Strafkammer, 22 October 1949.

[77] IfZ, MA 293, IKL Befehlsblatt, 4 June 1937, s. 2550182.

circulars suggest that the most common occasions for these measures were conversing with prisoners, tardy implementation of orders, drunkenness, and reporting late for roll call.[78] Beyond this, the only substantial sanctions the SS had against guards were demotion in rank, with the financial penalty this also brought, or dismissal from the organization. There were two types of dismissal. The first was temporary or permanent 'exclusion' (*Ausschluss*) and could be imposed by *Gruppenführer*. It included reduction to the rank of SS *Mann* and was applied to serious disciplinary infractions, mutiny, and particularly egregious damage to the reputation of the SS. The second, imposed only by Himmler himself, was permanent 'expulsion' (*Ausstossung*). This was accompanied by expulsion from the NSDAP and applied to the most serious of misdeeds: robbery, murder, and embezzlement.[79] For some SS men there was a path back from 'exclusion', though not from 'expulsion'. In July 1938, Himmler ordered the creation of a special 'Education Platoon' in Sachsenhausen near Eicke's offices in Berlin for former SS men to work their way back into the fold. By the outbreak of the war some seventy-three former SS men were detained here in comparatively comfortable conditions, their uniforms marked with crossbones as a reminder of their disgrace. Although only a small number were from the Death's Head units, the 'education' section of the platoon included men who had committed military infractions on guard duty, and its 'correction' section guards who had fraternized with inmates in some way.[80]

Eicke made quite regular use of the one-way tool of expulsion and depicted it in the starkest of terms as a psychological and social catastrophe for the guard concerned.[81] An individual who deserted, applied for a position outside the guard units behind his superior's back, or committed a serious disciplinary infraction at his post, he warned, would be expelled from the Death's Head units. The process would be emotional and humiliating. First, the man concerned would be demoted and expelled in front of his former comrades. He would find himself removed from a select minority and thrown back into the 'nameless mass'. He would discover that he was no longer a 'free' man, but an 'unfree, pitiful civilian'. The taint of expulsion would follow him everywhere: marked as unreliable, rarely would such a man find work. The SS, the regular police, and the Gestapo would keep a file on him and he would be permanently excluded from any position in the movement. All awards and decorations would be rescinded. Eicke concluded his dystopian narrative with the fervent hope that in the future he would no longer find himself obliged to hand out this most draconian of 'hard fates'.

Yet even Eicke did not suggest that expulsion would lead to physical retribution against the guard concerned. He would simply forfeit the financial security, prestige, and comradeship he supposedly enjoyed in the Death's Head units. The allure of conformity and belonging, set against the spectre of exclusion, should not

---

[78] IfZ, MA 293, IKL Befehlsblatt, 1 July 1937, s. 2550161.
[79] SAM, NSDAP 750, Gruppenbefehl Nr 5, 27 October 1933.
[80] Nikolaus Wachsmann, 'KL: A History of the National Socialist Concentration Camps' (Unpublished MS), ch. 2; Goeschel and Wachsmann, *Nazi Concentration Camps*, pp. 165–6.
[81] IfZ, MA 293, IKL Befehlsblatt, 1 March 1937, n.p.

be underestimated as an integrative force.[82] In the absence of coercive instruments, it was fundamental to command and compliance among concentration camp guards. Milgram's 'obedience to authority' studies are of particular relevance here. A staple of universalist perpetrator literature, they command broad recognition in the field of social psychology and have been replicated many times.[83] One replication carried out with male volunteers in Munich elicited 85 per cent compliance, higher even than Milgram.[84] Among historians, conversely, Milgram's conclusions meet heavy criticism: some well-founded, some rather desperate.[85] At first glance, the notion of 'obedience' seems incongruous, distasteful even, when applied to Nazi perpetrators. Defendants at Nuremberg, Dachau, Jerusalem, and Frankfurt readily alighted on the defence that they had merely been obeying orders, whereas scholarship on Holocaust perpetrators has documented a protracted excess, zeal, initiative, and creativity which map poorly to a narrowly defined concept of 'obedience'.[86] Acts of violence and murder by guards at the Dachau School, too, were generally encouraged implicitly rather than ordered explicitly.

No tenable case could be made that Milgram's work fully 'explains' the conduct of perpetrators of violence, National Socialist or otherwise. His later proposition that subjects enter a discontinuous, almost robotic 'agentic state' under authority is unconvincing.[87] Instead, and more directly than the Stanford Prison Experiment (see Chapter 4), Milgram registered the contribution of social and

---

[82] Historians have of late applied this much more broadly to Nazi German society. See Michael Wildt, *Volksgemeinschaft als Selbstermächtigung: Gewalt gegen Juden in der deutschen Provinz 1919–1939* (Hamburg, 2007); Thomas Kühne, *Belonging and Genocide: Hitler's Community, 1918–1945* (Yale, 2010).

[83] See the interesting scholarly biography by Thomas Blass, *The Man Who Shocked the World: The Life and Legacy of Stanley Milgram* (New York, 2004), here pp. 309–11; Arthur G. Miller, 'Reflections on "Replicating Milgram" (Burger, 2009)', *American Psychologist*, Vol. 64, No. 1 (2009), pp. 20–7. See also the excellent discussion of Milgram in Welzer, *Täter*, p. 107ff. The broader relevance of Milgram's work also reflects the fact that he deliberately avoided using college students: his subjects were highly heterogenous—see the (often insensitive and judgemental) character sketches by Milgram in *Obedience*, pp. 45–55; 74–91.

[84] David Mark Mantell, 'The Potential for Violence in Germany', *Journal of Social Issues*, Vol. 27, No. 4 (1971), pp. 101–12.

[85] For a positive assessment, see Browning, *Ordinary Men*, pp. 171–6; for a measured critique, see the comments by Richard Overy in conversation with Haslam and Reicher: 'Milgram and the Historians', *The Psychologist*, Vol. 26, part 9 (September, 2011), pp. 662–3. For hostile reception from an influential particularist, see Cesarani, *Eichmann*, pp. 15, 352–6. For the more hysterical, see Omer Bartov, *Germany's War and the Holocaust: Disputed Histories* (USA, 2003), p. 182 as well as his uncharacteristically rambling critique of Sofsky in the same volume, pp. 99–111. Bartov complains that Milgram's 'is a behaviourist explanation *par excellence*'. It is not. Behaviourism, dominant in the social sciences in the first half of the twentieth century, regarded human behaviours as (largely) involuntary functional responses to environmental stimuli and 'reinforcers'. In our context, this would imply that anyone could have sat in Milgram's teacher's chair, or been posted as a concentration camp guard, and acted in a cruel manner. Milgram claims no such thing and nor could he, given that in his main experiment one third of subjects refused to follow his instructions to the end. Milgram's subjects were agents and *decided* to comply with the experiment, often with considerable stress. On behaviourism, see John A. Mills, *Control: A History of Behavioural Psychology* (New York, 2000).

[86] For all its myriad shortcomings, Goldhagen's *Hitler's Willing Executioners* is indispensable in this regard.

[87] For a critical discussion, see Waller, *Becoming Evil*, pp. 173–5.

institutional setting to compliant behaviour: it is worth remembering that the obedience experiment was inspired by Solomon Asch's studies of social conformity.[88] Indeed, it is perhaps most useful to think of Milgram as having exposed the social and psychic costs of *disobedience*, of non-compliant behaviour. His subjects entered the laboratory as volunteers, sympathetic to the stated pedagogic objectives of the experiment and earning a fee for their time. They were inclined to identify with the experimenter as a man of status and to seek his approval. In doing so they were entering into an authority situation, one predicated on *an* orientation to authority.[89] As with most recruits to an unfamiliar environment with strong authority structures, it was difficult to discern whether the first instructions they were given were legitimate. Thus not a single subject refused to administer the first purported shocks: as is well-known, some two-thirds continued right to the end of the dial.

Perhaps the most powerful finding of the experiment was the extent to which participants found it difficult to disengage after taking these first steps. If the Dachau School was limited in its range of disciplinary instruments against guards, Milgram lacked any kind of coercive means. Most of his subjects expressed strong misgivings during the experiment and many exhibited symptoms of extreme stress.[90] Yet the majority either perceived no way to extricate themselves from the situation or evaluated the social costs of exit as too high. The earlier a subject expressed misgivings, the likelier it was that he or she would eventually defy the experimenter.[91] Yet as with Eicke's comments on 'grousing' at orders, the situation was perfectly able to navigate a strong element of dissent. The social tug of compliance and loyalty to the experimenter increasingly placed the confederate learner beyond the primary social field. 'For many subjects', Milgram concluded, 'the learner becomes simply an unpleasant obstacle interfering with the attainment of a satisfying relationship with the experimenter'.[92]

---

[88] Blass, *Man Who Shocked the World*, pp. 26–30. Milgram worked as Asch's research assistant in the academic year 1955 to 1956.

[89] Milgram, *Obedience*, pp. 141–4. 'An authority system . . . consists of a minimum of two people sharing the expectation that one of them has the right to prescribe behaviour for the other' (p. 142). Milgram uses the example of spectators at a military parade, who have not entered into an authority relation with the Colonel barking instructions, so do not respond to them. More broadly on this important point see Herbert C. Kelman, 'Violence without Moral Restaint: Reflections on the Dehumanization of Victims and Victimizers', *Journal of Social Issues*, Vol. 29, No. 4, pp. 25–51.

[90] As has been pointed out, for this reason the experiments raise a series of pertinent issues even in their institutional conception, funding, and organization. Given that Milgram's two paid—civilian—'confederates' were inflicting substantial psychic stress on hundreds of naive subjects, their own motivations and relationship to Milgram are themselves highly pertinent to the very issues (trust, responsibility, fragmentation, dissonance, devaluing of subject) explored by the experiment. The confederates evidently believed either that the interests of psychology outweighed the distress of the victims, or that their fee was more important. Milgram himself privately experienced inner conflict between the (self-interested) claim of science, and the human claim of his subjects: and seems himself to have 'blamed the victim' (in this case the 'naive subjects'). See Nestar John Charles Russell, 'Stanley Milgram's Obedience to Authority Experiments: Towards an Understanding of their Relevance in Explaining Aspects of the Nazi Holocaust' (PhD thesis submitted to Victoria University of Wellington, 2009), pp. 171–90.

[91] Blass, *Man Who Shocked the World*, p. 104.     [92] Milgram, *Obedience*, p. 146.

A key feature of training at Dachau was to break down residual cognitive interference. Here the binding factors were also of course much stronger in the first place. Dachau recruits were much younger on average than Milgram's subjects, in a pseudo-military environment, and subject to the pull of comradeship and tough, masculine norms. They were also entering into the more anticipated and predefined role of concentration camp guard. Yet, like Milgram's subjects, they passed through a series of 'escalating commitments'.[93] After volunteering they were brought into the controlled environment of Dachau and visually marked for their role with an SS uniform and military haircut. They were then pushed through the resocializing drill and training processes. The recruit was placed on a probationary period of three months as an SS Death's Head candidate. During this period he could be released at any time and Eicke reported five releases of candidates, for example, during April 1937.[94] During this period they were posted as sentries but initially only under close supervision. Eicke threatened with expulsion an SS officer who had left *blutjunge* SS men unattended together on a sentry post and Simon, too, stressed the need to mix up green and seasoned SS men on guard duty.[95] Observational learning and imitative performance of the role of sentry, under the watchful eye of more experienced and hardened seniors, furthered internalization of the accompanying values and the normalization of Dachau guard culture. Comradely recognition reinforced and rewarded compliant, normative behaviour. Once socialized into the attitudinal and performative aspects of the role, the recruits were posted independently around the prisoner compound or at external work details. As they gathered experience and demonstrated their commitment they became eligible for promotion and the financial rewards this brought. Eventually, the most experienced and committed sentries could be brought onto the commandant's staff.

In Milgram's much more telescoped situation, the escalating commitments were compressed into the incremental electric shocks. He identified a paradox of 'sequential action' in which the fact of compliance with earlier steps complicated the process of disengagement at the next.[96] Each previous commitment had confirmed the existing authority structure and its construal of the situation. To determine that the next step was too daunting or objectionable, or to entertain a crisis of confidence or conscience, required confronting both a legitimized authority structure and the moral propriety of the commitments hitherto undertaken. The impulse to disengage was therefore 'collapsed', to use Erving Goffman's terminology, into the situation.[97] Throughout the process the subject was hampered by the desire not to renege on the initial voluntary commitment to the experimenter. Interestingly, when the latter was physically absent from the experiment and relayed instructions

---

[93] See the useful theoretical discussion in Waller, *Becoming Evil*, pp. 230–42.

[94] IfZ, MA 293, IKL Befehlsblatt, 1 May 1937, s. 2550182.

[95] IfZ, MA 293, IKL Befehlsblatt, 1 May 1937, s. 2550190; BAB, NS4 Da/30, Richtlinien für Ausbildung, 15 April 1939, s. 3. The same principle was applied with trainee female guards at Majdanek: Koslov, *Gewalt*, p. 157.

[96] Milgram, *Obedience*, pp. 150–1; see also the cogent discussion in Bauman, *Modernity*, pp. 157–8.

[97] Erving Goffman, *Asylums: Essays on the Social Situation of Mental Patients and Other Inmates* (New York, 1961), p. 41.

over a telephone, compliance not only sank, but many subjects also merely acted out their role without actually administering the agreed level of purported shock to the learner.[98] Milgram also noted a gathering tendency for subjects to blame the victim—the accomplice 'learner'—for their actions. Processes of cognitive dissonance led them to 'harshly devalue the victim as a consequence of acting against him'.[99] Even during the brief duration of Milgram's experiment the adversarial mindset of institutions and impulse to pathologize their inmates began to take hold (see Chapter 4). The key point is that Milgram's subjects acted as conscious deliberative agents, rather than as helpless subordinates or passive receptacles of anonymous forces: this was an intersubjective social field.[100]

Again, all of these countervailing pressures against exit from the situation, against even countenancing an 'open break with authority', were present for recruits to the Dachau School and many more besides. They could seek to leave at any time but only in the face of rapidly accumulating social and situational inhibitions. To seek release would be either an admission of weakness or appear to cast implicit judgement on one's comrades and, in turn, the entire regimental history of the Dachau SS. For the early years of the camp, when the incremental commitments outlined above were still developing, there is also evidence of more practical 'binding mechanisms'. The personnel file of a guard who joined in December 1933 contains a series of sworn statements and incentives to keep him at the camp. On arrival he signed a declaration pledging to remain with the guard detail for a minimum of three months, and that he would give at least twenty days' notice of his intention to leave thereafter.[101] On 5 February 1934, at the conclusion of this initial spell, he was awarded the formal black ceremonial SS uniform. He now signed a further declaration that it would become his personal property only after another four months of service: should he cease employment as a guard before this it had to be handed back undamaged.[102] The guard concerned remained at Dachau until 1940, when he transferred to Neuengamme. These social and material binding incentives may appear insubstantial, even trivial, when viewed independently as explanatory variables for service as a concentration camp guard. Yet while they do not wholly account for personnel retention in an environment with few formal sanctions, any analysis omitting or dismissing them would be inadequate. They take their place alongside the cultural and situational stimuli discussed hitherto, and the training and leadership to be discussed next.

## LEADERSHIP

The 'leadership principle' (*Führerprinzip*) was fundamental to National Socialist authority structures, and above all in its volunteer paramilitary formations. Like

[98] Milgram, *Obedience*, pp. 62–3.
[99] Milgram, *Obedience*, p. 11. Emphasis in original.     [100] Welzer, *Täter*, p. 109.
[101] BAB, BDC RS B223 Albert E., Verpflichtung, 6 November 1933.
[102] BAB, BDC RS B223 Albert E., Bestätigung, 5 February 1934.

those other hallowed concepts of comradeship and community, it drew on an idealized view of aspects of German military culture and a visceral loathing of the supposedly rootless and calculating individualism of Weimar German 'society'.[103] The *Freikorps* were an important historic referent. These volunteers were said to have been driven and disciplined by intense personal devotion to officer and Fatherland rather than formal hierarchies of command.[104] The modern *Freikorps* recruited in the wake of the German Revolution of 1918, too, were mobilized and affiliated to charismatic commanders like von Epp and only loosely integrated into a military hierarchy. As will be seen, many of the senior personnel at Dachau had served in the *Freikorps* and the imagery of the charismatic, mobilizing leader of men found fertile soil there.

Great importance was therefore attached to the character and pastoral aptitude of these men. A *Führer* in the right-wing German paramilitary milieu had a status rather different from that of an *Offizier*, with its class connotations, in the army.[105] His authority was said to be conferred less by rank than by the character and charisma which pushed him to command through 'self-selection' (*Führer-Selbstauslese*). In an environment of voluntary discipline and allegiance, leadership was dependent upon assertion and affirmation: this goes some way to accounting for the restless dynamism of Nazi political culture.[106] As in the *Freikorps*, during the Nazi 'time of struggle' charisma and leadership were measured partly by recruitment. Men like Eicke and Dietrich, successful SS recruiters in an era when competition for volunteer manpower was intense and opportunists nowhere to be seen, were revered after 1933. The ideal paramilitary *Führer* was gregarious and paternalistic: like Eicke, Dietrich made great play of dining in the rank-and-file mess hall with his men.[107] The ideal paramilitary *Führer* inspired and developed his men. Like Hitler, whose virtues he transmitted, he had a sense of theatre and the ability to connect and communicate.[108] He was 'authority' in Milgram's sense, but as much as the embodiment of the values of the movement as a formal superior. He was a role model whose approval recruits would naturally and ardently seek. Eicke's 'Papa' soubriquet was held very much to be a product of these twin processes of assertion and affirmation. As he wrote, with customary self-regard, to Himmler in August 1936:

---

[103] Paul Brooker, 'The Nazi Fuehrerprinzip: A Weberian Analysis', *Political Science*, Vol. 37, No. 1 (1985), pp. 50–72; see also the lively, if dated, Joseph Nyomarkay, *Charisma and Factionalism in the Nazi Party* (Minneapolis, 1967), pp. 9–51. On Hitler and charismatic leadership, see Ian Kershaw, *The Hitler Myth: Image and Reality in the Third Reich* (Oxford, 1989), passim, esp. pp. 8–14.

[104] Mosse, *Fallen Soldiers*, pp. 23–8.

[105] Reichardt, *Faschistische Kampfbünde*, pp. 418–26, 492–7; Hein, *Elite*, pp. 57–8.

[106] See the collection of documents from the late Weimar era in Noakes and Pridham, *Nazism*, Vol. 1, pp. 50–4.

[107] James Weingartner, *Hitler's Guard: The Story of the Leibstandarte Adolf Hitler 1933–39* (London, 1974), p. 17. See also Hein, *Elite*, p. 146.

[108] Excellent discussion in Reichardt, *Faschistische Kampfbünde*, pp. 472–516; a vivid literary example of the construction of this ideal by a participant is the *Freikorps* veteran Ernst von Salomon, *The Outlaws* (London, 1931), pp. 342–71.

If my men call me Papa in their barracks, then this is the finest expression of a heart-felt community found only when a superior is constantly in touch with his men, when they know that he does not simply command but also cares about them.[109]

Eicke expected his own officers to follow suit and frequently reminded them that their relationship with their men, too, should be personal and emotional, extending beyond formal working hours:

The good officer is also the good spirit of his unit . . . officers and their deputies must ensure always that they retain the loyalty and affection of their men . . . For an SS officer there is no such thing as hours on duty; he is always on duty and never stands alone, for he is to be there for his men from dawn till night.[110]

Aloof commanders acting like officers in the army, Eicke warned, would be transferred to the General SS. Simon, too, stressed that a Dachau guard officer had a personal, elemental connection to each and every man under his command whether on or off duty.[111]

This cult of leadership ensured that officers in the Dachau Death's Head units wielded great influence over the culture of the guards, and in turn the experiences of inmates. The process started at the top with the post of 'Commander of the Guard Troops' (*Führer der Wachtruppe*). The first incumbent was Erspenmüller, whose path to the early Dachau SS was traced in Chapter 1. His impact on the camp was toxic and his brief tenure, lasting only until July 1933, was characterized by relations of suspicion and loathing with the State Police, the commandant staff, and the prisoners. His relationship with both concentration camp commandants in this period, Wäckerle and Eicke, was notably poor and highlighted immanent tensions between the command staff and guard formations. Erspenmüller was the ranking officer from Standarte Munich and Wäckerle the same for Standarte Augsburg. This geopolitical rivalry contributed to the chaotic culture of early Dachau. As early as 11 April, the very same day the SS took over the prisoner compound from the State Police, Wäckerle wrote to Malsen-Ponickau requesting Erspenmüller's transfer.[112] A number of irresolvable 'differences of opinion' had emerged between them. Guard platoons, he complained, were routinely late to arrive for sentry duty and their predecessors therefore had to stand guard for six hours or more without relief. Erspenmüller himself was frequently absent from his post. This was setting a demoralizing example and impeding much-needed training. Even when on site, Erspenmüller and his Munich cronies were often drunk, leaving everything to the unqualified NCOs of the guard platoons. Wäckerle requested a new commander of the guard troops who could be trained by the State Police if necessary and then remain in the camp as his duties required.[113]

---

[109] In René Rohrkamp, *'Weltanschaulich gefestigte Kämpfer': Die Soldaten der Waffen-SS 1933–1945* (Paderborn, 2010), pp. 226–7.

[110] IfZ, MA 293, IKL Befehlsblatt, 7 July 1937, s. 2550161.

[111] BAB, NS4 Da/30, SS-TK Oberbayern, Auszüge aus den Richtlinien für Ausbildung im Winter 1937/38, s. 1.

[112] BAB, BDC SSO Erspenmüller, Wäckerle to Führer der Politischen Hilfspolizei Bayerns, 11 April 1933.

[113] BAB, BDC SSO Erspenmüller, Wäckerle to Führer der Politischen Hilfspolizei Bayerns, 11 April 1933.

The Dachau commandant evidently had second thoughts, however, believing that a veteran National Socialist like Erspenmüller should be given another chance to prove himself. Yet the underlying problems simply festered. Eicke wrote to Malsen-Ponickau with identical complaints on 3 July 1933 and demanded Erspenmüller's transfer back to the Munich SS.[114] Despite many 'comradely' discussions, Erspenmüller continued to absent himself from the guard troops with comrades from Munich. On 1 July he had embarked on a marathon drinking session in the city, returning to the camp only in the early hours of 3 July. Eicke had therefore been obliged to take command of the guard units in addition to his many other duties as camp commandant. Again, Erspenmüller's behaviour was setting a deleterious example to his NCOs, who showed signs of demoralization on guard and in training. Eicke signed off his letter requesting the immediate recall of Erspenmüller, 'the final hindrance' to an efficacious reordering of the Dachau SS. As so often, he got his way. Erspenmüller was transferred back to Munich.[115]

His successor was Michael Lippert, a man with an eventful future in the SS. Born in 1897 in a small village in Upper Franconia, Lippert was a 1914 volunteer and saw action on the Western and Eastern fronts.[116] After demobilization he made his way, like so many future SS officers, to the Bavarian State Police. There he was well-regarded: a report on his eight-year tenure praised him as a 'faultlessly reliable and punctual, devoted, dutiful and indefatigable policeman . . . a skilled horseman and an outstanding cavalry instructor'.[117] In June 1930, Lippert joined the NSDAP and then the SS with the prestigiously low SS membership number of 2,968: lower even than Erspenmüller's 3,528. His personnel file does not explain his path to Dachau on 10 July 1933, but Lippert soon caught Eicke's eye as a capable officer with military experience. He was formally appointed the new commander of the guard troops on 3 August. Eicke depicted Lippert as the ideal National Socialist leader and an antitype to the disloyal Erspenmüller. He was quickly recommending an extraordinary promotion from *Sturmführer* to *Sturmbannführer*:

> Lippert, who in a short space of time has been able to turn a rather loose guard detail into a tight troop should also be recognised externally as the commander of the guard units. In Lippert I have an extremely valuable support on whom I can rely in every way; in his capacity as commander of the guards he relieves me of a great burden and forms the bridge between guards and commandant. In addition to his moral qualities his knowledge of his duties is faultless, as every superior requires. I have complete faith in his loyalty.[118]

Lippert was involved far less than Erspenmüller in the daily lives of the prisoners, devoting his time to moulding the Dachau sentries into a self-consciously

---

[114] BAB, BDC SSO Erspenmüller, Eicke to Führer der Politischen Hilfspolizei Bayerns, 3 July 1933.

[115] Erspenmüller eventually transferred to the SS Verfügungstruppe where he was killed commanding an artillery regiment during the French campaign: SAM, StA 34461/4, Max von Dall-Armi, Bilder und Skizzen aus dem Konzentrationslager, 13 April 1951.

[116] BAB, BDC SSO, Lippert, Lebenslauf, n.d.

[117] BAB, BDC SSO Lippert, Landespolizei Regensburg Beurteilung 1929.

[118] BAB, BDC SSO Lippert, Eicke to Malsen-Ponickau, 26 July 1933.

professional corps of gaolers, with local group loyalties subordinated to collective identity. He played a central role in the purge of the SA, to be discussed below. There are indications that his conduct was not quite as remote from Erspenmüller's as Eicke implied: a written rebuke from Himmler cites drunken parties outside his Dachau flat in the company of persons 'not morally desirable'.[119] Lippert was reprimanded for this lapse in self-restraint which had, in the familiar formula, 'damaged the reputation of the SS'. Yet Eicke continued to hold Lippert in the highest regard as a vector of militarism and professionalism, and appointed him commander of the guard formations at later camps as they were set up, including Sachsenhausen and Buchenwald.[120] Eicke's power to appoint and transfer within the guard formations proved a highly effective mechanism for spreading the 'Dachau spirit' throughout the Reich.

Lippert's successor at Dachau was Ernst Schulze, of whom little is known. Höß describes him as a Prussian drill fanatic dispatched to Dachau by Eicke to keep the guards from regressing to their native Bavarian training preference for the 'jolly' and 'comradely', for 'plenty of sociable evenings and a lot of Bavarian beer'.[121] A police captain, Schulze does not appear to have been a member of the SS, which no doubt contributed to the 'ill-feeling' Höß recalls towards him among the Dachau sentries.[122] According to Höß the guards managed to obstruct the 'Prussian pig' to the extent that he was moved on in 1936. Schulze was replaced by another obscure figure, *Obersturmbannführer* Otto-Friedrich Augustini. Born in 1891 in Minden, Augustini's SS number suggests that he joined the organization in 1932. He was an officer at the SS Training School at Bad Tölz from April 1934 to July 1935, when he came to Dachau as leader of a guard battalion. He was promoted to command the entire guard contingent in April 1936.[123] The appointment probably stemmed from him being the highest-ranked officer in the guard units, but given that both camp commandants during his tenure held the far loftier rank of *Oberführer* his overall influence on camp life was muted. The military exercises he arranged for the Dachau SS have been appraised as 'extraordinarily amateurish in conception and execution' by one historian.[124] Nevertheless, Augustini eventually left Dachau at his own request in 1937 and joined the Wehrmacht.

His successor, *Standartenführer* Max Simon, was a very influential figure in the history of the Dachau guard units and the Waffen SS. Born in Breslau in 1899, like most concentration camp guard commanders Simon was a member of the 'front generation'.[125] In 1917 he joined the Imperial Army and claimed to have served in Macedonia and France, winning the Iron Cross 1st Class for gallantry under

---

[119] BAB, BDC SSO Lippert, Himmler to Lippert, 30 October 1934.
[120] Wachsmann, 'KL: A History of the Nazi Concentration Camps', ch. 2.
[121] Höß, *Commandant*, p. 237.
[122] Schulze is listed in the 1936 Dienstaltersliste as a *Sturmbannführer* but with no SS number.
[123] BAB, BDC SSO Augustini.
[124] Franz Josef Merkl, *General Simon: Lebensgeschichte eines SS-Führers* (Augsburg, 2010), pp. 96–7.
[125] Orth has found that 58 per cent of the men in this post had front experience of some kind. Orth, *Konzentrationslager SS*, p. 76.

fire.[126] Simon may well, however, have been indulging in the biographical spin of war record so common among Nazis: his biographer doubts that he saw front-line action.[127] After the German capitulation he volunteered with the *Freikorps* on the Eastern border battling alleged 'Polish insurgents'. Between 1919 and 1929 he served in the Reichswehr, leaving to take up the civil service post to which he was then entitled. Simon came to the NSDAP in April 1932 via the National Socialist Civil Servant League and joined the SS in May 1933. In 1934 he was granted leave from his job to take command of the SS formation at Sachsenburg, where he apparently greeted the camp's assembled prisoners with the observation that the 'good times' were over for them.[128] With this outlook, and experience in the Reichswehr, Simon was a man after Eicke's own heart and rose swiftly in the Death's Head units. In May 1937 Eicke appointed him to command a Dachau guard battalion.

Within seven weeks he had replaced Augustini as commander of the entire guard formation, where his promotion seems to have been welcomed.[129] Eicke's annual appraisals of Simon were as glowing as those of Lippert and identified him as just the man to drive the militarization of the Death's Head units. His grasp of comradeship was exemplary, his 'rough manner' balanced by an 'inner warm heartedness'. In ideological matters Simon was apparently 'fired by the ideas and objectives of the movement and prepared always to commit himself mercilessly to these goals'. Eicke's disdain for the class-ridden Wehrmacht is evident in the judge-ment that Simon's 'men would go through fire for him . . . he is a soldier, loves all to do with weapons, but hates the military'.[130] Simon did indeed insist that the 'SS officer is in the first instance a National Socialist, in the second a soldier' but devoted greatest energy to bringing the guard battalions up to scratch as a mili-tary, field-worthy phenomenon.[131] He was a key force in the militarization of the Dachau guard units, both inside and outside the camp.

With the large expansion of the Dachau guard personnel from 1936, discipli-nary and operational leadership was shared with three battalion (*Sturmbann*) com-manders who oversaw guard duty in weekly rotation.[132] At least four SS men held this role and they had widely divergent paths to the camp. Heinrich Scheingraber had been Wäckerle's adjutant in the early Dachau SS. Born in Munich in 1900, Scheingraber served on the Western Front from July 1917 and won the Iron Cross, 1st Class.[133] After demobilization he volunteered for the *Freikorps* von Epp and fought in the crushing of the *Räterepublik*. He then found a position with a Munich newspaper, before losing his job in October 1931. In July of the same

[126] BAB, BDC SSO Simon, Lebenslauf; see also Sydnor, *Soldiers*, pp. 48–9.
[127] Merkl, *General Simon*, p. 28f. Further examples of such CV-enhancing among senior Dachau figures are given in Chapter 3.
[128] Goeschel and Wachsmann, *Nazi Concentration Camps*, p. 73.
[129] Merkl, *General Simon*, p. 97.
[130] BAB, BDC SSO Simon, Beurteilung, 29 September 1940.
[131] Merkl, *General Simon*, p. 99.
[132] BAB, NS4 Da/30, Richtlinien für Ausbildung, 15 April 1939, s.2; IfZ, Fa54, Bericht SS Hauptscharführer Hans Jüng, n. d., s. 6.
[133] BAB, BDC SSO Scheingraber, Abschrift des Lebenslaufes, n.d.

year he joined the NSDAP and SS: another veteran of the formative stage of the Bavarian SS. On 25 March, Malsen-Ponickau assigned him to Dachau as adjutant, a position he filled until Eicke's arrival before switching to the guard troops. In September 1938 he transferred for reasons unknown to the General SS. A stinging annual report from the latter in 1939 suggests waning commitment to the cause: Scheingraber is accused of introspection, ideological indolence, and failings of comradeship, among the worst shortcomings imaginable in the SS.[134]

Scheingraber was succeeded as battalion commander in the Dachau guard units by Karl Künstler. Born in Zella in 1901, the son of a barber, Künstler volunteered for the Reichswehr in 1919 and completed his twelve-year stint in April 1931.[135] He joined the NSDAP and SS in May 1932 and, no doubt in view of his military background, was quickly appointed commander of an SS Sturm in Glogau. On 4 May 1935 he moved to the 'Brandenburg' sentry units at Columbia House as guard commander, and soon after to the SS cadet school at Bad Tölz as an instructor. In the summer of 1937 he seems to have fallen into bad odour at Bad Tölz, but was welcomed back to the Death's Head fold by Eicke. After a probationary spell he was appointed a company commander in the Dachau sentry units. Appointed to succeed Scheingraber, Künstler received a glowing first report from Simon, who recommended his formal promotion to *Sturmbannführer*. In December 1938, however, he fell under a cloud at Dachau too, engaging in unspecified drunken misdemeanours with two other guards. Eicke immediately placed him on leave and penned a highly damning, if typically paternalistic, critique to Simon:

> SS Stubaf Künstler has not behaved like an SS officer, but like a brewer's drayman (*Bierkutscher*). This kind of example ruins the troops . . . It was a grave mistake to promote K to Stubaf. Whoever succumbs to alcohol is unreliable and will lose his Death's Head officer insignia . . . Künstler has sunk in my estimation, and if I give him another chance despite his disgraceful behaviour, it is because of his little lad, whom I met at Christmas.[136]

Tellingly, Künstler was indeed given another chance to prove himself in service to Eicke, but not in the Dachau guard troops. Instead, on 1 May 1939, he was appointed camp commandant of Flossenbürg. There he once more enjoyed glowing appraisals, although inmates are united in the view that he was a brutal and drunken tyrant. But such behaviour was tolerable in dealings with prisoners as it was not in providing leadership to SS soldiers.[137]

Eduard Deisenhofer, born in 1909 in Freising, had a very different career in the SS. He joined early, in October 1930, earning the low membership number of 3,642. He volunteered for Dietrich's Leibstandarte in February 1934 and then for the

---

[134] BAB, BDC SSO Scheingraber, Personalbericht July 1939.
[135] Johannes Tuchel, 'Die Kommandanten des Konzentrationslagers Flossenbürg—Eine Studie zur Personalpolitik in der SS', in Helge Grabitz, Klaus Bästlein, and Tuchel (eds), *Die Normalität des Verbrechens: Bilanz und Perspektiven der Forschung zu den nationalsozialistischen Gewaltverbrechen* (Berlin, 1994), p. 207.
[136] Tuchel, 'Flossenbürg', p. 208.
[137] Tuchel, 'Flossenbürg', p. 209.

Verfügungstruppe. He rose very rapidly for his age to *Obersturmführer*, but in 1935 fell foul of uncomradely intrigue. He was assigned by Himmler to remedial training in the Dachau guard units for three months as a rank-and-file private, on the equivalent pay.[138] Himmler depicted this not as a punishment but rather standard procedure for officers not yet fully attuned to the exacting leadership requirements in the SS. Deisenhofer, however, was outraged. From Dachau he penned a lengthy complaint on the matter, which he ascribed to the machinations of a malicious rival and former subordinate.[139] He found it painful to have to wear the uniform of a humble private, rather than his *Obersturmführer* stripes. He objected to the risible pay, unimpressed by the argument that Dachau finances did not stretch to the remuneration appropriate to his rank. In response, a memo noted wearily of his new posting that he was essentially too young to be an officer in the Verfügungstruppe, that he had dealt clumsily with subordinates, and that he had repeatedly been seen drunk.[140] He was entitled to wear his *Obersturmführer* uniform at Dachau when off-duty. Yet Deisenhofer clearly reconciled himself to his new environment and to the slight in honour of transfer to the concentration camp troops which lurks unarticulated in his correspondence. After brief postings in Columbia Haus and Sachsenhausen he returned to the camp for the remainder of the Dachau School era. He went on to have a meteoric career in the Waffen SS and was one of fourteen Death's Head personnel to be awarded the Knight's Cross medal.[141]

Hellmuth Becker also arrived at Dachau from the Verfügungstruppe under a cloud. He enjoyed, however, exactly the right kind of CV for advancement in the camp guard formations. Born in 1902, Becker was a volunteer in the *Freikorps* Grothe and served in the 5th Prussian Infantry Regiment of the Reichswehr from 1920 to 1929. His passing out papers commend him as 'physically strong, mentally sharp and in body and soul a soldier'.[142] Becker then spent several years as a civil servant and joined the SS in February 1933. In 1934 he volunteered for the Verfügungstruppe in Hamburg. His passing out report from here was less fulsome. It acknowledged his military aptitude and claim to leadership but insisted that it would have to be elsewhere. Becker had been the leader of a 'clique' in the officer corps which adversely affected the morale and performance of the entire unit.[143] The brief report found space to note tartly that he also wore glasses: aways negatively construed in the SS. Becker transferred to the Dachau guard formations in July 1935 as commander of the 9th platoon where he was once more highly regarded. His 1936 annual appraisal lauded the 'spirit' in his guard battalion and Becker's achievement in instilling this despite limited resources.[144] Becker is described as a devoted father and as passionately committed to the Dachau

---

[138]  BAB, BDC SSO Deisenhofer, Schmitt to Deisenhofer, 27 February 1935.
[139]  BAB, BDC SSO Deisenhofer, Beschwerde, 2 April 1935.
[140]  BAB, BDC SSO Deisenhofer, Aktenvermerk Munich, 12 April 1935.
[141]  French L. MacLean, *The Camp Men: The SS Officers Who Ran the Nazi Concentration Camp System* (USA, 1999), p. 272.
[142]  BAB, NS4 Da/38, Persönliche Unterlagen des SS-Untersturmführer Hellmuth Becker, s. 145.
[143]  BAB, BDC SSO Becker, Versetzung Hamburg, 26 April 1935.
[144]  BAB, BDC SSO Becker, 1936 Beurteilung.

SS Sports Association, a site of comradeship and physical conditioning in which Simon invested great importance. Like Deisenhofer, Becker thrived in the less demanding military world of the concentration camp guard units and Death's Head Division, becoming the latter's final commander and surrendering it to the USA in May 1945.

Some common characteristics can be identified among these guiding figures in the Dachau guard units, the ill-documented Schulze excluded. All had experience in the army. While every overall commander of the guard units, except Erspenmüller, was a member of the 'front generation', each of the battalion commanders hailed from the 'war youth cohort'. They tended to go on to have highly 'successful' careers either in the camps or the Waffen SS, with service in the Dachau School a springboard. Most striking of all is an early commitment to the Nazi movement, with each officer joining either the SS or NSDAP well before the 'seizure of power', generally in 1930 or 1931. This early commitment and purported prescience afforded them great prestige in SS circles and among their men. It was held to equip them with the cultural capital to militarize the guard units in the spirit of the political soldier facing the 'enemy within'.

The next layer of authority in the Dachau guard troops comprised the leaders of the companies who performed sentry duty in rotation. With the departure of the Bavarian State Police, the early Dachau guard companies were led by Anton Waldmann, Karl Fritzsch, Wilhelm Breimaier, and Max Koegel. All four, like the officers discussed above, were veterans of the SS and NSDAP, having joined the latter in 1930 or 1931. Koegel and Waldmann had served as volunteers in the Imperial Army, while Fritsch and Breimaier were of the 'war youth' generation. Himmler was so impressed with their collective achievement under Lippert with the guard troops, when he visited Dachau in January 1934, that all four were promoted.[145] Fritzsch and Koegel are examples of early guard personnel who went on to have high-profile careers on the command staff of Dachau and later concentration camps: Koegel became commandant of Ravensbrück, Majdanek, and Flossenbürg, Fritzsch compound leader in Flossenbürg and Auschwitz. Breimaier and Waldmann remained with the concentration camp guard units.

Breimaier offers an illustrative case study in the failings of paramilitary leadership. Although a veteran party member with a low SS number, he lacked the character and charisma to lead even within the Death's Head units. Eventually, in 1937, Eicke asked the SS Personnel Office to transfer Breimaier back to the General SS as, although a worthy 'old fighter', he was 'no longer able to meet the heavy expectations for an officer of a professional (*kasernierte*) unit'.[146] The details are furnished by a report from the guard commander of Buchenwald.[147] While hard-working and conscientious, Breimaier lacked ideological clarity, charisma, and leadership skills: above all the ability to make decisions on the spot. In this he was frequently upstaged by his NCOs, whom he accordingly lacked the

---

[145] BAB, BDC SSO Koegel, Letter Eicke to SS Oberabschnitt Süd, 10 January 1934.
[146] BAB, BDC SSO Breimaier, Eicke to Chef des SS-Personalamtes, 25 October 1937.
[147] BAB, BDC SSO Breimaier, Führer des SSTV Thüringen to Eicke, 21 October 1937.

**Table 2.2** Dachau guard troop officers by SS membership.

| SS Numbers | 1934 | 1935 | 1936 | 1937 | 1938 | Grand Total |
|---|---|---|---|---|---|---|
| SS Founders (membership <10,000) | 6 | 10 | 9 | 7 | 4 | 36 |
| Old Fighters (10,000–70,000) | 3 | 4 | 11 | 17 | 26 | 61 |
| From March 1933 (>70,000) | | | 5 | 19 | 63 | 87 |
| Grand Total | 9 | 14 | 25 | 43 | 93 | 184 |

presence to train and develop. This, the report continues, was only to be expected in the Death's Head units, the home of such select and demanding material. Perhaps most seriously, the performance of Breimaier's company on parade before Hitler and Mussolini had embarrassed Himmler and the Death's Head formations. Breimaier, at this point back in Dachau for remedial training, conceded that his subordinates had lost the requisite deference to him.[148] He attributed this to his inability to maintain the distance from the rank-and-file necessary of an SS officer: comradely, but not friendly. One of his NCOs, *Hauptsturmführer* S., had in consequence been undermining his standing with the men, insinuating that Breimaier's unusually friendly relations with them were an attempt to disguise his lack of leadership skills. Breimaier was tormented by the thought that his company had dishonoured the Death's Head formations in front of the *Führer* and the *Duce*. If Himmler and Eicke had lost confidence in him as a leader of men, he asked to be released from the SS.[149]

The machinations of *Hauptsturmführer* S., similar to those leading to Deisenhofer's transfer to Dachau, are significant. While in the regular army patterns of deference and compliance were governed by hierarchy, in the SS a subordinate had far more scope to press a rival claim to leadership. By this time many 'old fighters' in the guard formations were falling by the wayside, supplanted by a younger and more adroit generation of officers. The gradual eclipse of the founding generation of the SS, and the decline of 'old fighters' from the Weimar era in the Dachau guard troops, is evident from Table 2.2.

As will be seen in the next chapter, founders and 'old fighters' were still given paid roles in the concentration camps, but increasingly only on their command staff, where the stress was less on leadership and soldiering than on terrorizing camp inmates. In demographic terms, too, the clock was ticking for SS veterans among the Dachau guard troops with the beginning of rapid expansion in 1936. By the end of the 1930s even the 'war youth' generation of officers was giving way to a post-war cohort born after 1910 with little memory of the Great War and greater socialization in the Third Reich itself.[150] Table 2.3 provides a breakdown of

[148] BAB, BDC SSO Breimaier, Breimaier to Führer der SSTV und Konzentrationslager, 24 September 1937.

[149] For a similar example of failings of paramilitary leadership see Hein, *Elite*, pp. 58–9.

[150] For an analytical summary of the key generations of Nazi leaders, see Ulrich Herbert, 'Drei politische Generationen im 20: Jahrhundert', in Jürgen Reulecke (ed.), *Generationalität und Lebensgeschichte im 20: Jahrhundert* (Munich, 2003), pp. 95–114.

Table 2.3 Dachau guard troop officers by generation.

| Generation | 1934 | 1935 | 1936 | 1937 | 1938 |
|---|---|---|---|---|---|
| Front Generation (b. <1900) | 27% | 38% | 12% | 8% | 15% |
| War Youth Generation (b. 1901–1910) | 4% | 4% | 23% | 30% | 40% |
| Post-war Generation (b. >1910) | 0% | 2% | 9% | 24% | 65% |

Dachau guard officers, excluding overall commanders and battalion leaders, during the Dachau School.

Complaints from SS 'old fighters' about a lack of preferential treatment in posts and promotions became common in the mid-1930s.[151] Yet the implication that later arrivals to the SS were mere opportunists is not borne out by the CVs of Dachau School officers. One statistical indication of the ideological commitment throughout its officer corps is that just fifteen men were not members of the NSDAP as well as the SS. Party membership did not follow automatically from joining the SS and had to be applied for individually.[152] Moreover, like all Germans, SS men could not join the NSDAP between May 1933 and April 1937 because of the freeze on new members. Applying to join the Party much later, once the ban was lifted, was then an entirely separate decision from joining the SS, an independent statement of enhanced *political* commitment.

An example of the new generation of *Führer* in the guard units is Georg Bochmann. Born in 1913, he was evidently a young and dashing Death's Head officer deemed fully to command the personal devotion of his men. His annual appraisals laud his dependability, ideological clarity, energy, comradeship, intelligence, and 'steely diligence'.[153] He excelled in the all-important 'toughness', had a mature 'outlook on life', was socially adroit, decisive, and an excellent developer of men. By 1939, Simon concluded, Bochmann was a 'capable and proven company commander despite his tender age. His company is in every respect the finest in the Standarte and he is a role model for the younger officers'.[154] Bochmann's legend as a Dachau guard commander was nourished during the war. A hagiography in *Das Schwarze Korps*, to commemorate him being awarded the Knight's Cross for gallantry, interviewed 'an old *Rottenführer*' from Dachau who recalled, obligingly:

> Our company was always the best in the SS Death's Head Upper Bavaria. At Reich Party Rallies we always shone when marching in front of the *Führer*. Once we were given special holiday in reward. That was the 'Bochmann School.'[155]

*Das Schwarze Korps* presented this stellar performance in the Dachau School as the natural preamble to Bochmann's feats in the French campaign and the 'war of annihilation against Bolshevism'. In the familiar imagery, the paper lauded him as

---

[151] Boehnert, 'Sociography', p. 43ff.    [152] Riedle, *Angehörigen*, pp. 76–7.
[153] BAB, BDC SSO Bochmann, Beurteilung Dachau, 30 December 1935.
[154] BAB, BDC SSO Bochmann, Beurteilung Dachau, 30 December 1935.
[155] BAB, BDC SSO Bochmann, 'Das war Schule Bochmann' (undated).

an officer of 'iron toughness, steely will and the highest daring'. Bochmann is an exemplar of a generation of youthful and 'starry-eyed' SS officers who rose to field command in the final years of the war and led the fanatical resistance against the Allied armies.[156]

It was Simon's intention that every guard platoon (*Zug*) at Dachau would be led by an officer with Bochmann's pre-war rank of *Obersturmführer*. A guard company (*Hundertschaft*), comprising three platoons, would be led by a *Hauptsturmführer*.[157] This was still a work-in-progress as of September 1938, but without exception every platoon was commanded by an SS man of officer rank. With the responsibilities of guard leadership came financial reward. Even the lowest commissioned rank of *Untersturmführer* attracted monthly remuneration of least 221 Reichsmark, a substantial increase on the top NCO pay set out previously. An *Obersturmführer* earned 311 Reichsmark per month and a *Hauptsturmführer* up to 420 Reichsmark, the level of a top civil servant.[158] This was an appealing remuneration package for those personnel with the extensive army service that Himmler and Eicke were trying to recruit to the Death's Head units in the late 1930s. The rewards available to such volunteers, who could be commissioned directly upon enrolment, were extravagant and expeditious. Otto Haslreiter, for example, born in 1906, came to Dachau in 1938 as a sergeant with twelve years of military service behind him. After serving a four-week probationary spell on guard duty he was immediately appointed to the rank of *Obersturmführer*.[159]

## TRAINING

The imagery of the 'Bochmann School' illustrates the emphasis in the Death's Head sentry formations on practical leadership and example, on ceaseless proactivity in personnel development. 'As a rule', wrote Simon, 'every young SS man is eager to learn'.[160] He was quickly demoralized, however, by slovenly or uncommitted officers and comrades. His general outlook developed from the practical example of his commander, who was to provide ideological sustenance to his men just like a field chaplain in war.[161] For this reason it was vital that officers were fully up-to-date on political issues and that they develop themselves intellectually 'through reading good books, watching plays and *good* films, going to museums'. Every Friday evening between eight and ten Simon led 'ideological development' seminars for all officers.[162] They were exhorted to lead as National Socialists rather than soldiers, with ideological guidance in no sense restricted to the nominal hours

---

[156] Gerald Reitlinger, *The SS: Alibi of a Nation 1922–1945* (London, 1956), p. 86.
[157] BAB, NS4 Da/30, Personalbefehl Nr. 63/38, 20 September 1938.
[158] IfZ, Fa 127, Appeal to General SS for Technical Officers for Death's Head Formations, s. 149; Buggeln, *Arbeit*, p. 401.
[159] BAB, BDC SSO Haslreiter, Eicke to SS Personnel Office Berlin, 22 June 1938.
[160] BAB, NS4 Da/30, Auszüge aus den Richtlinien für Ausbildung im Winter 1937/38, s. 1.
[161] BAB, NS4 Da/30, Richtlinien für Ausbildung, 6 January 1939, s. 11.
[162] BAB, NS4 Da/30, Richtlinien für Ausbildung, 15 April 1939, s. 2. Emphasis in original.

devoted to it in the training programme. There was after all little point, continued Simon, in guards attending lectures on race and honour when the very same evening they forgot themselves and grabbed at any passing girl. He expected his officers to be aware of where their men spent their free time. Meal times, too, required his presence. For what was the use of a motivational address on the Four Year Plan, Simon concluded, when at lunchtime no officer was with the men and they gorged themselves like pigs? Sport, too, was a form of training and one in which Simon invested great importance. In another example of rhetorical invitation to leave guard service, he warned that any officer who felt that sport was 'superfluous' should immediately apply for a transfer, which he would gladly authorize.[163]

It was also deemed essential that all officers were present at ideological schooling sessions for enlisted men so they could tailor their leadership to the topics addressed. It was from this area of the Dachau School curriculum that the finer details of the guard 'world view' were built. A minimum of two hours every week was devoted to intensive schooling, whether or not the guard platoon in question was on sentry duty.[164] It was conducted by specialist Death's Head 'schooling officers'. Eicke instructed them to divide the time between discoursing on the current 'political situation' and the key tenets of SS ideology.[165] Topics included the history of the NSDAP and its struggle for power, its transformative impact on the people and state, and the 'spiritual revival' of the 'Aryan' race. Emphasis was laid on the history of the SS as both 'protective wall' and shock troops of National Socialism, the front line soldiers in Germany's military and racial renaissance. The importance of the strict SS principles of selection, marriage regulations, and the relation between 'blood and soil' were to be explored in depth. It went 'without saying that during this period the men read and discuss the Führer's *Mein Kampf'*. Communal perusal of *Das Schwarze Korps* was likewise essential. According to Eicke, the Dachau sentries distinguished themselves in zeal to spread the ideological word beyond the camp through circulation of the newspaper, 'the spiritual weapon of the SS'.[166] The guards had arranged a block subscription and then, having perused and digested the content, sent them back to friends and family in their home towns. In this way, the commendation continues, an additional 500 copies per week found their way to 'national comrades'.

Finally, and perhaps most pertinent of all to concentration camp guards, they were to discuss the many enemies of National Socialism. These ran, in order, Jewry, freemasonry, Marxism and Bolshevism, the Church, and reaction in all its forms. Revolutionary anticlericalism was particularly fervent in the Death's Head troops. Eicke devoted several pages of his April 1937 orders of the month to the Catholic

[163] BAB, NS4 Da/30, Richtlinien für Ausbildung, 15 April 1939, s. 5. On the importance of sport in the SS, see Bahro, *Der SS Sport*; Hein, *Elite*, pp. 213–25; Veronika Springmann, '"Sport machen": eine Praxis der Gewalt im Konzentrationslager', in Wojciech Lenarczyk et al. (eds), *KZ-Verbrechen: Beiträge zur Geschichte der nationalsozialistischen Konzentrationslager und ihrer Erinnerung* (Berlin, 2007), pp. 89–101.

[164] BAB, NS4 Da/30, Auszüge aus den Richtlinien für Ausbildung im Winter 1937/38, s. 4.

[165] IfZ, MA 293, IKL Befehlsblatt, 1 June 1937, s. 2550172.

[166] IfZ, MA 293, IKL Befehlsblatt, 1 June 1937, s. 2550159.

Church and its 'monstrous thirst for power'.[167] Guards were vehemently encouraged to renounce Catholicism. Most did so, which can only have enhanced their cognitive dependence on the SS. By the end of 1939 80 per cent of the Death's Head personnel had no confessional affiliation, compared to 56 per cent in the SS Verfügungstruppe and just 26 per cent in the General SS.[168]

What impact this ideological emphasis had on guard conduct is difficult to gauge. The SS continued to issue propaganda leaflets, and the Death's Head units to prize exhortatory lectures and ideological discussions, throughout the Third Reich, which suggests that Himmler and Eicke considered it worth investing scarce resources in. The youth of Death's Head personnel may be pertinent to assessing their susceptibility to this aspect of the Dachau School. For the young men of the 'post-war generation', socialized in the Hitler Youth and barely touched by the German humanist tradition, it was no doubt a powerful influence when aligned to social pressures to performative and discursive compliance.[169] Yet SS ideology in the everyday life of the camps was lived rather than theorized. It offered a filter and framework to interpret the camps and their context, the construal and 'definition of the situation' in Milgram's terms.[170] It lessened inhibitions and provided retrospective clarity to situational violence. As one historian has written, among National Socialists the 'deed preceded the thought, constantly molding and confirming it . . . acting in a manner perceived as necessary for the situation, one expected and actually created that situation, confirming one's expectations and justifying one's actions'.[171]

## EVERYDAY VIOLENCE

Vigilance and distance from inmates were the daily watchwords for the rank-and-file camp guard, as the punishments handed out by Eicke make clear. Aptitude and ideological commitment were measured in tough, proactive conduct, in assimilation to the Dachau habitus. When not in training, life as a pre-war Dachau guard entailed daily tedium enlivened occasionally by cruel pieces of public theatre. The most amenable guard duty, recalled one young recruit, was in the guard towers or at the gates where sentry posts were rotated every two hours.[172] The worst was at external, prisoner work details which might entail a long march to the site of

---

[167] fZ MA 293, IKL Befehlsblatt, April 1937, s. 2550187

[168] In Höhne, *Order*, p. 277.

[169] Browning's analysis of the contribution of propaganda and ideological instruction to the behaviour of Police Battalion 101, for example, accords it little weight because the perpetrators concerned were older, and socialized in an earlier age. Browning, *Ordinary Men*, pp. 176–84. Sofsky, necessarily, downplays the contribution of ideological training, of hazy cod philosophy and 'sundry legends' from the *Kampfzeit*. He suggests that schooling sessions were probably greeted with at least as much fooling around and grinning insincerity as they are in any organization. This, however, would seem incongruous with the 'bright-eyed' self-conception of the troops. Sofsky, *Order*, p. 110.

[170] Milgram, *Obedience*, p. 146. See also Welzer, *Täter*, passim, esp. pp. 48–75.

[171] Omer Bartov, *Hitler's Army*, p. 107.

[172] Michaelis, *Waffen SS*, p. 309.

work, and then eight hours at their post during the working day. Intermediate was watching over smaller groups of prisoners in camp workshops, the *Übungslager*, and over repair details in the prisoner compound.

In Dachau, sentries were generally in closer spatial contact with the prisoners than in more expansive camps such as Buchenwald or Auschwitz and this may have contributed to the proactivity of its guard culture. Just as Dachau prisoners were almost always in the line of sight of sentries, so too were the guards in that each other and their superiors. This panoptical effect reduced the scope for shirking or mere performative compliance in contrast to the vast forests of Buchenwald or under-staffed wartime satellite camps, in a manner redolent of Milgram's findings on the phenomenon.[173] Neurath, persuasively, foregrounds the situational in most cases of sentry chicanery: the guards were bored, unable to move around, standing for hours on end in the unpredictable Bavarian weather; even the prisoners could move around.[174] Sometimes they were hungover or otherwise indisposed from the previous day's drill. Pieces of social theatre, which could also be construed as signifiers of ideological zeal, alleviated the shared tedium. Demonstrative acts of violence could earn the perpetrator a certain social capital: here the prisoners were props rather than subjects. Yet often, writes Neurath, guards

> looked upon what they did to the prisoners less as an act of fiendish cruelty than as a boyish joke: You yelled at a man and the man began to run. You yelled some more, and he got frightened and ran some more. You could feel like a young puppy, barking with joy at an object that moved.[175]

This gamesome tyranny, also on some level a ritualization of power, pervaded the everyday life of the prisoners. They were often forced to collude in the theatre, chuckling appreciatively at the wit and imagination of the guard in question since, they soon realized, in the grotesque power relations of Dachau it was in the victim's interest to cede to the guard the recognition he believed he had earned.[176] A staple of the genre was the 'pretending not to hear' game, in which prisoners seeking permission to go to the toilet would be ignored. Inmates had to abject themselves in this situation, maintaining a prescribed distance from the guard who, accordingly, by rotating himself by 90 degrees, would force the prisoner to run around to face him.[177] Of course, what started off as an exuberant prank or mirthful theatre could spiral into unrestrained or lethal violence. Another initiative evident across all camps was for sentries to toss bread, or inmates' caps, into the neutral zone within the perimeter walls to entice inexperienced prisoners into entering it. They might then be shot 'trying to escape'.[178]

---

[173] On disinterested sentries, see Neurath, *Society*, pp. 101–5; Buggeln, *Arbeit*, pp. 412–13; Cohen, *Human Behaviour*, p. 255.

[174] Neurath, *Society*, p. 74.     [175] Neurath, *Society*, p. 74.

[176] Kay, *Dachau*, p. 113.

[177] Hübsch, 'Insel', p. 57; Neurath, *Society*, p. 74; WL, Herbert Seligman, 'Drei Jahre hinter Stacheldraht' (1945), p. 17.

[178] Schwarz, 'Wir haben', p. 53; Schnabel, *Frommen*, pp. 46–7; Zámecník (ed.), 'Aufzeichnungen', pp. 175–6; Röder, *Nachtwache*, p. 24.

For the inmates, much could depend on the mood of guards. Laurence recalls that the majority of sentries caused few problems when they were relaxed and 'at ease'.[179] In such a situation, a sentry was almost as likely as the prisoners to hope for the morning or afternoon to pass smoothly, without having to expend energy disciplining them or later filling out reports for formal punishments. Prisoners became skilled at discerning guards' moods from the very outset of shifts, and indications of a hungover or irritable sentry would send their spirits crashing. On these occasions the guard 'might not even let us take our tools out without previously having ordered us to lie down and roll in the dirt'. It is impossible, naive even, to propose a discrete linear 'motivation' for the countless indignities and petty cruelties meted out to prisoners of every category every day. Primo Levi addressed the topic with customary erudition and concluded that, ultimately, such violence was social in meaning.[180] It documented the subjugation of the prisoners and the power of the SS.

The somewhat generic, non-biographical character of this discussion is reflective of the available source material. Particularly towards the end of the Dachau School, the guard personnel were simply too numerous and anonymous to find any detailed description in prisoner memoirs. Neurath, once again, puts it best:

> To the prisoners, the guards were a great herd of animals without any individuality. Usually weeks would pass before one would see the same guard a second time. And usually prisoners did not recognise the guards unless one had been mistreated by a guard in a rather spectacular way. After all, you don't remember every dog that barks at you in the streets, but you will certainly remember the one that bites you.[181]

Even when an atrocity was so 'spectacular' that the sentry in question was remembered, and when in most unusual addition the event was investigated in depth after the war, the evidence points to toxic environment rather than dispositional pathology as the primary cause. This is illustrated by an incident from May 1934 which was pursued by Naaff's team. The perpetrator was Maximilian Seefried, a 20-year-old guard with six months' experience in the camp. It was dusk, around six in the evening, between roll call and lights out, and the scene was typical of this era, one slightly less draconian than most under the comparatively restrained tenure of commandant Deubel. The prisoners were mingling on the road between their barracks.[182] Some were polishing shoes, some cleaning clothes, some playing football, others just chatting and exchanging jokes. Two inmates were scuffling in good humour on the street. Seefried, meanwhile, was on sentry duty in a zone about 100 metres wide just outside the barbed wire of the prisoner compound.[183] According to his first testimony to American investigators, he espied the two scrapping prisoners forty metres away and, since fighting was forbidden by camp regulations, shot them. He added that he had been afraid of the consequences had he not acted according to the camp regulations and used his rifle.[184]

[179] Laurence, 'Out of the Night', p. 57.     [180] Levi, *Drowned*, pp. 83–101.
[181] Neurath, *Society*, p. 76.
[182] SAM, StA 34402, Vernehmungsprotokoll Johann Kaltenbacher, 2 February 1948.
[183] SAM, StA 34402, Protokoll Maximilian Seefried, 30 September 1948.
[184] SAM, StA 34402, Record about Produced Person, 31 May 1947.

Four months later, the case having been passed as murder to the Munich judiciary, it had clearly occurred to Seefried or his legal counsel that his invocation of camp regulations did not provide the *carte blanche* he had initially assumed. His next account of the incident was a cacophony of self-exculpation and muddled logic:

I was on guard duty and patrolling up and down my allocated sentry zone outside the barbed wire. My field of vision encompassed the barracks and the road between them, and I noticed that two prisoners were scuffling. It was forbidden for prisoners to fight. Our orders were to use our weapons in the event of fights or gatherings of prisoners in the camp. This was a secret directive we had been told about in a lecture. If I hadn't stopped these two prisoners scrapping and been caught, I would have been dismissed and perhaps imprisoned for three weeks in punishment. This was a real risk at that time of day, when the duty officer usually did his rounds in the camp. The fight took place around 25 meters away from my sentry zone. I was not allowed to call out when on guard duty, so I raised my hand to order them to stop. I don't know if they saw my signal. I can't be sure if they even saw me, but at any rate they didn't stop fighting. So finally I used my rifle. I only wanted to injure one of them so I aimed for his arm. I dispute that I wanted to kill anyone. However, I couldn't aim too far away from them as they were surrounded by a crowd of other prisoners and I might easily have hit one. As I had to use my weapon, I was pretty flustered. After the shot both fell immediately to the ground. I then realised that I must have hit them both. However, they weren't killed immediately as one grabbed his leg and the other raised his hand to his head. Our orders back then were very strict. We weren't allowed to issue warning shots, or to shoot in the air, or to shout out when on sentry duty. We had to use our weapons as soon as gatherings or fights took place in the camp, since there was the danger that prisoners could try to escape. Also, if we were required to use our weapons, one had at least to hit home.[185]

There are many contortions in Seefried's account. On the one hand, Eicke's regulations instructed guards to shoot, and kill, without warning. On the other, Seefried is anxious to avoid the capital charge of murder, which is based among other things in the German Penal Code on intent to kill. Seefried offers as an explanation for shooting his fear of not complying with the regulations, but waving his arm in the air by way of warning was likewise contrary to them.[186] Aiming merely to hit the arm, as he claims, was too, particularly in view of the informal rule cited that shots fired had to hit home. Moreover, if Seefried had nonetheless genuinely wished to warn the prisoners before shooting, how would raising a hand in the air so far away from two men engaged in a fight have helped? This no doubt explains the reduction in stated distance from the incident from forty to twenty-five metres in his second testimony. Furthermore, Seefried cites the regulations banning 'gatherings' (*Ansammlungen*) of prisoners as the reason he was compelled to shoot. Given that other prisoners were chatting and playing football which, as he admits in subsequent testimony, was customary under Deubel, this is nonsensical.[187] Did two prisoners scuffling in the camp street really represent a

---

[185] SAM, StA 34402, Protokoll Maximilian Seefried, 2 February 1948.

[186] BAB, R3001/21167, Dienstvorschriften für die Begleitposten und Gefangenenbewachung, 1 October 1933, ss. 62–9.

[187] SAM, StA 34402, Protokoll Maximilian Seefried, 30 September 1948.

more alarming 'gathering' than the customary scenes at dusk at this time, a critical mass of trespass against the regulations? This in turn dilutes the underlying argument that guards had no choice and no personal scope for discretion in interpreting the regulations. The case brings into focus the contribution of the apparently all-encompassing regulations to muddying the sentries' sense of personal accountability, as well as the fundamental lack of protection from judicial competence they provided: it was political clout alone that kept the judiciary at bay from Dachau (Chapter 6).

Yet this was scarcely an intentional or premeditated murder. It was also highly unusual, which is why it was remembered by inmates and Munich prosecutors alike. There are no other violent incidents on Seefried's file. He volunteered for the SS only in March 1933, having previously worked for the Red Cross as a driver and nurse. Seefried's concern about the scheduled appearance of authority, his company leader, seems the most plausible explanation for his action. The incident was atypical but played out in a normalized social field of pathologized inmates and unbound, desensitized guards who were constantly instructed that tolerance and hesitation were unworthy of an SS man.[188] As has been seen, Seefried's stated concern about being dismissed or imprisoned is plausible. Dachau sentries were disciplined formally, culturally, and socially but, as his action shows, retained a broad margin for personal discretion (*Handlungsspielraum*) commensurate with a very personal and moral agency.

## BEYOND THE BARBED WIRE

'Guard duty', wrote Eicke in June 1934, shortly before the event which would define his career,

> is a service of honour to the Fatherland. Performing it demands an elevated sense of duty. We are not prison wardens but political soldiers and the Führer's bodyguard . . . We are the representatives of the National Socialist revolution and the most loyal defenders of its state . . . But we shall never become officials, we will remain men of action and shock troops in black . . . In times to come we will be needed with our merciless spirit of attack. We rally around our Führer and whenever the interest of the Movement requires us, we must act.[189]

For the first fifteen months of the camp's existence, its SS stood formally among the Brownshirts as the sentinels and conscience of the Nazi seizure of power. Röhm had extensive ambitions for the SA and SS, inspired by the conspiratorial paramilitarism of early 1920s Bavaria.[190] He saw them as a people's army, the vanguard of the remilitarization of German society with the Reichswehr reduced to

---

[188] More generally on situational sentry violence, see Buggeln, *Arbeit*, pp. 480–4. On pathologized inmates, Chapter 4 of the present book.

[189] Commandant Order 1/34, June 1934. Printed in Goeschel and Wachsmann, *The Nazi Concentration Camps*, pp. 150–1, here p. 150.

[190] Longerich, *Geschichte*, pp. 186–7.

an advisory, technical role. When Hitler decided the time had come to act against Röhm, Himmler's ambition and the precedents of the early 1930s ensured that the SS would play a central role. And the Dachau SS, as the historian Wachsmann observes, would prove 'Hitler's most energetic executioner'.[191]

Contingent preparations in Bavaria began in early June when Eicke oversaw a practice exercise with SS troops around Munich.[192] In the days leading up to the purge, Lippert and other senior Dachau figures were brought into the planning. Sentries were despatched to secure sensitive locations in Munich: four guards, for example, were deployed to watch over Rudolf Hess's villa.[193] On the morning of 30 June Eicke led several hundred Dachau guards, armed with machine guns from the guard towers, out on trucks and buses to rendezvous with a detachment of the Leibstandarte. Detailed as backup, they missed out on involvement in Röhm's arrest only because Hitler had arrived before the scheduled time at Bad Wiessee. Instead they followed his motorcade back to Brown House in Munich, where Eicke was evidently primed to prepare Dachau for the murder ahead. At least twenty people were shot in the camp between 30 June and 2 July, the most prominent the elderly Gustav von Kahr whose role in betraying the Munich *Putsch* in 1923 had not been forgotten.

According to Steinbrenner, Kahr's arrival fired up the SS, who bundled him violently across to where Eicke was sat smoking in a chair outside his office. Savouring the moment, the Dachau commandant turned his right thumb downwards to signal Kahr's fate. The 71-year-old was probably executed in the *Bunker*. Although the SS played loud music to disguise the gunfire, the prisoners endured sleepless nights that Saturday and Sunday, tormented by gunshots, searchlights, and the 'Indian war-whoops' of the Dachau SS as another alleged traitor was dispatched.[194] An inmate from the first company caught watching proceedings through his barrack window was apparently shot at by a sentry, and a party of guards charged into the barracks in a 'blood rush'. The SS used the occasion of the Röhm purge opportunistically to murder five inmates in solitary confinement in the *Bunker*. To forestall any political or judicial complications, Eicke told Himmler that these prisoners had announced their support for Röhm's plot.[195] It also seems that Dr Flamm, a State Court physician who had carried out the autopsies on inmates murdered by the early Dachau SS, escaped death only by chance thanks to being at his mother's in Augsburg.[196]

On the evening of 1 July Eicke, Lippert, and SS *Gruppenführer* Heinrich Schmauser, the liaison officer between the SS and army for the purge, set out for Stadelheim prison. The two Dachau men murdered Röhm in his cell and returned to the camp with four more Brownshirts who, stripped to the waist, were shot on

[191] Wachsmann, 'KL: A History of the Nazi Concentration Camps', ch. 2.
[192] Longerich, *Himmler*, p. 173.
[193] SAM, StA Vernehmung Karl Minderlein, Weissenburg, 25 July 1949. The following from Wachsmann, 'KL: A History of the Nazi Concentration Camps', ch. 2.
[194] *Nazi Bastille Dachau*, pp. 100–1; Richardi, *Schule*, pp. 237–8.
[195] Wachsmann, 'KL: A History of the Nazi Concentration Camps', ch. 2.
[196] SAM, StA 34832/3, Zeugenvernehmungsprotokoll Friedrich Döbig, 21 August 1951.

the SS shooting range near the *Bunker*. The assembled SS men gave a round of applause.[197] According to a prisoner who worked in the SS canteen, the Dachau SS staged a Homeric 'victory celebration' to mark the purge in which they got through some 1,400 litres of beer.[198] Eicke was confirmed as Reich 'Inspector' of the concentration camps, and in late 1934 Himmler promoted the guard formations to the status of a separate force within the SS. This aside, in the distribution of the spoils the Dachau SS was overshadowed by the generous rewards bestowed on Dietrich's Leibstandarte for its role in events.

A creeping sense of being undervalued in comparison to other SS formations is important to understanding the desperate striving for status and esteem by the concentration camp troops. On 17 March 1933, around the same time as the piecemeal formation of the early Dachau SS, Hitler had instructed Dietrich to set up a ceremonial guard for the Reich Chancellery.[199] Initially classified, like the Dachau guard troops, as an auxiliary police formation, on 1 October it was decided to fund it centrally on exactly the same pay scale as the Reichswehr. Unlike the Dachau SS, the thousand or so men of the SS Leibstandarte now enjoyed Reichswehr perks, such as half-price fares on the German railways. Himmler attempted to secure the same for SS camp guards but met with a telling and symbolic lack of success.[200] Steinbrenner, characteristically, later looked back on the contrasting treatment of the Leibstandarte and camp SS with bitterness and self-pity.[201] In 1935 an SS guard from Columbia House in Berlin, too, complained to an SPD exile newspaper that morale there was poor because they were 'not treated as a force should be treated', unlike the 'pampered' Leibstandarte.[202] Many concentration camp guards sought without success to be transferred to the latter which, in accordance with supply and demand, was able to insist on physical minima for recruits that the Death's Head sentry formations could barely dream of. The Leibstandarte also came to enjoy largely cordial and cooperative relations with the army, in contrast to the respectively dismissive and chippy relationship which developed between the latter and the Death's Head formations.[203] Adding insult to injury, Hitler, after the 'Night of the Long Knives', authorized the formation of further units on the model of the Leibstandarte, stationed throughout the Reich and likewise paid, trained, and equipped on the lines of the army. It was these units, initially known as 'political emergency squads' (*politische Bereitschaften*), together with the Leibstandarte, which formed the SS Verfügungstruppe.[204] All were financed by the Reich Ministry of the Interior and paid as per army personnel. Thus, until April 1936, the concentration camp guard

[197] Goeschel and Wachsmann, *Nazi Concentration Camps*, p. 77; Wachsmann, 'KL: A History of the Nazi Concentration Camps', ch. 2.

[198] SAM, StA, 34832/5 Zeugenvernehmung Fritz Hugo, 6 February 1963.

[199] James Weingartner, 'Sepp Dietrich, Heinrich Himmler, and the Leibstandarte SS Adolf Hitler, 1933–1938', *Central European History*, Vol. 1, No. 3 (Sep., 1968), pp. 264–84.

[200] Weingartner, 'Leibstandarte', p. 271.

[201] DaA, Steinbrenner, 'Hinter den Kulissen', s. 5.

[202] In Goeschel and Wachsmann, *The Nazi Concentration Camps*, p. 71.

[203] Weingartner, 'Leibstandarte', p. 273.          [204] Weingartner, 'Leibstandarte', p. 274–9.

units alone of the 'active', barracks-dwelling SS formations were denied the remuneration and resonant status of soldiers.

Rendering this slight all the more visible at Dachau, one Verfügungstruppe unit, Standarte Deutschland, was stationed at the SS complex there before moving to Munich in 1938. Worse yet, many Deutschland personnel were drawn from another SS formation based at Dachau whose relationship with the concentration camp's guard units had seldom been neighbourly. This was the Austrian SS, whose presence in the Dachau complex illustrates the geopolitical significance of Bavaria in the Third Reich. In April 1933 the Austrian Nazi Party, energized by the advent of Hitler's regime in Germany, won 41 per cent of the vote in a municipal election. Hitherto miniscule, it soon numbered some 70,000 members, and the reactionary clerical regime of Engelbert Dollfuss feared that it, too, might soon come to power via the ballot box. In panic, Dollfuss suspended elections, banned the wearing of paramilitary uniforms, and closed down Nazi newspapers and headquarters. Austrian Nazis retorted with an escalation of street violence and a bombing campaign, with the perpetrators flocking over the border to the sanctuary of Bavaria.[205] A battalion of Austrian SS, the Austrian Legion, was stationed at Dachau where it was involved in smuggling arms and fugitives in both ways over the border.

By July 1933 there were some 130 Austrian SS men at Dachau, organized by the Bavarian State Police into a camp sentry platoon.[206] There was an SS Relief Station (*Hilfswerk*) providing welfare to refugees under the supervision of the future Dachau commandant Loritz, who complained bitterly to Eicke about the indiscipline and corruption of its Austrian personnel.[207] Among the arrivals was a young SS man from Linz, Adolf Eichmann. After a few months helping the smuggling initiatives he transferred to the 'Austrian Legion', the incipient battalion of Deutschland. In the run up to the bungled 1934 July *Putsch* against Dollfuss in Vienna, the Austrian SS trained in Dachau but the Legion was not called into action.[208] After the *Putsch*, the Relief Station premises were taken over by the Bad Tölz SS Cadet School for practical training. As would be expected, there was plenty of social interaction between the camp guard units and the other SS formations at the site.[209] In the interests of oversight and coherent comradeship, a ranking SS officer was nominated as garrison commander (*Standortführer*). Two Dachau camp commandants held this position in succession: Deubel and then Loritz. According to an SPD exile publication, relations between the Austrian and German SS at the camp were far from fraternal, spilling over into fights in local taverns.[210]

The presence of the Austrians, of the Verfügungstruppe, and of SS cadets was a particularly immediate and visible reminder of the relatively lowly status of the concentration camp guard units within an increasingly heterogeneous SS. Unlike the Death's Head formations, the Verfügungstruppe, and especially the

---

[205] Cesarani, *Eichmann*, pp. 35–8.
[206] DaA 16.112 Wimmer to Kommando des Landespolizei Munich, 17 July 1933.
[207] BAB, BDC SSO Loritz, Loritz to Eicke, November 1933.
[208] Casarani, *Eichmann*, pp. 37–8.
[209] Riedel, *Ordnungshüter*, p. 161.  [210] *Nazi Bastille Dachau*, pp. 59–60.

Leibstandarte, were lavishly trained and equipped by the army and organized on formal military lines, with machine gun companies, infantry companies, reconnaissance battalions, and field medics.[211] The 1935 accounts for the Dachau sentry units, submitted to the Bavarian State Chancellery by the Ministry of the Interior, lament in stark contrast a lack even of reserve ammunition.[212] They had just two cars, no motorcycles, no horses, no kit for the SS Revier, and the guard barracks were in urgent need of replacement. Meanwhile, the Leibstandarte barracks at Lichterfelde in Berlin, according to their historian, were fast acquiring 'an international reputation as the last word in modern military installations'.[213]

Even the Dachau sentries' organizational affiliations to the General SS undercut their aspiration to be viewed as soldiers. With the reintroduction of conscription in 1935, the General SS, like the SA, was fast losing any privileged claim to military status.[214] Even after the decision in April 1936 to finance the Death's Head troops from the Reich Finance Ministry, the latter still modelled pay scales on those of civil servants, that is to say jailors rather than soldiers.[215] Most wounding of all, perhaps, until 1939 Death's Head personnel, unlike their Verfügungstruppe brethren, were liable to be called up for military service at any time. All this is overlooked by writers who, to varying extents, buy into Eicke's desperate attempts to depict the Death's Head formation as an elite within the SS, as a 'crack' formation.[216] These were compensatory discourses fuelled by wounded pride. In August 1936, for example, Eicke looked forward to the forthcoming Party Rally in decidedly gloomy terms:

> For the second time since the formation of the SS-Death's Head formations, the Führer is giving his *Totenkopf* battalions the opportunity to march past him. He will see us, will know who we are and will remember the services we have rendered in the last year. Once more we shall be struggling for our recognition and acknowledgment of our existence.[217]

Party rallies were important occasions for the Death's Head troops; before the 1935 rally, Eicke had gathered his sentries from across the Reich in Dachau for weeks of rehearsal.[218] Yet they remained a rare moment in the sun for the guard troops. It is difficult, for example, to imagine a film being made about them as was done for the Leibstandarte in 1935.[219] While impossible to quantify, this lack of external prestige, even within the SS, undoubtedly contributed to the remorseless tyranny exercised by the guards inside the camps, in a compensatory localized

---

[211] Weingartner, 'Leibstandarte', p. 278.

[212] BHSA, StK 6300, Haushaltsangaben für 1936 KZ Dachau, 19 October 1935.

[213] Weingartner, *Leibstandarte*, p. 18. The sporting facilities at Lichterfelde were similarly lavish: Bahro, *Der SS-Sport*, p. 93.

[214] Koehl, *Black Corps*, p. 338.     [215] Wegner, *Waffen*, p. 98.

[216] Rupert Butler, *Hitler's Death's Head Division: SS Totenkopf Division* (Barnsley, 2004); Sydnor, *Soldiers*, pp. 23–36; even, on occasion, Segev, *Soldiers*, pp. 128–37.

[217] Hans Buchheim, 'The SS: Instrument of Domination', in Buchheim et al., *Anatomy*, pp. 125–301, here p. 261.

[218] Wachsmann, 'KL: A History of the Nazi Concentration Camps', ch. 2.

[219] Weingartner, *Leibstandarte*, p. 28.

self-aggrandisement. Bitterness over lack of prestige was nurtured in turn by the conviction that, unlike the more presentable SS formations, it was the Death's Head personnel who daily performed dangerous and unpleasant tasks for the Third Reich. They were its only soldiers perpetually at the 'front', 'holding the line' against the enemy within. This was a message hammered home in a special edition of the *Illustrierter Beobachter* on Dachau in December 1936.[220] One particularly striking photograph was taken from inside a guard tower, just behind its sentry and fixed machine gun. The logistics for such a shot must have been difficult to arrange, and it is obviously an invitation to readers to picture themselves in the demanding position of a Dachau guard. Lest anyone miss the point, the piece opined that 'the service of the SS is tough, standing here at lonely outposts on guard duty for the People's Community'.

Nevertheless, the Death's Head troops were slowly becoming beneficiaries of the militarization of the SS. The assumption by the Reich budget of the salaries of the guards gave them a more discrete identity from the camp SS in general, and they now answered to the commandant only when assigned to him for sentry duty. And as Hitler embarked on a radical trajectory in foreign policy in late 1937, Himmler became more vocal in his insistence that an armed SS would be needed to maintain domestic order in a coming war to avert a repetition of 1918. In his speech to the Wehrmacht in 1937, Himmler foresaw Death's Head personnel between the ages of twenty-five and thirty-five protecting the home front against the predations of Communists, saboteurs, and enemy parachutists.[221] There would of necessity, he added rather defensively, be some rotation of wounded personnel between the Verfügungstruppe at the front and Death's Head and police personnel at home. He explained that this would also avoid the problem, seen in the Imperial navy during the last war, of units stranded on the home front and becoming demoralized.

Himmler's opportunity to press more assertive military ambitions for the Death's Head troops arrived early the following year with the humbling of the Wehrmacht in the Blomberg-Fritsch crisis, in which the SS had played an ignoble role.[222] After a summer of lobbying by Himmler, in August 1938 Hitler promoted the guard troops to the status of 'standing armed force' at his personal disposal, part neither of the police nor army.[223] While time in the guard units would still not count as military service, Eicke was now permitted to recruit Wehrmacht personnel whose service there would count towards their period of enlistment in the Death's Head formations. This gave him another modest but tangible extrinsic inducement. Hitler's decree also provided for the so-called 'police reinforcement' of the Death's Heads units, in the event of their mobilization, by reservists aged twenty-five to thirty-five in the General SS. These men, part of a cohort of German males who had missed out on military service due to the Versailles Treaty, would

[220] *Illustrierter Beobachter*, 3 December 1936.
[221] IMT, Vol. XXIX, 1992 (A)-PS, Himmler speech to Wehrmacht on the Nature and Purpose of the SS and Police, ss. 231–2.
[222] For a useful summary, see Kershaw, *Nemesis*, pp. 49–57.
[223] The following from Wegner, *Waffen*, pp. 106–19.

receive preparatory training in peacetime at the camps. In the autumn of 1938, and again after January 1939, reservists from the General SS were duly called up for training in the camps. A supplementary Hitler decree of May 1939 ordered that Death's Head personnel would also act as replacements for casualties in the Verfügungstruppe: the first public confirmation of their envisaged front-line function. Bowing to the inevitable, in June 1939 the Wehrmacht instructed army corps headquarters to involve Death's Head officers and NCOs in training courses.

By this time, however, Dachau guards had already participated in their first armed excursion beyond Reich borders during the annexation of Austria in March 1938. Simon received a glowing report from the Wehrmacht for the 'exemplary' and 'comradely' support provided by the three Dachau Death's Head battalions during those 'demanding days'.[224] Their role in the Sudetenland crisis later that year was much greater. One of the more unusual external engagements for Dachau sentries was to act as guard of honour for British Prime Minister Neville Chamberlain at the Hotel Dreesen in Bad Godesberg during the Munich crisis: another moment in the limelight.[225] Far more substantial and significant, however, was the role of the Dachau guard contingent in the ranks of Josef Henlein's Sudeten German *Freikorps*.[226] In mid-September 1938, Hitler ordered the 1st and 2nd Dachau guard battalions, under Becker and Deisenhofer respectively, to slip over the Czech border and reinforce Henlein's supposed 'ethnic self-protection squads'. They were forbidden to leave Dachau with any identification papers in case they were captured by the Czech army. On 26 September, kitted out in grey uniforms and equipped with modern rifles and tank destroyer pieces, the two Dachau battalions were conveyed to Asch on a German postal train. Taking up positions among the *Freikorps*, they exchanged fire with the Czech military and it seems likely that one of the two 'Sudeten' volunteer fatalities was actually a Dachau guard.[227] The clandestine Dachau personnel remained in the so-called 'Free State of Asch' for a full week before the Wehrmacht rolled in under the terms of the Munich agreement and on 3 October staged a victory parade which was reviewed by Hitler, Rommel, and Reichenau. Simon recommended twenty-six officers, ninety-five NCOs, and 531 Dachau SS men for the 'Medal of Remembrance for 1st October 1938'. At yet another victory celebration twelve days later, Deisenhofer gave a heartfelt public speech celebrating the recognition won by his 'notorious Dachauers'.[228]

Hitler was able to send Death's Head personnel on this covert mission because, under the decree of August 1938, they were personally subordinated to him alone and therefore beyond the purview of the state executive. The Dachau guards were essentially illegal foreign partisans: the damage to the Nazi and Sudeten German cause had their identity been exposed would have been immense. It seems likely

---

[224] BAB, BDC SSO Becker, Schörner to Simon, 31 March 1938. For detail on the involvement of the Death's Head and Verfügungstruppe in the annexation, see Koehl, *Black Corps*, pp. 141–5.

[225] Merkl, *General Simon*, pp. 126–7.

[226] The following from Merkl, *General Simon*, pp. 128–32. See also Martin Broszat, 'Das Sudetendeutsche Freikorps', *Vierteljahrshefte für Zeitgeschichte*, Vol. 9, No. 1 (1961), pp. 30–49.

[227] Merkl, *General Simon*, p. 131, fn. 1.

[228] Merkl, *General Simon*, p. 133.

that they were sent to provide Hitler with a pretext for war should he need it even after the agreement reached at Bad Godesberg.[229] The spectacle of Czech troops firing on supposed Sudeten German nationalists would have offered the international rationale for a German invasion and likely war with Britain in France. Hitler's use of Death's Head personnel in this regard was a precedent for the macabre theatre staged in East Silesia on 1 September 1939, where the SS dressed up murdered concentration camp prisoners in Polish army uniforms as 'evidence' of Polish border violations against Germany.[230]

By the outbreak of the Second World War, then, Eicke's 1934 prophecy that his camp guards would be needed as soldiers 'in times to come' had been fulfilled. In the final dash towards the war which would eventually destroy the Third Reich, the camps' sentry units had been rapidly militarized. The net result of the reinforcements and frenzied recruitment of volunteers was that by mid-1939 the nominal SS headcount at the camps was some 22,033 men: slightly more than the total inmate population. Many of these were reservists undergoing three-month training courses, but even the permanent Death's Head staff had grown to some 12–13,000.[231] They had been provided with light military equipment from the Wehrmacht and SS officers were flowing into the Death's Head units from Bad Tölz: in 1938 17.7 per cent of graduates deployed to the formation, compared to 9.6 per cent the previous year.[232] Many Dachau guards had experienced front-line action in the Sudetenland. The camp sentry formations seemed finally to have established a quasi-military status, with 1938 marking a watershed. As the Sudeten crisis and police reinforcement programme make clear, this owed more to the radical political trajectory of the regime than to the intrinsic role of concentration camp guard. And now the older, incoming reinforcements needed to be socialized very swiftly into the terror values of the service: here seasoned personnel from the Dachau School commandant staff stood ready to offer behavioural cues.

[229] Merkl, *General Simon*, pp. 131–2.
[230] For detail, see Wachsmann, 'KL: A History of the Nazi Concentration Camps', ch. 4.
[231] Wachsmann, 'KL: A History of the Nazi Concentration Camps', ch. 3; Sydnor, *Soldiers*, p. 34.
[232] Wegner, *Waffen SS*, p. 142.

# 3

# The Dachau Commandant Staff

The commandant staff (*Kommandantur*) personnel managed the Dachau protective custody compound. Unlike the guard units, deployed in rotation as sentries around its perimeter, these men worked daily inside. Identified by the letter 'K' on the right-hand shoulder of their service uniforms and numbering 165 men by June 1939, the majority were employed in clerical roles little preserved in the historical record.[1] At the apex of the commandant staff, however, were found those few dozen key SS men who oversaw daily life in Dachau. It was these men, from the camp commandant down to the block leaders who supervised inmate barracks and work details, whom prisoners needed to watch, appraise, and adapt to in order to make it through the day. Many were gratified by this attention, and to them the Dachau prisoner compound was a stage, a theatre of power. If prisoners adhered at all times to the hard-won wisdom not to 'stand out' from the mass (see Chapter 4), for ambitious commandant staff personnel the agenda was quite the opposite: very much to stand out to inmates, comrades, and superiors alike. For them, standing out might bring status, prestige, and rapid promotion. Their whims and idiosyncrasies, their carefully nourished stage personae, could soon tip a day in Dachau from miserable to truly hellish. They were men bound by comradeship, patronage, and group complicities, yet riven by rivalries and resentments. Unlike the guard units, whose militarization introduced constraints on personnel policy, there were few demographic or technical restrictions to service on the command staff. Even more than the sentries, commandant staff personnel were the protagonists and vectors of the 'Dachau spirit'.

SS men came to the Dachau commandant staff by three main routes. The first was outright appointment from the General SS, often 'old fighters' of the movement with low SS membership numbers for whom a post on the staff was a reward and sinecure. The second was transfer from other concentration camps, from whence ambitious SS men throughout the pre-war era came to prove their Nazi mettle in the Dachau School. The third recruitment channel was the Dachau guard units, the most experienced and proactive of whose bright-eyed volunteers frequently secured transfer into the command staff. The key stakeholders in commandant

---

[1] SAM, StA 34686, Vernehmungsniederschrift Matthias Pfeiffer, 9 January 1967; personnel figures in BAB, NS4/Da 40, Commandant Staff Dachau, 30 June 1939, s. 199–202.

**Table 3.1** Dachau key commandant staff by generation.

| Generation | 1933 | 1934 | 1935 | 1936 | 1937 | 1938 | 1939 |
|---|---|---|---|---|---|---|---|
| Front Generation | 40% | 25% | 29% | 29% | 16% | 20% | 7% |
| War Youth Generation | 52% | 61% | 61% | 57% | 65% | 62% | 68% |
| Post-war Generation | 8% | 14% | 10% | 14% | 19% | 18% | 25% |

**Table 3.2** Dachau key commandant staff by SS membership.

| SS Cohort | 1933 | 1934 | 1935 | 1936 | 1937 | 1938 | 1939 |
|---|---|---|---|---|---|---|---|
| SS Founders | 36% | 33% | 25% | 18% | 16% | 21% | 15% |
| Old Fighters | 48% | 59% | 61% | 64% | 55% | 49% | 48% |
| From March 1933 | 16% | 8% | 14% | 18% | 29% | 30% | 37% |

staff personnel policy were Himmler, Eicke, and the concentration camp commandant himself, though Eicke was dominant.[2] Himmler allowed him a largely free reign in the first years of Dachau, and his organization of the commandant staff into seven departments—commandant, adjutant, sentries, prisoner compound, medical, economic and administrative, and political—was a key feature of the 'Dachau model'.[3] Commandant staff personnel lists are seldom preserved in SS documentation and must be derived instead from personnel files and inmate testimony.[4] Even these contain little data on medical and administrative staff. This chapter will confine itself to the key positions which most immediately shaped life in the prisoner compound: the commandant, adjutant, compound leader, report leader, and block leader, along with the place of the Political Department in the camp.

Before exploring the composition and biographies of the seventy pre-war personnel identified as meeting the above criteria, it is worth setting out some overall demographics (see Table 3.1). Their most striking feature, compared to the guard personnel, is the relatively small presence of the post-war generation.[5] The persistence, until the final year of the Dachau School, of older men from the front generation is also conspicuous and reflects the tendency for them to be given roles on the commandant staff rather than in the guard formations. This is also captured in the length of SS service among these key personnel, in Table 3.2.

---

[2] Wachsmann, 'KL: A History of the Nazi Concentration Camps', ch. 2; Tuchel, *Konzentrationslager*, pp. 238–43.

[3] On the 'Bavarian' and 'Prussian' models for concentration camps, see Tuchel, *Konzentrationslager*, pp. 148–52.

[4] Günter Morsch, 'Formation', pp. 87–194, here p. 156.

[5] This contrasts with Riedle's demographic analysis of the commandant staff at Sachsenhausen, where over half the personnel came from the post-war generation. However, Riedle's is a sample of all the personnel on the Sachsenhausen commandant staff (including, for example, clerical roles), rather than the key, prisoner-facing disciplinary personnel addressed here whom I feel are the more historically important subjects. See Riedle, *Angehörigen*, pp. 69–75.

Men joining the SS after 1933 were far less likely to secure a key position on the commandant's staff than among the sentry units. The commandant staff required ideological zeal and political reliability, and ideally experience from the street-fighting years of the Weimar Republic which continued to guide Eicke's construal of the concentration camps. Military aptitude and experience in themselves were much less important: the emphasis for these political soldiers was very much on the 'political' and almost all this sample were also members of the NSDAP.[6]

## DEPARTMENT I: COMMANDANT AND ADJUTANT

### Commandants

A concentration camp commandant was responsible for all the departments on the commandant staff. His personality and outlook had a decisive impact on the SS culture of a camp. Primarily a product of the SS ethos of personal leadership, it also reflected his influence on the distribution of subordinate posts and oversight of disciplinary measures against SS staff.[7] A change in commandant often brought dramatic changes to life in Dachau and takes a prominent place in prisoner literature. The character of a commandant's tenure was the product of an interplay between disposition and structure, between bureaucratic and charismatic authority, and between prisoner demographics and instructions from above at the IKL.

The arrival and departure of Wäckerle, Dachau's first commandant, was traced in the first chapter. On the whole his tenure functioned for his successor as an object lesson in how not to run a concentration camp, though Wäckerle left several enduring legacies to Dachau. One was the administration of corporal punishment with whips, which would remain a nightmarish topos throughout the camp's existence. With its rustic heritage, the whip was rich in *völkisch* semiotics and iconic among National Socialists: for over a decade Hitler had embarrassed and titillated patrons in Munich high society by sporting a whip in their well-heeled drawing rooms.[8] According to Steinbrenner, Wäckerle introduced 'welcome beatings' by whip with the observation that this had long been standard in penitentiaries, German and English, before a judicial system 'poisoned' by 'sentimental humanitarianism' withdrew this 'pedagogic' tool.[9] The use of whips was common among SA and SS guards throughout the early camps, an extremely painful form of violence bearing no risk of physical discomfort to the perpetrator.[10] Wäckerle's 'special regulations' foreshadowed many of the disciplinary preoccupations of the Dachau School. More tyrannical and murderous in tone than those in other early camps,

---

[6] Seventy-eight per cent can be identified as being Party members. Given that only around 80 per cent of NSDAP membership files survived the war this is very close to total. See the apposite discussion in Riedle, *Angehörigen*, p. 76.

[7] Günter Morsch, 'Organisations', pp. 58–75, here p. 62.          [8] Kershaw, *Hubris*, p. 188.

[9] DaA, DA 19.862, Hans Steinbrenner, 'Hinter den Kulissen', s. 8.

[10] Wachsmann, 'KL: A History of the Nazi Concentration Camps', ch. 2.

their very first measures provide for the shooting 'without warning' of attempted escapees that offered such expansive opportunities for the murder of prisoners.[11] They introduced solitary confinement, a graduated system of treating inmates, and insisted that every prisoner had to work on pain of condign penalties. They included capital punishment for mutiny, an illegal provision preserved in Eicke's regulations. They also established a fixed distinction between commandant staff and guard troops which was one of the defining features the 'Dachau model'. Less tangible but equally important was Wäckerle's paramilitary leadership: given Erspenmüller's absenteeism, he was the only SS man in early Dachau of officer rank. By appointing and goading the violent NCOs of the early Dachau SS he did much to launch the camp's lethal course. Yet in doing so he failed to strike what would become a critical balance in the operation of an early camp: to terrorize and kill without leaving traces sufficient for the judiciary to build an investigation from. It would be left to his successor to reconcile these cultural inheritances and environmental pressures in a superficially stable and organized model.

Theodor Eicke did not object to brutality or to the murder of prisoners. He sought merely to make it more discreet, less likely to leave a trail for the judiciary. According to Steinbrenner, Eicke observed the 'welcome beating' ritual and announced that it would be stopped in favour of administered floggings (*Prügelstrafe*) for documented transgressions of camp rules.[12] The advantage of this, from Eicke's point of view, was to remove the appearance of arbitrariness, of personal intent: to deindividuate the perpetrator. His new regulations of October 1933 offered great latitude to SS men in terms of finding transgressions.[13] They underpinned a vicious cycle in the camp, for the stricter the definition of order, the greater the scope and incidence of prisoner disorder and in turn the demand for watchfulness against recalcitrant prisoners. Eicke's regulations also introduced an 'incidental punishment' of 'tying to stakes' which had a particularly grim future in his concentration camps. A venerable field punishment, its immediate carceral heritage lay in the First World War when *Entente* governments had made repeated complaints about the German practice in POW camps of fastening prisoners to poles with their hands tied behind their backs.[14] Known as 'pole' (*Pfahl*) or 'arm-tying' (*Armbinden*), it became an international symbol of German depredation until abolished in May 1917. It is unclear whether the punishment was enforced in Dachau during Eicke's tenure as commandant: his successor, with grotesque lack of linguistic awareness, claimed that Eicke (as Reich Inspector) inaugurated it in Dachau 'behind my back'.[15] It soon became one of the most dreaded disciplinary measures in the camps, where the horrific refinement was added of

---

[11] IMT, Vol. XXXVI, Document 922-D, pp. 6–10, here p. 7; Wachsmann, 'KL: A History of the Nazi Concentration Camps', ch. 1.

[12] SAM, StA 34462/7, Fortsetzung der Beschuldigtenvernehmung Hans Steinbrenner, 29 June 1951.

[13] BAB, R3001/21167, Dienstvorschriften für die Begleitposten und Gefangenenbewachung, 1 October 1933, ss. 62–9.

[14] Ute Hinz, *Gefangen im Grossen Krieg: Kriegsgefangenschaft in Deutschland 1914–1921* (Essen, 2006), pp. 156–8.

[15] SAM, StA 34462/3, Beschuldigtenvernehmung Heinrich Deubel, 6 December 1949.

raising prisoners in the air on a spike, chains tied behind their backs, their feet unable to touch the ground.[16] Frequently, *Kapos* or SS personnel swung the inmates from side to side, making an ordeal which might last one or two hours more agonizing still. Also known in the camps as 'tree-hanging' (*Baumhängen*), inmates in its aftermath were usually unable to use their arms again for days. So debilitating was this punishment that it was eventually officially banned by Himmler in 1942 as incompatible with the new philosophy of (ostensibly) extracting the maximum labour possible from inmates.[17]

Dall-Armi, an early protégée of Eicke in Dachau, ascribed his mentor's fanaticism to his Alsatian background, hailing from the border area annexed by Bismarck in 1871 and returned to France at Versailles. There is probably something in this. A striking proportion of senior Nazi perpetrators came from the 'lost' and demilitarized German territories and from 'threatened' German border areas.[18] Other observers, however, saw Eicke more as a cynical careerist. Steinbrenner, while subscribing to the myth of Eicke's Rhineland insurgency, believed that he was fired above all by the ambition of outdoing Hitler's favourite Sepp Dietrich of the Leibstandarte.[19] Höß was of the opinion that Eicke's tirades against camp prisoners 'had the sole purpose of keeping the SS men on their toes at all times'.[20] Yet, important as they were, Eicke's personal motivations and individual agency can be over-weighted. He, too, was a product of environment and situation. He met a demand in the camp SS for a tough role model and charismatic father figure, for an ongoing rationale for hatred of concentration camp inmates long after the patent consolidation of the Third Reich. Dependent on Himmler's backing, he responded to the latter's need for a more canny and efficient brand of brutality. Eicke was a construct, 'a personality as much as a person', as Dall-Armi put it.[21] As has been pointed out, in organizational terms his Dachau model was not spectacularly different from that used by the SA at Oranienburg.[22] But the narrative of Eicke, like one of the great Prussian military reformers, bringing order and professionalism to the camps and their staff, flattered the SS as it distanced itself from the SA. Eicke seems in darker moments to have been aware of the limits to his indispensability. Paranoid and embittered, ever sensitive to real and imagined slights, he personified the insecurities and over-compensatory self-assurance of the concentration camp personnel.[23] His SS guards, he once wrote, were 'dearer to me than my wife and family': a rhetorical flourish perhaps, but indicative of a hollow personal life.

[16] For a vivid testimony on the experience see Erhard Klein, *Jehovas Zeugen im KZ Dachau: Geschichtliche Hintergründe und Erlebnisberichte* (Bielefeld, 2001), pp. 146–7.
[17] Zámečnik, S., *That Was Dachau 1933–1945*, p. 232; Broszat, M., 'The Concentration Camps 1933–45', p. 225.
[18] Michael Mann, 'Were the Perpetrators of Genocide "Ordinary Men" or "Real Nazis"?', pp. 139–75.
[19] DaA, 19.862, Hans Steinbrenner, Hinter den Kulissen von Dachau, 31 January 1962, s. 7.
[20] Höß, *Commandant*, p. 80.
[21] SAM, StA 34461/4, Max von Dall-Armi, Bilder und Skizzen aus dem Konzentrationslager, 13 April 1951.
[22] Morsch, 'Organisations-und Verwaltungsstruktur', p. 58.
[23] Segev, T., *Soldiers of Evil*, p. 147.

Eicke was killed in February 1943 flying a reckless reconnaissance mission for the Death's Head Division on the Eastern Front. Despite a series of hasty, last-minute exhumations during the lengthy retreat from Russia, Eicke's remains were eventually overrun in 1944 in the Ukraine, leaving him entombed in the soil of the state he so fanatically detested.[24]

Eicke, the man and the construct, was a tough act to succeed, and his successor as Dachau commandant had a very different personality and leadership style. Heinrich Deubel was born in 1890 in Ortenburg in lower Bavaria.[25] After nine years of schooling he joined the Fürstenfeldbrück military academy, signing up as a professional soldier in 1909. During the Somme offensive in July 1916, Deubel was knocked unconscious by a shell and buried alive before being taken prisoner by the British; he claimed still to be plagued by headaches in 1949. He was released from captivity in November 1918 and from the army in 1919. Deubel was a true veteran of the German Right, with the kind of prestigious nationalist CV Eicke lacked: a volunteer in the *Freikorps* von Epp, a participant in the Kapp *Putsch*, a member of the NSDAP from 1923 and of the SS from 1926. His SS membership number of 186 was the third lowest to be found anywhere in the concentration camp system: Deubel had impeccable credentials.[26] His professional life was more prosaic and Deubel worked as a customs official from 1920 until his appointment to Dachau in 1934. His boss in the customs service recalled him with evident affection as a diligent and reliable deputy, always ready to help out those in need— save when Nazi politics called him away from his desk.[27] Promotion in the SS came quickly even by its generous standards and within five years of joining he reached the rank of *Standartenführer*. After the seizure of power, as a senior SS man, Deubel was called away more and more from his desk. In October 1934 he was transferred, against his wishes, to command the SS Relief Station at Dachau. Deubel had been anxious to preserve his state pension, and at this time the SS was unable to offer pension benefits.[28] However, after a mismanaged attempt in the same month by Himmler to parachute in another worthy but wayward senior SS man, *Oberführer* Alexander Reiner, to replace Eicke, Deubel was now the only SS officer in Dachau of adequate seniority to command the concentration camp.[29] This, then, was an ad hoc appointment; SS personnel policy did not extend to succession planning.

Nor were the handover arrangements indicative of such a policy. According to Deubel, Eicke simply passed him a folder containing the service regulations and advised him to read it thoroughly.[30] He was told nothing about his responsibilities and duties, which were instead set out by his first adjutant, Wilhelm Noetzl. This

---

[24] Sydnor, *Soldiers of Destruction*, p. 273, fn. 26; Rohrkamp, '*Weltanschauulich gefestigte Kämpfer*', p. 226.

[25] SAM, StA 34462/3, Beschuldigtenvernehmung Heinrich Deubel, 6 December 1949.

[26] MacLean, *Camp Men*, p. 275.

[27] SAM, StA 34462/4, Zeugenvernehmungsprotokoll Andreas Baierl, 29 December 1949.

[28] SAM, StA 34462/3, Beschuldigtenvernehmung Heinrich Deubel, 6 December 1949.

[29] Johannes Tuchel, 'The Commandants of the Dachau Concentration Camp', in Wolfgang Benz and Babara Distel (eds), *Dachau and the Nazi Terror: Studies and Reports* (Dachau, 2002), pp. 232–5.

[30] SAM, StA 34462/3, Beschuldigtenvernehmung Heinrich Deubel, 6 December 1949.

informality ceded Deubel the space to relax some of the draconian conditions in the camp. He claimed to have assembled the Dachau SS and to have warned them that mistreatment of prisoners would be punished and referred as necessary to SS or civilian courts. He introduced work-free Saturday afternoons, sports, better footwear and clothing, and improvements to the medieval conditions in the *Bunker*. Prisoner testimony tends to back him up in all this, and the 'Deubel era' appears in memoirs as one of relative moderacy sandwiched between two harsh regimes. Ludwig Schecher recalls a 'camp school' in the tenth barracks where, under the oversight of an SS NCO, inmates of lesser educational attainment were given lessons in German, stenography, civil law, and arithmetic.[31] Schecher himself was a guest speaker on maths and law. Deubel even came to sit in on the school in civilian attire on one occasion, chatting with the prisoners and doling out cigarettes.[32] In December 1935 he arranged a Christmas tree with fairy lights for the camp, while presents were handed out to the inmates. Deubel also arranged a special festive meal and an alcohol-free punch.[33]

Behind the scenes, none of this sat well with the traditionalists of the Dachau SS. Deubel asserted that Eicke often came to the camp and spoke with them behind his back, bemoaning the un-National Socialist character of the new regime.[34] He added that Eicke protected favoured block leaders from his own time as commandant; it was these men, in Deubel's admittedly self-serving account, who introduced the 'pole' punishment without his consent. Deubel also recalled having to ban Steinbrenner from making unauthorized visits to the prisoner compound to catch up with comrades from the early Dachau SS. Collective dismay among the traditionalists at what one described at the time as the 'disgusting humane treatment' (*ekelhafte humane Behandlung*) of the inmates seems to have reached a critical mass in spring 1936.[35] The exact reasons for Deubel's transfer at the end of March that year are not preserved in his personnel file and most of the official calumny for his allegedly indulgent reign seems to have fallen upon his compound leader. Nevertheless, Deubel's proposal to send a Communist inmate on a Strength Through Joy vacation brought home to Eicke the 'depths' to which Deubel, too, had sunk.[36] Deubel was moved on to command Columbia House in Berlin until it closed in November 1936, when he returned to his post with the customs service. He was the only Dachau commandant available to the post-war Bavarian authorities to investigate; the others were all dead by the late 1940s. The case was dropped because there was no evidence for charging him with murder, and lesser offences under his reign were no longer prosecutable under the statute of limitations.[37]

[31] Schecher, 'Rückblick', pp. 35–8; SAM, StA 34414, Zeugenvernehmungsprotokoll Karl Mausner, 6 March 1950; SAM, StA 34414, Zeugenvernehmungsprotokoll Ludwig Scharnagel, 6 March 1950.
[32] Schecher, 'Rückblick', p. 38.      [33] Schecher, 'Rückblick', p. 38.
[34] SAM, StA 34462/3, Beschuldigtenvernehmung Heinrich Deubel, 6 December 1949.
[35] BAB, BDC SSO D'Angelo, Driemel to Guthardt, 30 April 1936.
[36] Tuchel, 'The Commandants', p. 235.
[37] Edith Raim, 'Westdeutsche Ermittlungen und Prozesse zum KZ Dachau und seinen Aussenlagern', in Eiber and Sigel, *Dachauer Prozesse: NS-Verbrechen vor amerikanischen Militärgerichten in Dachau 1945–1948* (Göttingen, 2007), p. 214.

Deubel's relative restraint should not be overstated, for some eighteen prisoners died during his tenure.[38] Yet the suffering for which he was individually, as opposed to executively, responsible was indeed small compared to his predecessors, and brings into focus the authority, the scope for leadership, enjoyed by concentration camp commandants even in the face of resistance by subordinates.

The same could be said, in a wholly negative sense, of his successor Hans Loritz, Dachau's final pre-war commandant. Born in 1895 in Augsburg, the son of a policeman, Loritz trained as a baker before volunteering for the Bavarian Army in August 1914.[39] He was wounded several times on the Western Front, including a gassing which was to hinder him for the rest of his life. In 1917 he switched to the prestigious ranks of the Air Service although, contrary to later boasting, it seems that he served as a tail gunner rather than a pilot.[40] In July 1918 Loritz's plane was shot down over French territory. He was seriously injured and seems to have been treated harshly by French farmers before being handed over to the army as a POW.[41] Loritz worked at a labour camp on the Somme river until his repatriation in September 1920, when he followed his father into the police. In 1930 he joined the Augsburg NSDAP and SS, and was instrumental in building up the Augsburg SS *Standarte* which provided so sizeable and violent a proportion of the early Dachau SS. On 15 December 1933, Loritz was given leave from the police to take up a position commanding the SS Relief Station at Dachau. Himmler assigned him to the relief station as a punishment for squabbling with a senior SA leader at the 1933 Nuremberg rally, but it was a decisive moment in his career. For it was at Dachau that he first came into contact with Eicke, his future patron in the SS. Loritz wrote a mildly repentant letter to Himmler outlining his achievement in transforming the idle, undisciplined, and obstreperous Austrians into an orderly and cohesive formation.[42] He requested assignment to the concentration camp itself, where Eicke was seeking able personnel. Loritz argued that working with prisoners would be easier on his health and that his experience as a police officer offered sound preparation. Instead, on 9 July 1934, he was assigned to command Esterwegen concentration camp as part of Eicke's project to bring SA-run camps under SS control on the model of Dachau. Eicke was soon lauding Loritz in familiar imagery for turning an unreliable guard formation into committed professionals, a chaotic institution into a model of order and control.[43] It was no coincidence that Esterwegen endured a rising crescendo of violence under Loritz: five inmates were murdered between March and May 1935 alone. As a reward, Himmler promoted him to *Oberführer* and then transferred him to Dachau in April 1936 to replace Deubel. Loritz was the first Dachau commandant with experience in another concentration camp.

At Dachau, Loritz consciously constructed his tenure as a return to the traditional values of the Dachau School. He wrote to Eicke that the Deubel regime had

---

[38] Zámečnik, *Dachau*, p. 82.     [39] For detail, see Riedel, *Ordnungshüter*.
[40] Information provided to the author from Dirk Riedel.     [41] Segev, *Soldiers*, p. 199.
[42] BAB, BDC SSO Loritz, Loritz to Himmler, 9 January 1934.
[43] Tuchel, 'The Commandants', p. 238.

been 'lazy', that he would be ashamed to be 'loved by his enemies', that he was not surprised that prisoners no longer sought to escape from such a convivial environment.[44] He fumed that some of his new subordinates seemed more concerned with avoiding 'atrocity propaganda' about Dachau than with keeping the prisoners in line. Loritz's compound leader, Jakob Weiseborn, worried that Dachau was no longer respected as an institution by miscreants. 'Nearly always', he reported, 'released prisoners say that things had been good in Dachau, and that they would not mind in the slightest if they were sent back'.[45] This had to change. Schecher encountered Loritz, a 'powerful-looking man with a brutal face and rough manners', in his first days, stalking around the camp and familiarizing himself with it as Eicke had in 1933.[46] Loritz introduced himself formally to the prisoners with an act of theatre Schecher likens to Wagner. As a warning of what to expect, seven inmates were given twenty-five lashes on the spot. The block leaders administering the beatings quickly began to 'work towards' the commandant, devising new and energetic ways to impart the blows.[47] The camp school, a symbol of the tolerant depredations of Deubel's regime, was closed down. Smoking regulations were tightened up, as were barracks inspections. Facial hair was banned. Even the food, in Schecher's account, soon became scarcer and lower in fat.[48] In marked contrast to his predecessors, Loritz seems also to have had a hands-on approach to violence, as part of a lovingly nurtured public persona as a 'tough' man of action. Neurath recounts Dantean scenes:

> To us prisoners he appeared as a brutal and uneducated man, who raced through the camp on his motorcycle like a whirlwind, raising hell here and there, and then disappearing again. He loved his dog and his swan. Once we watched him trample a prisoner half to death and, while still wiping blood from his boot, whistle for his beloved dog and pet him.[49]

Loritz led through example, patronage, and exhortations to brutality. Schecher, working in the laundry detail, overheard 'judicial and sociological expositions' to younger SS men as though in a 'criminal law seminar' at Munich University.[50] Eicke saw Loritz as a strong, charismatic SS leader who shared his own values, the ideal candidate to oversee the Dachau School. While he dismissed fully half of all incumbent commandants during the consolidation of the SS concentration camp system from 1936, Loritz was kept in his post until 1939.[51]

Yet Loritz was not simply a bright-eyed idealist. His extensive career in the camps was dogged by suspicions of corruption dramatically revealed in 1942

---

[44] BAB, BDC SSO D'Angelo, Loritz to Eicke, 29 April 1936. More detail below, see also Riedel, *Ordnungshüter*, pp. 141–59.
[45] BAB, BDC SSO D'Angelo, Memo Weiseborn, 2 May 1936.
[46] Schecher, 'Rückblick', p. 42.
[47] Schecher, 'Rückblick', p. 46. On Ian Kershaw's influential hypothesis of 'working towards the Führer' as an explanation for the escalating radicalism of the Nazi regime, see *Hubris*, pp. 527–91. The concept of anticipatory compliance (taking actions without explicit instruction) is equally applicable to the SS. See the discussion in Hein, *Elite*, pp. 92–5.
[48] Schecher, 'Rückblick', p. 43.     [49] Neurath, *The Society of Terror*, p. 80.
[50] Schecher, 'Rückblick', p. 59.     [51] Riedel, *Ordnungshüter*, p. 149.

when Himmler uncovered evidence of gargantuan embezzlement during his tenure at Dachau. In 1938, shortly after the annexation of Austria, Loritz purchased a lakeside plot of land near Salzburg in the village of St Gilgen, where he planned to build a luxurious new home.[52] In the summer of 1938 a small detachment of prisoners, mainly Jehovah's Witnesses, were sent there as a private work detail and housed overnight in the town prison. Much of the building material, too, was sourced from the Dachau complex. With the villa complete, selected Dachau block leaders were invited to spend their holidays at St Gilgen.[53] A small community of senior SS figures from the camps bought plots there, safe from Allied bombing raids. All this was an open secret in the SS up to the summer of 1942 when it was exposed amid great scandal. Contrary to Himmler's many homilies on the self-sacrificing and austere lifestyles of the SS, petty corruption was widespread in the camps. It seems that he decided to make an example of Loritz at a sensitive time in the war when public disquiet about the privileges enjoyed by dignitaries of the regime was on the rise.[54] Yet Loritz was not even expelled from the SS: he was transferred to Norway to set up a cluster of forced labour camps and committed suicide in Allied custody in 1946.

These four pre-war Dachau commandants share some striking common characteristics, suggesting that personnel policy was not quite as haphazard as is sometimes suggested.[55] All were born in the 1890s and as such, like most senior Nazis, were members of the 'Front Generation'. All had seen action on the Western Front in the heady, myth-laden days of 1914 either as volunteers or professional soldiers. All joined the NSDAP very early indeed, on average in December 1926. By the time of their appointment as Dachau commandant, they had served the movement for an average of eight years. With SS numbers under 10,000 they were among the founding cohort of the SS, joining on average in February 1930. They had been instrumental in building up their respective *Standarten*, and risen to the senior rank of *Standartenführer* or *Oberführer* by the time of their appointment as Dachau commandant. This high rank is a further indicator of the importance of Dachau in the pre-war concentration camp system: other camps tended to be commanded by officers of less elevated rank.[56] All except Wäckerle were in their forties by the time of their appointment, and all except Wäckerle continued in the post of commandant elsewhere in the camp system. All had a decisive impact on the operational culture of Dachau, and prisoner memoirs are frequently structured in terms of their respective tenures. In addition to their personal, charismatic leadership, one reason was their influence over subordinate appointments, to positions intimately entwined in the daily lives of inmates and SS personnel. It is to the first of these, their adjutants, that the next section turns.

---

[52] Riedel, *Ordnungshüter*, p. 209f. Picturesque photographs of the holiday home on pp. 278–9.
[53] Riedel, *Ordnungshüter*, p. 213.
[54] Wachsmann, 'KL: A History of the Nazi Concentration Camps', ch. 7.
[55] Tuchel, *Konzentrationslager*, pp. 160–5.     [56] Tuchel, 'Commandants', p. 244.

## Adjutants

Adjutants generally have a modest presence in inmate testimony, but theirs was a key role in the concentration camps. The adjutant, in the words of one organizational memorandum, was responsible for 'the quickest and most precise execution of the commandant's orders'.[57] He oversaw all personnel matters pertaining to the commandant staff and acted as point man in its liaison with the guard troops.[58] The adjutant was often de facto deputy for the commandant in his absence, since he usually had a fuller grasp of his duties than the 1st compound leader who was his nominal deputy. The role was a key springboard for future careers in concentration camps' commandant staffs.[59] Adjutants also wielded significant soft political power in their control of access to the commandant and the relationship between the two was almost feudal, with a change of commandant invariably accompanied by a change in adjutant. A commandant relied heavily on his adjutant and could be permitted to cause significant personnel upheaval in selecting a trusted candidate, as when Hermann Baranowski brought his paladin Höß from Dachau to become his adjutant at Sachsenhausen.

Eight SS men can be identified as having held the role of adjutant pre-war at Dachau. Wäckerle's adjutant was Scheingraber, who went on to command a guard troop battalion. His successor, Hans Weibrecht, came the other way, from the Dachau guard units. Born in the northern Bavarian city of Fürth in 1911, Weibrecht was a youthful member of the conservative paramilitary Stahlhelm before joining the SS in February 1933. In a letter penned later in the 1930s, Weibrecht recalled 'being transferred' to the Dachau guard troops in July 1933.[60] He spent three months on sentry duty before switching to the commandant staff to recover from an operation. At the start of 1934 he was appointed Eicke's adjutant. He was promoted quickly at Dachau and rose from private to *Oberscharführer* in less than a year. Eicke clearly valued his work, reporting that Weibrecht 'yields to no one as stenographer and typist' and taking his adjutant with him to the IKL.[61] Yet Eicke also came to fret that Weibrecht's office duties there were making him soft, 'indolent and comfortable' like a civil servant. In 1936 he accordingly transferred Weibrecht back to the 'front' as a sentry. Weibrecht was evidently displeased and requested, successfully, to be transferred back to the General SS. Yet his avoidance of the more violent duties of the camp SS did not in the end keep him clear of murderous criminality: from August 1941 to April 1942 he was a member of Einsatzgruppe D, operating behind the lines of the 11th Army in the Ukraine.[62]

Deubel's first adjutant was Wilhelm Noertzl, of whom nothing is known. His successor was an altogether better-known figure: Karl Koch who served a two-week spell as Deubel's adjutant in 1935. He is included here, then, less for his material

[57] IfZ, Fa54, Bericht SS Hauptscharführer Hans Jüng (undated), s. 3.
[58] Morsch, 'Organisations-und Verwaltungstruktur', p. 62.
[59] Morsch, 'Organisations-und Verwaltungstruktur', p. 63.
[60] BAB, BDC, SSO Weibrecht, Weibrecht to General SS Standarte 80, 11 January 1937.
[61] BAB, BDC SSO Weibrecht, Eicke to Schmitt, n.d. (1936).
[62] Tuchel, *Konzentrationslager*, p. 393.

contribution at Dachau than for the light his appointment and departure might shed on personnel policy and preferred adjutant biography. Koch was born in 1897 in Darmstadt, the son of a customs official.[63] He volunteered for the army and fought on the Western Front where he was taken prisoner by the British: another senior figure from the concentration camp SS to have experienced captivity as a POW. A prosaic petit bourgeois life working in a bank and supporting a young family was abruptly severed in 1931 when both bank and marriage collapsed. In the same year Koch joined the NSDAP and SS. After the 'seizure of power', Koch was rewarded for his services with an appointment to organize the auxiliary police in Kassel, his route to the concentration camps. His career there was at first nomadic, taking in Sachsenburg, Esterwegen, Lichtenburg, Dachau, Columbia House, and Sachsenhausen before settling down as a notoriously cruel and corrupt commandant of Buchenwald.[64]

His successor as Dachau adjutant was *Obersturmbannführer* Walter Gerlach. Gerlach was born in 1896 in Lebus, Brandenburg, and served in the Imperial Army from 1914 to 1918.[65] Together with his brother, he then took over his father's carpentry factory until spiralling debt forced its closure in 1930. He joined the NSDAP in September of the same year, the SS in February 1931. Gerlach was another senior figure on the Dachau commandant staff who had been instrumental in building up his local SS *Standarte*, Frankfurt am Oder, which he commanded from August 1932. In July 1934, at the instigation of Sepp Dietrich, Gerlach transferred to the Gestapo prison at Columbia House. On 1 December 1934 he moved to Sachsenburg, and on 20 April 1935 to Dachau in place of Koch. When Loritz took over as Dachau commandant, Gerlach was already under a cloud for his role in a major Dachau SS traffic accident in central Munich (see Chapter 6) where prosecutors were preparing a case against him.[66] Loritz also regarded him as complicit in the iniquitous softness of Deubel's regime. The two were unable to establish a working relationship and in July 1936 Gerlach requested transfer back to the General SS, which Loritz was only too happy to approve. As he wrote to Eicke:

> On the basis of my observations, today I even incline to the view that *Standartenführer* Gerlach was just as responsible for the mess which ruled here as the commandant was, for he certainly knew what was going on but never queried it . . . After he noted that I did not set great store in this advice and take care of my own work, he sees himself as being superfluous.[67]

Eicke was blunter still. 'I approve the request', he wrote, 'on the grounds that SS *Standartenführer* Gerlach had previously been assigned as a support to the work-shy SS *Oberführer* Deubel'. He rejected, however, Loritz's request to bring in the skilled Weibrecht as a replacement. The position went instead to one Max von Lachemair,

[63] Detailed biographies of Koch in Segev, *Soldiers*, pp. 179–89; see also Morsch, *Sachsenburg*, passim.
[64] Segev, *Soldiers*, pp. 179–81.
[65] Following from Tuchel, *Konzentrationslager*, pp. 375–6.
[66] Riedel, *Ordnungshüter*, pp. 147–8.        [67] Tuchel, 'Commandants', p. 236.

of whom little is known save that he was born in 1901, joined the SS in October 1932, and lasted only six months in the role.[68] In January 1937 Max Koegel, an old crony from Loritz's Augsburg days, took over as Dachau adjutant, having served in the same position at Columbia House and Sachsenhausen. Koegel will be discussed in more depth below as he went on to become Dachau compound leader before graduating to other senior positions throughout the camp network.

He was replaced by Martin Weiß, like Koegel an example of an ambitious SS officer whose spell as Dachau adjutant proved the ticket to a career at the apex of the concentration camp network. Weiß was born in 1905 in Weiden, a small town in the Palatinate. He attended a mechanical engineering school and then the College of Technology in Bad Frankenhausen where he stayed on as an assistant after completing his engineering exams.[69] He was an early devotee of the Nazi movement, joining the NSDAP in the summer of 1926 and becoming a founding member of the Weiden SA.[70] In April 1932 Weiß lost his job and decided, along with a few local friends, to found a Weiden SS: among them was Richard Baer, the future commandant of Auschwitz. During the Nazi takeover of Bavaria, Weiß enlisted with the Weiden auxiliary police and came in this capacity to the early Dachau SS on 11 April 1933. After three months training under the State Police, Eicke brought him into the Technical Department of the commandant staff to make use of his engineering background.[71] In 1936 he was made head of the department, and in July 1938 Loritz's adjutant in succession to Koegel. In early 1940 Weiß embarked on a peripatetic career as commandant of various concentration camps; Neuengamme, Arbeitsdorf, Dachau, Majdanek, and Mühldorf. The headline defendant in the US Dachau Trial (see Figure 3.1), Weiß, despite considerable supportive testimony from former inmates, was sentenced to death and hanged in May 1946.[72]

Weiß is an interesting figure; an intelligent and companionable man who presided over incalculable suffering as a commandant. Weiß was Schecher's supervisor in the Dachau Technical Department and seems to have latched onto the 52-year-old jurist as a cultured interlocutor. Schecher, adhering to what he describes as 'the first law of life as a slave . . . no personal relations to an SS superior', relates their one-sided conversations with customary wry humour.[73] Weiß's intimate discourses, he recalls, were met with a resolute and succinct 'Jawohl, Herr *Sturmführer*' or 'Nein, Herr *Sturmführer*'. Undeterred, Weiß confided that he was torn between using his training as an engineer with the German railways or remaining in the camp system, where Himmler had plans for him. His dilemma and doubts seem to have been silenced by a lucrative promotion to *Obersturmführer* in 1937 and then Dachau adjutant the following year: an important reminder that early identification with the Nazi movement could still intersect with a calculating careerism.[74] Had Weiß moved to work in the railways he would have forfeited not only the

---

[68] BAB, BDC SSO von Lachemair, Dienstlaufbahn, n.d.
[69] Tuchel, 'The Commandants', p. 241.     [70] Orth, *Konzentrationslager SS*, p. 96.
[71] Orth, *Konzentrationslager SS*, p. 136.     [72] Orth, *Konzentrationslager SS*, p. 284.
[73] Schecher, 'Rückblick', p. 81.
[74] See also Wildt, *Unconditional Generation*, pp. 433–44.

**Figure 3.1** Martin Weiß takes the stand in the Dachau trial in 1945. He was found guilty of 'common design' to violate the laws of war and was hanged in May 1946 at Dachau. USHMM Photo Archives 61,092.

pleasures of officer rank, but also the security of a fixed place of work; he had married in 1934.[75] It is further credit to Schecher's humanity that on hearing of Weiß's execution in 1946 he wondered if he should have engaged more evenly with him, and tried to guide him towards the railways. As he rightly concludes, however, it was scarcely felicitous for a concentration camp inmate to give career advice to an SS officer.[76]

Considering the pre-war Dachau adjutants as a collective, excluding the undocumented Noetzl, few common properties of the type so evident with their commandants can be identified. Their ages were evenly distributed between 1896 and 1911; four had front experience and three did not. Most were in their thirties at the time of their appointment. All joined the SS in the early 1930s, on average in January 1932, with a mean service of three and a half years prior to their appointment as adjutant. They had joined the NSDAP on average in August 1930 at the age of twenty-nine, although this figure is skewed by Weiß's very early age of joining. Weiß, Koegel, and Koch went on to have highly 'successful' careers at the apex of the concentration camp network, whereas the others were ultimately found

[75] Orth, *Konzentrationslager SS*, p. 137.     [76] Schecher, 'Rückblick', p. 82.

wanting and transferred out to the backwaters of the General SS. Department I of the Dachau commandant staff, then, was headed by a mixture of seasoned SS commandants and rather younger men who oversaw the execution of their orders, and for whom the position of adjutant was of useful career potential provided that they could navigate the high politics of the concentration camp SS.

## DEPARTMENT II: THE POLITICAL DEPARTMENT

The Political Department was the only division of the commandant staff which did not fall under the direct supervision of the Concentration Camp Inspectorate. It was headed by Gestapo officials and staffed by a mixture of policemen, SS men, civilians, and inmates. From September 1939 it reported to Heydrich's RSHA. The Political Department was the gateway to the wider world of Nazi persecution, the area of the camp least compatible with the hypothesis of the 'closed' perpetrator world.[77] Its duties were manifold. The Political Department registered new inmates, ensured paperwork was in place and up to date, carried out interrogations of inmates and staff, liaised with judicial and administrative authorities outside the camp, dealt with the formalities and correspondence attending prisoner accidents and deaths, and oversaw the details of releases.[78]

Dachau had a political department from the earliest days of the camp, although it is unclear at what point it was given this specific name. It was a product of the particular political circumstances in Bavaria. Himmler's appointment as acting Munich police president during the takeover of Bavaria put him in charge both of the imposition and execution of protective custody. There were three types of policemen in Dachau in the early months, all of whom reported to him: the SS auxiliary police who provided the commandant staff and guards, the Bavarian State Police, who provided training for the SS and oversaw external security, and the political department under the Bavarian Political Police, which oversaw the details of 'protective custody' beyond the prisoner compound.[79] It was this unique alignment of personnel and powers that provided Himmler's political 'springboard' to national control of the police and persecution apparatus, first in Bavaria and then the other German states.[80] This process was accelerated after the 'Night of the Long Knives' and completed in June 1936 with his appointment as Chief of the German Police.

Very little information survives on the staff of the pre-war Dachau Political Department save for the early years investigated by Naaff's team. Its head then was Josef Mutzbauer, a middle-aged career policeman who had lived in Dachau since 1931, presumably a key factor in his appointment.[81] Mutzbauer was heavily

[77]  For this concept and literature, see Chapter 6, fn. 4 and fn. 9.
[78]  SAM, StA 34881/9, Politische Abteilung Arbeitsplan, 1 September 1937.
[79]  Tuchel, *Konzentrationslager*, pp. 141–52.
[80]  Longerich, *Himmler*, pp. 148–55.
[81]  SAM, StA 34462/1, Stadtpolizei Dachau to Staatsanwaltschaft, 21 June 1949.

implicated in covering up the early murders in the camp, and was one of the officials against whom Wintersberger issued an arrest warrant for obstruction on 1 June 1933.[82] Under Eicke, with whom his relations were generally poisonous, he was also involved in arranging inmate murders. Rudolf Dirnagel, an early Dachau SS sentry, recalled being summoned to the Political Department in August 1933.[83] Here Mutzbauer informed him that Eicke had ordered that Franz Sterzer, a Reichstag deputy currently in the *Bunker*, be taken outside for a walk. As deputy duty officer for the guard troops that day, it was Dirnagel's responsibility to accompany prisoners outside the compound. Dirnagel duly reported to the lockup and, along with Kantschuster, led Sterzer outside the camp. Kantschuster then dismissed Dirnagel and shot Sterzer 'whilst trying to escape'. Eicke and Kantschuster sought without success to get Dirnagel to take the blame. Mutzbauer attempted to cajole him in terms suggestive of the bracing cynicism which could shape the conduct of the police in Dachau:

> My dear Dirnagel, I know that, but I have been ordered by *Brigadeführer* Eicke to note in the protocol that you shot the prisoner as he tried to escape and confirmed as much under questioning. What's the point of us swimming against the tide? We'll only both be bumped off ourselves another day. Eicke has expressly ordered that Kantschuster can't be named to the Public Prosecutor because he was for the same thing a week ago. It would be too conspicuous.[84]

It was Koegel, in the end, who interceded to prevent one of his sentries taking the rap for this murder. Mutzbauer's words were in some ways prophetic, however, for he was himself found dead in the Dachau *Bunker* in April 1935 under circumstances which remain unclear. The Social Democratic underground (Sopade) believed that Mutzbauer's constant pilfering of incoming money for inmates had finally forced an internal investigation, to protect himself from which he committed suicide.[85] Hans Brücklmayr, a court official well-informed about events in Dachau, also recalled a corruption racket involving prisoner food. He had viewed Mutzbauer's corpse, chained still by the foot to the floor of the *Bunker*, and concurred that the disgraced head of the Political Department had indeed hanged himself.[86] Dall-Armi, on the other hand, suggested that Mutzbauer knew too much for Eicke's comfort and had announced once too often on duty that he could easily 'bring down' the Inspector of the Concentration Camps.[87] In Dall-Armi's view, Eicke had had Mutzbauer imprisoned in the *Bunker* and throttled.

This dramatic event aside, little documentation exists on the pre-war personnel of the Dachau Political Department; its papers were burned very carefully in 1945.

---

[82] DaA, 18.723, Wintersberger to OLG Munich, 1 June 1933.

[83] SAM/St 34461/2 Auszug aus der Vernehmungsniederschrift des Amtsgerichts Arolsen vom 22.11.1949 in der Strafsache gegen Rudolf Dirnagel wegen Mordes.

[84] SAM/St 34461/2 Auszug aus der Vernehmungsniederschrift des Amtsgerichts Arolsen vom 22.11.1949 in der Strafsache gegen Rudolf Dirnagel wegen Mordes.

[85] DaA, A4071, Deutschland-Berichte der Sozialdemokratischen Partei Deutschlands (Sopade) 1934–40, s. 1.

[86] SAM, StA 34461/4, Zeugenvernehmungsprotokoll Hans Brücklmayr, 27 June 1951.

[87] SAM, StA 34461/3, Zeugenvernehmungsprotokoll Max v Dall-Armi, 12 January 1951.

From 1935 to 1937 it was headed by Valentin Schelkshorn, hitherto Mutzbauer's deputy. From 1937 until almost the end of the war the incumbent was Johann Kick, who was tried by the USA at Dachau for his role in organizing the execution of Soviet POWs near the camp. He was also implicated in the selection of enfeebled inmates for the gas chamber at the Hartheim 'Euthanasia' Institute in Austria under the 14f13 programme.[88] Kick, another Dachau miscreant whose CV included a spell in the Bavarian State Police, was sentenced to death at the Dachau Trial and hanged in May 1946.[89] The everyday violence and bureaucratic spite of the pre-war Dachau Political Department, however, was out of statute by the time the West German authorities came to investigate it. The same was not true of the final department to be considered in this chapter, where the judiciary rightly sought those primarily responsible for the murder of prisoners throughout the camp's existence.

## DEPARTMENT III: THE PROTECTIVE CUSTODY COMPOUND DEPARTMENT

Department III, the largest on the command staff, was 'the centre of real power' in the concentration camps.[90] Whereas the inmates' personal exposure to their camp commandant was generally fleeting, they encountered the personnel of Department III every day: the compound leaders in charge of the prisoner zone, the report leaders who organized the interminable daily roll calls (see Figure 3.2), and the detail and block leaders who oversaw order and cleanliness in their barracks. Terror professionals one and all, their foibles and moods indelibly shaped everyday life as a Dachau *Häftling*.

### Compound Leaders (*Schutzhaftlagerführer*)

Compound leaders had such a domineering and malevolent presence in prisoner life that memoirs towards the end of the 1930s sometimes mistake them for the commandant himself.[91] They were, wrote Eugen Kogon, 'the absolute overlords of the prisoners'.[92] By the end of the war, there could be up to four compound leaders per camp, depending on its size.[93] Even by 1938, Dachau had two. They oversaw the enforcement of camp regulations at ground level, monitored the report and block leaders, issued permits for entrance to the prisoner compound, and implemented punishments handed down from the IKL in Berlin. During the day they patrolled prisoner work sites to collect reports from sentries on prisoner

[88] For detail see Orth, K., *Das System der nationalsozialistischen Konzentrationslager: Eine politische Organisationsgeschichte*, pp. 114–21.
[89] IfZ, MB 21/3, Interrogation Johann Kick, ss. 334–68.          [90] Sofsky, *Order*, p. 106.
[91] Kay, *Dachau*, p. 74; more broadly see Morsch, 'Organisations', p. 67.
[92] Kogon, *The Theory and Practice of Hell*, p. 51
[93] Orth, *Konzentrationslager SS*, p. 41.

**Figure 3.2** Dachau inmates stand to attention as a protective custody compound staff member cycles leisurely past, 1938. Bundesarchiv, image 152-23-34A.

transgressions.[94] The commandant depended heavily on his compound leader to ensure that his directives were being enforced. As with adjutants, a change in commandant frequently entailed a change in compound leader, and the relationship is frequently narrated by inmates as a malevolent double act. The role of compound leader in the Dachau School was the most reliable route to securing appointment as camp commandant; of the ten pre-war Dachau compound leaders, seven went on to head a concentration camp. Sachsenhausen, the next most productive environment for compound leaders, saw seven of its fifteen in total win promotion to commandant by 1945.[95] Yet not all incumbents were able to perform the role to the IKL's satisfaction.

All ten pre-war Dachau compound leaders were seasoned National Socialists and often relatively old by the standards of the movement and SS by the time of their appointment. This flags the function of the position of compound leader, even more than commandant, as a stipend for worthy, genuinely 'old' fighters of the movement. The role does not seem to have existed under Wäckerle and was created during Eicke's reorganization of Dachau in spring 1934. The first incumbent was Günther Tamaschke. Born in 1896 in Berlin, Tamaschke saw action on the Western Front in the Great War and, like Deubel, was taken prisoner during the Somme campaigns. On return from captivity, where he later claimed that he and his fellow prisoners had spent their time plotting a racial renaissance of

---

[94] Hübsch, 'Die Insel des Standrechts', p. 70.      [95] Orth, *Konzentrationslager SS*, p. 63.

Germany, he too took part in the Kapp *Putsch*.[96] Initially an adherent of the liberal German Peoples' Party (DVP), Tamaschke was apparently drawn to the Nazi movement by the *Völkischer Beobachter* and by Hitler's performance at the trial for the Munich *Putsch*.[97] In 1926, Tamaschke joined the reconstituted NSDAP and was a founding member of the SS in Berlin with the membership number of 851, the eighth lowest in the camp system.[98] He lost his job working for his father-in-law's business at the end of 1932 due to the economic crisis, but found a position with the Neukölln local authorities in Berlin. This he held until May 1934, when he was appointed compound leader in Dachau as a reward for his work in building up the Berlin SS.[99] He won Eicke's favour at Dachau, and in March 1935 returned to Berlin to join the staff of the IKL. On 1 December 1937 he was appointed commandant of the newly opened women's concentration camp at Lichtenburg.

His successor was another SS veteran, Karl D'Angelo. Born in Osthofen in September 1890, D'Angelo saw front line service in the war, including a spell as a fighter pilot.[100] Initially a supporter of the conservative nationalist DNVP, he seems to have been radicalized by the French occupation of the Ruhr in 1923, where a French court handed him a 3,000 Reichsmark fine and two year prison sentence for sabotage. He served twenty months in prison before being released in November 1924 in line with the Dawes Plan. He joined the reconstituted Nazi movement in November 1925 and served as a senior local functionary (*Ortsgruppenleiter*) from 1925 until 1930 when he also volunteered for the SS. He represented the NSDAP in the Hessian state parliament and later apparently pursued a political grudge nurtured there by terrorizing a deputy who was imprisoned in Dachau.[101] Yet on the whole, despite his longstanding and evidently deep commitment to Nazism, D'Angelo did not evince the hatred and violence of so many of his peers in the camp environment. He was appointed the 1st commandant of his hometown Osthofen concentration camp in March 1933. Here the inmates recall that D'Angelo earnestly attempted to convert them to the National Socialist cause.[102] As a worthy 'old fighter' in need of a post after Osthofen's closure, D'Angelo was transferred to Dachau as compound leader in February 1935 in succession to Tamaschke. The 'Deubel–D'Angelo era' at Dachau was looked back on by inmates as one in which the violence had considerably abated. That D'Angelo, even more than Deubel, incurred the IKL's opprobrium for this illustrates the importance attached to the role of compound leader in maintaining discipline in a camp. The accusations levelled against him included allowing foreign language lessons in the camp school, appointing a returned Jewish emigrant as a

[96] BAB, SSO Tamaschke, Lebenslauf, 22 June 1936.
[97] BAB, SSO Tamaschke, Lebenslauf, 22 June 1936.		[98] MacLean, *Camp Men*, p. 275.
[99] Orth, *Konzentrationslager SS*, p. 134.
[100] Volker Gallé, 'Karl d'Angelo: Lagerleiter des Konzentrationslagers Osthofen', in Hans-Georg Meyer (ed.), *Die Zeit des Nationalsozialismus in Rheinland-Pfalz*, Vol. 2, (Mainz, 2000), pp. 69–79. I would like to thank Kim Wünschmann for this information.
[101] SAM, StA 34832/3, Zeugenvernehmungsprotokoll Stefan Jakob, 10 October 1951.
[102] Gallé, 'Karl D'Angelo', p. 74; more broadly on Osthofen, see also Kim Wünschmann, 'Natürlich', pp. 97–111.

prisoner functionary, allowing inmates to work in sensitive clerical positions in the Political Department, and a thoroughgoing 'weakness of character' in delegating tasks rather than providing personal leadership.[103] Loritz added that he had once in D'Angelo's company espied prisoners openly lounging around during work time. Taking the compound leader to task, he was told that 'nothing could be done about it'. The net result of all this in Dachau, Loritz scoffed, was a penal environment no more effective than the 'famous judicial camps' against which they, the Nazis, had railed during Weimar.[104] On 24 April 1936 Eicke duly placed D'Angelo on leave and wrote to Himmler that 'as compound leader he is not only as soft as butter but completely lacking interest in this branch of the service'.[105]

His successor Jakob Weiseborn was of an altogether different hue, a true camp SS traditionalist. He was born in 1892 in Frankfurt am Main, the son of an unsuccessful carpenter.[106] In 1908 he volunteered for the Imperial Navy and served a full twelve-year stint with the 1st Torpedo Division in the Baltic, finishing at the NCO rank of Master Sergeant (*Oberfeldwebel*). It is unclear what occupation he pursued thereafter: his son described him as an accountant, and his SS file, vaguely, as a 'manager' (*Geschäftsführer*). In 1931 Weiseborn joined the NSDAP and SS, gaining a full-time position in the latter from 1933. His promotion to officer rank in April 1934 was supported by the observation that he was a committed National Socialist, adept at training underlings in the spirit of Nazi militarism.[107] Weiseborn, however, struggled to make ends meet in the General SS. The latter provided him with support payments totalling 150 Reichsmark in late 1934 but professed itself unable to continue to do so and requested that the 'old fighter' be found a salaried position elsewhere in the SS. In December 1934 Weiseborn was duly assigned to Dachau on a three-month probationary tenure as a platoon commander in the guard units. He clearly did enough here to satisfy Augustini, and in April 1935 was appointed commander of a guard company in the 'Brandenburg' guard troops at Columbia House. In May 1935, however, Weiseborn got senselessly drunk as duty officer with an NCO on the guard staff, Theo Dannecker, later to play a key role overseeing the deportation of West European Jews to Auschwitz. Dannecker was drummed out of the guard units and made his way to the SD, while Weiseborn was sent for remedial guard service at Esterwegen under the sure hand of Loritz. These two stalwarts of the SS front generation formed a close personal bond and Loritz brought him to Dachau as his compound leader in June 1936 to replace the disgraced D'Angelo.

The two are recalled in prisoner literature as an unholy double act, an antithesis to Deubel and D'Angelo. Loritz was known as 'Nero' to Weiseborn's 'Caesar'.[108] The combination proved mercifully short-lived, as high political wrangles among

---

[103] BAB, BDC SSO D'Angelo, Angriffpunkte gegen SS Standartenführer D'Angelo, undated (*c.* May 1936).
[104] BAB, BDC SSO D'Angelo, Loritz to Eicke, 29 April 1936.
[105] Gallé, 'Karl D'Angelo', p. 75.
[106] The following from Tuchel, 'Flossenbürg', p. 201–19, here pp. 201–6.
[107] Tuchel, 'Flossenbürg', p. 202.     [108] *Nazi Bastille Dachau*, p. 35.

the concentration camp elite saw Weiseborn transfer later that year to become compound leader at Sachsenhausen under Koch. This role had initially been earmarked for Baranowski. The latter's rank of *Standartenführer* was the same as Koch's, however, and it was felt that this would generate leadership problems. In another illustration of personal fealties, Weiseborn then accompanied Koch to Buchenwald as his compound leader in August 1937. In May 1938 he secured his first commission as commandant, at the newly opened Flossenbürg concentration camp. He died there under slightly mysterious circumstances in January 1939, officially of a heart attack.[109]

Hermann Baranowski was outraged at his transfer in November 1936 from the role of commandant at Lichtenburg to compound leader at Dachau. Loritz, however, both outranked Baranowski and possessed the steely will deemed necessary to keep this other veteran of the Imperial Navy, too, in line. Baranowski has a notably grotesque presence in Dachau memoir literature, as a man with a particularly keen sense of social theatre. Known as 'Der Staf', in abbreviation of his rank, or 'square', in allusion to his pot-bellied frame, one of his favoured pastimes was to ride around Dachau on his horse Liese, recapitulating in humorous fashion the place of the various prisoner groups in Nazi narratives of perdition. Hübsch recalls one performance with persuasive detail:

> 'Liese! Look over there. There stand the enemies of the state, the Bolsheviks, the arsonists of the Reichstag! Do not be afraid, they cannot harm you'. He rode on and pulled up his horse in front of the 'green' block. 'Careful, Liese! Those are the "Greens", the criminals, the murderers. Watch yourself, Liese!'. Then he rode on to the Jewish block: 'Stop, Liese! These are the Jews, the stinking Jews! Do you not smell, Liese, how they stink? Away, Liese, away from them!'.[110]

Baranowski delighted in showing off his repertoire to visitors to Dachau, among them SA commanders, students from the SS cadet school at Bad Tölz, dignitaries from the Labour Front, and Wehrmacht officers.[111] Roll calls in his era too were characterized by a hateful pantomime: bawdy jokes and the humiliation of prisoners who caught his attention, all lapped up by his devoted report leader Höß.[112] Dachau inmates were overjoyed to see the back of Baranowski when, rehabilitated in Eicke's eyes, he transferred to Sachsenhausen as commandant in March 1938.[113] He ran this camp with customary brutality until his death in February 1940. The funeral notice in a local newspaper requested, perhaps superfluously, that visits of condolence be abjured.[114]

In 1937 Dachau was accorded a 2nd compound leader, subordinate to Baranowski but sharing some of his duties. The first incumbent was Egon Zill. Born in 1906 in Plauen, near Leipzig, Zill was another veteran of the movement. He joined the SA and Nazi Party at the age of seventeen before switching to the SS in 1925, securing the membership number of 535, the sixth lowest in the

[109] Tuchel, 'Flossenbürg', p. 205.      [110] Hübsch, 'Insel', p. 28.
[111] Hübsch, 'Insel', p. 26.      [112] Schecher, 'Rückblick', p. 71.
[113] Hübsch, 'Insel', p. 80.
[114] BAB, BDC SSO Baranowski, Funeral Notice, 8 February 1940.

concentration camps.[115] A series of mundane jobs culminated in a position as a guard at a curtain factory, where he remained for seven years and met his wife.[116] In October 1934 Zill joined the 'Elbe' guard unit at Lichtenburg as the commander of a platoon, no doubt seeking to capitalize on, and monetize, his very early membership of the SS. There he did indeed rise at meteoric pace, promoted to *Obersturmführer* and then compound leader on the commandant staff on 1 November 1936.[117] In August 1937 he was promoted once again and assigned to Dachau as 2nd compound leader: another example of the transfer of a senior SS officer to a position in Dachau more lowly than he had held elsewhere. Zill then undertook a peripatetic career on the commandant staff of various concentration camps; first Buchenwald, then Lichtenburg women's camp and Ravensbrück, before returning to Dachau as 1st compound leader in December 1939, his first taste of heading a department. Three further years passed before he was entrusted with the position of commandant, at the SS 'special camp' Hinzert, and then at Neuengamme and Flossenbürg. His final role as an SS leader, commanding a unit in the Waffen SS, was an inglorious failure.[118] Zill was a small, cruel man, recalled by Dachau inmates with a shudder: Hans Schwarz regarded him as 'more dangerous than all the others'.[119] He was a particular devotee of the pole torment, and reports of proactive, imaginative, and murderous chicanery abound in prisoner testimony.[120] He was sentenced to lifelong imprisonment in 1955 by the Munich state court, reduced to fifteen years in 1961. Zill offers a compelling example of a hitherto marginal existence unbound in the toxic concentration camp environment, to which he evidently felt a lifelong affinity. After his release from prison he retired in Dachau, around a mile from the camp site, and resided there until his death in 1974.[121]

He was succeeded as 2nd Dachau compound leader by Hans Kreppel, whose fleeting tenure will be addressed in a later chapter (Chapter 5). At this point the Dachau compound leader picture becomes complicated. Several men are identified in inmate testimony or SS personnel files as having served as 1st and 2nd compound leader in various permutations from 1938 to 1939, but exact dates are not available. One was Bernhard Schmidt, another to fail in the role. Schmidt was born in 1890 in Pegnitz in upper Franconia.[122] He served in the Imperial Army from 1914 to 1918 and one year thereafter got married and took over the running of his parents-in-law's guest house. The business was in ruinous debt by 1933 as a consequence, Schmidt believed, of the malice of his political enemies. Schmidt was another Nazi stalwart, having joined the NSDAP in August 1925 and the SS in April 1930. Himmler seems to have been determined to find him a sinecure in concentration camps, and Schmidt was appointed the 1st commandant

[115] MacLean, *Camp Men*, p. 275.     [116] Karin Orth, 'Egon Zill', pp. 264–73.
[117] SAM, StA 34786, Feststellungen zur Person Zills (undated), s. 84.
[118] SAM, StA 34786, Feststellungen zur Person Zills (undated), s. 84.
[119] Schwarz, 'Wir haben es nicht gewusst', p. 213.
[120] Summarized in Orth, *Konzentrationslager SS*, pp. 138–42.
[121] Distel, 'Täter', p. 204.     [122] Tuchel, *Konzentrationslager*, p. 390.

of Lichtenburg concentration camp after Eicke's temporary stewardship in July 1934.[123] From April 1935 until July 1937 he was commandant of Sachsenburg, before appointment as compound leader in Sachsenhausen and Dachau. Schmidt was now the second Lichtenburg commandant, after Baranowski, to be transferred to a subordinate role in Dachau. Eicke eventually released him from camp SS duty in November 1938. Numerous later attempts to secure a commission in the Waffen SS met without success, and Schmidt died without having been troubled by the judiciary in September 1960.

Schmidt has little presence in inmate testimony from this period, where he is overshadowed by the grimly memorable Koegel. The post of Dachau compound leader is not listed in Koegel's personnel files, but inmate testimony and an SS report leader from this period identify him as the successor to Baranowski as 1st compound leader.[124] Koegel was not relieved officially of his role as Loritz's adjutant by Weiß until 1 July 1938; possibly he held a dual position as adjutant and compound leader while Weiß, coming from the relative backwater of the Technical Department, was trained up in the role. Koegel had been stationed with the Dachau guard troops from the earliest days of the camp. Having risen to *Hauptsturmführer* and company commander, he accompanied Deubel to Columbia House as adjutant in April 1936. When Deubel was placed on leave in September 1936, Koegel took over as acting commandant.[125] When Columbia House was closed in November of the same year, he returned to Dachau to become Loritz's adjutant. Sometime after Baranowski's departure in March 1938 he took over as compound leader.

Neurath recalls Koegel as a 'very capable organizer, who routinized the hell of Dachau into a well-rehearsed play'.[126] According to Hübsch, Koegel came into the role of compound leader resolved to make a managerial statement.[127] In his first few days he assembled the senior prisoner barracks functionaries, bribed them with sausage, and urged them to increase the volume of disciplinary punishments handed out to the inmates. Shortly afterwards, Koegel switched from the carrot to the stick, identifying petty infractions the functionaries had failed to report and imposing 'punishment exercises' and hours at the pole on them. For good measure, he also transferred some *Kapos* from the comfort of their positions to the dreaded punishment battalion, a stark ritualization and reminder of the underlying balance of power between them and the SS. In early May Koegel moved on to the prisoners themselves, ordering a series of public whippings for purported offences which every prisoner barracks had to assemble and watch. The tough climate in the Dachau prisoner compound thus affirmed, in the summer of 1938 Koegel moved onto the role of 1st compound leader in Lichtenburg and thence to Ravensbrück, where he was promoted to Camp Director in succession to Tamaschke. In August

[123] Hördler, 'SS Kaderschmiede Lichtenburg', p. 81.
[124] Neurath, *Society*, p. 80; Schecher, 'Rückblick', pp. 81–2; SAM, StA 34590, Vernehmungsprotokoll Franz Hofmann, 22 April 1959.
[125] Tuchel, 'Flossenbürg', p. 212.    [126] Neurath, *Society*, p. 80.
[127] Hübsch, 'Insel', pp. 81–3.

1942 he transferred to Lublin and took command of the concentration camp at Majdanek, before appointment as commandant of Flossenbürg in May 1943. Koegel committed suicide in court custody on 27 June 1946.[128]

His replacement as 1st Dachau compound leader was Alex Piorkowski. Born on 11 October 1904 in Bremen, Piorkowski trained as a mechanic and spent the 1920s as a travelling salesman.[129] In 1929 he joined the SA and NSDAP, switching to the SS on 1 June 1933. Piorkowski eventually succeeded Loritz as Dachau commandant, and is another example of a commandant who had made a name building up his local SS: in this case in Bremen, whose *Standarte* he commanded from July 1935. In 1936 Piorkowski was placed on leave from the General SS for health reasons that were also to hamper his tenure in Dachau. After a lengthy break he was appointed compound leader in Lichtenburg alongside Zill in February 1937 and made acting commandant in June.[130] From then until his transfer to Dachau in August 1938, Piorkowski was deputy director of the Lichtenburg women's camp. Piorkowski was now the third Lichtenburg commandant to be appointed to the supporting role of compound leader in Dachau, casting doubt on the assertion that Lichtenburg was the 'elite school' (*Kaderschmiede*) of the pre-war concentration camp system.[131] He remained compound leader in Dachau until February 1940, but was also temporary commandant from July 1939 when Loritz departed to oversee the restive Austrian SS in Graz.[132] It says much about Piorkowski's regime that Dachau inmates recall little improvement in the atmosphere of the camp. His tenure was characterized by a dramatic worsening of living conditions as well as an avid implementation of orders from above for the execution of captured Soviet POWs and the transportation of 'invalid' prisoners to Hartheim.[133]

The final pre-war Dachau compound leader identified is Adam Grünewald. Born in 1902 in the Bavarian village of Frickenhausen near Würzburg, he was the son of a carpenter who died when Grünewald was eight years-old.[134] Grünewald trained as a baker but came onto the labour market just as the Imperial Army demobilized and was unable to find a job. Instead he joined the *Freikorps* and then the Reichswehr, completing his twelve-year stint in 1931 at the NCO rank of sergeant. In the same year he joined the NSDAP and SA, the latter in a salaried position where he reached officer rank. After the Röhm purge, Grünewald switched to the SS and joined the Lichtenburg guard contingent, where he rose to become guard troop commander.[135] In spring 1938 Eicke assigned him to Dachau along with Kreppel as a rival candidate for the post of 2nd compound leader.[136]

[128] Tuchel, 'Flossenbürg', p. 213.      [129] Tuchel, 'Commandants', p. 239.
[130] Hördler, 'SS Kaderschmiede Lichtenburg', p. 85.
[131] Hördler, 'SS Kaderschmiede Lichtenburg'.
[132] Hördler, 'SS Kaderschmiede Lichtenburg', p. 85. Tuchel makes a rare empirical error in dating Loritz's departure to October 1939, with the temporary dissolution of the Dachau *Schutzhaftlager* for the equipping of the *Totenkopf* Division: Tuchel, 'The Commandants', p. 239.
[133] For a detailed précis of Piorkowski's trial, see Martin Gruner, *Verurteilt in Dachau: Der Prozess gegen den KZ-Commandanten Alex Piorkowski vor einem US-Militärgericht* (Augsburg, 2008).
[134] Segev, *Soldiers*, p. 93.      [135] Hördler, 'Kaderschmiede', p. 80.
[136] Riedel, *Ordnungshüter*, p. 157.

Unlike Kreppel he was soon much-feared by the inmates, but Loritz was still not convinced after his three-month probation that he had the 'required enthusiasm' for serving on the commandant staff. It seems likely that Grünewald secured the post in September 1938 largely through Kreppel's deficiencies rather than Eicke and Loritz's approval.[137]

Although nominally his subordinate, Grünewald's theatrical persona sees him more vividly recalled in prisoner literature than Piorkowski. Grünewald in his early days prowled around the camp getting acquainted with his new environment but, unlike his predecessor Koegel, looked to frame his chicanery within a discursive rubric of fairness and honour. Neurath even has wryly warm words for him as a man who 'in comparison to Koegel seemed almost human'.[138] Other prisoners recall Grünewald with horror. One signature foible was to leave the exhausted prisoners at roll call for hours before gracing them with his presence.[139] Schwarz focuses on him setting his dog against prisoners.[140] Karst narrates a 'master of life and death, a god-like creature . . . one of the most dangerous bloodhounds of the SS'.[141] Grünewald belatedly found a use for his professional training when he took part in the French campaign with the Death's Head Division, commanding a regimental bakery.[142] He returned to the concentration camp network in 1943, initially as 2nd compound leader at Sachsenhausen and then commandant of the Herzogenbusch concentration camp in occupied Holland. Grünewald ended his concentration camp service here in early 1944 with a notorious atrocity. In retribution for a collective protest by female inmates, he ordered his adjutant Hermann Wicklein, another Dachau School graduate, to cram seventy-four female prisoners into a small cell overnight. Ten suffocated.[143] Occurring on the soil of a fellow 'Aryan' nation, this was too much even for the SS and the two were removed from their posts. Grünewald was assigned back to the Death's Head Division where he was killed in action in 1945.

An aggregate analysis of these ten central SS figures in the Dachau commandant staff reveals some striking commonalities and characteristics. On average, they joined the NSDAP very early, in April 1928, well before its electoral breakthrough.[144] They did so, moreover, at the relatively advanced average age of thirty-three. Seven were of the front generation, and just three from the war youth cohort. On average they joined the SS in February 1930, at the age of thirty-five. All had served the movement for a long time before appointment as Dachau compound leader, the NSDAP on average for nine years, and the SS for seven.[145] By the time of their appointment, they were on average just over forty. These men,

---

[137] As Riedel writes, the 'Inspector of the Concentration Camps preferred a dim-witted sadist over a melancholy neurotic'. Riedel, *Ordnungshüter*, p. 158.

[138] Neurath, *Society*, pp. 81–2.        [139] Kay, *Dachau*, p. 102; Hübsch, 'Insel', p. 110.

[140] Schwarz, 'Wir haben', p. 211.        [141] Karst, *Beasts*, p. 102.

[142] Schwarz, 'Wir haben', p. 211.

[143] Hans de Vries, 'Herzogenbusch (Vught)—Stammlager', in Benz and Distel, *Ort des Terrors*, Vol. 7, pp. 136–8.

[144] This excludes Grünewald, whose precise dates of joining the NSDAP, SA, and SS are unclear.

[145] Excluding Schmidt, the date of whose appointment as Dachau compound leader is unknown.

then, were seasoned National Socialists who had proven themselves in other camps and were now assigned to the Dachau School as candidates for commandant positions in the future. Hardy veterans of the paramilitary scene, such men were well-versed in the expectations of leadership. Their histrionic comportment, their 'exquisite devilishness', as Neurath puts it, attests to the highly performative, theatrical nature of the role of compound leader, leading protagonists on the captive stage of the Dachau compound.[146] Radical, proactive, and imaginative brutality earned career capital and was construed as an expression of ideological zeal and vigour. The role of compound leader was key to entering the rarefied circles of the SS concentration camp aristocracy: only D'Angelo, Kreppel, and Schmidt failed to secure a posting as commandant in the system after their spell as compound leader in the Dachau School.[147]

## Report Leaders (*Rapportführer*)

The report leaders were the immediate subordinates of the compound leaders. The role is less well-documented than compound leader and seldom detailed even in such SS personnel lists as survive: it is unclear even when it was created. It was one analogous in many ways to the battalion leaders in the guard troops, although report leaders tended to be only of SS NCO rank. The report leader formed an intermediate link between the compound and block leaders. He produced the monthly block leader service schedule, carried out prisoner roll calls, produced daily, weekly, and monthly reports on prisoner numbers, and was responsible for the security of external worksites.[148] According to one inmate, these positions in Dachau 'were without exception filled by the very worst beasts, and neither is any humane report leader known from any other concentration camp'.[149] An analysis of the four SS men identified as having held this role in pre-war Dachau endorses this evaluation. And all, having proven their aptitude in the role, went on to to senior positions elsewhere in the concentration camp system.

The first is the most infamous graduate of the Dachau School, Rudolf Höß.[150] His memoirs are the most valuable ego-document preserved from a concentration camp perpetrator. Self-serving and frequently mendacious, they nevertheless offer unique and unintended glimpses into the relationship between disposition and environment in the camps. Born in Baden-Baden in 1900, Rudolf Franz Ferdinand Höß was the son of a devout and cheerless businessman who hoped that he would become a priest. Höß tries to present his childhood as austere and neglected but, even judging from the text, seems to have enjoyed considerable freedom to pursue his youthful enthusiasms.[151] After suffering a spiritual crisis

---

146 Neurath, *Society*, p. 78.
147 More broadly on the importance of the role see Orth, *Konzentrationslager SS*, pp. 138–42.
148 IfZ, Fa54, Bericht SS Hauptscharführer Hans Jüng (undated), ss. 17–18.
149 Schnabel, R., *Die Frommen in der Hölle*, pp. 48–9.
150 Höß refers to a predecessor as *Rapportführer* from 1935, but it is not possible to identify him. Höß, *Commandant*, p. 66. He may well have meant Max Dall-Armi, see below.
151 One of the most acute analyses of Höß's memoirs remains Joseph Tennenbaum, 'Auschwitz in Retrospect', here p. 204.

when his priest betrayed a confession, Höß volunteered in 1914 to serve with the Red Cross. He was enchanted by the company of wounded veterans whose gruff humour, he wrote, awakened 'the soldier's blood that ran through my veins'.[152] At the age of sixteen he managed to wangle his way into the regiment in which his father and grandfather had served, and was sent to the brutal Iraqi front. By the time of the German armistice, Höß had been awarded the Iron Cross 1st and 2nd Class. Unable to adjust to demobilized life, he soon volunteered for the *Freikorps* Rossbach, where he partook in hellish violence in the Baltic as well as the *Feme* murder discussed previously (Chapter 1). For the latter he was sentenced to ten years in Brandenburg prison and wrote in great detail of the experience in his autobiography.

The orderly, homosocial environment of the prison was not unconvivial to Höß. In a passage bringing to mind the cynical barracks pedantry he was to participate in as Dachau report leader, Höß recalled that his cell 'was a model of neatness and cleanliness and even the most malicious eyes could see nothing there with which to find fault'.[153] He was indeed a model prisoner and beneficiary of the 'stage' system, writing proudly that he had risen to the uppermost tier where he was entrusted with paid work in the prison store.[154] It was in prison, too, that Höß developed his purported insights into criminality, comradeship, and male homosexuality (see Chapter 5). In 1928 he was released under one of the amnesties for political murder which so clearly documented the cheapening of the value of human life in the Weimar Republic. He soon joined the Artaman league, a *völkisch* sect of youthful, earnest farmers which counted Himmler among its devotees. Höß, who already knew Himmler from his time in the Nazi movement in the early 1920s, joined the part-time SS in September 1933. In December 1934, at Himmler's invitation, he moved to a salaried position in the Dachau guard units. Material considerations certainly played a role in his decision: early Nazi membership and military experience guaranteed rapid promotion.[155]

After just four months with the guard units, Höß was brought onto the commandant staff as a block leader. According to his account, Eicke had decided that all older officers and NCOs from the guard units were to be transferred to positions in the commandant staff.[156] We know this was not fully the case as Koegel, five years Höß's senior, remained with the guard formations. Höß claims to have secured a personal audience with Eicke to request exemption, where he was told that his prison experience was an ideal background for the role of block leader. Höß recalls that he and the other newly-appointed block leaders were 'let loose' on the prisoners with little supervision. His 'stony mask' developed only gradually:

> I felt quite embarrassed as I stood in front of the prisoners committed to forced labour who had been entrusted to my care, and noticed the curiosity with which they eyed their new company leader, as block leaders were then called. Only later was I to understand the searching expression on their faces.[157]

[152] Höß, *Commandant*, p. 35.        [153] Höß, *Commandant*, p. 54.
[154] Höß, *Commandant*, p. 59.        [155] Höß, *Commandant*, p. 64.
[156] Höß, *Commandant*, p. 68.        [157] Höß, *Commandant*, p. 69.

Soon enough, in Höß's account, the barracks he oversaw were as tidy and orderly as his Brandenburg prison cell. He censored his prisoners' mail, he suggests, with the sure touch of a man versed in human nature and psychology and claims that the mocking aphorism 'Work Brings Freedom' on the camp's gates was well-intentioned.[158] The endemic violence in the camp he attributes to a small minority of pathological guards, while a benign majority seek to bring the inmates to a recognition of their errant conduct. The year 1936 was an important one in Höß's new career, for he was promoted once again to report leader and given commissioned SS rank. His dog-like devotion to the charismatic Baranowski was rewarded in 1938 when the latter brought him with him to Sachsenhausen as his adjutant and then compound leader.

Soon after Baranowski's death in 1940 Himmler assigned Höß to command the new concentration camp at Auschwitz, where he became one of the great mass murderers in history. Höß penned his memoirs, in small, neat handwriting, under no illusions about his fate and is generally anxious to please his reader with clichés of a wholesome life led astray. He blames his decision to join the Dachau SS for setting him on an 'intricate course' of 'destiny' which he could not have foreseen.[159] This is a vanishingly rare moment of agency in an account otherwise characterized by blaming others, whether Eicke, Himmler, or the prisoners, for his plight. Yet his autobiography is studded with casual and unknowing outbursts of antisemitism and he describes himself without reflection as a 'fanatical National-Socialist' as though this were a given, a constant, a phenomenon beyond personal choice.[160] For in reality, of course, Höß's journey from Dachau sentry to Auschwitz commandant was driven less by the soldierly stoicism he conveys than by ruthless, consuming ambition and no little ideological investment in destroying the purported enemies of Nazism. The extermination of the Jews, Höß now believed, had been 'fundamentally wrong'. Wrong not in the sense of being a crime, but wrong because through 'these mass exterminations, Germany has brought upon herself the hatred of the entire world. It in no way served the cause of anti-Semitism, but on the contrary brought the Jews far closer to their ultimate objective'.[161]

Höß would be assisted in these myopic endeavours by a host of personnel from the Dachau School, among them another sentry brought with him onto the command staff as block leader in March 1935. Johann Schwarzhuber was born in Tutzing in Upper Bavaria in 1904. His background was unusually privileged for this milieu. He attended a Munich *Volksschule* for eight years and then a vocational printers' college for another four.[162] As a consequence of the hyperinflation he was unable to find a job when his apprenticeship finished in 1923. A range of menial jobs saw him through the 1920s but he became unemployed once again in 1931. Apparently at the suggestion of an SS acquaintance, he joined the SS and NSDAP on 8 March 1933, just one day before the Nazi takeover in Bavaria. Two months later he transferred, probably via the auxiliary police, to the early Dachau SS.[163]

158 Höß, *Commandant*, p. 77.    159 Höß, *Commandant*, p. 64.
160 Höß, *Commandant*, p. 131.    161 Höß, *Commandant*, p. 178.
162 BAB, BDC SSO Schwarzhuber, Lebenslauf, 1 December 1935.
163 BAB, BDC SSO Schwarzhuber, Lebenslauf, 1 December 1935.

His time as Dachau block leader and then report leader, however, is little documented in inmate testimony at a time when there were, as has been seen, many picturesque competitors for space in these narratives. Höß claims that Schwarzhuber shared his delicate aversion to corporal punishment.[164] If so, then like Höß, Schwarzhuber soon overcame his inhibitions. From 1942 he was compound leader at Auschwitz where his annual reports laud him as an officer of comradely warmth and humour, dextrous with subordinates and of sure ideological grasp.[165] Among his vile deeds in Birkenau was a macabre piece of theatre staged in summer 1944, when he forced Soviet prisoners to dance by the electric fence for the entertainment of his wife and children.[166] Later that year, Schwarzhuber returned to Dachau to command the Kaufering satellite camp, and from January 1945 until the German defeat was compound leader at Ravensbrück. He was captured by the British and sentenced to death in the Hamburg-Ravensbrück trial, being hanged in May 1947.

Report leader Albert Lütkemeyer also had an eventful criminal career in the concentration camps. He was born in 1911 in Wellingholz, a small farming village near Osnabruck. The whole village is said to have been proud of Albert's important job at Dachau.[167] Lütkemeyer joined the NSDAP and SA in 1933, switching to the SS after the Röhm purge. Around the same time, he signed up for the guard units at Esterwegen, where his vigilance earned him the nickname of 'the dead-shot of Esterwegen'.[168] He came to Dachau on 1 June 1936, as part of Loritz's new, 'tough' contingent of block leaders and in inmate testimony is conspicuous for chicanery even in this company. Karl Röder recalls the arrival of a new block leader with a kind mien and 'playful eyes' who moved with 'cat-like sleekness' through the camp.[169] Some lovingly nurtured eccentricities were soon evident, however. Lütkemeyer was agitated by the sight of prisoners with hands in their pockets. Rather than the customary beating, he would take the offenders to the roll square or hospital and force them to drink castor oil.[170] This was a cultural peculiarity imported from the Italian Blackshirts, who often force-fed socialists sickly castor oil to symbolize their internal cleansing.[171] Lütkemeyer also became a devotee of 'taking sports' on the roll call square, painful and humiliating repetitive exercises: rolls, frog jumps, springs, and somersaults, until the participants, already weakened by labour and poor diet, could barely stand up.[172] This was another form of torment framed in positive, re-educative imagery, and indebted to the highly politicized nineteenth-century German gymnastics movement. It suggested, as one historian observes, the strengthening of the body, while being intended to weaken and oppress.[173] It was also public theatre, a ritualization of SS power. Indeed, some prisoners suggest that Lütkemeyer derived an almost sexual gratification from his power. One describes him as 'a dandy', another as 'a sadist among sadists'.[174]

---

[164] Höß, *Commandant*, p. 67.     [165] BAB, SSO Schwarzhuber, 1944 Beurteilung.
[166] Wachsmann, 'KL: A History of the Nazi Concentration Camps', ch. 7.
[167] Eickmann, *Der KZ Gärtner*, pp. 192–3.
[168] DaA, 27.897 Deposition Albert Lütkemeyer, 17 August 1946.
[169] Röder, *Nachtwache*, p. 252.     [170] Röder, *Nachtwache*, p. 253.
[171] Reichardt, *Kampfbünde*, p. 128.     [172] Röder, *Nachtwache*, p. 254.
[173] Springmann, '"Sport machen"', pp. 89–101.
[174] Kay, *Dachau*, p. 74; Karst, *Beasts*, p. 103.

After his promotion to report leader in 1938, recalls Hans Schwarz, Lütkemeyer had free reign to indulge his humorous idiosyncrasies throughout the camp;

> He was forever inventing new forms of abuse, new tortures. You had to hand it to him, he was inventive. And he was more intelligent than his companions, who were merely stupid, brutal and lazy . . . 'his' methods were systematic, that's why he was so dangerous. But he had humour.[175]

In November 1939 Lütkemeyer married a girl ten years his junior in a Dachau registry office.[176] In 1940 he transferred to Neuengamme as report leader where he remained until the end of the war. He was tried by the British and executed in April 1947. His final letter to his sister assured her that he was not 'some contemptible criminal or base murderer', but had just 'followed orders, like any soldier at the Front'.[177]

The final identifiable pre-war Dachau report leader was the only one to evade the hangman's noose. The British psychologist Henry Dicks was not taken with Franz Hofmann when he came to interview him in a Bavarian prison in 1967 during a project on Nazi war criminals:

> the most repulsive among even this group; a huge, fat, coarse 'butcher' with bloated features and a thick neck. His pale, grey eyes had a hostile expression which could only be called baleful as well as suspicious. His complexion was 'beery' and his voice screechingly hoarse, like a worn-out sergeant's.[178]

Hofmann was born in 1906 in the small Franconian village of Hof. He worked as a bellboy in various Bavarian establishments before running out of employment in 1931.[179] He then returned to Hof and lived in his father's guest house, a favoured haunt of local Nazis. Hitherto, in Hofmann's account, he had not been interested in politics. After the seizure of power he enlisted with the auxiliary police, where he came to the Dachau guard troops on 1 September 1933. Hofmann spent a year as a rank-and-file sentry before being transferred to the lower reaches of the commandant staff as a telephonist. He worked there until September 1937, when because, he claimed, he was relatively old, he was appointed a block leader for political prisoners and returned emigrants. In the summer of 1938 he was promoted to report leader when Schwarzhuber went on leave; this promotion Hofmann attributed to his numerical faculties. Now ten barracks and a range of Dachau block leaders reported to him, while he was accountable in turn to Baranowski and Koegel. Hofmann had also reached the senior NCO rank of *Hauptscharführer*. He and Lütkemeyer quickly developed a grotesque double act, and in the summer of 1938 tormented at least one Austrian Jewish inmate into 'running to the wire': into the neutral zone by the camp perimeter, where he was duly shot by a sentry for 'trying to escape'.[180] In the days following the November pogrom, Hofmann

175 Schwarz, 'Wir haben', p. 243.
176 SAM, StA 34590/3, Memorandum Bayerisches Landeskriminalamt, 6 November 1962.
177 DaA, A3841, Letter Albert Lütkemeyer to family, Hamburg, 9 June 1947.
178 Dicks, *Licensed*, p. 119.
179 SAM, StA 34590/3, Vernehmungsprotokoll Franz Hofmann, 22 April 1959.
180 SAM, StA 34590/7, Vernehmungsprotokoll Franz Hofmann, 7 July 1964.

murdered the 64-year-old Jewish businessman Hermann Fuld in the washroom of his barracks on the unlikely grounds that Fuld had assaulted him.[181] Such vigilance clearly impressed his superiors, as following Grünewald's departure to the front, Hofmann was appointed 2nd compound leader. In December 1939 Hofmann married the 21-year-old Anna Marie Zillinger, with whom he had three children during the war.[182]

Prisoners recall Hofmann as a rustic Bavarian thug, all broad shoulders, uncouth utterances, and gratuitous violence meted out with his beloved truncheon. He spat constantly.[183] His Dachau comrades were little more enamoured of him. Hofmann was transferred to Auschwitz in December 1942 because, in his recollection, other officers on the Dachau commandant staff resented the fact that he had been at the camp since its early days and had not been inconvenienced by moving.[184] At the Auschwitz trial of 1963, Hofmann achieved media notoriety for having taken exhausting 'sports' with the camp's inmates.[185] He told his interrogators that he had known at the time that what was going on in the camp was 'pure murder', but that he had lacked the courage to do anything about it.[186] He was sentenced to life imprisonment. When Dicks visited him in 1967, he expressed contempt for Himmler, but became gushing when recalling Eicke: 'quite different—[he] was "Papa" to us all. Ah! He died a hero's death at the head of his troops on the Russian front'.[187] He depicted his leaving the Catholic Church as a matter of honour, since 'you couldn't believe in Christ, who was a Jew, while attacking his race'.[188]

Hofmann was the only Nazi criminal visited by Dicks whom he believed was pathological. But there was nothing in his pre-Dachau background to portend this. Hofmann moved up swiftly through the ranks of the Dachau SS, far more swiftly than his mediocre education and abilities would have enabled elsewhere. Throughout the concentration camp system, the position of report leader seems to have brought out the very worst in often already temperamentally violent men.[189] It involved constant interaction with prisoners, arranging and monitoring work details, and dealing with problems and security at work sites, as well as orchestrating the daily climaxes of theatre and torment at roll calls. As for each of these pre-war Dachau report leaders, the post was a stepping stone to even greater power in the camps. These men were younger than the Dachau compound leaders and came from the 'war youth "generation"', although Höß had seen front-line service at a very young age. The position of report leader offered social mobility and great localized power over inmates. All displayed an initiative and performative zest; what they lacked in the longer-term immersion in the movement characteristic

---

[181] SAM, StA 34590/2, Vernehmungsprotokoll Franz Hofmann, 4 December 1959.
[182] SAM, StA 34590/1, Memorandum Stadtpolizei Dachau, 14 June 1957.
[183] SAM, StA 34590/1, Vernehmungsprotokoll Franz Sippel, 3 June 1958.
[184] SAM, StA 34590/1, Vernehmungsprotokoll Franz Hofmann, 22 April 1959.
[185] Rebecca Wittman, *Beyond Justice: The Auschwitz Trial* (Harvard, 2012), p. 186.
[186] SAM, StA 34590/1, Vernehmungsprotokoll Franz Hofmann, 22 April 1959.
[187] Dicks, *Licensed*, p. 122.        [188] Dicks, *Licensed*, p. 123.
[189] Buggeln, *Arbeit*, pp. 480–3.

of their superiors, they made up for in a zeal and voluntarism for which none expressed the slightest contrition.

## Block Leaders (*Blockführer*)

For those yet to reach the executive heights of compound or report leader, the position of block leader offered a more delineated empowerment. The term 'block' leader seems not to have been used at Dachau until 1937, as part of a discursive demilitarization of the inmates (Chapter 5). An alternative appellation, 'commando leader' (*Kommandoführer*) was also used to denote SS NCOs who oversaw work details, rather than allocated barracks of inmates. The block leaders had intimate, daily contact with the prisoners. Initially this contact was of an immediate and often violent nature: with the increasing delegation of quotidian torment to the *Kapos* it became more panoptical, although outbursts of hands-on abuse still peppered the working day. Block leaders were not micromanagers, delegating the minutiae of order and organization to senior inmate functionaries in each barracks. At any point, however, they could choose to enforce a lapsed or forgotten rule, to peer into a dark corner and find some transgression of the latitudinous regulations. This latent danger haunted the daily lives of Dachau inmates: as Bruno Bettelheim recalled, although many got through their time in the camp without severe corporal punishment, 'the screamed threat that they were going to get twenty five on the behind rang in their ears several times daily'.[190]

'Bed-making' (*Bettenbau*) was a cherished tool of psychological terror for block leaders. A staple of hazing in total institutions (see Chapter 4), it developed into a cruel cult in the concentration camps as a bedrock of their 'useless violence'. Bed-making pitted the camp SS narrative of idle, cheeky prisoners against the latter's desperation to avoid giving block leaders any pretext for collective punishment. It is evident from the earliest years in Dachau.[191] Every bunk bed comprised a blanket and a paillasse whose straw had to be spread out evenly to its edges. The mattresses were sweaty, fetid, poorly-stuffed, and deeply uncomfortable: 'outwardly smooth and minutely ordered, filthy on the inside—the beds symbolised the whole system', as one Dachau inmate put it.[192] It could take even an experienced prisoner ten to fifteen minutes to make his bed with the process particularly awkward for those on top bunks. The barracks itself had to be faultlessly swept and the inmate lockers had to look, another recalled, as if 'fresh from the carpenter's plane'.[193] It was largely down to the mood of the block leader whether a barracks passed muster or was declared a 'pig-sty', but bed maintenance was a constant source of divisive recrimination among prisoners. It was part of the daily theatre of torment in Dachau and the high water mark of power for the SS block leaders.

It is impossible to identify every Dachau block leader because the position was generally held only by lower-ranked SS men with modest presence in SS

---

[190] Bettelheim, *The Informed Heart*, p. 132.  [191] Hornung, *Dachau*, p. 53.
[192] Adam, *Nacht über Deutschland*, p. 33.  [193] Heilig, *Men Crucified*, p. 99.

documentation.[194] But many block leaders etched themselves into the memories and memoirs of inmates. Lowly as they may have been in the SS hierarchy, their localized power was near absolute. As Sofsky points out, '[n]o officer in the modern military can walk through his men's barracks and choose summarily to drown a recruit on the spot in a latrine'.[195] Yet usually block leaders did not murder their prisoners but dealt instead in kicks and so-called 'boxes round the ears' (*Ohrfeigen*). The latter, prevalent in German, as in British, pedagogy were an assertion of seniority, status, and authority.[196] However savage in practice, they could be accommodated in narratives of re-education and rehabilitation. Eicke, even as he warned against their use outside the enclosed stage of the prisoner compound, depicted them as a wholesome expression of National Socialist pedagogy:

> Upon the arrival of a prisoner transport some SS men handed out boxed ears to a few particularly cheeky prisoners. Although as a National Socialist I have every sympathy for such behaviour, I can and must not tolerate it as it brings the risk that the Ministry of the Interior will decide that we are not capable of dealing with prisoners.[197]

Behind the discursive fig leaf of boxed ears, of course, lay all manner of depredations: clubbing with rifle butts, blows to the face, breaking jaws and teeth. The same applied to so-called 'kicks' (*Fußtritten*), a more distant form of violence, entailing less physical discomfort, less touching, for the perpetrator due to the stout boots worn by the SS.[198] It is all too easy, when reading inmate memoirs and testimony, to become desensitized to this daily violence. Yet Wilhelm H., for example, was a robust 29-year-old when he was imprisoned in early Dachau. He was kicked in the stomach by Steinbrenner, his block leader, for failing to offer an appropriately deferential greeting. Wilhelm H. was unable to eat for weeks and spent the next several years coming in and out of hospital for treatment on his stomach. In 1944 he was declared a full invalid and underwent a further serious operation after the war: all the consequence of one otherwise unremarkable 'kick' from a block leader.[199]

Dachau block leaders in their testimony frequently defend the 'boxed ears' and 'kicks' they handed out as objectively compassionate, perpetrated instead of filing an official report which might well have resulted in a much more dangerous flogging or hour at the 'pole'.[200] The motivation for not filing a report was more usually bureaucratic indolence. Constantly exhorted to vigilance, moreover, the block leader had to appear responsive to supposed transgressions or lose credibility with his compound and report leaders. The same dynamic helps to account for the 'terrible zeal' prisoners identified in newly appointed or candidate block leaders

[194] Riedle's admirably forensic study of Sachsenhausen encountered the same problem. Riedle, *Angehörigen*, p. 59.
[195] Sofsky, *Order*, p. 116.
[196] Koslov, *Gewalt*, pp. 413–20; Buggeln, *Arbeit*, 433–52.
[197] IfZ MA 293, Befehlsblatt, 1 March 1937, s. 2550207.        [198] Koslov, *Gewalt*, p. 419.
[199] SAM, StA, 34462/1, Zeugenvernehmungsprotokoll Wilhelm H., 4 November 1949.
[200] SAM, StA 34686, Vernehmungsniederschrift Matthias Pfeiffer, 9 January 1967; DaA, DA 6.454, Vernehmungsniederschrift Hans Steinbrenner, 19 August 1948; IfZ, MB 37, Clemency Appeal for Alois Hipp, 28 June 1947, s. 967.

Table 3.3  Dachau School block leaders by generation.

| Generation | 1933 | 1934 | 1935 | 1936 | 1937 | 1938 | 1939 |
|---|---|---|---|---|---|---|---|
| Front Generation | 8 | 4 | 4 | 3 | 2 | 2 | 1 |
| War Youth Generation | 12 | 15 | 15 | 15 | 16 | 15 | 14 |
| Post-war Generation | 1 | 3 | 3 | 4 | 5 | 5 | 6 |
| Total | 21 | 22 | 22 | 22 | 23 | 22 | 21 |

for whom 'great diligence' in abusing prisoners was the path to promotion and social status.[201] This performative quality was sometimes invoked by prisoners as a defence of Dachau block leaders in post-war proceedings. Alois Hipp, for example, who replaced Hofmann as block leader in 1937, was supported by an inmate thus:

> In no case were the crimes committed by Hipp the product of his own brain, but always the result of instructions previously issued or of his unconditional obedience owing to cowardice and fear. If Hipp was alone in the camp on a Sunday, felt he was not being watched by superiors . . . one must admit that we, the prisoners, also had peace.[202]

This is another reminder of the salience of Milgram's findings on the role of authority's gaze. Yet block leaders on the whole were less captives of the Dachau habitus than its ground-level protagonists, their conduct driven by ambition, routinization, and ideological investment, and particularized by carefully nurtured idiosyncrasies.

Forty-nine Dachau SS men can be identified with reasonable certainty as having held the role in the pre-war period (see Table 3.3). Their exact dates of service are unknown, but the sample is broad enough to gain an oversight of the type of man appointed and to offer some illustrative biographies.

The war youth generation remained dominant at this lowliest rung of the key commandant staff personnel. The most substantial change in demographic terms occurred during Eicke's tenure with the departure of unsuitable older men like Vogel and Ehmann. Although not captured in the above statistics, the next purge of block leaders was led by Loritz in 1936 as part of his shake up of key personnel in the wake of Deubel's tenure. The final section of this chapter will consider two biographies from before the purge, the purge itself, and then some examples of block leaders who either survived it or were appointed by Loritz.

The most infamous of all Dachau block leaders was Hans Steinbrenner. Many inmates report being struck by his winning appearance. Röder recalls 'a tall, extraordinarily handsome man in his SS uniform'[203] and Johann Barth a 'burly, smart, good-looking man' whose brutality seemed so at odds with his appearance.[204] All witnesses testify to his intelligent yet 'unpredictable' (*unberechenbar*) nature. Johann Treitinger relates a characteristic incident from June 1933 when he

---

[201] Quotes from Neurath, *Society*, p. 77; see also Orth, *Konzentrationslager SS*, pp. 130–2.
[202] IfZ, MB 37, Statement Heinrich Tuting, s. 953.    [203] Röder, *Nachtwache*, p. 265.
[204] SAM, StA 34462/7, Zeugenvernehmungsprotokoll Johann Barth, 26 February 1951.

was a member of a party of inmates with whom Steinbrenner was standing around cracking jokes, a scene more redolent of a scout camp than the most murderous venue of extra-judicial confinement in Nazi Germany.[205] Perhaps discomforted by such dissonance, Steinbrenner abruptly lashed out at his chuckling audience, knocking Treitinger to the floor before picking him up and laughing dementedly in his face. Another inmate, Karl Seeser, offered a more prurient reading:

> As soon as Steinbrenner came out of a cell after abusing someone he made for the telephone to ring his wife in Munich. He would then talk to her in the most tender manner. Later his wife came to live with him at Dachau and we observed that after ill-treating inmates he went straight home to his flat. This was very conspicuous to us.[206]

While a sexual pathology cannot be excluded in Steinbrenner's case, this kind of testimony is impossible to verify and almost certainly stems above all from prisoners' understandable tendency to demonize their tormentor-in-chief. Steinbrenner's notoriety, moreover, was such that it is difficult to isolate the man from the myth. There are, for example, reports from inmates of having 'without doubt' encountered him among the SS personnel at Auschwitz.[207] Steinbrenner, however, was never posted at Auschwitz. After rejoining the Dachau guard troops in autumn 1933 he remained there as an instructor and then medic, and was attached in the latter capacity to the Death's Head Division throughout the war. He survived the Eastern Front and was captured by the Americans in 1945. The German judiciary was perplexed by Steinbrenner, a man of well-above average intelligence who had offered such assertive and brutal leadership to his peers.[208] This reflected, of course, the immediate post-war impulse to present Nazi perpetrators as social failures. During marathon interrogations, Naaff's team invited Steinbrenner to respond to over 600 incriminating testimonies. The process was frequently interrupted as he was overwhelmed by outrage and tearful self-pity at the mendacities therein, and the fact that he was carrying the can for a collective practice.[209] Steinbrenner, like Höß, wrote that he had become criminal by twist of fate: the fate of passing by Erspenmüller's grey omnibus in March 1933, and the fate of being versed in weaponry and thus selected for the first Dachau commandant staff.[210] He also claimed that he had acted in the belief, which he still held, that the contemporary Munich judiciary had been 'in agreement with the necessity of these revolutionary events'.[211]

The Munich state court was not impressed by these rationalizations. Steinbrenner was convicted of the murders of Hausmann and Wilhelm Aron, a Jewish inmate

---

[205] SAM, StA 34462/6, Zeugenvernehmungsprotokoll Johann Treitinger, 5 June 1950.
[206] SAM, StA 34462/6, Zeugenvernehmungsprotokoll Karl Seeser, 6 July 1950.
[207] SAM, StA 34462/2, Angabe Hans Mentler, 22 July 1948; SAM, StA 34462/5, Niederschrift Amtsgerichts Vilshofen Ludwig Mittermeier, 19 May 1950; SAM/StA 34462/6, Zeugenvernehmungsprotokoll Fritz Busching, 7 June 1950.
[208] DaA, DA3856, Urteil Landgericht Munich II, 25 April 1952.
[209] SAM, StA 34462/7, Fortsetzung der Beschuldigtenvernehmung Steinbrenner, 21 June 1951.
[210] SAM, StA 34479/1, Erweiterer Lebenslauf des Hans Steinbrenner, 3 January 1953.
[211] DaA, DA3856, Vernehmungsniederschrift Hans Steinbrenner, 19 August 1948.

beaten over days to a sickening death, as well as nine counts of bodily harm. He was sentenced to lifelong imprisonment in Landsberg before being released in 1962. Steinbrenner spent his twilight years in a nursing home in, of all places, Berchtesgaden. He had found God again in prison, and his priest recalled him living a reserved, pious life in Berchtesgaden, attending mass every Sunday and sitting alone in the choir stalls.[212] His spiritual calm seems to have been disturbed when brought once more before the judiciary as a witness in Franz Hofmann's trial. On 13 June 1964, Hans Steinbrenner hanged himself in his care home, one of the later Nazi suicides. The suicide note was inaccurate: 'I have never killed anyone' it finished, 'this I can say with a clear conscience'.[213]

Max von Dall-Armi spent longer on the Dachau commandant staff than Steinbrenner. Dall-Armi was born in Landsberg in 1912.[214] After attending *Volkschule* and *Mittelschule*, he trained as a salesman and worked in his uncle's shop. In 1932 he joined the SS 'out of idealism'. This led to friction with his uncle, who was not enthusiastic about Nazism. During what he refers to as the 'days of subversion', the Nazi takeover of Bavaria, Dall-Armi signed up with the Munich auxiliary police, in which role he came to Dachau on 27 March. After six weeks' training by the State Police he was brought onto the commandant staff as a telephonist. In the summer of 1933 Eicke appointed him 'work service leader' (*Arbeitsdienstführer*), tasked with organizing the prisoners into work details at roll calls, a duty later assumed by the report leader. It entailed standing daily on a podium in the roll call square with the guard contingent stationed behind, allocating the assembled prisoners notionally according to their skills. This was a task with limitless potential for public theatre and Dall-Armi took advantage to such an extent that political prisoners, steeped in the social prejudices of the era, are certain that he was homosexual.[215] The asking after occupations was replete with sarcastic humour, boxed ears, and petty humiliations.[216] The fresh-faced Dall-Armi was known by inmates as 'the little bug' (*Lausbub*) and himself later sought to account for his 'excesses' in terms of 'youthful foolishness'.[217] Prisoners offer other explanations. Xaver Schwarzmüller puts Dall-Armi's conduct down to burning ambition, the chance quickly to become a 'somebody', at the dawn of what he truly believed would be a 'thousand year Reich'.[218] Dall-Armi was perhaps alluding to such imponderables when he prefaced his memoirs on Dachau with a pithy aphorism: 'Clearly sees he who looks on from afar but only foggily, he who takes part'.[219]

---

[212] DaA, 6454, Erkundigungsnotiz in der Sache des KZ-Mörders Hans Steinbrenner, 11 November 1984.
[213] DaA, 6454, Erkundigungsnotiz in der Sache des KZ-Mörders Hans Steinbrenner, 11 November 1984.
[214] SAM, StA 34453/1, Protokoll Spruchkammer Darmstadt Lager, 18 April 1948.
[215] SAM, StA 34453/1, Zeugenaussage Karl Geist, 18 April 1948.
[216] SAM, StA 34453/1, Zeugenvernehmungsprotokoll Ferdinand Wünsch, 17 January 1950.
[217] SAM, StA 34453/1, Protokoll Spruchkammer Darmstadt Lager, 18 April 1948, s. 4.
[218] SAM, StA 34452/1, Xaver Schwarzmüller, Darmstadt Spruchkammer, 18 April 1948, s. 14.
[219] SAM, StA 34461/4, Max von Dall-Armi, Bilder und Skizzen aus dem Konzentrationslager, 13 April 1951.

Dall-Armi, at any rate, seems to have tired of the intoxication of power and Nazism by the mid-1930s, for he was among the Dachau block leaders purged by Loritz for softness and complicity in the indolently benign Deubel regime. To substantiate long-held rumblings at the IKL and among Dachau SS traditionalists about this turn in camp culture, Loritz was able to elicit obliging testimony in Augsburg from a former inmate on Dachau block leaders negligently 'popular' among the camp's prisoners.[220] Max Reindl was a stalwart of the movement, an SS NCO and former comrade of Loritz briefly imprisoned in Dachau as a result of a seedy corruption scandal. Loritz went personally to speak to him in Augsburg. Deubel and D'Angelo, Reindl averred, 'were very popular' among Dachau inmates, while nine Dachau block leaders, although less cherished, were nonetheless 'highly regarded'.[221] Dall-Armi was among those and as a consequence moved on from Dachau, in his case to Esterwegen and then to the General SS.

In the wake of this exemplary punishment four of the named block leaders were allowed to remain at their posts to prove themselves to the new commandant. One was Vincenz Schöttl, later a compound leader at Auschwitz/Monowitz. Schöttl was born in Appersdorf in 1905. He was a veteran of the movement, having joined the NSDAP in November 1928 and the SS in January 1931.[222] He was a member of the early Dachau SS, and stood sentry alongside Steinbrenner in the very first days of the camp. At some unidentified point under Eicke he transferred to the commandant staff as a block leader. Here one of his charges was Laurence, whose description of him belies Reindl's testimony:

> A giant with reddish hair, heavily built with enormous hands . . . Schöttl was the kind of Bavarian backwoodsman whom the humorous weekly *Simplicissimus* used to portray and quote every week . . . When angry he was absolutely like a giant wild animal, one did not know how to escape his furies and feared for one's very life. Of all the block leaders he was probably the most dangerous, probably chosen for the Jewish block just for that reason. He was worst when under the influence of alcohol . . . yet could be friendly and smiling on occasion too . . . He had numerous family and a great pride in his Bavarian homeland. At the end of his life he returned to being a most observant and pious Catholic.[223]

Schöttl's peer Wolfgang Seuss was a man even Reindl would have struggled to present as 'popular' among the prisoners. Born in Nuremberg in 1906, Seuss was one of three brothers to serve in the Dachau SS. He attended elementary school with modest success before training as a metalworker.[224] In 1928 he was released and spent the next five years unemployed. In 1932 he volunteered for the SS along with his brothers hoping, he claimed, to find employment. After the seizure of power he sought a job in the State Police, but was sent instead to be trained by them in the Dachau guard units. In 1934 he was brought into the commandant

[220] BAB, BDC SSO D'Angelo, Vernehmungsniederschrift Max Reindl, 28 April 1936.
[221] BAB, BDC SSO D'Angelo, Vernehmungsniederschrift Max Reindl, 28 April 1936.
[222] BAB, BDC RS F562 Schöttl, Fragebogen (n.d.).
[223] Alfred Laurence, 'Dachau Overcome', pp. 34–9.
[224] SAM, StA 34570, Urteil in der Strafsache gegen Wolfgang Seuss, 22 June 1960.

staff to supervize a work detail, and in 1935 secured promotion to block leader.[225] He remained in the camp until 1942 and prospered there financially, his salary increasing from 600 Reichsmark in 1934 to 3,000 Reichsmark in 1939.[226]

Seuss was a malicious and violent man. His antisemitism was ardent even by the standards of the Dachau SS, reflecting perhaps his political socialization north of the Danube where *Gauleiter* Streicher's notably putrid antisemitism had so long poisoned the waters. Hans Schwarz attributes a gamut of unpleasant antisemitic innovations to Seuss including special 'sports' forcing Jewish prisoners to crawl along on their stomachs, followed by a refusal to allow them into the infirmary on the basis that 'Jewish swine can die outside'.[227] He was a block leader after Loritz's own heart, capable of sending prisoners scurrying for cover with his very approach. It is possible that Seuss had been promoted to report leader by the outbreak of war; if so he certainly adheres to the pattern identified previously for this group.[228] His legal counsel, however, contended that the motives for Seuss's many antisemitic outrages in Dachau 'lie not in hatred of Jews, but in a painstaking and conscious adaptation' to a prevailing culture of violence.[229]

A similar legal defence was offered by Josef Voggesberger, another block leader very much in the Loritz spirit. Voggesberger is remarkable, however, for the rustic Bavarian candour of his post-war testimony, strikingly unguarded by the standards of the genre. He was born in 1908 in Tiefendobel, joined the SA and the NSDAP in 1927, and switched to the SS in Landshut in August 1931.[230] On 20 April 1933 he arrived at Dachau with the auxiliary police and was assigned to the guard detail. In 1937 he transferred to the commandant staff and was appointed a block leader in January 1938, a position he retained until his transfer to Sachsenhausen in November 1941. His first deposition, to the Viennese judiciary, was frank. It is clear from inmate memoirs that certain prisoners were picked out by the SS as targets for abuse and murder on given days. Voggesberger made abundantly clear this was an intricate, bureaucratic process when he reflected on death sentences passed on 'seven or eight' of his prisoners:

> Early in the morning at the march out to work the block and commando leaders attended a so-called 'lecture' (*Belehrung*) delivered by the report or compound leader. This usually consisted of telling us that we were too kind to the prisoners, and then which inmates were to be 'finished off' (*fertig-gemacht*). We received slips from the report or block leaders with the prisoner numbers of the relevant inmates. There were no particular remarks on these, but every block and commando leader knew well what they meant: in the evening these prisoners were to be returned dead or nearly dead and should not be rescued from torment. These slips were handed out two to three times a week. The SS men carried out these orders themselves, or delegated it to the

[225]  SAM, StA 34570, Beschuldigtenvernehmung Wolfgang Seuss, 22 February 1960.
[226]  SAM, StA 34570/1, Spruchkammer Bergedorf Akten, s. 3.
[227]  SAM, StA 34570, Zeugenvernehmungsprotokoll Hans Schwarz, 19 October 1954.
[228]  SAM, StA 34570, Anklageschrift Landgericht Munich II Wolfgang Seuss, 11 March 1960.
[229]  SAM, StA 34570, Dr Kurt-Otto Scholz to Schwurgericht beim Landgericht Munich II, 6 September 1960.
[230]  SAM, StA 34452/2, Vernehmungsniederschrift Josef Voggesberger, 24 October 1946.

appropriate *Kapo*. I won't deny that I was involved in this kind of abuse, but not out of sadism, I was just following the orders of the camp leadership. Sometimes inmates slated for 'finishing off' would also be chased out into the so-called 'sentry chain'.[231]

Voggesberger's rare initial candour before the judiciary clearly sent his legal counsel into panic. Six months later the above procedure is narrated very differently. The Viennese judiciary now learn that Voggesberger merely passed nebulous slips on to SS NCOs who went themselves to the report and compound leader to find out what they entailed.[232] His personal participation in the killings fades likewise from the scene. These retractions, however, did not convince the Vienna state court. Appalled by his nonchalant testimony, it rightly concluded that he demonstrated 'not the slightest trace of disquiet' about his actions, indeed 'he gives the impression that it is self-explanatory'.[233]

The court alighted here on a very salient point. Like Maximilian Seefried, Voggesberger had misjudged the enormity of what had happened in Dachau, and the moral and legal implications of his participation. This despite sitting, for his testimony, in the environment most likely to encourage calculation and restraint. Yet while his candour was unusual, the residual institutional mentality it betrayed was not. Few of the perpetrators discussed in this chapter expressed contrition after the war, nor is it likely they felt any. The casual, tone-deaf character of so many of their writings and statements registered their deep habituation to terror and violence on the Dachau command staff. Here personal conduct was gauged not against universal ethics or 'sentimental' judicial precepts, but relative to peers in a localized manner. This was characteristic of 'vanguard' National Socialist institutions, and a driving force of 'Dachau spirit'.[234]

Instead, these roles became public performances in terror and domination. For command staff personnel, the Dachau prisoner compound was a stage with multiple audiences. There were the prisoners, whom they sought to terrorize and appal in a ritualization of the power relations in the camp. Then there was the commandant and Eicke's IKL, who controlled the levers of patronage and promotion. Third, their own subordinates and peers, for whom they offered leadership and behavioural cues. Up in the galleries, too, the bored sentries were there to be entertained. A carnival of humiliation and violence, orchestrated by comrades in SS uniforms and *Kapo* extras, might break out at any moment, lending a sense of unpredictability to the temporally regimented working day. One reason for the unpopularity of Deubel's regime with Dachau traditionalists was the constraints placed upon this stage, the absence of acclaim and of incidents to induct into the Dachau SS equivalent of regimental history.

Many commandant staff personnel, as has been seen, consciously moulded their stage personae and worked hard at the projection of an 'exquisite devilishness'.

---

[231] SAM, StA 34452/2, Vernehmungsniederschrift Josef Voggesberger, 24 October 1946.

[232] SAM/StA 34452/1, Vernehmung des Beschuldigten Josef Voggesberger, 17 April 1947.

[233] SAM/StA 34452/1, Urteil Landesgericht Wien, 24 April 1948.

[234] On the mentalities of Nazi vanguard institutions, see Wildt, *An Unconditional Generation*; Bloxham, *Final Solution*, pp. 267–72.

Acts of demonstrative chicanery earned the perpetrator career capital and could be framed as appropriate responses to 'cheeky' transgressions of the camp regulations. These commandant staff personnel, moreover, came daily into intimate contact with prisoners and the pressures for compliance were at their strongest here: an uncommitted or 'soft' block leader was a good deal more conspicuous than an equivalent sentry. So although a maximalist role account on the lines advanced by Zimbardo is to be resisted (see Chapter 4), these key disciplinary positions placed the perpetrators in situations even within an environment of violence which encouraged terroristic theatre.[235] The reciprocal relationship between belief and deed was hastened in these highly proactive roles on the commandant's staff. Bettelheim put this point well: '[o]nly dimly at first, but with ever greater clarity, did I also come to see that soon how a man acts can alter what he is'.[236] Bettelheim had his fellow prisoners in mind, but the aphorism seems more applicable to the perpetrators.

Closely linked to the theatre of terror among the key commandant staff was their shared complicity. Hilberg surmised of the bureaucrats of the Final Solution that there 'was nothing so irksome as the realization that someone was watching over one's shoulder, that someone would be free to talk and accuse because he was not himself involved'.[237] A member of the Dachau command staff, too, who avoided getting his hands dirty, cast implicit judgement on his peers. He would be tainted as a loner, one of the few things beyond the pale in these comradely circles. Only a vanishingly small number of commandant staff personnel held themselves clear of these centripetal dynamics and the pleasures of power. These rare specimens were known by inmates as 'white ravens', and lavish speculative mythologies were spun around their reasons for being in the camp.[238]

Hans Mursch was a 'white raven'. Born in Munich in 1900, Mursch came to Dachau in September 1933 and worked in the SS sick bay for three months before Eicke put him in charge of prisoner property.[239] He stayed in the role until 1941 when he was appointed camp registrar, where his duties included registering deaths in the camp with the town municipal administration. Hans Mursch was never seen insulting, let alone mistreating, inmates. For the thousands of prisoners humiliated and abused by Kick during their registration with the Political Department, Mursch was a sincere and courteous face in the adjoining property office. In the prisoner compound, he was known to warn inmates when they were scheduled to be called to the Political Department for questioning and to brief them on what to expect.[240] Prisoners detailed to him in the property office were allowed to rest up during the day in the cellar below. Röder, imprisoned in Dachau for eleven years,

---

[235] On this, see also Buggeln, *Arbeit*, pp. 479–84.
[236] Bettelheim, *Informed Heart*, p. 24. More broadly on this point see the insightful analysis in Bloxham, *Final Solution*, pp. 264–7.
[237] Hilberg, *Destruction*, p. 50. See also Kühne, *Kameradschaft*, pp. 55–94.
[238] Neurath, *Society*, p. 78. Neurath identifies one anonymous 'white raven' in Dachau, and one in Buchenwald.
[239] SAM, StA 34462/4, Zeugenvernehmungsprotokoll Hans Mursch, 27 June 1950.
[240] Buzengeiger, 'Tausend Tage Dachau', p. 21; Röder, *Nachtwache*, pp. 275–7.

even believed that Mursch responded to events in the camp 'like a prisoner . . . he was one of us'.[241] According to Reimund Schnabel, Mursch was once locked up for several weeks for failing to beat a refractory inmate. He wept openly on the camp thoroughfare when a transport of Hungarian gypsies arrived at Dachau in 1944.[242] Since it was clearly not ideological commitment which kept Mursch at Dachau, the reasons must be sought in the livelihood it provided and the difficulty of exit: he was medically unfit for service at the front. He and his wife had three children at Dachau during the 1930s, born in 1934, 1936, and 1941. His wage as a married *Oberscharführer*, as has been seen, put him comfortably above the average salary of a German worker. Mursch is a reminder both of the behavioural agency of Dachau SS men and of the fact that the running of the camp was perfectly able to accommodate a degree of dissent. He also illustrates the importance of role held: his non-key, largely clerical positions had lesser behavioural minima than a block leader. Of course, by working at the camp for twelve years, Mursch remained situatively complicit, at the very least, in its criminality. Our focus on his behavioural restraint merely highlights the caprice and voluntarism of his peers, who committed themselves so avidly to the institutional norms of the Dachau School.

---

[241] Röder, *Nachtwache*, pp. 276–7.      [242] Schnabel, *Frommen*, p. 47.

# 4

# The Dachau SS and the Prisoners

Paul Martin Neurath was burning anti-fascist literature in his flat in Vienna when the Gestapo arrived.[1] Two days previously, on 11 March 1938, the Austrian Chancellor Kurt von Schuschnigg had resigned, brow-beaten by Hitler, diplomatically iso- lated, and exhausted by domestic turmoil. The motorized vanguard of the invad- ing Wehrmacht was followed by Himmler's agents, eager to secure the files of the Austrian police. Arrest lists of Schuschnigg functionaries, Communists, and Socialists were swiftly drawn up and Neurath's name was among them. A scion of the Jewish intelligentsia, his father Otto had travelled to Munich in 1919 as an economic advisor to the *Räterepublik*. Neurath's stove was 'glowing deep red' when the Gestapo pulled up in the courtyard. He managed to slip away but it is indicative of the times that he was harried and denounced at every turn by hostile and officious citizens. Neurath was eventually arrested some five days later within sight of the Czech border and taken into police custody. With no judicial process, he was transported to Dachau on 1 April 1938 in the first cohort of Austrian political prisoners.[2] Some 3,500 more would follow to 'Dora', the Viennese Gestapo's code word for the camp, in the ensu- ing months. A Social Democratic publication was soon reporting that '[n]o word creates more terror in Austria than Dachau'.[3]

The Austrians caught up in the *Anschluß* dragnet included a remarkable cross-section of Viennese political and intellectual life. They have left a rich, contemporary, and analytical body of memoirs on Dachau which marks the first concerted—and in some ways unsurpassed—engagement with its inner life as a social phenomenon.[4] Their

---

[1] Neurath, *Society*, pp. ix–xiii.
[2] On this first transport see Wolfgang Neugebauer, 'Der erste Österreichertransport in das KZ Dachau 1938', in Wolfgang Benz and Angelika Königseder (eds), *Das Konzentrationslager Dachau: Geschichte und Wirkung nationalsozialistischer Repression* (Berlin, 2008), pp. 193–205. Construction work on an Austrian concentration camp at Mauthausen began in the same month.
[3] *Nazi-Bastille Dachau*, p. 13. The records of the International Tracing Service suggest that around 2,000 of these men were Jewish: Wünschmann, 'Jewish Prisoners', p. 173, fn. 667.
[4] In addition to Neurath, these 'participant-observer' texts include Bettelheim, *The Informed Heart*; Adam, *Nacht über Deutschland*; Peter Wallner, *By Order of the Gestapo: A Record of Life in Dachau and Buchenwald Concentration Camps* (London, 1941); Rudolf Kalmar, *Zeit ohne Gnade* (Vienna, 1946), Benedikt Kautsky, *Teufel und Verdammte: Erfahrungen und Erkenntnisse aus sieben Jahren in deutschen Konzentrationslager* (Zurich, 1946). Eugen Kogon, whose sociology of Buchenwald is much better known, was also interned after the *Anschluß*. Despite their later dates of publication, Neurath and Bettelheim also wrote up their camp experiences in the 1940s.

specific experiences in the camp stemmed, like those of all inmates, from a complex of interrelated factors. On a situational level, these included the prevailing ideological direction of the Nazi regime, the size and taxonomy of the inmate population, and the profile of the SS personnel. On an individual level, the most decisive were duration of imprisonment, the ability to adapt to a pathological environment, and—not least— sheer luck in dealings with guards and fellow inmates. The following chapter focuses on the relationships between the SS and the inmates inside the Dachau protective custody compound. It identifies a radicalizing tension in this hands-on aspect of the Dachau School between the drive to homogenize and pathologize the inmates as a collective 'other', and the impulse to categorize, to divide the inmates among themselves and to express the specificities of the SS world view. As has been seen, the camp and its culture were deeply marked by events beyond the barbed wire. This was particularly true of its inmate profile, substantially more diverse by the outbreak of war than in the days of the early Dachau SS. Political prisoners were very quickly joined by so-called 'professional criminals', social outsiders, homosexuals, Jews, and Jehovah's Witnesses, all marked and grouped under an intricate taxonomy. This heterogeneity complicated the operation of discipline, distance, and power in the camp: the fundamental daily responsibility of every SS man and a matter as much of creativity and personal initiative as of official regulations. Nor, as the Austrian memoir literature makes particularly clear, should the inmates be seen simply as passive objects of this power. As historical subjects navigating and constitutive of a dynamic situation, they often exercised a greater direct and indirect influence on the conduct of the guards than scholarly literature on the concentration camps suggests.[5]

## HOMOGENEITY

### Inmate and Institution

For all their soldierly trappings and aspirations, the primary function of the pre-war concentration camp SS was to sequester, subjugate, and punish the camps' inmates. This permanent structured conflict was fundamental to its processes of group formation: the SS 'we' explored throughout the present book was dependent on the production of 'them', the concentration camp prisoners. This dualism, while by no means always as 'absolute' in practice as some writers have claimed, underpinned the curriculum of the Dachau School. Here the Manichean properties of the SS world view, indebted to the front imagery characteristic of National Socialism, were expressed in the constructed, mythical figure of the *Häftling* (inmate). This was a creature of low animal cunning whose perfidy demanded constant vigilance from guards unburdened by the cognitive strain of disciplining him on a case-by-case basis. As such, with a very few privileged exceptions, every Dachau prisoner

---

[5] More broadly on these issues of construal and agency, see Alf Lüdtke's influential concept of 'Eigensinn', introduced in Alf Lüdtke, *Eigen-Sinn: Fabrikalltag, Arbeitererfahrung und Politik vom Kaiserreich bis in den Faschismus* (Hamburg, 1993).

was potentially exposed to what they often referred to in their post-war testimony as 'the usual camp treatment' (*die übliche Lagerbehandlung*).[6] This spectrum of torment ranged from verbal harassment through incidental violence to regulated, bureaucratic punishments for supposed disciplinary transgressions. Death in the pre-war period remained the exception, but was sufficiently in evidence to keep inmates in a state of chronic anxiety. In sum, incarceration in Dachau was a spell of institutionalized terror and the fact that an inmate was in the camp was considered reason enough to beat him: this was one of most important principles of the camp SS.

Indeed, one type of explanation for the rhythms of conflict and cruelty in Dachau would focus on this institutional setting. The sociologist Erving Goffman argued that 'total' institutions such as asylums, prisons, and concentration camps inherently create an adversarial mindset.[7] Their inmates are depersonalized and discursively pathologized merely by being in such an institution, while this devaluation generates a superior, even predatory, self-conception among the staff. It is customary for personnel in total institutions to communicate with inmates exclusively through shouting.[8] The latter are organized into blocks and live under constant surveillance, ensuring that any infraction of the rules 'is likely to stand out in relief against the visible, constantly examined compliance of the others'.[9] Infractions in turn bring the risk of physical sanctions from the staff, which can quickly escalate out of control in a process Goffman terms 'looping'. Here any conscious or instinctive act of self-defence on the part of the inmate might be construed both as a refusal to recognize the initial offence and as a wilful challenge to the authority of the perpetrator and, in turn, of the entire staff.[10] This potentially brings the full force of institutional violence on to the victim. As will be seen, situational 'looping' brought the very real potential for death in Dachau, where guards enjoyed an untrammelled right to be capricious and were instructed to use their guns in the event of the slightest resistance.

[6] SAM, StA 34832/2, Zeugenvernehmung Eduard Baar-Baarenfels, 14 August 1950; SAM, StA 34832/3, Zeugenvernehmungsprotokoll Josef Eckstein, 22 November 1951; SAM, StA 17445/1 Aussage Ferdinand Wünsch, 17 January 1950.

[7] Goffman, E., *Asylums: Essays on the Social Situation of Mental Patients and Other Inmates* (New York, 1961). Goffman argued that all institutions have 'encompassing tendencies', but among the closest to totality were concentration camps: 'The central feature of total institutions can be described as a breakdown of the barriers ordinarily separating . . . spheres of life. First, all aspects of life are conducted in the same place and under the same single authority. Second, each phase of the member's daily activity is carried on in the immediate company of a large batch of others, all of whom are treated alike and required to do the same thing together. Third, all phases of the day's activities are tightly scheduled, with one activity leading at a prearranged time into the next, the whole sequence of activities being imposed from above by a system of explicit formal rulings and a body of officials. Finally, the various enforced activities are brought together into a single rational plan purportedly designed to fulfil the official aim of the institution' (p. 17).

[8] Goffman, *Asylums*, p. 19.    [9] Goffman, *Asylums*, p. 18.

[10] Goffman, *Asylums*, p. 41: 'The individual finds that his protective response to an assault upon self is collapsed into the situation: he cannot defend himself in the usual way by establishing difference between the mortifying situation and himself'. The phenomenon is also stressed by Buggeln: Buggeln, *Arbeit*, pp. 335–484, esp. pp. 346–7.

Goffman's 'total institution' manifestly has some applicability to Dachau, where the prisoners and guards, as Höß puts it, constituted 'two hostile and opposing worlds'.[11] It would form the basis of an account foregrounding role and environment, rather than the disposition of the SS personnel, in Dachau's culture of violence. The most extreme, maximalist, position on this is taken by the social psychologist Philip Zimbardo, whose Stanford Prison Experiment (SPE) of 1971 features much more prominently than Goffman in universalist perpetrator literature.[12] Given the expansive claims made for the SPE as an explanation of carceral tyranny, it is worth considering it in some detail. A group of eighteen young male volunteers, screened against antisocial values, were split randomly into prisoners and guards. Initially self-conscious and rueful, within days the imbalance of situational power had apparently created a vicious circle of tyrannical guards and subjugated, apathetic prisoners. The experiment famously had to be aborted after just six days of its scheduled fourteen duration. As such, according to its convenors, the SPE demonstrated that extreme aggression and cruelty were 'a natural consequence of being placed in the uniform of a guard and asserting the power inherent in that role'.[13]

This proposition, however, is strongly contested in the field of social psychology. There are two key objections. The first concerns the use of the word 'natural'. In a laboratory or field study, the analysts and observers are obliged to do everything possible to minimize the potential impact of their presence. Above all, they should take care not to communicate their hopes or expectations to the participants.[14] Yet Zimbardo is on record exhorting his 'guards' to aggression and to maintaining 'total power in the situation'.[15] With regard to the status of the 'prisoners', too, the 'natural' claim is questionable. Dressed in a 'smock, like a tan muslin dress' with no trousers or underwear, their very uniforms were designed by the experimenters to communicate degradation.[16] They wore rubber clogs with a heavy chain locked around one ankle, making their movements awkward, and women's nylon

[11] Höß, *Commandant*, p. 75.

[12] Zimbardo, P., *The Lucifer Effect: How Good People Turn Evil* (London, 2007); Browning, C. R., *Ordinary Men: Reserve Police Battalion 101 and the Final Solution in Poland* (London, 2002 [1991]), pp. 167–9; Bauman, Z., *Modernity and the Holocaust* (Cambridge, 2000 [1989]), pp. 166–7; Waller, J., *Becoming Evil: How Ordinary People Commit Genocide and Mass Murder* (Oxford, 2007), pp. 236–40.

[13] Craig Haney, Curt Banks, and Philip Zimbardo, 'A Study of Prisoners and Guards in a Simulated Prison', *Naval Research Reviews*, Vol. 9 (1973), pp. 1–17, here p. 12.

[14] Ross, L., and Nisbett, R. E., *The Person and the Situation: Perspectives of Social Psychology* (New York, 1991), p. 157.

[15] See also Welzer, H., *Täter: Wie aus ganz normalen Menschen Massenmörder werden* (Frankfurt am Main, 2005), p. 283 fn. 283. Zimbardo is on record as priming the guards as follows: 'We can create boredom. We can create a sense of frustration. We can create fear in them, to some degree. We can create a notion of arbitrariness that governs their lives, which are totally controlled by us, by the system, by you, me . . . They'll have no privacy at all, there will be constant surveillance—nothing they do will go unobserved. They will have no freedom of action. They will be able to do nothing and say nothing we don't permit . . . In general, what all this should create in them is a sense of powerlessness. We have total power in the situation. They have none'. Zimbardo, *Lucifer Effect*, p. 55. Waller is, then, considerably wide of the mark in contending that '[n]either group was given any instructions on how to behave': Waller, *Becoming Evil*, p. 236.

[16] Zimbardo, *Lucifer Effect*, p. 40; photograph of the 'prisoners' on p. 66.

stockings over their heads, supposedly as a simulation of shaven hair. The present chapter will argue that the visual properties of inmates play an important psychological role in the habitus of their captors, but the grotesque appearance of the SPE inmates scarcely corresponded to the normative prison situation its convenors claimed to be simulating. Even in Nazi concentration camps, prisoners did not wear heavy chains to sleep unless they were in punitive solitary confinement in the *Bunker*. The SPE inmates were also under constant surveillance, forbidden from talking during meals and in the exercise yard, and forced to address *one another* by number, rather than name, in their cells.[17] It is hardly surprising that as they became immersed in the environment—and everything suggests that they did—they felt degraded and humiliated, ceding the social psychological initiative to the more proactive and probing of the immaculately dressed, disinhibited guards. Their situation was more akin to an Orwellian nightmare than even the most unreconstructed of Western penal institutions.

This introduces the second, related, objection. Spurred on by a distorted situation, these subjects were being encouraged to act out an understanding of the 'role' of the prison guard marked by the embattled campus values of the early 1970s.[18] For his critics, Zimbardo's priming of their behaviour amounts to a kind of unethical entrapment, even puppetry.[19] In an analogous experiment conducted with the BBC in 2001, the social psychologists Stephen Reicher and S. Alexander Haslam created a less engineered simulation of the prison situation.[20] Male volunteers were assigned on the basis of representative cognitive variables to groups of prisoners and guards. The prisoners in this experiment were attired conventionally and not subjected to the exaggerated regimen of the SPE. In this very different cultural context, and with less intrusive experimenters, the 'guards' by no means identified reflexively with their roles. On the contrary, they 'felt (and were) weak, inconsistent, and ineffective as a group'.[21] The prisoners did not experience themselves as depersonalized or pathologized in their situation: on the contrary they were able to exercise an increasingly dominant influence on the culture of the simulated prison.

It is difficult to avoid the conclusion that the experimenters' interventions in the SPE violate its universal claim as a situational explanation of institutional tyranny.[22] Intended as a liberal critique of the corrosive effects of incarceration, it

---

[17] Zimbardo, *Lucifer Effect*, p. 44.

[18] They were even given mirror sunglasses from the 1967 film *Cool Hand Luke*.

[19] See the acrimonious exchange between Zimbardo and the convenors of the BBC's prison 'experiment' in the pages of the *British Journal of Social Psychology*. Stephen Reicher and S. Alexander Haslam, 'Rethinking the Psychology of Tyranny: The BBC Prison Study', *British Journal of Social Psychology* (2006), Vol. 45, pp. 1–40; Philip Zimbardo, 'On the Psychology of Imprisonment: Alternative Perspectives from the Laboratory and TV Studio', *British Journal of Social Psychology* (2006), Vol. 45, pp. 47–53; Reicher and Haslam, 'Response. Debating the Psychology of Tyranny: Fundamental Issues of Theory, Perspective, and Science', *British Journal of Social Psychology*, Vol. 45, pp. 55–63. It must be said that Zimbardo does not come out well from the exchange.

[20] Haslam and Reicher, 'Rethinking', p. 11.

[21] Haslam and Reicher, 'Rethinking', p. 15.

[22] Not to mention Zimbardo's later judicial attempt to use the SPE, barely modulated, to account for the abuses by US service personnel in Abu Ghraib in Iraq: summarized in Zimbardo, *Lucifer*, pp. 324–442.

better exposes the potential for engineering cruelty through leadership and permissive environment. Rather paradoxically, this preserves some of its explanatory force for institutional violence in Dachau. First, Zimbardo's heavy-handed interventions mirror, in a much milder form, the exhortations and command culture in the camp: from Malsen-Ponickau's motivational address to the early Dachau SS through to the ideological and behavioural reinforcers noted in previous chapters. Second, the behaviour of the SPE guards reminds us once again of the potential contribution of a malevolent theatricality in an institutional setting. As has been seen, this was visible in the conduct of Dachau sentries and, even more so, the commandant's staff.

Perhaps the most striking theme common to the three studies outlined above—Goffman, the SPE, and the BBC experiment—is the extent to which the habitus of institutional personnel is shaped by the status of the inmates. This status is defined both internally, in the rules and customs of the institution, and externally, in norms and values drawn from its broader cultural context. It is important nevertheless to reiterate that the social field facilitates, rather than instigates, the conduct of personnel. With this in mind, the following will consider this relational property at Dachau in greater depth, in the devaluation of the concentration camp inmate and its impact on what the social psychologist Harald Welzer terms the perpetrators' 'frame of reference'.[23]

## Framing the Inmate

The pre-war concentration camps played a highly visible role in the progressive exclusion of outsiders from the People's Community and its universe of moral obligation.[24] The concentration camp inmate in this sense came to embody—and to unite—the political, social, and racial ills supposedly besetting German society. Indeed, like the camps themselves, he or she was a symbol of the ongoing presence *of* those very ills. This broader societal stigmatization of concentration camp imprisonment complemented more localized processes of devaluation inside the camps. Two entangled and interdependent projects will be explored here. The first is the discursive pathologization of the Dachau inmate as a danger to community and guard alike. The second is the process of his visual and physical production whose outcome, for community and guard alike, worked to validate the first.

A progressive demonization of inmates can be traced in the Dachau regulations. While those of the Bavarian State Police have little to say about the prisoners, Wäckerle's 'special regulations', issued around the same time in May, take a far warier tone. The inmates are depicted as likely to engage in partisan subterfuge, to disobey orders, to attack guard personnel, and to engage in collective resistance.[25]

[23] Welzer, *Täter*, passim.
[24] Robert Gellately, *Backing Hitler: Consent and Coercion in Nazi Germany* (Oxford, 2001), pp. 51–69; Kim Wünschmann, 'Cementing the Enemy Category: Arrest and Imprisonment of German Jews in Nazi Concentration Camps, 1933–1938/39', *Journal of Contemporary History*, Vol. 45, No. 3 (July, 2010), pp. 576–600.
[25] IMT, Vol. XXXVI, Dokument 922-D, Sonderbestimmungen, May 1933.

Thus, in a gesture towards proportionality characteristic of Nazi persecution, the declaration of martial law in Dachau stems from the dangerous nature of its inmates. Eicke's regulations of October 1933 mark a further sharpening of tone.[26] Here the prisoners appear as wily, perfidious, and above all fanatical enemies of everything German, bitterly beholden to Marxism or liberalism, as unscrupulous agitators, inveterate plotters, and mutineers. They are warned that any stepping out of line 'will be dealt with by your own methods', a vivid example of the ongoing myth of commensurate violence. The direct correlation in these regulations between the political security of the Nazi regime, and the demonization of the prisoners, was by no means anomalous. After all, ran another narrative that was to endure throughout the Third Reich, reformed prisoners had been released by now. Those remaining after the *Führer's* magnanimous amnesties were an obstinate and dangerously distilled insurrectionary threat.[27] As such, in a self-referential, even circular, argumentation characteristic of the concentration camps, the fact *of* the inmates' exclusion became the rationale for continued, ever more vigilant, exclusion.

Eicke continued to invoke and refine his construct of diabolical prisoners throughout the pre-war period. Some of the formulations from his Dachau School are preserved in Höß's memoirs:

> out there, beyond the wire, the enemy is lurking: he is watching all your doings in order to profit from your weaknesses. Do not therefore display any weakness, show the enemies of the state your teeth![28] . . .
>
> It was not for nothing that they wore the death's head badge and always kept their weapons loaded! They were the only soldiers who, even in peacetime, faced the enemy every hour of the day and night—the enemy behind the wire.[29]

The *Totenkopf* guard Hans B. recalled of his training as late as 1937 that 'again and again the dangerousness of the job was emphasized'.[30] In the same year Himmler told the Wehrmacht that no service in the Third Reich was 'more devastating and strenuous for the troops than that of guarding villains and criminals' and that the camps' guard towers were fitted with machine guns 'so that every attempted mass revolt—which one must always reckon with from such people—can be crushed immediately'.[31] Höβ believed these narratives had been internalized by guards, and himself imparts in the manner of a bold insight and confession that, contrary to Eicke's depictions, he felt that the majority of the prisoners were 'harmless and peaceable men'.[32] An element of cognitive dissonance may have been at work here, for the SS did not consider itself immoral: quite the contrary, it held itself to be honourable and 'decent'. Recent scholarship has stressed that Nazi perpetrators

---

[26] BAB, R3001/21167, Dienstvorschriften für die Begleitposten und Gefangenenbewachung, 1 October 1933, ss. 62–9.

[27] Schecher, 'Rückblick', pp. 97–100. See also Himmler's speech to Wehrmacht in January 1937: IMT, Vol. XXIX, Dokument 1922-A, January 1937, ss. 219.

[28] Höß, *Commandant*, p. 236.     [29] Höß, *Commandant*, p. 68.

[30] In Rolf Michaelis, *Die Waffen SS: Mythos und Wirklichkeit* (Berlin, 2006), p. 310.

[31] IMT, Vol. XXIX, Dokument 1922-A, January 1937, s. 222.

[32] Höß, *Commandant*, p. 78.

often framed and perceived their actions in idealistic moral terms.[33] The virtuous self-conception of the concentration camp SS should not be underestimated. As the historian Claudia Koonz points out, 'the road to Auschwitz was paved with righteousness'.[34]

The importance of the myth of the lethality of the concentration camp inmate is perhaps best illustrated by the response to the one pre-war instance in which a guard did indeed 'fall' on duty. This exception, in the SS universe, endorsed the rule. The incident occurred at Buchenwald in May 1938. Two prisoners managed to overpower a guard, beat him to death with a shovel, and make a bid for freedom. Himmler and Eicke seized on this isolated event with alacrity and a barely concealed sense of excited vindication. What Goebbels had achieved with the martyring of Horst Wessel in 1930, the SS emulated with SS *Rottenführer* Albert Kallweit. The reportage in *Das Schwarze Korps* was particularly lurid, indignant but not surprised that two of the 'subhumans' guarded by the SS in the camps had behaved in this murderous fashion:

> He died for us!
>
> On 13 May 1938 SS *Rottenführer* Albert Kallweit of the 3rd SS Death's Head Standarte 'Thüringen', while doing his duty at a lonely post in the Thüringen Forest, fell victim to an insidious, cowardly attack . . . While the German nation is peacefully going about its daily work, the SS man of the Death's Head unit is permanently in contact with the enemy.[35]

The *Thüringer Gauzeitung* drew obliging parallels between Kallweit's demise and his father's death at the front in the Great War, casting both as martyrs in 'the eternal struggle of good and evil'.[36] In Dachau, too, the reverberations of the event were soon felt. On 14 May, Hübsch reports, a platoon of Dachau SS guards armed with carbines marched into the camp and trained their guns menacingly onto the prisoners.[37] Sentries minding external work details no longer kept rifles over their shoulders, but in ostentatious readiness under their arms. Himmler took the opportunity presented by his deceased guard to write to the Minister of Justice, Franz Gürtner, using the incident to indemnify the brutal and murderous treatment meted out in the concentration camps, as well as the shooting of two further prisoners in the aftermath.[38] The value of the incident as propaganda for the SS assumed an international dimension following the escape of one of the fugitives across the Czech border. The Nazis demanded his extradition, which was granted in

[33] Koonz, *Nazi Conscience*, passim; Welzer, *Täter*, pp. 37–63; Gross, *Anständig geblieben*. The Auschwitz survivor Elie Cohen made the same point in the psychoanalytical terminology of the SS 'super-ego'. Elie A. Cohen, *Human Behaviour in the Concentration Camp* (London, 1988 [1954]), pp. 231–3. The concept of 'decency' in the SS will be explored in Chapter 5 of this book.
[34] Koonz, *Nazi Conscience*, p. 3.
[35] *Das Schwarze Korps*, 26 May 1938. See also Himmler's letter to Reich Minister of Justice Gürtner of 16 May 1938, printed in Goeschel and Wachsmann, *Nazi Concentration Camps*, p. 435.
[36] *Thüringer Gauzeitung*, 18 May 1938. My thanks to Paul Moore for this reference.
[37] Hübsch, 'Insel', pp. 82–3.
[38] Goeschel and Wachsmann, *Nazi Concentration Camps*, p. 261.

December 1938. In the febrile atmosphere following the Munich agreement, Peter Forster's subsequent execution was widely reported in the international press.[39]

That Kallweit's murderers were respectively a 'professional criminal' and a political prisoner in protective custody was in many ways felicitous for the SS narrative of the pathological inmate. *Das Schwarze Korps* opined that on both their faces, 'Nature' had written 'crime'.[40] The notion that criminality was hereditary and biologically determined long predated Nazism and was part of the discourse of 'racial hygiene' that informed the eugenic legislation of the Third Reich.[41] It was taken up with great enthusiasm by the SS and given ever greater prominence from the mid-1930s. Bolstered by Himmler's takeover of the German police in 1936, the organization presented itself as a 'state protection corps' defending the German racial body against toxins of all political, social, and racial strains. With this increasingly essentialist and biological tinge, the terms 'enemies of the state', 'criminals', and 'subhumans' became interchangeable with 'inmates' in SS discourse.[42] All concentration camp prisoners, after all, had placed themselves outside the national community, suggestive in itself of an underlying pathology. As Himmler remarked to his audience of Wehrmacht officers, 'none of them has been put there unjustly. They are the dregs of humanity . . . a demonstration of the laws of heredity and race . . . a crowd of racially worthless scum' (see Figure 4.1).[43]

### Producing the Inmate

The framing of the inmates as a toxic, unitary other was complemented and validated by more tangible processes of physical, visual production. Here too, Dachau was part—and beneficiary—of a broader social and institutional context. Most prisoners spent at least a few days in detention in Stadelheim, Eichstätt, or the Ettstraße police prison before transportation to the camp; some spent many years in judicial confinement and were brought to Dachau on release from prisons and penitentiaries as part of Nazi 'corrections' of legal sentences (see Chapter 6). Although physical abuse elsewhere in the web of Nazi persecution was less prevalent than in the camps, inadequate food provision and psychological stress contributed to eroding the resilience of the inmates on their path to the camp. Particularly in the early years, protective custody prisoners had to reckon with abuse from SA and SS auxiliary police during their arrest and transport to the camps. High-profile

[39] Paul Moore, 'German Popular Opinion on the Nazi Concentration Camps, 1933–1939', (PhD Dissertation, University of London, 2010), pp. 200–2.

[40] *Das Schwarze Korps*, 26 May 1938.

[41] For a succinct summary see Jeremy Noakes, 'Nazism and Eugenics: The Background to the Nazi Sterilization Law of 14 July 1933', in Roger Bullen et al. (eds), *Ideas into Politics: Aspects of European History 1880–1950* (London, 1984), pp. 75–94.

[42] Ulrich Herbert, 'Von der Gegnerbekämpfung zur "rassischen Generalprävention". "Schutzhaft" und Konzentrationslager in der Konzeption der Gestapo-Führung 1933–1939', in Herbert, Orth, and Dieckmann (eds), *Die nationalsozialistischen Konzentrationslager*, pp. 60–81. More broadly on Himmler's project to unite all toxic elements into a 'subhuman' coalition, see the excellent discussion in Longerich, *Himmler*, pp. 192–251.

[43] IMT, Vol. XXIX, Dokument 1922-A, January 1937, ss. 219.

**Figure 4.1** SS *Reichsführer* Heinrich Himmler surveys a prisoner in Dachau. Bundesarchiv, image 152-11-12.

prisoners were often paraded through towns decked in sandwich boards announcing their misdeeds and destination. Here the pre-modern customs of spectacle and pillory were revived and repackaged as a 'consensus-building exercise in *Schadenfreude*'.[44] The more fortunate individual prisoners and small groups were guarded by regular police-men and prison officials and generally not mistreated physically en route.

The experiences of the *Anschluß* prisoners in 1938 were a particularly grotesque exception. To ensure the docility of these first mass international transports in the history of the concentration camps, the Dachau SS developed a bespoke pro-gramme of preparatory terror that has been documented vividly by the Austrian memoirists. The Death's Head troops came to Vienna in person to pick up the pris-oners from the Westbahnhof. Having already been subjected to a public violence and humiliation which shocked even seasoned observers of Nazism,[45] the prison-ers were herded onto the trains with great brutality. Throughout the eleven-hour train journey to Munich they were forced to stare unblinkingly into the carriage lights, or into the eyes of the man opposite.[46] Meanwhile incidental humiliations were enacted by drunken guards on alternating two hour shifts. Individual inmates were beaten and introduced to the principle of 'looping'. Carriages were forced to perform exercises, to slap or to spit at one another. Bettelheim received a bayonet wound to the face.[47] The net death toll in the transports from Vienna to Dachau

[44] Moore, 'Popular Opinion', p. 33.
[45] Gedye, *Fallen Bastions*, pp. 308–17; Shirer, *Rise and Fall*, pp. 351–2.
[46] Bettelheim, *Informed Heart*, pp. 124–7; Neurath, *Society*, pp. 252–3.
[47] Bettelheim, *Informed Heart*, p. 125.

in the spring and summer of 1938 was twelve, nine of whom were Jewish.[48] Even after months inside the camp, Austrian inmates continued to discuss the overnight train journey from Vienna to Dachau as the high water mark of their suffering at the hands of the SS. There can be little doubt that this was the product of a concerted plan, rather than an opportunistic response on the part of the Dachau guards to a permissive situation. As Bettelheim recalled, when thousands of the Austrian inmates were transported to Buchenwald six months or so later, they viewed the prospect of another train journey with sickening dread. But no one was injured on this one: the SS knew that seasoned concentration camp inmates did not require an induction.[49]

Regardless of the mode of transport, inmates faced initiation processes on arrival designed to cement the power relations in Dachau. Prisoners from all early camps recalled improvised degradation rituals.[50] What had started in 1933 as a biographical rite of vengeance soon commended itself as an important management technique in its own right. The Dachau SS were aware of the psychological significance of the prisoners' initial encounter with the camp regime and devoted resources accordingly. The first hours in Dachau have a prominent place in all inmate testimony and memoirs: much depended on how prepared the individuals were for what lay in store.[51] Sometimes groups of prisoners had been primed by their escorts to respond to SS instructions without hesitation and to be prepared to run.[52] Prepared or not, on disembarkation they ran a gauntlet of bawling Dachau SS, who clubbed and kicked them as sentries nearby shook with laughter.[53] The situation understandably appeared chaotic and irrational to the inmates, but for the SS it was part of a calibrated process of destroying the vestiges of sovereignty among arrivals, of introducing them to the concentration camp prisoner's 'condition of constant punishability'.[54] After this, reaching the Dachau protective custody compound often seemed like a sanctuary, but they were soon disabused of this notion. The malevolent theatre continued with a hateful address from the camp commandant or compound leader, in which the so-called 'order to shoot' (*Schießbefehl*) took pride of place.[55] The 'order to shoot', a legacy of Eicke's regulations, concerned the duty of the Dachau sentry to use his rifle in the event of a range of inmate infractions. A selection of these were relayed to the fresh arrivals with the invariant suffix 'will be shot'.

Aggregate violence and threats towards the arrivals were sometimes followed by calculated and exemplary individualized humiliation: it was at this point that

[48] Wünschmann, 'Jewish Prisoners', p. 175.
[49] Bettelheim, *Informed Heart*, pp. 124–5. Bettelheim added that 'initiated' prisoners among 'new' groups were also generally left alone by the SS on the inward journey.
[50] Goeschel and Wachsmann, *The Nazi Concentration Camps*, pp. 29–48.
[51] See the psychonanalytical discussion of this point in Cohen, *Human Behaviour*, pp. 115–24.
[52] Kay, *Dachau*, p. 30; Wiener Library Report 227, s. 1.
[53] Burkhard, *Tanz Mal*, p. 42; Ecker, 'Hölle', pp. 24–6; Neurath, *Society*, p. 248; WL 227.
[54] Sofsky, *Order*, p. 215.
[55] Detailed descriptions in Röder, *Nachtwache*, pp. 12–14; Hübsch, 'Insel', p. 11; Viktor Matejka, *Widerstand ist Alles: Notizen eines Unorthodoxen* (Vienna, 1984), pp. 78–82; Neurath, *Society*, p. 251.

a certain rhetorical heterogeneity towards the prisoners made its first appearance. Not yet assigned to a Dachau inmate category, newcomers were asked what their jobs had been and why they had been brought to the camp:

> The SS man begins to ask questions. 'What is your profession?' . . . One man is beaten for having been a worker—'So you are a Communist, you criminal, you!' Another for not having been a worker—'So you enjoyed life at a desk while others did the hard work!' One is kicked for having been an intellectual—'Perhaps you believe that you're somebody? We'll disillusion you. Here you are nobody'. Another receives the same kick for having been nobody—'So you have been loafing around while we have been working!' To have been sent as a professional criminal is reason for getting beaten. Not to know why one was sent to camp is also reason for mistreatment. To be rich is bad, but to confess poverty is not good either, because of course that would be a lie.[56]

This torment, the climax of introductory theatre, had a number of social functions. It flagged the arbitrary and unbound nature of the power of the SS over the prisoners, for there were of course no 'right' answers. It was an opportunity for the perpetrator to display his ready wit, stock of replies, and virtuosity in crisp, efficient violence to his comrades. And, above all, it ensured that any nascent solidarity or social identity within the group was shattered.[57] Neurath notes that a group of 300 Austrian gypsies, whose violent anti-establishment culture and history of fighting with the police led prisoners and SS alike to assume they would put up resistance, was likewise quickly shocked into apathy.[58]

Physical violence and humiliation were followed by the bureaucracy of the Political Department. One prisoner recalled that nowhere in his life did he encounter as much 'red tape' as in Dachau.[59] Each of the admissions procedures identified by Goffman as characteristic of 'total institutions' was present in Dachau and other camps, but here they assumed a predictably malevolent quality.[60] By the late 1930s, even the photographing procedure had acquired a seemingly superfluous malice; many prisoners report the use of a chair with a remote controlled needle jabber in the seat to eject the photographee without the tiresome effort of a verbal instruction.[61] The arrivals were assigned prisoner numbers—in keeping with the bureaucratic orderliness even in early Dachau, prisoner no. 1 was allocated to the trainee lawyer Claus Bastian by alphabetical order.[62] Inmates were also divested of other markers of individuality; hair styles, facial hair, possessions, and clothing. This was a key stage in the physical production of the anonymous inmate 'other'.

---

[56] Neurath, *Society*, p. 13; detailed descriptions of earlier forms of this process see Beimler, *Four Weeks*, pp. 21–4; Schecher, 'Rückblick', pp. 52–3.

[57] See the discussion in Sofsky, *Order*, pp. 82–7.        [58] Neurath, *Society*, pp. 254–5.

[59] Karst, *Beasts of the Earth*, p. 42.

[60] Goffman, *Asylums*, pp. 25–6: 'taking a life history, photographing, weighing, fingerprinting, assigning numbers, searching, listing personal possessions for storage, undressing, bathing, disinfecting, haircutting, issuing institutional clothing, instructing as to rules, and assigning to quarters . . . shaped and coded into an object that can be fed into the administrative machinery of the establishment, to be worked on smoothly by routine operations'.

[61] Kay, *Dachau*, pp. 53–4; Schecher, 'Rückblick', p. 116; Fred Pelican, *From Dachau to Dunkirk* (London, 1993), p. 12.

[62] Richardi, *Schule*, pp. 48–53.

Prisoners' hair seems to have been cut short from early on in Dachau, ostensibly on hygiene and security grounds, but also as a means of degradation and of enhancing distance from the guards who often knew them personally.[63] Until the issuing of the standard concentration camp striped clothing in the summer of 1938, Dachau prisoners wore a medley of uniforms, either produced in the camp or obsolescent attire from the Weimar-era police and army.[64] Redolent of the sartorial semiotics of the SPE, it was a particular enthusiasm of the SS to ensure that new inmates were assigned grotesque or ill-fitting uniforms. Beyond the obvious visual degradation, this made their movements tiring and their gait awkward, likely to attract the attention of the sentries. In time, they would be able to trade these for better-fitting garments, but for now, clean and misallocated attire—along with high inmate numbers—marked them out for the particular chicanery reserved for 'new arrivals' (*Neuzugänger*). These prisoners needed to learn fast the overriding and hard-won wisdom for staying alive in Dachau: *nicht aufzufallen* (not to 'stand out').

The final process of initiation to Dachau, of the resocialization from new arrival to inmate, also staked a priority claim on Dachau SS personnel resources: special manual labour. Right from the early months, new arrivals were allocated to a 'newcomer company' (*Zugangskompanie*).[65] The newcomer company always worked inside the camp perimeter on exhausting work commandos. One benefit of this, for the SS, was that there was no potential public gaze to inhibit violence. From the mid-1930s it was standard practice for newcomers to be assigned to the gravel pit work detail under the particularly vicious *Kapo* Sterzer, a career criminal who evidently took pride in his fearsome reputation for violence.[66] While this sequence of processes varied over time and was the product of trial and error by the SS, it appeared to prisoners as an elaborate and diabolical programme. As Neurath puts it:

> After a few days with the officers or Sterzer, the new men are assumed to have learned their lesson. They are now expected to behave as depersonalised numbers with no more thought of resistance left in them. They are now attached to regular working groups, like the old prisoners. The initiation is over.[67]

Forced physical labour remained central to the discursive framing and physical production of the Dachau prisoner. Work structured daily life in Dachau. The cynical and mendacious aphorism 'Work Brings Freedom' welded onto the Dachau gates was adopted by a number of later concentration camps, including Auschwitz under Höß. From the perspective of the prisoners, of course, the motto was nothing more

---

[63] Judging from photographs, hair was kept short rather than shaved in the early years. There were differences between camps in this regard. See Wachsmann, 'KL: A History of the Nazi Concentration Camps', ch. 2.

[64] Paul Neurath, Interview with Christian Fleck and Albert Müller, 12 July 1989. Cited in Christian Fleck and Albert Müller, 'Bruno Bettelheim and the Concentration Camps', *Journal of the History of the Behavioral Sciences*, Vol. 33, No. 1 (Winter 1997), pp. 1–37; Heilig, *Men Crucified*, p. 15.

[65] Richardi, *Schule*, pp. 72–4.

[66] On Sterzer see especially Wallner, *By Order of the Gestapo*, p. 59.

[67] Neurath, *Society*, p. 249.

**Figure 4.2** Prisoners toil at hard manual labour under oversight of an SS NCO, May 1933. Bundesarchiv, image 152-01-26.

than a mocking torment.[68] For the SS, the malleable concept of work provided the principal site of terror against the prisoners and embedded the various narratives of punishment, deterrence, and re-education operative in the framing of the camps.[69] Forced labour always formed an important aspect of propaganda about Dachau, as when the *Dachauer Zeitung*'s piece in May 1933 rejoiced that the hubristic revolutionaries of 1919 were now 'performing honest work'. Wäckerle's internal regulations, too, committed every prisoner to 'labour service whose duration is determined by the commandant'.[70] It would be a defining principle of the Nazi concentration camp system right to the end that formal exemption from labour was the greatest privilege, reserved in practice only for the very sick, and a small number of *Kapos* and prominent prisoners.[71] This group apart, the fact that the SS was the only party which did not have to perform manual work in the camps was another marker of the chasm between prisoners and guards.

[68] The 'Dachau Song' composed by the Anschluß Austrian inmates Jura Soyfer and Herbert Zipper in 1938 (darkly) lampooned the motto: 'We have indeed learned the motto of Dachau, and it made us hard as steel; Be a man, comrade, stay a man, comrade; do a good job, get to it, comrade, for work, work makes us free!'. Full text at <http://www.gedenkstaettenpedagogik-bayern.de/dachaulied> [accessed 18 October 2014].

[69] Jane Caplan, 'Political Detention and the Origin of Concentration Camps in Nazi Germany, 1933–1935/6', in Neil Gregor (ed.), *Nazism, War, and Genocide: Essays in Honour of Jeremy Noakes* (Exeter, 2005), p. 33.

[70] On forced labour in prisons and penitentiaries, see Wachsmann, *Hitler's Prisons*, pp. 95–102.

[71] Sofsky, *Order*, p. 185.

Generally in the first years of the concentration camp system, labour was a vehicle for torment rather than production. It was the context and pretext for disciplinary power rather than the prosocial redemption trumpeted by propaganda. It furnished the guard personnel with a rehabilitative, self-righteous rhetoric and virtuous self-conception. Heavy manual labour was the norm, reflecting the principal, long entrenched in the German prison system, that hard work was both punishment and effective deterrent.[72] Undermechanized work also assuaged the traditional concerns of the private sector about competition from inmate labour and, for camp guards, was ideally suited for the exercise of terror. It required little technical nous on their part and placed few practical, situational restraints on arbitrary violence.[73] Manual labour in details exposed supposed idlers, for a slower swing of a shovel 'stood out' and was, of course, a matter of subjective interpretation. Prisoners unfortunate during the distribution of tools at the start of work were in particular danger of being singled out as a 'loafer' that day.[74] In the era of the Dachau School, this bully labour took place primarily in the gravel pit, in heavy roller brigades, and in the so-called 'Moor Express' details. In the latter, groups of prisoners pulled enormous iron carts usually drawn by horses or tractors, a prime example of deliberate undermechanization (Figure 4.2).

Yet work is another sense in which Dachau should be regarded as pioneering in the SS camp system: the extent to which some inmate labour was used for productive, as well as disciplinary, purposes.[75] Even in 1933 more than 300 of the camp's prisoners were deployed in workshops to meet its internal demand for uniforms, clogs, and bedding. They also attended to the general maintenance of the camp: cooking, baking, laundry, carpentry. Mechanization came rather quickly to this area of Dachau and inmates endured long shifts in the workshops from seven in the morning until ten at night.[76] According to one memoirist, the demand for skilled labour in the workshops was such that protective custody prisoners in the regular penal system were poached for Dachau on this basis. He claims, in addition, to have seen correspondence from the Dachau commandant staff to one prisoner's wife admitting that although the inmate's conduct had been faultless, he could not be released as his skills were indispensable.[77] Sopade also believed these factors influenced releases from Dachau, but this is impossible to verify.[78]

For the SS, inmate labour also served the inestimable productive virtue of constructing the vast SS installation at Dachau. In the concentration camp system as a whole, the shift in emphasis from terror towards productivity in inmate labour is generally dated to April 1938, with the establishment of the SS limited company

---

[72] Wachsmann, *Hitler's Prisons*, pp. 97–8.

[73] See the insightful discussion in Sofsky, *Order*, pp. 187–91.

[74] Kogon, *Theory and Practice*, p. 89

[75] The best overall monograph, from a crowded field, on the deployment of concentration camp labour is Kaienburg, *Die Wirtschaft der SS* (Berlin, 2003); esp. pp. 114ff.

[76] Ecker, 'Die Hölle Dachau', p. 35; Neurath, *Society*, p. 36.

[77] Ecker, 'Die Hölle Dachau', p. 35.

[78] Sopade report on Dachau, May 1937. Printed in Goeschel and Wachsmann, *The Nazi Concentration Camps*, pp. 134–5.

**Figure 4.3** Command staff personnel oversee the reconstruction of the Dachau protective custody compound in June 1938. Throughout the camp system, construction work was more feared and lethal than production commandos. Bundesarchiv, image 152-23-07A.

'German Earth and Stoneworks' (DESt).[79] At Dachau, however, the serial development of internal workshops, construction of the SS training camp, and rebuilding of the concentration camp proper (see Figure 4.3) in 1937/8 meant that productivity was a salient concern throughout the era of the Dachau School. From the spring of 1938, too, a large plantation was built under infernal work conditions on the eastern side of the camp's site to grow medicinal herbs and domestic substitutes for imported spices such as pepper.[80] This unyielding programme contributed to Dachau's lethality: generally in the SS concentration camp system construction work details—with poorer safety and more manual processes—were more feared and lethal than production commandos.[81] Nevertheless, as recent historiography has stressed, productivity and persecution were far from mutually exclusive in the camps.[82] The call for output was a rationalization for remorseless pressure on the prisoners, for squeezing ever more working hours from their day. During the reconstruction of the protective custody compound between July 1937 and May 1938, inmates recalled not a single day free from work except Christmas Day.[83] Loritz inspected progress almost daily

---

[79] Wachsmann, 'Dynamics', pp. 24–5; Kaienburg, *Die Wirtschaft der SS*, pp. 455–551.

[80] For detail, see Robert Sigel, 'Heilkräuterkulturen im KZ: Die Plantage in Dachau', in *Dachauer Hefte* 4 (1988), pp. 164–73.

[81] Wachsmann, 'KL: A History of the Nazi Concentration Camps', ch. 9.

[82] See the historiographical discussion in Jens-Christian Wagner, 'Work and Extermination in the Concentration Camps', in Caplan and Wachsmann, *Concentration Camps*, pp. 126–48.

[83] Schecher, 'Rückblick', p. 72; Alfred Hübsch report (*c.* 1960). Printed in Goeschel and Wachsmann, *The Nazi Concentration Camps*, p. 90.

and introduced 'lightening punishments' (*Blitzstrafen*) for inmates he deemed not to be working ardently enough, circumventing the usual bureaucratic conventions for formal punishments.[84]

Forced labour of all kinds marked and depleted the body of the Dachau prisoner, another of its contributions to his visual production. As in all concentration camps, the most onerous work details tended to comprise new or particularly stigmatized prisoners, since more experienced political inmates were generally able to extricate themselves from these jobs over time.[85] Those inmates not accustomed to tools and manual labour soon bore its marks. As Neurath, a doctoral student, recalled:

> The skin on our hands and shoulders was still tender. Unaccustomed to pickaxe, shovel, and wheelbarrow, our hands were covered with blisters within a few hours. Since they were not cared for, the blisters burst and the skin came off. Dust and dirt got into the open wounds. They began to fester and large sores developed . . . Some of us were lucky, and no serious infections developed. Others, whose wounds grew worse, finally had their hands bandaged, but they had to keep working. Two of our group each lost a hand within the first few weeks.[86]

It was difficult for ordinary prisoners to get treatment in the Dachau infirmary, harder still to secure a temporary exemption from work on medical grounds. To access the infirmary, which contained just a few dozen beds for an institution with thousands of inmates, one often had, in the mirthless prisoner parlance, 'to report carrying your head under one arm'.[87] Even 'invalids' and very elderly prisoners were required to carry out lighter manual work throughout the day.[88] The combination of tough physical labour with poor-quality tools, perfunctory medical provision, and the extremities of the Bavarian climate inevitably took a toll on the bodies of the prisoners.

This was much aggravated by the meagre food and water provision in Dachau. Although the situation seems to have been rather better than in other camps, and immeasurably preferable to the wartime era, in the pre-war period inmates were still marked by invariant nutrition wholly inadequate for heavy manual labour. The quantity and quality of food seem to have declined sharply in the mid 1930s. The usual fare was monotonous, sloppy and tasteless soups and stews. Dachau's prisoner canteen, which offered butter, biscuits, sugar, and various tinned goods did to an extent mitigate this, while ensuring a thick profit margin for the SS.[89] But due to the hard work most prisoners were constantly hungry and the poor nutritional value of the food left them vulnerable to illnesses and complications. Prisoners who spent extended periods of time in the camp invariably lost weight: the case documented by an exile publication of a young man whose body weight fell from 79 kg to 49 kg during two years of protective custody in Dachau was grimly typical.[90] This was lost neither on the SS nor the broader public, who could recognize

---

[84] Riedel, *Ordnungshüter*, p 189.       [85] Kogon, *Theory and Practice*, p. 82.
[86] Neurath, *Society*, p. 27.       [87] Kalmar, *Zeit*, p. 88.
[88] Neurath, *Society*, pp. 35–7.       [89] Neurath, *Society*, pp. 42–3.
[90] Goeschel and Wachsmann, *The Nazi Concentration Camps*, p. 199.

released concentration camp prisoners by their gauntness.[91] One young Czech man recalled the pitiful state of his father after imprisonment in Dachau in the late 1930s: 'a skeleton. He wasn't ill but he was just very, very thin'.[92] A former SS man was denounced to the Munich police for discussing the physical condition of Dachau inmates in his new, civilian workplace. He admitted to having 'told my colleagues at work that if anyone arrives in the camp with a fat belly, he loses it in an astonishingly short period' but defended himself on the basis that this was 'universally known among the Dachau population and can be heard in every tavern'.[93] Alfred Laurence was shocked to see that his temples were grey when his hair grew back after release from Dachau in 1937. He was twenty-six years old.[94]

Physical depletion thus branded the body of the Dachau prisoner as a concentration camp inmate, taking its place alongside other the visual markers discussed above. It exposed less denuded prisoners to the attention and predation of the SS as newcomers or purported exploiters of their fellow inmates. Inevitably, it also degraded the psychic resilience of inmates, who found themselves embroiled in endless conversations and squabbling about food. The fantasy of the first meal after release was staple of camp discourse and memoirists remark that they had experienced this as degrading at the time.[95] The importance of food to daily life ensured that it also became a tool of domination for the SS. Thus new arrivals were often denied food, or given only half rations.[96] The punitive withdrawal of food (*Essenentzug*) was a much-feared sanction throughout the camp's existence. Eicke's regulations were particularly draconian in this regard, restricting inmates in solitary confinement to a diet of bread and water with warm food every four days. An important consequence of all this was to reinforce and magnify the distinction and distance between the inmates and the 'well-fed, broad shouldered, ruddy-faced lads', as one put it, who guarded them.[97] The SS, which sought to recruit only tall young men, must have appeared to many prisoners even bigger and more powerful physically than it was.[98]

This, then, was the baseline condition for the Dachau inmate. He was discursively pathologized, physically degraded, denuded of the markers of his individuality, thrust into and constitutive of a situation which exposed him to the arbitrary violence of SS guards. The outcome, and function, of such processes of devaluation and exclusion is often described in the vocabulary of 'dehumanization'.[99] In

[91] Moore, 'Popular Opinion', pp. 87–8; 92.
[92] IWM Interview, Catalogue Number 18573, Reel 1.
[93] SAM, Sta 4849, s. 10. My thanks to Paul Moore for bringing this document to my attention.
[94] Alfred Laurence, 'Out of the Night', p. 141.
[95] Neurath, *Society*, pp. 41–2; Röder, *Nachtwache*, p. 71; Bettelheim, *Informed*, p. 229.
[96] Zámečnik, *Dachau*, p. 54.     [97] Schecher, 'Rückblick', s. 5.
[98] Bettelheim discusses the tendency of some prisoners to inflate the SS into superhuman beings at great length, but does not consider this physical dimension: Bettelheim, *Informed*, pp. 213–21.
[99] Herbert Kelman, 'Violence Without Moral Restraint: Reflections on the Dehumanization of Victims and Victimizers', *Journal of Social Issues*, Vol. 29, No. 4, (1973), pp. 25–61; Albert Bandura, 'Moral Disengagement in the Perpetration of Inhumanities', *Personality and Social Psychology Review*, Vol. 3, No. 3 (1999), pp. 193–209; Zimbardo, *Lucifer*, pp. 307–16; Waller, *Becoming Evil*, pp. 205–11; Tzvetan Todorov, *Facing the Extreme: Moral Life in the Concentration Camps* (London, 1999), pp. 158–78; Staub, *Roots of Evil*, pp. 100–10.

terms of perpetrator violence, the concept proposes that recognition of the shared humanity of others has a powerful inhibiting and morally censoring effect on social interaction. Conversely, as its leading theorist puts it, when these same others are deprived of their individuality and human status, 'the principles of morality no longer apply to them'.[100] In the context of National Socialism, the nadir of these processes would be reached at Auschwitz, whose inmates were tattooed with numbers and herded, exploited, and exterminated at will. The pitiful figures of the camp's 'drowned' *Muselmänner*, its emaciated, apathetic, shuffling corpses, haunt the historical consciousness. For the perpetrators, this was a dialectical process: by inducing such behaviour they validated their superior world view and, in turn, their treatment of these inmates. Höß's comments on the 'selfishness' of the starved Soviet POWs in the camp, 'no longer human beings' but 'animals, who sought only food', are notorious even in this grim field.[101]

Nevertheless, as ever the distinctions between the pre-war and wartime concentration camps need to be kept in mind. For all its misery and privation, *Muselmänner* were not a feature of pre-war Dachau. And the broader concept of 'dehumanization' seems less convincing here, where German (and often Bavarian) guards oversaw largely German (and often Bavarian) inmates. That the Dachau School was structured on a distancing and othering of the inmates is not in doubt: we need only recall Malsen-Ponickau's exhortation to the early Dachau SS that they had not been assembled 'to treat these swine like human beings'. Nazi discourse abounded in such malevolent devaluations of its enemies, with the categorization of Communists as 'subhumans' widespread by 1933.[102] But, as has been seen, the early, defining violence in Dachau was profoundly biographical and anything but impersonal. As the social psychologist Johannes Lang argues, the framing and visual degradation of camp inmates bolstered the self-esteem of the perpetrators and the concept of 'dehumanization' probably masks more quotidian and relational operations of power and social distance.[103]

The 'dehumanization' of the Dachau inmates is perhaps better thought of as a perverse ideal, a cluster of cognitive and physical processes, than as an achieved or perceived condition. Certainly, the dichotomy between guard and inmate characteristic of SS discourse and much inmate literature disguises a liminal territory which was often highly unstable. The following section will explore some of the more intersubjective social transactions between guards and inmates in Dachau. The devaluation processes noted above set the profoundly disadvantageous and asymmetrical social field in which they took place. But by focusing on the occasions

[100] Kelman, 'Violence without Moral Restraint', p. 48.

[101] Höß, *Commandant*, pp. 123–4.

[102] See, for example, Diels, *Lucifer*, p. 194; Werner Schäfer, *Konzentrationslager Oranienburg: Das Anti-Braunbuch über das erste deutsche Konzentrationslager*, p. 162; more broadly, Evans, *Coming of the Third Reich*, pp. 331–4.

[103] Johannes Lang, 'Questioning Dehumanization: Intersubjective Dimensions of Violence in the Nazi Concentration and Death Camps', *Holocaust and Genocide Studies*, Vol. 24, No. 2 (Fall 2010), pp. 225–46. Lang's contention that his analysis can also be applied to the Nazi extermination camps is, however, questionable.

when the 'front' mentality preached by the Dachau School proved brittle, we can discern fragments of a complex social psychology otherwise obscured by the reductive tendencies of the historical record.

## Beyond Dehumanization

The emphasis in the curriculum of the Dachau School on the sustenance of distance from and indifference to the inmates has parallels with the customary preoccupation of military authorities with the danger of fraternization. Here interpersonal contact with members of an enemy group against whom soldiers have been indoctrinated is regarded as jeopardizing the state of moral disengagement conducive to military discipline and lethal violence. Eicke's Dachau service regulations warned guards that 'addressing as *Du* equals fraternization'. The guard was exhorted to be watchful but aloof, alert to the insidious and hypocritical entreaties of the inmates. As Höβ put it, unrepentantly, in his memoirs:

> Every prisoner tries to improve his lot and to make the conditions of his life more tolerable. He will exploit kindness and understanding. Unscrupulous prisoners will go to the limit and try, by evoking sympathy, to get the better of their guards . . . A single gesture of human understanding towards a strong-minded prisoner will often initiate a series of lapses on the part of the guard that can only end in the most severe punishment.[104]

Despite the many discursive and visual disfigurements imposed on the Dachau inmate, his subjective properties could still unsettle the resolution of the guard. His gaze, above all, might disturb the autonomy of SS power. Eyes, the prime vectors of non-verbal communication, were critical organs for the prisoners in Dachau. They learned to 'work with the eyes' (*mit den Augen arbeiten*), which meant conserving energy by moderating their pace of work according to the proximity of SS personnel.[105] They learned to 'keep the eyes wide open', to size up their immediate environment and thus avoid scenes of confrontation or looping which might escalate.[106] Yet, twinned with the camp injunction not to 'stand out' was another, apparently contradictory, principle: 'see nothing' or 'don't dare to notice'.[107] One of the greatest situational dangers for inmates was to be caught watching SS mistreatment of a fellow prisoners. This was perilous in two senses: it brought the immediate risk of being drawn into the violence, and the post-situational risk of being regarded by the perpetrator as a potential witness. For all the arbitrary terror in Dachau, its guards were not wholly insensitive to the potential for released prisoners to spread purported 'atrocity propaganda', nor to judicial complications.

---

[104] Höβ, *Commandant*, p. 73. For Eicke's orders see BAB, R3001/21167, Dienstvorschriften für die Begleitposten und Gefangenenbewachung, 1 October 1933, ss. 62–9.
[105] Schwarz, 'Wir Haben es nicht Gewusst', p. 196; Schecher, 'Rückblick', p. 79.
[106] DaA, A 3255, Polnische Häftling Hnaupek Walter Bericht, s. 8. This was part of Hnaupek's 'Philosophy of Life in the Camp'.
[107] Bettelheim, *Informed*, pp. 153–6.

As has been seen, not until 1940 did the camp SS win complete independence from the judiciary.

There was a difficult balance to be struck by inmates here between acquiring the knowledge of the camp and their immediate situation necessary to avoid 'standing out', and being seen to be unduly observant. Again, this might have seemed irrational to newcomers but was not to the SS, for whom it was part of the Dachau habitus, of the conventions of status and power. Bettelheim provides an interesting illustration:

> An SS man might seem to have gone berserk about what he viewed as some resistance or disobedience, and in this state beat up or even kill a prisoner. But in the midst of it he might call out a friendly 'well done' to a passing column who, having stumbled on the scene, would fall into a gallop, heads averted, so as to pass by as fast as possible without 'noticing'. Obviously their sudden break into running and their averted heads showed clearly that they had 'noticed': but that did not matter as long as they had also showed so clearly that they had accepted the command not to know what they were not supposed to know.[108]

To approach this contorted balance between being observant enough to avoid trouble, but not conspicuously watchful, the Dachau inmate needed to learn the art of the 'swift look' (*kurzer Blick*). Seasoned prisoners could spot new arrivals by their tendency to observe camp goings-on attentively.[109] Another vulnerability of the non-adapted inmate was his propensity to look and react visibly, which might be construed as evidence of internalization of the scene. Control over the principles of looking and looking away was part of the definition of status in Dachau. The SS reserved the right to determine what the inmates should watch. Perhaps the most striking and grotesque example was public corporal and, in the wartime era, capital punishment. An inmate caught by the SS averting his gaze might well himself be added to the line of victims.[110] Schecher reports an incident shortly after the arrival of the Austrians in 1938. The whipping block was brought out to the roll call square and the newcomers were forced to watch as luckless delinquents from their ranks were given twenty-five lashes each. A number of newer German prisoners, evidently from morbid curiosity, also decided to attend the event. They were somehow identified by the SS and added to the queue.[111] It was this arrogation by the SS of the right to decide what inmates should watch and remember which lent such resonance to the impulse of survivors to 'bear witness' to the horrors of the camps in their entirety.

In this testimony, inmates sometimes comment on the gaze and eyes of the SS personnel themselves. The 'animal-like' savagery of a block leader's eyes, the 'dimming' of another's as he trampled on an inmate, even a fleeting spark of compassion or despair: these take their place in the remembered visual landscape of the camp.[112] Kaspar Drexl, a block leader in Dachau until 1936, is said always to have

---

[108] Bettelheim, *Informed*, p. 154.　　　[109] Röder, *Nachtwache*, p. 15, pp. 44–5.
[110] Sofsky, *Order*, pp. 219–20; Hübsch, 'Insel', p. 82.
[111] Schecher, 'Rückblick', pp. 111–12.
[112] Respectively, Burkhard, *Tanz Mal*, p. 58; Neurath, *Society*, 74; Röder, *Nachtwache*, p. 260.

'entered the camp with his head to the ground, not once looking left or right, and departed in the same fashion'.[113] A number of memoirs report that direct eye contact with aggressor guards, while still on the whole best avoided, could create a mitigating intersubjective reaction. Neurath's first experience of looping during work came a few weeks into his time in Dachau. An SS officer decided that he had acted inappropriately to being yelled at and slapped his face:

> I decided to take it on the chin. I stood straight and stared into the officer's eyes. They are cowards. They can't bear you staring into their eyes. Stare an SS man in the eyes and he will behave like a dog when you stare into its eyes. The dog will bite you or howl at you or pull his tail in and get off. The SS man will either kick you or beat you, just to get rid of your eyes, or he will howl at you, 'Don't you dare look at me! (*Schau mich ja nicht an!*)'. This one hit me once more. I did not move but kept staring into his eyes. A third slap I took in the same manner. Then the dog pulled in his tail and went off.[114]

Neurath, characteristically, asserts that during this incident he had 'felt more like the observer of a psychological experiment than a victim in the hands of tormenters'.[115] Yet even the fearsome Hans Steinbrenner, it seems, struggled with eye contact. Hugo Burkhard was brought to Dachau in June 1933 and, as the only Jewish prisoner on his transport, was singled out on arrival by Steinbrenner as a 'rapist of Aryan maidens'. He was led off, kicked, punched, and bullwhipped, before being taken to the inmate infirmary by fellow prisoners to recover. When he came round groggily the next morning, Burkhard was horrified to see Steinbrenner standing over him:

> He just stared at me, without saying a word; this time I held his hard stare and looked back directly into his eyes; he hung his head and left my bed. What had taken place inside him? . . . As I later found out from my comrades, he could not bear the gaze of a *Häftling* and often got nervous and let his victim go . . . perhaps his guilty conscience tormented him.[116]

It is important when reading such material to resist any temptation to conceptualize confrontations in a concentration camp as some kind of 'duel', as Primo Levi put it, however unequal, between inmate and guard.[117] Survival in this arbitrary realm was not merely a matter of will and initiative. Generally, if stirred emotionally, the SS felt sorry for themselves for having to be so tough, and resented the prisoners for this. But, as the preceding discussion has highlighted, the liminal domain between prisoners and guards was more complex than the static 'dehumanization' trope favoured by some literature suggests. The same caveat applies to the following discussion of resistance in Dachau, and its potential impact on guard behaviour.

---

[113] SAM, StA 34462/4, Zeugenvernehmungsprotokoll Heinrich Ultsch, Nuremberg, 6 March 1950.
[114] Neurath, *Society*, p. 264.      [115] Neurath, *Society*, p. 265.
[116] Burkhard, *Tanz Mal*, p. 26.
[117] Levi, *Drowned*, p. 22; see also the essay 'Stereotypes' in the same volume, pp. 121–36.

The situational potential for physical resistance to SS domination was practically nil in Dachau. If looping could, and did, have lethal consequences, actual violence against guards certainly would. The Kallweit incident at Buchenwald was exceptional for the pre-war period, and the Dachau memoir literature contains nothing comparable. Karl Röder, however, did witness one fatal instance of retaliation by an inmate.[118] Watching a group of enfeebled prisoners being transported, as he later found out, to a so-called 'euthanasia' facility in 1941, Röder recalled reflecting on the absence of physical resistance to the SS in Dachau. It was only conceivable among newcomers not yet resocialized into camp culture, as in the incident from the mid-1930s that came to his mind. An SS block leader had been hauling a new arrival, recognizable as such by his civilian attire, through the main camp gate. An oldish man, he reacted with outrage to a boot in the back—no more than the 'usual camp treatment'—and shouted at a second SS officer minding the gate that he should warn the perpetrator not to push his luck. Initially stunned and dumbfounded by this unheard-of reaction, the SS men stared wide-eyed at the new inmate and then collapsed into laughter. The block leader recovered his composure, grabbed the prisoner by the coat, and slapped him heartily around the face: a 'boxed ear' in camp discourse. His blood still up, the prisoner retaliated and struck back in a manner which reminded Röder of a father disciplining a wayward son. The block leader did indeed apparently step back with an expression akin to a 'tearful grimace', before the SS officer at the gate drew his pistol and shot the prisoner. Röder, watching perilously intently, registered the brief expression of astonishment on his face before he collapsed to the floor.

To be sure, the assertion that an inmate had been shot while 'attacking' a guard was common, but this was simply a vague disguise for murders such as Lehrburger's at the hands of Steinbrenner. In fact, the nature of the concentration camp situation was such that physical resistance by a prisoner would have been regarded as reprehensible even by his fellow inmates. It would be seen not only as suicidal but even selfish in bringing the risk of collective reprisals by the SS. It would, moreover, have been interpreted as casting implicit judgement on an entire population of males that did not 'hit back' at guards, despite the countless indignities and episodes of arbitrary violence it endured in Dachau.[119] What was admired was enduring a beating in a composed, resilient, and masculine fashion. There were also sound practical considerations to this: staying on one's feet greatly reduced the risk of a much more dangerous trampling from the perpetrator's sturdy SS boots.

Historians of the concentration camps thus prefer to discuss inmate resistance in terms of 'self-assertion' and solidarity.[120] Given that prisoners were placed in

---

[118] The following from Röder, *Nachtwache*, pp. 54–5.

[119] Bettelheim, *Informed*, p. 167; Neurath, *Society*, pp. 256–67.

[120] Falk Pingel, *Häftlinge unter SS-Herrschaft: Selbstbehauptung, Widerstand und Vernichtung im nationalsozialistischen Konzentrationslager* (Hamburg, 1978); Johannes Tuchel, 'Selbstbehauptung und Widerstand in nationalsozialistischen Konzentrationslagern', in Jürgen Schmädeke and Peter Steinbach (eds), *Der Widerstand gegen den Nationalsozialismus: Die deutsche Gesellschaft und der Widerstand gegen Hitler* (Munich and Zurich, 1985), pp. 938–53; Detlev Garbe, 'Selbstbehauptung und Widerstand', in Benz and Distel, *Der Ort des Terrors*, Vol. 5, pp. 315–46.

Dachau in order to break their spirit, those vestiges of culture and moral sovereignty they were able to retain did indeed represent a limit to SS power and deserve commemoration.[121] An interesting, and unusually powerful, example of such self-assertion attended the unveiling in the camp of a memorial to the Nazi hero, Albert Leo Schlageter, in 1933 on the tenth anniversary of his execution by French troops. The entire camp, prisoners and SS, was assembled and Wäckerle, seeking to wring maximum humiliation for the prisoners from the ceremony, ordered the Jewish lawyer and inmate, Dr Albert Rosenfelder, to deliver the eulogy to Schlageter. The adroit Rosenfelder duly offered a stirring reflection on the virtues of comradeship and martyrdom in adversity for a greater cause, whose potential double meaning was lost on no one present.[122] Rosenfelder here was making immaculate, and courageous, use of a favourable socio-cultural situation, for in order to preserve the saccharine solemnity of the occasion the Dachau SS was obliged to endure his performance in silence.

A more structural and enduring form of self-assertion was the extent to which the inmates were able to make use of the so-called 'self-administered' aspects of life in Dachau.[123] Almost from the start, the early Dachau SS delegated certain administrative and supervisory tasks to selected prisoners as company 'sergeants' (*Feldwebel*), principally oversight of order and tidiness in the prisoner barracks.[124] In time, inmates were also appointed as foremen of work details to free SS personnel from the burden of micro-management. The most senior of these 'prisoner-functionaries' were known as *Kapos* and would become a defining feature of the SS concentration camp system. Reflecting the profile of its inmate population, most *Kapos* in Dachau were Communists, although in the course of time purportedly 'criminal' prisoners were also used, particularly for the most manual work commandos. Their presence muddied the sharp division between personnel and inmates characteristic of 'total institutions' and of the binary thinking of the Dachau School. In the interests of the smooth operation of the camp, the SS was obliged to develop a working, even symbiotic, relationship with these figures although it preserved the right to depose—and to kill—them at will.[125]

Political prisoner memoir literature from the pre-war camps tends to stress the resistance by *Kapos* drawn from its ranks against the SS.[126] And there is certainly evidence that Dachau prisoner-functionaries could use their position to mitigate the conduct of the SS towards the inmates. A skilled barracks functionary could deflect the critical gaze of an SS block leader from an imperfectly made bed by engaging him in conversation and creating a more amicable atmosphere.[127] SS

[121] Todorov, *Facing the Extreme*, pp. 31–43.
[122] Hornung, *Dachau*, p. 112; Grünwiedl, *Dachauer Gefangene*, p. 12.
[123] Sofsky, *Order*, pp. 130–44.
[124] See the typically generous discussion of early Dachau *Kapos* in Richardi, *Schule*, pp. 155–61.
[125] For this reason, as the Auschwitz survivor Hermann Langbein pointed out, the concept of 'self-administration', still to be found in the literature on the camps, is misleading. Hermann Langbein, 'Work in the Concentration Camp', in Wolfgang Benz and Barbara Distel (eds), *Dachau and the Nazi Terror*, Vol. 1 (Dachau, 2002), pp. 64–74, here 64–7.
[126] Pingel, 'Social Life', pp. 60–6.          [127] Neurath, *Society*, p. 29.

personnel, after all, had few managerial 'carrots' at their disposal even if they wanted them and the most powerful was the discretion to ignore disciplinary infractions. A familiar relationship between a barracks senior and block leader might even reduce the incidence of ad hoc inspections. Networks of political functionaries could occasionally transfer favoured or vulnerable prisoners to less onerous work details, albeit at some risk to the network itself. Neurath contends that a struggle developed between the Dachau camp leadership, anxious to break up any nascent solidarity among longer-term work details and 'red' functionaries who were able to play on the desire of the more production-orientated SS work supervisors for stable and efficient commandos.[128]

At work, a decent *Kapo* foreman could discreetly warn his charges of the approach of SS personnel and ensure that the detail appeared to be running smoothly, in no need for them to intervene. He could also create the impression of a work party suitably terrorized by the 'Dachau spirit'. The *Anschluß* inmate, Peter Wallner, had initially been horrified and bewildered by the rough treatment meted out by political *Kapos*. Yet

> [a]s the weeks passed it gradually dawned upon me that this or that apparently brutal and bestial gang leader was, in reality, intensely human. Some only beat the members of their gang when a barrack officer came in sight, in order to save them from a more brutal chastisement. Indeed, a time came when I realised that the life of many a prisoner was saved in this way.[129]

It was rare indeed for a Jewish prisoner to be appointed to the post of *Kapo*. Yet the one documented pre-war exception, Heinz Eschen—a highly controversial figure in Jewish remembrance of Dachau—was able to an extent to insulate the members of his Jewish company from the predations to which they were particularly exposed, as Jews, from the Dachau SS.[130] In sum, given that working life by most accounts was even worse in concentration camps such as Buchenwald and, particularly, Flossenbürg, where political prisoners held fewer key functionary positions, the contribution of some political *Kapos* in Dachau should not be underestimated.[131]

Yet there was also a darker, complicit side to the *Kapo* system. While some did what they could to shield the inmates from the SS, others revelled in their delegated power. They acted, as one historian puts it, 'the part of medieval fiends in a Last Judgement painting, stoking up the fires of hell'.[132] Determined to preserve their privileged position, and the gratifying retinue of sycophants and enforcers

---

[128] Neurath, *Society*, p. 170.    [129] Wallner, *By Order of the Gestapo*, p. 58.

[130] Eschen, an interesting and controversial figure, is ably discussed in Karl-Heinz Jahnke, 'Heinz Eschen: Kapo des Judenblocks im Konzentrationslager Dachau bis 1938', in *Dachauer Hefte* 7 (1991), pp. 24–33; and Wüschmann, 'Jewish Prisoners', pp. 167–72.

[131] Pingel, 'Social Life', pp. 60–6. Kautsky wrote that '[i]f the concentration camp in itself was already hell, camps under the control of criminals were hell increased a thousand times': Kautsky, *Teufel und Verdammte*, p. 203. It is worth emphasizing, however, that the extent to which Kapos, rather than resources and SS personnel, shaped overall conditions in any given camp is frequently exaggerated by memoirists.

[132] Reitlinger, *Alibi*, p. 258.

which surrounded it, some *Kapos* exceeded the SS in arbitrary violence. Many inmates reserved particular bitterness towards functionaries after the war since their conduct could not, like that of the SS, be explained as an expression of fascist ideology. Eleven Dachau *Kapos* were tried in the US-led proceedings, one of whom, Christof Knoll, was sentenced to death.[133] Many prisoner memoirists from the pre-war period of the Dachau School point to a thoroughgoing identification by *Kapos* with its values. The mid-1930s *Kapos* Sterzer and Zock, both imprisoned as 'politicals', were notorious for murderous violence and particularly eager to play up to the antisemitic passions of spectating SS sentries.[134] Yet such mimesis was not dependent on an SS audience. On Christmas Day 1938, with the SS nowhere in sight, *Kapo* Sebastian Ebenburger, distributing the evening meal, compelled his company to submerge their heads in the toilet bowl after receiving their food and to shout 'we thank our *Führer*' before eating it.[135] The Austrian inmate, George Karst, recounts a similar example of the internalization of SS 'humour'. In his first week in the camp he was hauled from his work detail by an SS block leader for a torment. Having dug, as instructed, a grave 60 centimetres deep he was ordered to walk back to his barracks:

> I put down the spade and marched away with the uncertain feeling that a bullet might strike me from behind. I staggered back to the barracks. When I got there the block-elder and my room-elder were standing at the door.
> 'What did he want?' they asked.
> 'I had to dig a grave, my own' I answered, and wanted to pass them by.
> Both of them were old camp hands, Communists, who have spent years in Dachau and in jails. They grasped the idea immediately, howling with laughter.[136]

This apparent mimesis between perpetrators and victims would clearly fall into the 'grey zone' of Primo Levi's moral map of the concentration camps. The camp in this sense was a pathogenic, as well as pathological, situation and the 'Dachau spirit' was not necessarily confined to the guard personnel. Bettelheim, indeed, believed that the *Kapos* were merely an extreme expression of certain psychological tendencies among the prisoner community towards the SS, the tip of an iceberg. His observations in Dachau and Buchenwald led him to conclude that behavioural compliance by the inmates developed, over time, into 'identification' with the language, values, and behaviour of the SS.[137] Hannah Arendt, albeit without the same first-hand data, made a similar point.[138] This is not the place to be drawn into hazardous generalizations on the internal psychology of Dachau's inmates, save to point out that such adjustments represented above all the effects of a pathological

---

[133] See the useful summary by Michael Bryant, 'Die US-amerikanischen Militärgerichtsprozesse gegen SS-Personal, Ärzte und Kapos des KZ Dachau 1945–1948', in Eiber and Sigel (eds), *Dachauer Prozesse*, pp. 109–26.
[134] Drobisch and Wieland, *System*, p. 294; Heilig, *Men Crucified*, 63–67; Wallner, *By Order of the Gestapo*, pp. 120–3.
[135] SAM, StA, 34462/1, Zeugenvernehmungsprotokoll Leopold Figl, 16 September 1949.
[136] Karst, *Beasts*, p. 58.          [137] Bettelheim, *Informed*, pp. 168–74.
[138] Hannah Arendt, 'Social Science Techniques and the Study of Concentration Camps', *Jewish Social Studies*, Vol. 12 (1950), pp. 149–64, here p. 161.

situation. That prisoners often blamed the victims for the violence of the SS, or visited brutal punishments on wrongdoers redolent of the Gestapo's own methods, were adaptive behaviours reflecting the permutations of power and violence in Dachau rather than any concerted psychological emulation.[139] The Auschwitz survivor Viktor Frankl put this point succinctly: '[a]n abnormal reaction to an abnormal situation is normal behaviour'.[140]

This chapter has hitherto explored those many aspects of the relationship between the SS and inmates in Dachau informed by its dualistic institutional structure, and teased out some of the areas of liminality beneath this. Yet in line with the radical trajectory of the Nazi regime, Dachau was a dynamic institution which served manifold terror and disciplinary functions. Although the concentration camps developed an internal social system of power, they were also instruments of the state. Beneath, and very occasionally above, the 'usual camp treatment' were gradations of torment reflecting the granularities of SS ideology and the changing preoccupations of the Nazi regime. The following section will argue that the dwindling aggregate plight of the Dachau inmates reflected, in part, a creeping heterogeneity in the camp's population. Some of this heterogeneity was common to the whole pre-war concentration camp system, while other aspects were specific to Dachau, pioneering in a number of ways throughout the period of the Dachau School.

## CATEGORIZATION

### Regulations

The first official steps by the SS towards a moderate diversity in the treatment of the Dachau prisoners are contained in Wäckerle's regulations from May 1933. These set out a graduated 'stages' system for inmates similar to that piloted in Imperial prisons and operative for all inmates on long sentences in Weimar Germany by 1926.[141] Wäckerle's split Dachau's prisoners into three classes, with food provision already used as a form of structural violence. Most new arrivals were to be assigned to Class II, where they were told they could expect considerate treatment and adequate provision. Given diligence and good conduct they might be promoted to Class I, where they would enjoy pleasant treatment and ample provision. In Class III, however, comprising 'big shots' and inmates who had broken camp rules, they could expect harsh treatment and a miserable provision of no more than a quarter of the warm food allocated to inmates in Class II.[142]

It is not clear how faithfully the incentivizing features of this schema were applied in the camp, and whether the guard personnel had any meaningful interest

---

[139] Bettelheim's controversial interpretation is critiqued in Fleck et al., 'Bruno Bettelheim'.
[140] Frankl, *Man's Search for Meaning*, p. 20.
[141] Wachsmann, *Hitler's Prisons*, pp. 26–7.
[142] IMT, Vol. XXXVI, Document 922-D, 'Sonderbestimmungen', May 1933.

in them. One prisoner, nevertheless, testified to having reached Class I. This was Anton Schöberl, who—in another illustration of the role of inmate biography in the early years—attributed the privilege to having previously served with camp administrator Vogel in the navy.[143] He was appointed 'camp elder' (*Lagerältester*) and given a blue armband entitling him to roam relatively freely inside the camp, and even outside it on Sundays. The appointment was probably for presentational purposes, as the existence of a Class I prisoner lent apparent authority to Wäckerle's rehabilitation narrative. It also marked the beginnings of the *Kapo* system: the camp elder would be the most senior prisoner-functionary position in all SS camps.

The punitive Class III, on the other hand, was applied most concertedly and provided the basis of the 'punishment company' (*Strafkompanie*) overseen in the early Dachau SS by Heinrich Strauss. The punishment company was a disciplinary instrument with a long and lethal future in Dachau and later camps. Composed of inmates who had supposedly broken camp rules and particularly loathed prisoner groups, its food provision was restricted. After the rebuilding of the camp, the punishment company comprised multiple adjacent barracks and was used for large-scale manual enterprises such as the construction of the plantation, or the so-called Dachau 'game park' built for the recreation of the SS to the north of the prisoner compound.[144] Desperate with hunger, the inmates on this detail secretly ate animal fodder, wild berries, and even grass during the day.[145] Prisoners on the punishment company essentially endured an intensified programme of the 'usual' Dachau treatment, with its former block leader conceding in his testimony that they were consciously subjected to enhanced individual and collective punishment and humiliation for 'alleged' poor singing or disciplinary infractions.[146]

Eicke's regulations dispensed with the stages system, although they did reserve condign penalties for prisoner-sergeants and work foremen who exceeded their authority or tyrannized their fellow prisoners. Other exploratory efforts towards a rehabilitative stages system open to all prisoners are evident elsewhere in the early camps—such as at Fuhlsbüttel near Hamburg—but disappeared as Eicke gained control of the system from 1934.[147] A staged system, associated as it was with prisons, was incongruous with Eicke's conception of the concentration camps and their guard personnel as a military phenomenon. By placing a notional structural restriction on the 'usual camp treatment' on which the Dachau School curriculum was based, it was also a potential cognitive burden for guards. Eicke did not believe in disciplinary carrots for 'enemies of the state'. A much more salient factor in differentiated treatment of prisoners by the SS, and in the experiences of inmates, was the pattern of the total inmate population in Dachau.

[143] SAM, StA 34590, Vernehmungsniederschrift Anton Schöberl, 30 November 1959.
[144] On the game park see Dirk Riedel, 'Der "Wildpark" im KZ Dachau und das Außenlager St. Gilgen', *Dachauer Hefte*, 16 (2000), pp. 54–70.
[145] Erhard Klein, *Jehovas Zeugen*, p. 86.
[146] SAM, StA 34452/2, Vernehmung des Beschuldigten Josef Voggesberger, 13 December 1946.
[147] Address to Fuhlsbüttel prisoners 4 September 1933, printed in Goeschel and Wachsmann, *Nazi Concentration Camps*, pp. 17–19.

## Inmate Numbers

The function and long-term employment prospects for the Dachau SS hinged on the presence and quantity of prisoners in the camp. The early concentration camps were not intended to be permanent institutions but rather provisional instruments of revolutionary discipline and purported civil war. By the end of 1933, Dachau had registered 4,821 prisoners, some 1,860 arriving in a glut under Wäckerle in April and May.[148] Releases were frequent in the first years of the Third Reich, however, and the average inmate population of the camp at any given time was between 2,000 and 2,500 men.[149] Indeed, bucking the much more volatile trends at an aggregate, national level, the Dachau inmate population remained relatively constant right up to 1938, with between 1,500 and 2,500 prisoners housed in its ten inmate barracks.[150] During this period, too, releases were common, with newly registered prisoners accounting for between one and two thirds of the recorded inmate population. A core of unreleased prisoners, overwhelmingly Communists, had camp experience dating back to the early Dachau SS and have made a dominant contribution to inmate memoir literature. But even in Himmler's Bavaria, the camp's figures suggest most prisoners in these years were released after a matter of weeks or months. Overcrowding, and in turn SS personnel overstretch, was not an issue, particularly when the reconstruction of the Dachau protective custody compound in the winter of 1937 to 1938 increased the number of prisoner barracks from ten to thirty. Only in the summer of 1938 did this change.

The year 1938 was one of pronounced radicalization in the entwined racial, economic, and foreign policies of the Third Reich. The reverberations were felt, indeed sometimes anticipated, in its concentration camps. The 3,500 *Anschluß* prisoners transported to Dachau, largely in May and June 1938, more than doubled the population of the camp, which grew from 2,372 in January to 5,502 in July.[151] This first influx of foreign prisoners evidently caused bureaucratic disarray in Dachau's Political Department, where their 'citizenship' was variously recorded as 'D' for German, 'D.Ö' for Austrian-German, and 'Ö' for Austrian.[152] The sheer scale of the increase in inmate population brought unaccustomed challenges for the SS. The most striking was the phenomenon of unemployment among inmates, a contravention of the entrenched principle that the concentration camp inmate *worked*. This had not been an issue since Eicke's tenure as Dachau commandant, when inmates not assigned to work commandos had been forced to perform pseudo-military exercises throughout the day in order, as SS discourse had it, 'not to succumb to negative thoughts'.[153] The mass incarceration of the Austrians, coming as it did after the labour-intensive rebuilding of the protective custody camp, threatened to undermine the entire ecosystem of terror and discipline in Dachau.

---

[148] Richardi, *Schule*, p. 312 fn. 61, drawn from International Tracing Service (ITS) statistics.

[149] Richardi, *Schule*, p. 231; Pingel, *Häftlinge*, p. 71.

[150] Tables provided in Drobisch and Wieland, *System*, pp. 204, 271, 288; on aggregate national figures, see the table in Goeschel and Wachsmann, *Nazi Concentration Camps*, Appendix A.

[151] Drobisch and Wieland, *System*, p. 288.

[152] Wünschmann, 'Jewish Prisoners', p. 180.     [153] Richardi, *Schule*, p. 82.

Initially, the surplus Austrians were set to work aimlessly on an enormous pile of dirt and gravel they christened 'Mount Sinai', hauling debris from one side to another under the oversight of *Kapo* Sterzer.[154] When this cheerless theatre began to pall, the SS leadership hit upon another solution, familiar to the Third Reich: unemployment was to be rendered 'invisible'. Saturday afternoons and Sundays were once again declared work-free.[155] Barracks maintenance and drill, phenomena last seen in the early years of the camp, replaced work for some of the unemployed.[156] One inmate recalled that the net result was that his barrack only went out to work three days a week.[157]

The work situation in Dachau in 1938 was exceptional rather than, as Bettelheim assumed, characteristic of the camp.[158] It was still more exceptional in the context of the penal system in the Third Reich at the time. The unemployment of inmates in the regular prison system, a problem in the early years of the Third Reich, was almost unknown by 1938 when prisoners of all kinds were being squeezed brutally for labour.[159] The Four Year Plan, launched in 1936 to place the German economy on an autarkic war footing, had taken Nazi rhetoric about labour productivity to increased pitches of urgency. For the Dachau SS authorities, the situation was potentially embarrassing at a time when DESt had just been formed, and Heydrich was beseeching the Justice Ministry to transfer eligible inmates in the prison system to the granite quarries of the new concentration camps at Buchenwald and Flossenbürg.[160]

The pressure on Dachau's labour-based model of terror did not let up in 1938. Indeed, the influx of Austrians, which disproportionately affected Dachau, was followed shortly by two other mass campaigns which disproportionately affected Buchenwald and Sachsenhausen. The first, a 'Reich Work-Shy Campaign' in June brought some 10,000 social outsiders—itinerants, pimps, beggars, and casual workers, disproportionately Jewish—to the camps, 923 of them to overcrowded Dachau.[161] Even by National Socialist standards, it would appear particularly perverse to have imprisoned these men in Dachau as 'work-shy' when there was no work available in the camp. But beyond socio-racial hygiene, the motivation for the sweep was also deterrence, as the Nazi leadership was concerned that flagging labour discipline was undermining the momentum of the Four Year Plan.[162] Inside Dachau, a 'slave market' developed in the summer of 1938 comprising a vast reserve of unassigned prisoners available to augment existing manual work commandos, from where *Kapos* each morning would pick the least depleted inmates for their own details.[163] While the 'slave market' was the product of situational,

---

[154] Heilig, *Men Crucified*, p. 126.

[155] Wallner, *By Order of the Gestapo*, p. 144; Neurath, *Society*, p. 105; Wünschmann, 'Jewish Prisoners', pp. 186–7.

[156] Heilig, *Men Crucified*, pp. 123–6; Neurath, *Society*, p. 89.

[157] Heilig, *Men Crucified*, p. 126.        [158] Bettelheim, *Informed*, p. 134.

[159] Wachsmann, *Hitler's Prisons*, pp. 96–100.

[160] Heydrich to Gürtner, 28 June 1938, printed in Goeschel and Wachsmann, *Nazi Concentration Camps*, pp. 128–9.

[161] Wünschmann, 'Jewish Prisoners', p. 193.        [162] Wachsmann, 'Dynamics', p. 24.

[163] Neurath, *Society*, pp. 170–2.

demographic factors, it certainly fitted with the SS project to denigrate and deper-
sonalize the camp's inmates.

The final, and largest, mass imprisonment in Dachau in 1938 took place in
the wake of the November pogrom when around 30,000 male Jews, some 10 per
cent of the entire Jewish population, were transported to the concentration camps
on Hitler's personal order. In the course of a few days 10,911 Jewish men were
brought to Dachau—including a further 3,700 Austrians. Their experiences will
be considered in greater depth below; for now it is sufficient to note the many
logistical challenges these numbers presented to the SS. Initially the thousands
of Jewish men queued in vast rows outside the main gate to be registered by the
Political Department, but when night fell on 10 November they were brought into
the camp on security grounds to line up on the roll call square. The bureaucratic
challenge was immense: 'the clerks wrote day and night', recalled Hübsch, 'they
wrote and wrote'.[164] The scale of the arrivals also soon outstripped the SS supply
of prisoner uniforms, and the final 4,000 'November Jews' spent their time in
Dachau in their own clothes: a substantial advantage in view of the thin, rag-
ged quality of the camp-issued uniforms.[165] The Dachau inmate barracks, already
stretched beyond capacity, became overcrowded to an unprecedented extent, with
200 men per room, sharing four or more to a bed, the norm.[166] While the SS
had no objection to the appalling privations this inflicted on the Jewish inmates,
it did mean that the traditional Dachau terror instrument of barracks and 'bed-
making' inspections was unfeasible: it is striking in the context of Dachau inmate
literature how absent this is from Jewish testimony on the *Kristallnacht*. Only after
Christmas of 1938, by which time the great majority of the November Jews had
been released, were the SS block leaders able to restore barracks torment to its
traditional place in the camp.

The aggregate figures for 1938 are startling: whereas Dachau registered 2,151
new arrivals in 1937, in 1938 the figure was 18,712.[167] Most 'November Jews'
were released fairly quickly, however, in a matter of weeks or months. For the other
prisoners, releases were less frequent than in the early years of Dachau but still periodic, including amnesties such as that to mark Hitler's 50th birthday, when *Kapo*
Zock was among those released back into the racial community.[168] After this, prisoner numbers in Dachau dropped back to around 3,500, in line with the pre-war
average. Not until after the closure of the Dachau School at the start of the war,
and the reopening of the camp in February 1940, would the dire overcrowding of
1938 be approached again.

## Inmate Categories

The mass raids of 1938 altered the profile of the Dachau inmate population in
rather dramatic fashion and take an equivalently prominent position in the inmate

164 Hübsch, 'Insel', p. 117.   165 WL Report, no. 184, s. 2.
166 WL Report, no. 67, s. 1.   167 Drobisch and Wieland, *System*, p. 271.
168 Drobisch and Wieland, *System*, pp. 308–9.

literature on the camp. But contrary to certain commonplaces in the historiography of the pre-war concentration camps, and indeed the self-conceptions of Eicke's Dachau School, its population quickly ceased to be a relatively homogenous, political group.[169] While the great majority of prisoners up to 1937/8 were in 'protective custody', this category of detention was deployed with great elasticity in Bavaria. In the summer of 1933, to the glee of the local press, Himmler's police carried out a punitive campaign against so-called 'grand profiteers' (*Großschieber*) in Munich, which brought some seventy, generally small-scale, dairy merchants to Dachau.[170] At the same time, social outsiders were being persecuted, building on repressive instruments developed by the Weimar era police, judiciary, and welfare apparatus. The concentration camps as such contained outsiders defined on eugenic and criminological bases right from 1933.[171] In Bavaria, the authorities imposed protective custody for all manner of violations of social norms. An inventory of 'protective custody' prisoners in Bavaria drawn up in April 1934 reveals that some 2,009 of 2,500 persons were political opponents, 1,531 of them Communists. Yet already 441 persons were detained for such social disciplinary reasons as alcoholism, being 'workshy' or 'asocial', even two for poaching.[172] On 1 December 1934 a Dachau inventory records 338 inmates in the camp from the Rebdorf workhouse, due to its overcrowding, along with 21 men committed to the camp for compulsory labour under section 20 of the Reich Welfare Code.[173]

The source base for the Dachau inmate taxonomy between 1935 and 1938 is particularly meagre. In February 1935 the camp population was around 2,300 men accommodated in nine barracks.[174] Five barracks were occupied by political prisoners, with one 'punishment company', one barrack of purported 'asocials', one of Jews and sundry 'big shots', and a smaller one of emigrants who had left Germany after the Nazi takeover but returned. A British Legion delegation shown round Dachau in July 1935 was informed by the SS that of its 1,500 inmates, 950 were political cases. There were also 246 'professional criminals', 198 'work-shy' men, 26 'hardened criminals', 38 'moral perverts', and 85 returned Jewish emigrants.[175] After its inspection of the camp, the delegation apparently enjoyed a 'quiet family supper' with Himmler himself, in which he impressed upon them the ever-gathering menace of communism in Germany.[176]

[169] Wachsmann, 'Dynamics', p. 24. Due to the destruction of most concentration camp records with the approach of the Allied armies in 1945, it is impossible fully to reconstruct the inmate population of Dachau, although the memorial site is now developing a prisoner database.
[170] Moore, 'German Popular Opinion', p. 64; *Nazi Bastille Dachau*, pp. 66–7; photograph of closed-down premeses in Longerich, *Himmler*, p. 149
[171] Julia Hörath, 'Terrorinstrumente der "Volksgemeinschaft"? KZ-Haft für "Asoziale" und "Berufsverbrecher" 1933 bis 1937/38', *Zeitschrift für Geschichtswissenschaft*, Vol. 60, No. 6 (2012), pp. 513–32.
[172] BayHstA, StK 6299, Zusammensetzung der Schutzhäftlinge in Bayern, 10 April 1934.
[173] BayHstA, StK 6299, Staatsministerium des Innern an den Bay, Ministerpräsident, 3 December 1934.
[174] Hübsch, 'Insel', p. 6.
[175] Graham Wootton, *The Official History of the British Legion* (London, 1956), pp. 184–5.
[176] Wootton, *British Legion*, p. 185.

Table 4.1  SS inventory of Dachau by inmate category, April 1939.

| Inmate Group | Total |
|---|---|
| Protective Custody | 2,090 |
| Jehovah's Witnesses | 108 |
| Male homosexuals | 44 |
| Jews | 712 |
| Race defilers | 3 |
| Emigrants | 16 |
| *Ausweisungshaft* (awaiting deportation) | 22 |
| 'Work-shy' – local | 138 |
| 'Work-shy' – Reich | 296 |
| Police Preventive Custody (PV) | 50 |
| **TOTAL** | 3,479 |

The appearance of 'hardened criminals' in the information the British Legion were given is significant. For another contributor to the heterogeneity of the Dachau prisoners was the practice of taking recidivist criminals—without trial—into the concentration camps under 'preventive custody'. Although used on a much smaller scale in Bavaria—where 'protective custody' was so loosely defined—than in Prussia, 'preventive custody inmates' formed part of the Dachau population from January 1935 onwards.[177] The twenty-six reported to the British Legion had increased to forty-five by June 1936.[178] In May 1937, Sopade noted that these prisoners were accommodated in one room of the eighth barracks alongside the newcomers company. Three barracks comprised solely political prisoners, one 'asocials', one Jews, one prisoners detained in Dachau for a second time, one a mixture of politicals and alleged male homosexuals, and one a temporary 'invalid' company which included the future West German SPD leader Kurt Schumacher.[179]

On the eve of the *Anschluß* there were around 2,200 inmates in Dachau, of whom 1,200 were political prisoners, 200 'professional criminals', 400 'asocials', 50 emigrants, 150 male homosexuals, 150 Jehovah's Witnesses, and 50 race defilers.[180] The most detailed available inventory of prisoners was drawn up for Himmler's inspection of the Dachau School on 25 April 1939 (see Table 4.1).[181] With the partial exception of *Kapos*, prisoners from anywhere in this increasingly pedantic and intricate taxonomy were exposed to the Dachau SS 'usual camp treatment'. But this mistreatment could be intensified or reconfigured at any time for a given inmate group, according to the whim of the SS leadership or to instructions from outside the camp. The examples of the 'newcomer' and 'punishment' companies have already been encountered. This final section

[177] Hörath, 'Terrorinstrumente', p. 524.     [178] Drobisch and Wieland, *System*, p. 204.
[179] Sopade report on Dachau, May 1937. Printed in Goeschel and Wachsmann, *Nazi Concentration Camps*, pp. 235–8.
[180] Neurath, *Society*, pp. 111–12.
[181] BAB, NS19/1792, Minutenprogramm für den Besuch des KZs Dachau und der SS Standarte 'Deutschland' durch Reichsführer SS, s. 227.

will explore granularities in the treatment of various prisoner groups in the camp, bespoke refinements beyond the baseline camp treatment. Some of these disciplinary innovations reflect a process of cumulative radicalization familiar to historical scholarship on the Third Reich. The net result of the interplay between an evolving standard practice, prisoner numbers, and disciplinary innovation, was a spiralling in mortality in the camp. The camp recorded 22 inmate deaths in 1933, 17 in 1934, 12 in 1935, 11 in 1936, 41 in 1937, 240 in 1938, and 182 up to its temporary closure in September 1939.[182]

### Political Prisoners

The repression of political opposition, real or perceived, remained the primary—although by no means sole—function of Dachau for longer than any other concentration camp: the historian Karin Orth describes it as the 'traditional' SS camp.[183] The group of political prisoners in Dachau was at its most heterogeneous in 1933, tracking the high political consolidation of the Nazi dictatorship. While the first prisoners were overwhelmingly Communist, Social Democrats began to arrive in greater numbers after the crackdown on the trade unions in May and the banning of the SPD in June. They were by no means welcomed in an 'iron front' spirit of proletarian comradeship by the Communist majority in the camp.[184] Whilst the point should not be overstated, this lack of solidarity played into the hands of a Dachau SS keen to encourage animosity among inmates.

Although the institutions and personnel of the organized working class were the primary target of Nazi repression, political Catholicism, too, came under pressure from spring 1933. The first Catholic politicals in Dachau were paramilitaries from the BVP's Bavarian Guard (*Bayernwacht*). Rupert Berger was one of a number of its squadron leaders brought to the camp on 26 April.[185] They were beaten severely by Steinbrenner and Strauss on arrival and assigned to the punitive Class III category. Strauss explained to them that 'the People's Party need a serious kick up the arse to get the blood flowing to their heads; maybe then they'll become proper nationalists'.[186] Dachau SS attitudes towards these paramilitaries were rather more nuanced than towards Communist and *Reichsbanner* fighters. Many, like Steinbrenner, had grown up in BVP households. The BVP was ardently antisocialist and had voted enthusiastically for the Enabling Act to excise, as its Reichstag delegation explained, 'the shameful Revolution of 1918'.[187] The Bavarian Guard counted notable counter-revolutionary veterans in its ranks: Berger himself

---

[182] DaA, A2002, Todesfälle im KL Dachau 1933–1940. For a very persuasive deployment of Hans Mommsen's influential concept of 'cumulative radicalization', see Kershaw, *Nemesis*, pp. 3–60.

[183] Orth, *System*, p. 51.          [184] Ecker 'Hölle', pp. 45–51; Rubner, 'Dachau', p. 67.

[185] SAM, StA 34462/9, Zeugenvernehmungsprotokoll Rupert Berger, 13 March 1951.

[186] SAM, StA 34462/7, Bericht Rupert Berger, 2 May 1950.

[187] On the ambiguous stance of the BVP in the late Weimar Republic, see Klaus Schöhoven, 'Zwischen Anpassung und Ausschaltung: Die bayerische Volkspartei in der Endphase der Weimarer Republik 1932/33', *Historische Zeitschrift*, Vol. 224, No. 2 (Apr., 1977), pp. 340–78; here p. 372.

had served in the *Freikorps* von Epp. The day after his introductory beating he was called out from his heavy roller work detail by an unidentified SS man who, addressing him with the polite 'Sie', enquired about his background. On hearing his counter-revolutionary CV, he excused Berger from work and sent him back to his barracks. Berger was removed from Category III and soon released from Dachau in the amnesty on 1 May.[188] The detention of subsequent BVP personnel in Dachau was also relatively brief. On 26 June Himmler ordered that 'particularly active' members of the party be taken into protective custody. Apparently on Eicke's personal order, luminaries such as Alois Hundhammer and the two sons of Heinrich Held were placed in the punishment company on the grounds that they were 'no better than Jews'.[189] But almost all BVP inmates were released after a few days, once the party had agreed to dissolve itself.[190]

There were also a number of monarchists in Dachau. Erwein von Aretin, who had been taken hostage by the *Räterepublik* in 1919, was brought to the camp in November 1933 for his criticism of Nazis as a contributor to the *Munich Neueste Nachrichten*. Soon after arrival he was dragged to the prisoner canteen, surrounded by a party of SS men, and beaten in a manner which reminded him, with characteristic immodesty, of the Passion of Christ.[191] Throughout his spell in Dachau, the SS seem to have been eager to expose his lack of physical strength as an intellectual, assigning him along with other monarchists to washing up the heavy cauldrons in the camp kitchen.[192] Yet despite the particular animus of some elements of the SS towards his reactionary views, von Aretin emerged from the camp largely unscathed in May 1934. The political prisoner category in Dachau also included professionals like Schecher, a lawyer imprisoned from 1935 until the camp's liberation. Lawyers were particularly likely to be detained if they were Jewish. Some, like Rosenfelder and Hans Litten, had close links with the political Left, while others were simply taken into 'protective custody' on vague grounds which barely disguised the true antisemitic motivation.[193]

But while aristocrats, lawyers, and Catholic paramilitaries were to be found among the political prisoner category in Dachau, it was the activists of the working class, and particularly Communists, who dominated its SS stereotype. Initially it was communism, or 'Bolshevism', which most excited the hatred of the Dachau SS. This was manifested in the epithets reported from introductory beatings: 'Marxist swine', 'Bolshevik dog', 'Red scum', and so on, which, one memoirist suggested, 'evidently produced their own dynamic'.[194] The Bolshevik enemy trope (*Feindbild*) remained central to National Socialism throughout its existence, eliding anti-communism, antisemitism, and anti-Slavism: one of the myriad derogatory camp SS terms for Communist inmates was 'Russians'.[195] A key aspect of

[188] SAM, StA 34462/7, Bericht Rupert Berger, 2 May 1950.
[189] SAM, StA, Zeugenvernehmungsprotokoll Siegmund Herz, 4 September 1951.
[190] Tuchel, *Konzentrationslager*, pp. 153–5.
[191] Erwein von Aretin, *Krone und Ketten: Erinnerungen eines bayerischen Edelmannes* (Munich, 1954), p. 277.
[192] Aretin, *Krone und Ketten*, p. 290.     [193] Wünschmann, 'Jewish Prisoners', pp. 48–55.
[194] Hornung, *Dachau*, p. 76.     [195] Höß, *Commandant*, p. 79.

Himmler's pitch for the retention of the concentration camp system, in the face of opposition from senior officials in the Nazi regime, was that the Communist movement in Germany was in fact 'continually growing'.[196] So too, by extension, was the indispensability of his unflinching 'state protection corps'. In 1936 the *Reichsführer* wrote that it was the ongoing mission of the SS to ensure that 'never again in Germany, the heart of Europe, can a Jewish-Bolshevik revolution of sub-humanity be initiated, either from within or by outside agents'.[197]

There are nevertheless a few indications of a grudging respect for Communists not extended to other political prisoners. The KPD's Josef Zäuner was imprisoned in Dachau in May 1933 and subsequently chosen by Eicke for the most senior *Kapo* post of prisoner work sergeant. Zäuner quickly made himself a marked man by intervening and lodging official complaints when sentries mistreated prisoners at work.[198] The final straw came at the start of August when he became embroiled in a public row with a member of the commandant's staff. He was dragged off to the *Bunker*, beaten in the direst manner, then placed in solitary confinement for a barely imaginable seven months. When he was released, Eicke sent for him. According to camp lore, the Dachau commandant asked him whether he was still a Communist. Zäuner replied that he believed the only way to save Germany was through communism. Eicke is said to have been deeply impressed by this resilience, saying 'you are a man of character, Zäuner!', and later sent him a pipe as a present.[199] Although it is not possible to verify this incident, there is a broader sense that Nazi street fighters like Eicke saw something honourable in the fanaticism of Communists.[200] The Social Democrat Ecker even believed that the SS and Communists in Dachau had a 'mutual attachment'.[201] Yet however true this may have been on some subterranean, psychological level, political prisoners could expect little tangible magnanimity from the Dachau SS. And perhaps the most striking illustration of this is the appalling plight of political prisoners who were returned to the camp having previously been released.

## Second-timers

Blood-curdling threats from the Dachau SS about the consequences of being brought back to the camp were standard for inmates being released in the early years of the Third Reich. They were warned, often by the commandant personally, that even speaking about their experiences would see them re-arrested and brought back, never to emerge again. Eicke in particular displayed rhetorical ambitions for the longevity of Dachau befitting of a 'Thousand Year Reich': one party

---

[196] Himmler memorandum to to Gürtner, 28 March 1935, cited in Longerich, *Himmler*, p. 194.

[197] Himmler, *Die Schutzstaffel als antibolshewistiche Kampforganisation*, p. 16.

[198] Prisoner reports compiled by Richardi, *Schule*, pp. 158–9.

[199] Hornung, *Dachau*, 212–13.

[200] Paul Moore, '"The Man Who Built the First Concentration Camp." The Anti-Brown Book of Concentration Camp Commandant Werner Schäfer: Fighting and Writing the Nazi "Revolution"' (Unpublished MS), pp. 23–6.

[201] Ecker, 'Hölle', p. 46.

of prisoners was assured on release that the camp would still be around in 1960, another that Dachau had a good fifty years of service ahead of it.[202]

In the event, the first 'second-timers' seem to have arrived through police initiative rather than unguarded discussion of the camp. In July 1935 the shooting of two Communists caught smuggling underground literature over the Czechoslovakian border presented Himmler with an opportunity to dramatize the ongoing Communist menace in Germany. He ordered the Bavarian Political Police to round up 300 Communists for Dachau, and these included a number who had been in the camp before.[203] This inaugurated a renewed persecution of German Communists. The following March, Himmler issued detailed instructions for the treatment of the rising numbers of second-timers in the concentration camps. They were to be segregated from the rest of the inmates in 'special sections', to work a ten-hour day, to endure severely restricted mail privileges, and were forbidden to smoke. Most devastating of all, they were not even to be considered for release for three years.[204] That Himmler had Communists in mind may be ascertained from a speech he had given a few weeks previously, lamenting that the Nazis had been recklessly 'chivalrous' in assuming that

> a political adversary whom we have released would regard this as a sign of decency and would therefore no longer undertake anything because he felt he had to be grateful to us that, as a leading Communist, he was not executed by firing squad while, as he himself knows, if things had gone the other way, every leading National Socialist would have had to face death.[205]

These bespoke provisions for the treatment of second-timers are a striking example of cumulative radicalization in the treatment of concentration camp inmates. Second-timers were presented by the SS as not having learned their lesson through the normal 'camp treatment'. To mark this transgression, and to provide an additional deterrent to the other inmates, their plight had to be made materially worse than that of the 'punishment companies' which already existed in Dachau and other camps. The harsh treatment of second-timers in Dachau more than lived up to this billing. Fenced-off from the remainder of the camp, they were assigned to the most brutal block leaders and *Kapos*. One survivor of the pre-war Dachau second-timer company remembered that they were not only forced to work at twice the pace of other inmates, but received 'in compensation', as SS discourse had it, half the normal food provision.[206] They almost never had time off at weekends. The physical depletion of second-timers was appalling even by the standards of camp inmates. Sopade, all too cognisant of the horrors of Dachau, described the second-timers company of around 200 men as one of its very 'saddest' features,

---

[202] Hornung, *Dachau*, p. 79; Rubner, 'Dachau', p. 79.
[203] Drobsich and Wieland, *System*, pp. 199–200; Longerich, *Himmler*, pp. 194–5.
[204] Himmler to IKL, 23 March 1936. Printed in Goeschel and Wachsmann, *Nazi Concentration Camps*, p. 83.
[205] Transcript printed in Goeschel and Wachsmann, *Nazi Concentration Camps*, p. 82.
[206] SAM, StA 34462/3, Zeugenvernehmungsprotokoll Walter Czollek, 25 October 1950.

'regarded in the camp as hell'.[207] Its inhabitants 'look very ill. Their faces are marked by their strict detention'. Another mark of the intentionally dire conditions in this company is that Jewish second-timers were assigned here, rather than to the Jewish company: perhaps the only instance of their racial classification being overruled.[208] Many second-timers, if they survived at all, only emerged from the camps at liberation in 1945.

## Jehovah's Witnesses

Another well-documented prisoner category in Dachau regarded by the SS as ideological opponents was the Jehovah's Witnesses, or 'Earnest Bible Researchers'. The internationalism of this small Christian sect, numbering no more than 30,000 in Germany, was anathema to the *völkisch* world view. Pacifism and unwavering fealty to Jehovah also led male Witnesses to refuse to take the oath of obedience to Hitler and serve in the armed forces. This represented the rejection of a fundamental masculine duty to the People's Community. Given the total claim of Nazism, a confrontation was inevitable: in 1933 the Bavarian Minister of Culture opined that 'every pacifist deserves to be whipped out of the country'.[209] The Nazis tended to ascribe female opposition among Witnesses to religious stubbornness, that of male Witnesses to political dissent.[210]

The first Jehovah's Witnesses seem to have arrived in Dachau in December 1933, after refusing to vote in the Reichstag elections the previous month.[211] Their numbers in Dachau were low compared to other camps; just ten had been registered by the end of 1936, rising to around 150 by the closure of the Dachau School in September 1939.[212] Yet Dachau SS resources and imagination disproportionate to their numbers went into breaking them, for their ideological resilience potentially set an example to other prisoners. Jehovah's Witnesses were housed in the punishment company from the start. They were promised release if they would sign an oath undertaking, among other things, 'to defend my Fatherland with weapon in hand and fully join the People's Community'.[213] Very few availed of this opportunity. The derogatory SS repertoire for the Witnesses included 'heaven's comedians', 'birds of paradise', and 'bible worms'.[214] Höβ recalls the efforts made by the SS in the camps to expose contradictions in the bible and to engage the Witnesses in matters of theodicy.[215] One Jehovah's Witness in Dachau was forced to stand on a pile of gravel and shout 'I am the biggest idiot of the twentieth century'.[216] They

---

[207] Sopade Report May 1937, printed in Goeschel and Wachsmann, *Nazi Concentration Camps*, pp. 235–8.

[208] Kim Wünschmann, 'Before Auschwitz: Jewish Prisoners in Nazi Concentration Camps 1933–1939' (Unpublished MS), p. 186.

[209] In Kaplan, *Jewish Life*, p. 19.     [210] Caplan, 'Gender', p. 88.

[211] Drobisch and Wieland, *System*, p. 101.

[212] Detlef Garbe, 'Erst verhasst, dann geschätzt: Zeugen Jehovas als Häftlinge im KZ Dachau', in Benz and Königseder, *Das Konzentrationslager Dachau*, pp. 220–1.

[213] Garbe, 'Erst verhasst', p. 234.     [214] Garbe, 'Erst verhasst', p. 223.

[215] Höβ, *Commandant*, pp. 88–91.

[216] DaA, 37518, Aufzeichnungen des Alfred Hübsch, p. 5.

also endured bespoke restrictions on mail which attest to a cumulative radicalization here, too. From early 1939 they were allowed to write no more than twenty-five words and the card was stamped 'The protective custody prisoner is as before a stubborn Jehovah's Witness and refuses to renounce these mad doctrines'.[217] Their rations were cut, with the promise of a return to normal fare if they renounced their faith. Given their plight, the Witnesses in Dachau offered remarkably effective self-assertion bordering on outright resistance. They were almost never to be found in war-productive work details during the Second World War, despite the condign penalties applying to shirkers and saboteurs.[218] As Kogon wrote, 'psychologically speaking, the SS was never quite equal to the challenge offered by the Jehovah's Witnesses'.[219] Certainly the camp SS gave up on the idea of breaking them, and particularly during the war their utter trustworthiness saw them increasingly used for distant work commandos and domestic service, a compensatory project of feminization. The Witnesses, it was found, were dutiful, industrious, and compassionate individuals who never sought to escape. *Reichsführer* SS Himmler himself came to admire the ideological 'fanaticism' of the Jehovah's Witnesses and towards the end of the war even discussed the possibility of exporting their faith to occupied lands in the East.[220]

## 'Asocials' and 'Professional Criminals'

It is extremely difficult to reconstruct the treatment and experiences of men imprisoned in Dachau under the expansive umbrella of 'asociality'. Unlike political prisoners, they have left no memoirs and their presence in the testimony of other inmates is marked by the prejudices of their authors. Many political memoirists even believed that these inmates had been brought to Dachau simply to undermine the comradeship and self-esteem of the politicals.[221] A particularly heterogeneous group, some 1,800 to 2,000 'asocial' males in total had been imprisoned in Dachau for 'asocial behaviour' even prior to the mass campaigns of 1938.[222] In July 1936, 700 were arrested, just before the Olympics, and briefly comprised two prisoner companies. A further 900 arrived in the course of the 'Reich work-shy raid' in the summer of 1938 and wore a black badge under the standardized taxonomy rolled out that year. But, contributing to its status as the 'traditional camp' of the SS, Dachau's proportion of asocials at any one time was probably lower than in other camps.[223]

---

[217] Garbe, 'Erst verhasst', p. 225.     [218] Garbe, 'Erst verhasst', p. 227–9.

[219] Kogon, *Theory and Practice*, p. 34.     [220] Longerich, *Himmler*, p. 267.

[221] Characteristic is the report by Hans Schwarz printed in Goeschel and Wachsmann, *Nazi Concentration Camps*, pp. 250–2; writing some five decades later, Zámečnik was also unable to divest himself of this fallacy: Zámečnik, *Dachau*, p. 81.

[222] Annett Eberle, ' "Asoziale" und "Berufsverbrecher": Dachau als Ort der "Vorbeugehaft" ', in Benz and Königseder, *Dachau*, pp. 252–68, here p. 257.

[223] The historian Annette Eberle estimates that so-called 'asocials' comprised around 70 per cent of the entire national inmate population of the camps in October 1938, on the eve of the November pogrom: Anette Eberle, 'Häftlingskategorien und Kennzeichnungen', in Benz and Distel (eds) *Ort des Terrors*, Vol. 1, p. 97.

Qualitative information on the treatment of asocials is harder to find. SS men never comment on asocials in their testimony. Höß recognized, in his memoirs at least, that aside from a small number of 'notorious idlers and loafers and other types of a-social spongers' the great majority of 'asocials' and 'work-shy' men in Dachau were simply

> ashamed of being where they were, particularly older men who had not previously come into conflict with the law. Now all of a sudden they found themselves punished because, out of pigheadedness or Bavarian stubbornness, they had consistently shirked their work or shown an exaggerated fondness for beer.[224]

That the 'asocial' category contained men who had simply fallen foul of the Labour Service counsels against the extremely derogatory terminology used to describe the category in memoir literature. The same caveat applies very much to prisoners in Dachau held under the 'green' badge of professional criminals, which included men imprisoned for trifling offences. The idea of 'criminality' and 'asociality' as a biological destiny, rather than a product of choice or circumstance, implied that their concentration camp confinement could be a prophylactic measure at most. For the police and welfare organizations involved in combating these ills, concentration camp confinement became a welcome new disciplinary instrument to pursue longstanding goals frustrated by the liberal Weimar polity.[225]

As with purportedly 'asocial' prisoners, the number of 'professional criminals' in Dachau was lower than in other SS camps, although the overall figures are unreliable. In July 1938 there were 469 alleged criminals held in 'preventive custody' in Dachau, vastly outnumbered by the 4,155 categorized as politicals. At the same time, the proportion of political prisoners in Buchenwald was just 21 per cent.[226] It is customary for political memoirists to assert that the camp SS had a stronger affinity to the criminal prisoners than to the politicals, against whom they supposedly felt a sense of inferiority.[227] Certainly Höß believed he had got the measure of these men during his own time in prison in the 1920s, preparing him for dealing with them in his career in the concentration camps. His comments, however, are often barely distinguishable from those of political prisoners about 'professional criminals'. Höß believed he had peered 'into the minds and souls of these people and an abyss of human aberrations, depravities, and passions was opened before my eyes'.[228] He heard tales of pitiless murder and saw wardens attacked and corrupted by artful criminals. Höß concluded that the professional criminals in the camps were a far greater danger to the state than the political prisoners.[229] Yet while political prisoner memoirs are invariably at pains to stress an inmate hierarchy in Dachau with themselves at its apex, there is no concrete evidence to suggest that

[224] Höß, *Commandant*, p. 70.
[225] See especially the excellent monograph by Patrick Wagner, *Volksgemeinschaft ohne Verbrecher: Konzeption und Praxis der Kriminalpolizei in der Zeit der Weimarer Republik und des Nationalsozialismus* (Hamburg, 1996).
[226] Orth, *System*, p. 51.
[227] Schwarz, 'Wir haben es nicht gewusst', p. 192; Kogon, *Theory and Practice*, pp. 31, 287, 300.
[228] Höß, *Commandant*, p. 48.          [229] Höß, *Commandant*, p. 79.

'professional criminals' in Dachau were accorded treatment by the SS either above or below the 'usual' level of violence and terror.

## *Jews*

Jewish men were imprisoned in Dachau under the full range of detentive instruments and categories: as political prisoners, asocials, criminals, race defilers, and returned emigrants. Until early 1937, the number of Jewish prisoners in the camp at any one time was no more than seventy, around 2–3 per cent of the inmate population.[230] Yet even when their absolute numbers were relatively low, Jewish inmates were of extreme symbolic and cognitive importance to the Dachau School, their presence in the camp a purported validation of the antisemitic Nazi world view. Aspirational dehumanization was at its most concerted in the SS when it came to Jews, its *Reichsführer* urging in 1936 that 'we Germans must at last learn not to regard the Jews and Jewish-linked organisations as human beings who are members of our own species'.[231] Dachau's Jewish prisoners were marked with yellow spots superimposed on the normal categorized colours: thus political prisoners in protective custody wore red stripes with a yellow dot, Jewish 're-migrants' blue with a yellow spot, purported 'race defilers' yellow strips with a red dot.[232] The use of the colour yellow to identify and stigmatize Jewish inmates, redolent of medieval practices, was standard across the SS concentration camps.[233]

In February 1937, Reinhard Heydrich ordered the transfer of all male Jewish concentration camp inmates to Dachau. By the end of the year, they numbered some 300, around 12 per cent of the prisoner population.[234] Although it is not entirely clear why Dachau was chosen, recent research has stressed the camp's pioneering tradition of special treatment for Jewish inmates.[235] This stretched back to the days of the early Dachau SS, when Kantschuster had overseen a discrete Jewish company. In terms both of treatment and personnel, the boundaries in Dachau between the punishment and Jewish companies were blurred and porous but both were exposed to an intensified regimen of the 'usual camp treatment'. And in another example of sequential radicalization, the Dachau SS also introduced a grotesque punitive initiative for the Jewish company setting it apart even from the feared second-timer company. This was a periodic lock-in of the Jews to their barracks and was enacted on at least five occasions, lasting several months, between 1935 and 1937.[236] The pretext was invariably some kind of agitation against the Nazi regime in the foreign press, which the SS regarded as fresh evidence of the global Jewish conspiracy against Germany. The prisoners were thus deprived of contact with other inmates and of access to the canteen. The windows of their

[230] Wünschmann, 'Jewish Prisoners', p. 158.   [231] Longerich, *Himmler*, p. 198.
[232] Sopade Report on Dachau, May 1937. Reprinted in Goeschel and Wachsmann, *Nazi Concentration Camps*, pp. 235–8.
[233] Wünschmann, 'Jewish Prisoners', p. 159.   [234] Wünschmann, 'Jewish Prisoners', p. 158.
[235] Wünschmann, 'Jewish Prisoners', p. 166.   [236] Wünschmann, 'Jewish Prisoners', p. 164.

barracks were painted over, and inmates emerged only briefly in the mornings to undertake 'sport'.[237] With the concentration of all male Jews in Dachau in 1937, these terror initiatives secured optimal quantitative as well as qualitative impact.

Dachau, like other camps, had also long reserved particular incidental torments for Jewish prisoners. One regular spectacle was a game known as 'dance, Jew!'. In this, the SS drove a stake into the ground in front of a row of sentries. The Jewish prisoner was forced to 'dance' around it until dizzy on the understanding that if he strayed too close to the sentries, he would be shot for 'trying to escape'.[238] Another speciality particularly reserved for Jewish inmates was 'stomach crawling' (*Bauchkriechen*), in which they were forced to crawl face-down through puddles between SS block leaders.[239] A Jewish man from Würzburg was forced to eat his own excrement, and subsequently hanged himself in the latrine that night.[240] In a particularly notorious incident in November 1937, Kurt Riesenfeld, a Jewish lawyer from Breslau imprisoned for so-called 'race defilement', was spotted by commandant Loritz supposedly resting during work. He was thrown into a cement mixer by block leader Wolfgang Seuss and subsequently died of his injuries.[241] The SS also proved sensitive to the calendar of the Jewish faith, organizing particularly punitive labour on Yom Kippur in September 1937 as a mirthful play on this 'Day of Atonement'.[242] The special torment for Jewish inmates extended to their last moments in the camp. When Alfred Laurence emerged from eight months in Dachau his 'front teeth were all still somewhat shaky' from a savage blow he received from a passing SS NCO who had spotted the yellow patch on his uniform as he waited by the camp gate to be released.[243]

All in all, the Dachau School did not disappoint Heydrich with its murderous terror against the gathered Jewish prisoners: of the forty-one deaths recorded in the camp for 1937, fourteen were Jewish, a striking overrepresentation of an order not seen since the days of the early Dachau SS.[244] Yet the summit of lethal terror against Jews in Dachau was reached the following year in the aftermath of the November pogrom. This was the first time in the history of the concentration camps that membership of the Jewish 'race' alone was openly stated as a reason for imprisonment.[245] Hardened Dachau inmates were sickened by the SS violence against the 'November Jews'. As has been seen, the arriving Jews were forced to stand for hours on the roll call square. SS men patrolled the perimeter, lunging at the conspicuous or simply unlucky. In a kind of telescoping of the usual weeks of initiation, SS terror resources were focused on the most recent arrivals to the square. One witness observed that whenever an SS man seemed to be losing momentum in arbitrary violence, his supervisor would walk in his direction, reviving his ardour

[237] Wünschmann, 'Jewish Prisoners', p. 164.      [238] Burkhard, *Tanz Mal*, pp. 98–100.
[239] SAM, StA 34570, Zeugenvernehmungsprotokoll Hans Schwarz, 19 October 1954.
[240] Burkhard, *Tanz Mal*, pp. 52–4.
[241] SAM, StA 34570, Anklageschrift Landgericht Munich II Wolfgang Seuss, 22 June 1960; Riedel, *Ordnungshüter*, p. 190.
[242] Burkhard, *Tanz Mal*, 98–9.      [243] Laurence, 'Dachau', p. 6.
[244] Wünschmann, 'Jewish Prisoners', p. 162.
[245] Wünschmann, 'Jewish Prisoners', p. 215.

to curse and kick.[246] Röder describes SS men crashing their rifles into the heads of the massed ranks of Jews. He saw cracked skulls with torn hanging skin, prostrate Jews with broken arms and bleeding chests being trampled into the gravel. Nearby walls were splattered with blood, attracting a large group of off-duty SS officers to smoke and bawl encouragement to their comrades.[247] Schecher suggests that the advent of the November Jews was seen by ambitious SS personnel as an opportunity to demonstrate their Nazi ardour to superiors. In response to a Jewish man bold enough to make a complaint about his treatment, and to terrorize the arrivals, commandant Loritz despatched a pair of prisoners to retrieve the whipping block and whip from the *Bunker*. The complainant was placed over it. Suddenly one SS *Scharführer* with whom Schecher had long worked, 'in general a placid chap', hastened across to Loritz and volunteered to deliver the blows himself. Demonstrating his 'National Socialist heroism on the behind of a defenceless Jew', the NCO swung the whip 'with dedication'.[248]

By February 1939, 187 of the 10,911 Jews imprisoned in Dachau in the wake of the pogrom had been registered as dead by the camp authorities.[249] Most survivors were released after weeks or months on the expectation or undertaking that they would surrender their property to the Nazi state and emigrate. Throughout Germany Jewish men with shaven heads and anxious gait were visually marked as being on borrowed time in the Greater German Reich.[250] For the SS, the post-*Kristallnacht* imprisonment of male Jews was the most dramatic illustration to date of the versatility of the concentration camps and their staff as terror instruments for the regime. They had proven capable of absorbing and subjugating enormous numbers of inmates at short notice. A programme of terror developed in, and exported from, the Dachau School over the past five and a half years, with a few adaptations for an unprecedented quantitative situation, had the desired effect on German Jews able to leave the country.

This programme of terror embodied a range of social and cognitive stimuli. A dualistic institutional outlook, deliberately nourished in the Dachau School, played a central role. It was midwife to the 'usual camp treatment', the terror principle that a Dachau inmate might at any time be hectored, punched, kicked, whipped, and even killed, simply by dint of being a Dachau inmate. In practice, most prisoners got through the day without suffering physical violence from the SS. The personnel resources of the latter were inadequate to achieve the individualized, penetrative terror sometimes implied by an inmate memoir literature which understandably foregrounds set-piece atrocities. 'It is not these stories', writes Neurath, 'but the 120 loads of gravel and the roll call and the construction of the bed and other routine jobs, which dominate the prisoner's life'.[251] After creating

---

[246] WL Report, no. 68, s. 2.        [247] Röder, *Nachtwache*, pp. 41–2.
[248] Schecher, 'Rückblick', p. 123.   [249] Wünschmann, 'Jewish Prisoners', p. 215.
[250] Wolfgang Benz, 'Mitglieder der Häftlingsgesellschaft auf Zeit: "Die Aktionsjuden" 1938/39', in Benz and Koenigseder, *Das Konzentrationslager Dachau*, pp. 207–18, here pp. 217–18; Wünschmann, 'Jewish Prisoners', p. 219.
[251] Neurath, *Society*, p. 115.

a terroristic social field during the processes of admission and initiation, the SS relied partly on the *Kapos* for delegated, quotidian violence. Beyond this, the Dachau SS habitus rested on a quasi-Darwinian ethos, always central to Nazi practice, in which inmates who proved unable to adjust to concentrational behaviour, or were simply unlucky, 'stood out' and became susceptible to extreme, exemplary violence from the SS themselves. The SS also intervened in this selective process in countless arbitrary ways. These stretched from deliberately singling out individuals and groups for torment, to placing inmates in particularly attritional environments such as the punishment and second-timer companies, to locking Jewish prisoners into darkened barracks to break their health and prosociality. Such bespoke, sequential, punitive initiatives drove camp terror cumulatively in a radical direction. Yet despite a grotesquely asymmetrical social field, and despite the Dachau School's efforts to promote a dehumanization of the camp's inmates, it would be misleading to cast them as mere objects of violence. Although the source base sometimes works to conceal it, Dachau personnel and inmates also confronted one another on an intersubjective, even biographical, basis. The psychology of this engagement was complex and varied, impossible to capture in blanket generalizations of psychoanalytic or social psychological inspiration, nor in the search for a linear SS 'motivation'. The penultimate chapter will explore the contribution of ideals of masculinity to the SS habitus, where the camp was once again at the vanguard of wider cultural and political trends.

# 5

# 'Tolerance Means Weakness': The Dachau SS and Masculinity

The importance of masculinity as a social category and status in the Third Reich is hard to exaggerate. The Nazi state was an avowed 'masculine state' (*Männerstaat*), like other fascisms tracing its lineage back to a mythologized classical world.[1] 'Manliness' in this milieu entailed the glorification of militarism, toughness, loyalty, camaraderie, and youth. These ideals had increasingly been mobilized by European states in the nineteenth century for military recruitment, beginning with the revolutionary *levée en masse* decreed by the Jacobin National Convention in 1793. Shaken by defeat at the hands of this French army, Prussia, too, had introduced conscription in 1813 for the so-called 'Wars of Liberation' against Napoleon. The system was continued into peacetime when all Prussian men between the ages of fourteen and forty were required to serve in militia alongside the army. This universalization of military service helped turn it, in theory at least, from a dynastic affair of elites and mercenaries into the privilege and key manifestation of individual masculinity.[2] 'Military prepared-ness' (*militärische Bereitschaft*) was fundamental to German male identity in a manner absent, for example, in Britain, which retained the pre-revolutionary military model of a small, professional, non-conscripted army. Military service in the Prussian and German armies was regarded as the nation's 'school of manliness'.[3] The full resonance

---

[1] An excellent comparative study of the complex historical mythologies of the Italian and German fascist movements is Knox, *Threshold of Power*. See also Roger Griffin, *The Nature of Fascism* (London, 1991). On the importance of an idealized Ancient Greece to German nationalism and fascism, see especially George L. Mosse, *Nationalism and Sexuality* (Wisconsin, 1985), pp. 48–65.

[2] Mosse, *Fallen Soldiers*, pp. 18–22; Frevert, *Nation in Barracks*, passim. In *Mein Kampf* Hitler lamented the fact that he had not been born for the Wars of Liberation 'when a man . . . was really worth something': Hitler, *Mein Kampf*, p. 144.

[3] Frevert, *Nation in Barracks*, pp. 170–82. See also Hitler's ode to the Imperial Army in *Mein Kampf*, pp. 254–6. The literature on the genealogy of Nazi conceptions of masculinity is now exten-sive. See especially George L. Mosse, *The Image of Man* (Oxford, 1996); Karin Hagemann and Stefanie Schuler-Springorum (eds), *Home/Front: The Military, War, and Gender in Twentieth Century Germany* (Oxford, 2002); René Schilling, *'Kriegshelden': Deutungsmuster heroischer Männlichkeit in Deutschland 1813–1945* (Paderborn, 2004); Stefan Dudink, Karin Hagemann, and John Tosh (eds), *Masculinities in Politics and War* (Manchester, 2004); Frevert, *A Nation in Barracks*; Thomas Kühne, *Comradeship. Die Soldaten des nationalsozialistischen Krieges und das 20 Jahrhundert* (Göttingen, 2006); On post-First World War notions of tough, soldierly masculinity on the German Right, see the classic psychoana-lytical treatments of the *Freikorps* by Klaus Theweleit, *Male Fantasies. Volume 1: Women, Floods, Bodies,*

of the Dachau SS self-stylization as 'soldiers' can only be grasped with reference to the interaction between these *longue durée* ideals and the more immediate and particular gender discourses of Weimar and Nazi Germany. As has been seen, the supposed soldierly male values of toughness, ruthlessness, and comradeship framed guard service in the concentration camps, presented throughout the SS documentary record as the 'inner Front' of the People's Community. With this in mind, the following presents a concentric circle type of analysis, first looking—necessarily briefly—at the broader context of these ideals in Nazi Germany before moving piecemeal towards their localized iteration in Dachau and the Dachau School.

## MARTIAL MASCULINITY IN THE THIRD REICH

National Socialism emerged in the wake of a series of social disturbances—rapid industrialization and urbanization, war and defeat, inflation and depression— which had profoundly unsettled centuries of inherited thinking about gender roles.[4] The Great War's heavy demographic toll on young males had unbalanced the ratio between the sexes, with anxieties about the advent of the independent and enfranchised 'new woman' shared across the political spectrum of the Weimar Republic. This much-mythologized figure, harbinger of modernity, was a metonym for Weimar's gender crisis, 'the most readily available symbol of gender disorder'.[5] Conservatives and nationalists fantasized about deliverance from upheaval through the forging of the 'new man' to drive a reinvigorated patriarchy.[6] Then there was the blow to the German martial pedagogic tradition in the Versailles treaty, which reduced the army to a small core of 100,000 professionals enlisted for twelve years. Weimar politics was indelibly shaped by the struggle for custody of the values of manhood in the democratic, republican age. Those hegemonic in the Third Reich—toughness, militarism, comradeship, patriarchy—were far from uniquely National Socialist. Indeed, by commanding a much broader assent they brought an enhanced cultural legitimacy to the regime and offered a social dividend to males beyond its electoral constituency.[7]

This contest to define an honourable model of manhood was a central feature of the 'culture wars' which beset the Weimar Republic and contributed to

---

*History* (Minneapolis, 1987) and Theweleit, *Male Fantasies. Volume 2: Male Bodies: Psychoanalysing the White Terror* (Minneapolis, 2003).

[4] Raewyn Connell, 'Masculinity and Nazism', in Annette Dietrich and Ljiljana Heise (eds), *Männlichkeitskonstruktionen im Nationalsozialismus* (Frankfurt am Main, 2013), pp. 37–42, here p. 39.

[5] Kathleen Canning, 'Women and the Politics of Gender', in Anthony McElligott (ed.), *Weimar Germany* (Oxford, 2009), pp. 146–74, quote p. 167.

[6] See especially Mosse, *The Image of Man*, pp. 155–80.

[7] Theoretical literature on masculinity describes this social benefit as the 'patriarchal dividend'. On this and the broader notion of 'hegemonic masculinity' see R. W. Connell and James W. Messerschmidt, 'Hegemonic Masculinity: Rethinking the Concept', *Gender and Society*, Vol. 19, No. 6, (Dec., 2005), pp. 829–59.

its seemingly endemic crisis of legitimation.[8] The best-known engagement was fought in late 1930 over the German release of the film *All Quiet on the Western Front*. Erich Maria Remarque's novel had already sold over one million copies in Germany and proffered a bleak, naturalistic depiction of a life in the trenches in which conscripts feared, suffered, and despaired of their lot. German conservatives were incensed by Remarque's failure to grasp the nobility of purpose and heroism beyond the inescapable privations of war. Nationalists loathed him additionally for besmirching the comradely 'war experience' which underpinned their imagined classless People's Community. The Nazis, following their triumph in the 1930 Reichstag elections, chose a violent response to a discursive threat. Goebbels orchestrated a series of boisterous SA riots to disrupt the 'filthy' film's first public showings on Berlin's Nollendorfplatz.[9] In an eloquent and dire portent for the freedom of cultural expression, the film was banned at Hindenburg's personal approval a few days later. Remarque's book was among those burned on pyres at universities throughout the land on 10 May 1933, 'in the name', rejoiced Berlin students, 'of educating our people in the spirit of valour'.[10] During the Third Reich the regimentation of cultural life under Goebbels entailed less medieval forms of censorship. Liberal and pacifist literature was simply banned, while books and films towed the Nazi line by valorizing war, martial comradeship, and a concomitant female domesticity.[11]

In no danger of being burned or banned was a distinctively German genre of war narrative highly congenial to militarist nationalism: masculinist so-called 'heroic realist' literature.[12] Its high priest and star author was Ernst Jünger, an archetype of youthful soldierly fortitude, injured fourteen times and awarded Germany's highest war decoration, the Pour le Mérite. His self-published war memoir, *The Storm of Steel*, was a runaway success and emerged as the Right's countertype to Remarque to become a bestseller and 'cult book' of the Third Reich.[13] For Jünger, the Entente artillery's 'storm of steel' had wrought a 'chiselled' new generation of 'princes of the trenches, with hard, set faces, brave to madness, tough and agile to leap forward and back, keen with bloodthirsty nerves'.[14] A more eloquent anticipation of the 'hard look' (*forscher Blick*) of the implacable Waffen SS soldier, propounded in countless recruitment posters, is hard to imagine. Much of the iconography and vocabulary of Nazi paramilitarism was drawn from the 'storm' assault squads

---

[8] Succinct summary of Weimar's culture wars offered in Evans, *Coming of the Third Reich*, 118–38. See also Bessel, *Germany after the First World War*, pp. 254–84; Mosse, *Fallen Soldiers*, pp. 159–81.

[9] Eksteins, 'War, Memory, and Politics', pp. 71–2.

[10] Modris Eksteins, *Rites of Spring: The Great War and the Bith of the Modern* Age (Boston, 2000), p. 289–98.

[11] David Welch, *The Third Reich: Politics and Propaganda* (London, 2002).

[12] A useful monograph on this genre is Ann P. Linder, *Princes of the Trenches: Narrating the German Experience of the First World War* (Columbia, 1996). Theweleit's *Male Fantasies* volumes remain the most sustained and provocative analysis. For some links between this literature and the SS mindset, see the pioneering article by Buchheim, 'Command and Compliance', esp. pp. 321–32.

[13] Bernd Weisbrod, 'Military Violence and Male Fundamentalism: Ernst Jünger's Contribution to the Conservative Revolution', *History Workshop Journal*, No. 49 (Spring, 2000), pp. 68–94, here p. 71.

[14] Ernst Jünger, *The Storm of Steel* trans Basil Creighton (London, 1975), pp. 109, 235.

on the Western Front lionized by Jünger and his peers. Frontline newspapers celebrated their exploits and the squads awarded themselves romantic unit names, among them the Death's Head.[15] The units were said to have practised an egalitarian discipline, addressing their officers with the familiar 'Du', another convention picked up by the Waffen SS.

This mythologized 'trench socialism' was part of a broader discourse of male comradeship and camaraderie inherited and nurtured by the Nazis.[16] These concepts were fundamental to debates about German masculinity because they provided the context for so many other behavioural norms. Their mythology reached back to the Napoleonic era and to Ludwig Uhland's mawkish 'Song of the Good Comrade'. Penned during the Wars of Liberation, this was a patriotic bourgeois staple appropriated and subverted by the Nazis: concentration camp inmates would be forced to sing it.[17] The ideal of male comradeship reached a mythical apogee in Weimar politics as part of the search for consolation and redemption in defeat.[18] The Left fashioned a Remarquian narrative of rank-and-file soldiers bound in alienation from well-fed officers, closer in fraternal internationalism to the soldier workers in opposing trenches. It is in this spirit that Paul, the main character in *All Quiet*, wonders if 'there is anything more beautiful, more sacred in this world, than freely bestowed comradeship?'[19]

The Nazis, who profited from such implicit endorsement of their preoccupation with the front experience, promised to recover the sense of camaraderie and belonging squandered by the interest group politics of the Weimar Republic.[20] Comradeship prefigured a chauvinistic People's Community and restored masculine state. Rather than Remarque's aggregate of shared endurance, it was a collective and elemental will to achievement, suffused with German particularism. The German 'national awakening' on 30 January 1933 was choreographed as a masculine and comradely affair, with torchlit parades of thousands of uniformed men cheered on by admiring, awestruck crowds. The engorged war veterans' *Stahlhelm* rejoiced that 'comradeship has become the foundation of the new Reich'.[21] Artists, photographers, and sculptors hastened to produce monuments to male togetherness: taut, muscular bodies aligned in disciplined will.[22] The Hitler Youth, the Labour Service, and countless other sex-segregated organizations brought males together in earnest pseudo-military camps. The German army, too, invested considerable resources in fostering a Nazified comradeship in its ranks whose

---

[15] Robin Lumsden, *Himmler's Black Order: A History of the SS 1923–1945* (Somerset, 1997), pp. 2–3.

[16] An interesting monograph, albeit not without some fundamental flaws, is Kühne, *Kameradschaft*. It is baffling, for example, to read that an ideal based on loyalty and self-sacrifice in war 'was explicitly encoded as feminine'. See Thomas Kühne, 'Comradeship: Gender Confusion and Gender Order in the German Military, 1918–1945', in Hagemann & Schüler-Springorum, *Home/Front*, here pp. 233–4.

[17] Guido Fackler, *'Des Lagers Stimme'—Musik im KZ: Alltag und Häftlingskultur in den Konzentrationslagern 1933–1936* (Bremen, 2000), p. 134.

[18] Kühne, *Kameradschaft*, pp. 52–65.        [19] In Kühne, *Kameradschaft*, p. 61.

[20] Fritz, *Frontsoldaten*, p. 208–10.        [21] Kühne, *Kameradschaft*, p. 97.

[22] Jonathan Petropolous, *The Faustian Bargain: The Art World in Nazi Germany* (New York, 2000), pp. 218–53. Excellent photographic selection of sculptures in Mosse, *Nationalism*, pp. 96f.

contribution to the martial resilience of the Third Reich is still debated among military historians.[23]

Initially, however, it was paramilitary rather than military culture that defined and advertised the forms of masculinity and comradeship privileged in the nascent Third Reich. As has been seen, during the Weimar Republic a shared sense of comradely purpose as a 'fighting community' amid unemployment and privation had helped to bind paramilitaries together and sustain the dynamism of the movement. The Brownshirts' hostels and taverns, heavy with the fug of beer and cigar smoke, were key sites for expressing individual and collective masculinity. SA publications conceded that the public stereotype of the SA man was not far off the mark:

> Sure, he loves to drink a beer or two, sure he gets drunk sometimes and does stupid things playing cards instead of looking for work . . . of course his lifestyle isn't morally flawless—he is too full of life for that—he has his wife and perhaps another all too soon in colourful succession . . . sure, he gets into a row with other guests in a pub which leads to a punch-up . . . In short, he has a whole host of failings and weaknesses and makes no effort to disguise them. You love him nevertheless, once you know and understand him, because he embodies the very best of the German race.[24]

The SA man's supposedly loveable personal flaws became priceless political virtues in a comradely setting. His *Sturm* was a sturdy paramilitary shield against the predations of socialism, communism, and Jewry on the German streets—dark forces who respected nothing but the violence they themselves had wrought on Germany since 1918. Brownshirt togetherness was divided between such 'duties' and bespoke 'comradely' evenings, which frequently began with a lecture on honour, loyalty, or comradeship.[25] SA comradeship was depicted as the spearhead of the classless Third Reich, binding men of all backgrounds together, 'the one a factory worker, the other a student, the third a farmer's son, the fourth an engineer'.[26] Vast consumption of alcohol could fuel an intense, fiercely emotional camaraderie within local *Stürme*, banter and masculine horseplay to the fore. Heavy drinking sessions might spill over into 'punitive expeditions' to working-class enclaves and thence public violence.[27]

Yet while the Brownshirts' boozy camaraderie and public scuffling stood more or less within a broader tradition of raucous and youthful masculinity, other aspects of their comradeship were highly controversial. Röhm's homosexuality, and that of a number of his lieutenants, was no secret. Yet with his war-scarred, porcine face, earthy charisma, and distinguished military record he certainly fulfilled the Jünger criteria of manliness. In the twilight of the Weimar Republic, the

---

[23] See especially the classic analysis by Edward Shils and Morris Janowitz, 'Cohesion and Disintegration in the Wehrmacht', *Public Opinion Quarterly*, Vol. 12, No. 2 (Summer, 1948), pp. 280–315. Also Kühne, *Kameradschaft*, pp. 271–9; Fritz, *Frontsoldaten*, pp. 208–16. For a classic and stridently particularist reading focusing instead on ideology, see Omer Bartov, *The Eastern Front 1941–1945* (London, 1985).

[24] Longerich, *Geschichte*, p. 142.     [25] Longerich, *Geschichte*, p. 141.

[26] Longerich, *Geschichte*, p. 139.

[27] Longerich, *Geschichte*, p. 127; Hein, *Elite*, pp. 62–3. For a brilliant microstudy of one Berlin *Sturm*, see Reichardt, *Faschistische Kampfbünde*, pp. 422–32.

left-wing press devoted much space to advertising Röhm's sexual tastes and their reverberations in the NSDAP headquarters in Munich, dubbed the 'Brown House of Homosexuality'. Reichsbanner and communist Red Front paramilitary units taunted SA and SS foes by shouting '*Schwul Heil*' ('Hail Gay').[28] The Brownshirt weekly, *SA Mann*, gamely tried to turn Röhm's predilections, too, into a virtue, a mark of singular genius. In February 1933, the paper placed him in exalted company:

> Is Goethe less valuable to us because he was a known polygamist? Does Schopenhauer's misogyny lessen his genius? Should we admire Schiller less because this national hero was often inspired by the smell of rotting apples?[29]

Even within the Nazi movement, voices were raised against Röhm. Hitler, however, was unmoved. He pointed out that the SA was 'not a moral institution for the education of nice young girls, but a band of rough fighters'.[30] All this changed in 1934 when the slaying of Röhm and the SA leadership by the SS was presented to the public in terms of a moral cleansing, even a defensive measure against a plot to establish a homosexual dictatorship. Now Hitler told the party press that he 'would especially like every mother to be able to offer her son to the SA, the Party or the Hitler Youth without the fear that he might become morally or sexually depraved'.[31] Persecution of male homosexuality became an increasing preoccupation for the Nazi state, with the legal definition of 'unnatural vice' between men vastly expanded in 1935. Henceforth male homosexuality was kept in the public eye by regular outings of supposed pederasts in the Catholic Church and by the scandal in 1938 involving the Army's Commander-in-Chief Werner von Fritsch, dismissed on trumped-up allegations of homosexual relations with a male Berlin prostitute. The SS, the ideological cavalry of the Third Reich, increasingly took the lead on this issue.

## SS MASCULINITY

If the public face of the Nazi regime was 'intensely masculinized', the SS was ever more at the heart of its iconography.[32] In the wake of the Brownshirts' disgrace, Himmler's troops were the Third Reich's pre-eminent *Männerbund* (association of

---

[28] Reichardt, *Faschistische Kampfbünde*, p. 680. The SPD's *Münchener Post* ran a veritable campaign on this topic in 1931 (see for example 23 April 1931, 22 June 1931, 23 June 1931).

[29] In Longerich, *Geschichte*, p. 200.

[30] Evans, *Third Reich in Power*, p. 531. A detailed recent analysis is provided by Suzanne zur Nieden, 'Aufstieg und Fall des virilen Männerhelden: Der Skandal um Ernst Röhm und seine Ermordung', in zur Nieden (ed.), *Homosexualität und Staatsräson: Männlichkeit, Hompohobie und Politik in Deutschland 1900–1945* (Frankfurt am Main, 2005), pp. 163–76.

[31] Geoffrey J. Giles, 'The Institutionalization of Homosexual Panic in the Third Reich', in Robert Gellately and Nathan Stoltzfus (eds), *Social Outsiders in Nazi Germany* (Princeton, 2001), pp. 233–55; here p. 236.

[32] Connell, 'Masculinity and Nazism', p. 38. An interesting if sometimes speculative monograph on this topic is Paula Diehl, *Macht-Mythos-Utopie: Die Körperbilder der SS Männer* (Berlin, 2005).

males), a prestigious yet sometimes troubling responsibility for the *Reichsführer*.[33] Himmler's awkward adolescence had left him with hang-ups about intimacy and sexuality which would colour the negotiation of these issues in the SS.[34] In a lengthy speech to his lieutenants in February 1937, Himmler warned that there had been 'far too great a masculinization of our whole life'.[35] With the fate of the SA in mind, he worried that such 'exaggerated masculinization . . . provides fertile soil for homosexuality'. It was vital, Himmler cautioned, that young German males interact at an early age with girls, and with the very best girls at that. For once they had fallen in love, 'mutual masturbation with friends, male friendships, or friendships of this kind of sexual nature between boys are out of the question'. In the final analysis, male homosexuals were incapable of the true comradeship demanded by a *Männerbund*, for 'although these people like to pretend that they love one another, there is in truth no loyalty in the love of one man for another, whereas in other circumstances men are normally loyal to each other'.

In the same speech, Himmler set out his punitive policies on homosexuality within the SS. Contrary to an image which persists to this day, the SS was not a conspicuously homosexual organization. This erroneous and offensive trope was first popularized by the homophobic writings of literary exiles from Nazi Germany and Dachau inmate literature, too, teems with hostile speculation about the 'unnatural' sex lives of the SS.[36] But in the SS, male homosexuality was regarded as a defect of character, a eugenic sin to the perpetuation of SS racial stock, and a threat to the well-being of the German nation. In the speech, Himmler revealed that around eight to ten cases of homosexuality were found in the SS every year. Their ancient Germanic ancestors, he reflected, had solved the problem by drowning homosexual men in swamps, but this was no longer practical. Instead, from now on, every SS offender uncovered would be degraded, expelled, and passed to the courts for sentencing. After serving his sentence, the homosexual would be brought into a concentration camp and 'shot while trying to escape' by former comrades from his unit. It is doubtful that this was actually carried out; the two documented homosexual scandals in the Dachau SS ended simply with the expulsion of the culprits.[37] But the harsh rhetoric was no mere window-dressing, as the

[33] For great detail on the *Männerbund*, see Claudia Bruns, *Politik des Eros: Der Männerbund in Wissenschaft, Politik und Jugendkultur (1880–1934)* (Cologne, 2008). On the role of all-male associations in British and European masculine identities, see John Tosh, 'What Should Historians Do With Masculinity?', *History Workshop*, No. 38 (1994), pp. 179–202.

[34] Longerich, *Himmler*, passim.

[35] The following quotations from IfZ, MA311, Rede der RFSS to Gruppenführer-Besprechung, 18 February 1937, ss. 765–93.

[36] For example Burkhardt, *Tanz Mal*, p. 71; Otto Marx and Harry J. Marx, *Dachau, 1933–1935* (New York, 1987), p. 51. A recent contribution to this troubling trope is the bestselling 'perpetrator novel' by Jonathan Littell, *The Kindly Ones* (London, 2009), whose anti-hero has many homosexual affairs with SS comrades. See also Geoffrey J. Giles, 'The Denial of Homosexuality: Same-Sex Incidents in Himmler's SS and Police', *Journal of the History of Sexuality*, Vol. 11, No.1 (2002), pp. 256–90. Giles offers detailed examples of homosexual incidents in the SS—including a former Dachau guard—but rightly resists the notion that the organization was atypical in this regard. See also Hein, *Elite*, p. 101.

[37] DaA, A4102, Strafmaßnahmen gegen SS-Ange. Wilhelm S., s. 4; Edith Raim, 'Westdeutsche Ermittlungen und Prozesse zum KZ Dachau und seine Außenlagern', in Ludwig Eiber and Robert Sigel

appalling treatment of allegedly homosexual prisoners in Dachau, to be discussed below, shows. And in 1941 a new edict was issued in Hitler's name warning that an SS man who committed 'indecency with another man or allows himself to be abused in an indecent manner will be punished with death'. Although the edict was implemented unevenly, death sentences were carried out.[38]

Where did this leave the intimacies of male togetherness in the SS? Most unusually, Himmler personally made little effort to develop a distinctively SS understanding of comradeship to distinguish it from the SA. He remained uncharacteristically reticent on the topic in his speeches throughout the Third Reich.[39] But the term is prevalent elsewhere in the documentary record of the SS. An internal circular of 1936 explained that comradeship was 'the soul of the SS', uniting its members 'like a magic wand'. While warning that '[n]o book can teach you the rules of true comradeship: you must feel it in your heart', it went on to offer some practical pointers:

> One comrade has problems on his farm . . . His friends go to help with the harvest . . . You meet a drunk comrade at a bar. People are staring at him. True comradeship is to take him home, quietly . . . A comrade is sick . . . his friends come to visit . . . A poor comrade has become embroiled in a legal dispute: his friends collect money from among themselves in order to get him a good defence lawyer.[40]

Theodor Eicke was characteristically eager to promote a distinctive ethos of comradeship among his concentration camp guards. It was to be a familial, brotherly phenomenon under his personal tutelage. Eicke developed a consciously paternalist relationship with his troops, his 'Papa Eicke' soubriquet a vivid example of the patriarchal discourses which pervaded the Nazi *Männerstaat*. Just as a good father knows no favourites, Eicke claimed that his underlings were all equal to him. In his orders of the month for April 1937, Eicke reminded the Death's Head guards that 'the foundation of our cohesion is comradeship'. Invoking trench socialist mythology, he warned that even the youngest and rawest recruit was worthy of sitting next to the most senior officer in the SS mess hall, and that any officer or NCO who thought otherwise was 'living in another world'.[41] According to Höß, Eicke would sit with the sentries in their canteens and barracks in the evening, listening to their worries, and 'speaking with them in their own language'.[42] He even offered to take guards estranged from their families into his own home for vacations, although his housekeeper did not recall anyone taking him up on the offer.[43] Nevertheless, Eicke's function as an alternate paternal figure was important in a society with such a strong tradition of patriarchal authority (*Obrigkeit*). Even decades later, brutal concentration camp murderers could become hoarse with emotion as they looked back from prison cells on their beloved 'Papa' Eicke, killed leading his 'boys' in

(eds), *Dachauer Prozesse: NS-Verbrechen vor amerikanischen Militärgerichten in Dachau 1945–1948* (Dachau, 2007), pp. 210–36, here pp. 215–16.

[38] Giles, 'Denial', pp. 265–6.      [39] Longerich, *Himmler*, p. 308.
[40] Cited in Segev, *Soldiers*, p. 114.
[41] IfZ, MA 293, IKL Befehlsblatt, 1 April 1937, s. 2550195.
[42] Höß, *Commandant*, p. 236.      [43] Segev, *Soldiers*, p. 137.

Russia in 1943.[44] Loved for his protection, feared for his temper and discipline, Eicke performed his role with a stern paternal brow, a Virginia cigar at his lips.[45]

The ideal of comradeship clearly played a role in attracting young males to the SS in the first place. Many Dachau SS men, as will be seen, were to be disappointed by the quotidian realities beneath the myth. To others it was a genuine and integrative phenomenon. The widow of Josef Kramer, the Bergen-Belsen commandant who cut his teeth in Dachau, told Segev that what drew her husband to the SS

> more than anything else was the desire to be in the company of other young men, of his age, in the same situation. He found close friends in the organisation and their friendship was very dear to him. They would always enjoy themselves together . . . This joint effort, the new faith, brought them closer to each other. They had something to give each other. When I thought about that years later I said to myself that my Kramer felt more comfortable among men than among women.[46]

Höß, too, describes himself in his autobiography as a 'lone wolf . . . continually drawn towards the comradeship which enables a man to rely on others'.[47] The ties of paramilitary comradeship always existed relative to an 'other': generally to women and civilians (drawing on the supposed chasm between home and front in the Great War) but also, in the confrontational environment of the concentration camps, relative to the inmates in a kind of mutually reinforcing dynamic of inclusion and exclusion. In an aphorism which might serve as a lodestar for concentration camp guard masculinity, Eicke wrote that '[i]n service there is only merciless severity; outside service hours there is heart-warming comradeship'.[48]

Beyond a masculine comradeship drained discursively of any homoerotic subtext, the SS male ideal type cannibalized elements from assorted German masculine traditions. In its ceaseless invocation of 'honour' it aped the chivalrous Prussian norm also increasingly popular among bourgeois males towards the end of the nineteenth century.[49] The SS had its own 'court of honour' in Munich, modelled on those of the Imperial officer corps, to adjudicate in cases where an SS man felt his honour to have been besmirched. In 1938 it issued a verbose set of regulations setting out his path to 'satisfaction'.[50] Should a 'chivalrous' (*ritterlich*) exchange between the dishonoured and the injurer not settle matters, the dispute might be settled by armed duel subject to the approval of Himmler, himself a former member of a duelling fraternity in Munich. The extent to which duels were actually fought in the SS is unclear; certainly there is no evidence that any were conducted by Dachau personnel despite countless amply rancorous quarrels. The provisions were an attempt to promote a cohesive sense of eliteness to the organization. Traditionally elite pursuits such as fencing, boxing, rowing, climbing, and

[44] Dicks, *Licensed Mass Murder*, p. 122; Sydnor, *Soldiers*, p. 30, n. 72.

[45] SAM, StA 34461/4, Max Dall'Armi, Bilder und Skizzen aus dem Konzentrationslager, 13 May 1951.

[46] Segev, *Soldiers*, pp. 68–9.     [47] Höß, *Commandant*, p. 42.

[48] Special camp order 1 August 1934, in Goeschel and Wachsmann, *Nazi Concentration Camps*, p. 151.

[49] Ute Frevert, *Ehrenmänner: Das Duell in der bürgerlichen Gesellschaft* (Munich, 1991).

[50] IfZ, MA 847, Bestimmungen über die Erledigung von Ehrenhandeln, s. 2958662.

especially horse-riding were also much favoured in the SS, while its feudal trappings of castles and crusading Teutonic knights are well-known.[51] The requirement for all SS men to secure permission from above to marry, to be addressed in detail below, imitated the caste-conscious Imperial officer corps who also needed the permission of their superiors to wed: significantly, this ensured there were no Jewish wives amongst the officer caste.[52] Himmler told one well-heeled audience in 1933 that the SS could only secure elite status if its men

> brought to the social requirements of the present day the genuine military tradition, the distinctive outlook, bearing and breeding of the German nobility, and the creative efficiency of the industrialist, on the basis of racial selection.[53]

There were also distinctly bourgeois aspects to normative SS masculinity, reflecting its demographic profile, orderly self-image, and the earnest, moralizing character of its leader. Never fully freed from the Youth Movement's body purity ethic, Himmler was forever exhorting his men to forego alcohol and tobacco. 'My dear Toni', he wrote in 1937 to an underling he had imprisoned in Dachau, 'naturally you will be released . . . as soon as I am convinced you have renounced alcohol, which over the years has been a tyrant to you and your family'.[54] For uxoriousness too, despite Himmler's own marital infidelities, was much emphasized. All these aristocratic and bourgeois values, of course, were unmoored from their Christian-moral context, discursive fig leaves camouflaging an unprecedented criminality. In one of the most infamous speeches even in Nazi Germany, Himmler lauded his SS men for having carried out their 'difficult' genocidal work and yet 'remained decent'.[55]

'Decency' (*Anständigkeit*) is also the main theme, the guiding ideal, in SS marriage application files. Finding a bride had long been a key responsibility and expression of individual manhood, but in the totalitarian SS the familial and sexual were no private matter. From 1931 the aspirant SS husband was obliged to prove to the satisfaction of the 'clan department' (*Sippenamt*) of the SS Race and Resettlement Main Office (RuSHA) that no racial or eugenic pollutants were to be found in the couple's family trees.[56] He was also vetted for maturity and economic means, the bride for her compatibility with SS domesticity. A complete set of marriage paperwork ran to dozens of documents. The conditions for marriage approval were tightened further from 1935 to ensure that the SS remained at the racial vanguard of Nazism in the wake of the Nuremberg Laws.[57] And whilst

[51] For detail, see Bahro, *Der SS-Sport*. Bahro offers an impeccable organizational history of sport in the SS but is rather cursory on its function and implications, and on the relationship between sport and masculinity in particular. On this, see Daniel Wildmann, *Begehrte Körper: Konstruktion und Inszenierung des 'arischen' Männerkörpers im 'Dritten Reich'* (Würzburg, 1998), esp. pp. 18–27. See also Hein, *Elite*, pp. 213–25.

[52] Gudrun Schwarz, *Eine Frau an seiner Seite: Ehefrauen in der 'SS-Sippengemeinschaft'* (Hamburg, 1997), pp. 25–7.

[53] Höhne, *Order*, p. 132.

[54] BAB, NS19/1273, Himmler to Anton Lehner, June 1937, s. 1. The classic analysis of Himmler's petit bourgeois upbringing remains Angress and Smith, 'Diaries of Heinrich Himmler's Early Years'.

[55] In Jeremy Noakes and Guy Pridham, *Nazism 1919–1945*, Vol. 3, pp. 617–18.

[56] A fine monograph on the RuSHA is Heinemann, '*Rasse*'.

[57] Schwarz, *Frau*, pp. 31–2.

many SS regulations were meaningless in practice—not least in the concentration camps—when it came to ensuring racial purity the RuSHA could be punctilious in the extreme. According to one estimate, between 1932 and 1940 just 958 out of 106,304 marriage applications were turned down by the RuSHA, less than 1 per cent.[58] The personnel files of the Dachau SS, however, suggest the percentage was much higher in this lowly reach of organization, reflecting both its relative lack of political clout and the elevated eugenic expectations for professional SS units. Many applications in addition were granted only after Sisyphean paperwork trailing by guards, and then only 'provisionally' due to documentary lacunae. The process was expensive in terms of time, postal fees, and the hiring of professional researchers.[59] Parish and civilian record offices had to be cajoled and jostled; one officer lamented that he was still waiting for data on five of his fiancée's relatives despite threatening the priest concerned with a visit from the Gestapo.[60] As such it presumably worked to reinforce the guards' resentment of and antipathy to non-'Aryans', above all Jews and Jewish inmates. It also provoked tensions and jealousies belying the hallowed comradeship of the SS, as the following anonymous letter sent to the RuSHA in 1936 by a Dachau guard suggests:

> Several days ago SS *Rottenführer* Ludwig W. celebrated his second wedding anniversary and made light of the RuSHA, boasting that he did not need permission to marry and hadn't even bothered to submit the necessary paperwork . . . Are there different rules for this man, should he be allowed to continue to make a mockery of the RuSHA, without his black uniform being rescinded?[61]

For good measure the whistleblower added that Ludwig W. was a 'habitual drinker' who fed his baby son beer to help him sleep, and that the infant 'gives the impression of idiocy'. The transgression of SS masculine conduct here was twofold; not only a lamentable lapse of comradeship, but also the anonymous authorial voice. Eicke's monthly orders left their audience in no doubt about the gendered disgrace of such behaviour: 'It is both inappropriate to the SS and utterly unmanly ("*überhaupt unmännlich*") to write anonymous letters. In this case I was able to identify the heroic letter writer and to enlighten him accordingly'.[62] Eicke frequently feminized lapses of comradeship among his 'boys', attributing, for example, the continual grousing about his Dachau protégée Koegel to 'washerwomen in black uniform'.[63]

Masculinity is always constructed relative to a perceived femininity: the SS female ideal type is as such of great interest. In December 1939 the Dachau sentry Engelbert W. was in the field with the Death's Head Division when he received the following telegram from the RuSHA regarding his marriage application:

[58] In Noakes and Pridham, *Nazism 1919–1945*, Vol. 2, p. 494.
[59] Schwarz, *Frau*, p. 46.
[60] BAB, BDC, RS G5045, Weibrecht to Weist, 29 January 1936.
[61] BAB, BDC, RS G5199, Chef des Sippenamtes to Führer der SSTV, 22 April 1936.
[62] IfZ, MA 293, IKL Befehlsblatt, 1 May 1937, s. 2550182.
[63] Goeschel and Wachsmann, *Nazi Concentration Camps*, p. 170.

On submission of SS-*Untersturmführer* W.'s papers the *Reichsführer* SS was appalled to notice in the photos that the proposed bride is wearing lipstick. The *Reichsführer* SS was astonished at this. [*Der Reichsführer SS hat sich darüber sehr verwundert*].[64]

In Himmler's view, racially valuable women had no need for the frivolous sporting of lipstick, visual marker of the Weimar-era 'new woman'. In 1937 he told his leadership corps that he hoped one day their *Männerbund* would develop into a 'clan community' (*Sippengemeinschaft*) to which women would be 'required to belong just as much as men'.[65] This membership, however, was to be very much of the separate spheres variety, as fecund domestic saints and Madonna figures. It should not be difficult, Himmler continued, for SS suitors to identify them in advance. In a complicated analogy on dancehall protocol, he observed that 'racially valuable women' tended towards modesty and wholesomeness, and would as such be found among the 'wallflowers'. Their 'non-Aryan' peers would not evince such dignity. Himmler looked confidently towards a future in which the Nordic girl would dance and marry, while the other would be 'left to sit' on the sidelines.[66]

Nevertheless, even 'Aryan' brides had to prove to the RuSHA's satisfaction that they were cut out for SS domesticity. Among the documents SS men assembled for their marriage application were two questionnaires completed by worthy citizens attesting to the proposed bride's 'suitability to become the wife of a member of the SS'. The form asks for statements illuminating whether she is 'reliable or unreliable', 'fond of children or not', 'companionable or domineering', 'thrifty or extravagant', 'home-loving or fickle', and whether she is 'addicted to cleaning' (*putzsüchtig*). The referees are also asked to comment on whether her family is 'financially sound or unsound', whether 'the proposed bride and her family committed themselves to the NS awakening and are today reliable defenders of the NS worldview', and whether they 'know of any other reservations or unwelcome qualities in the bride'. The vast majority of responses are positive and succinct, and may be read as anticipations of what the respondents believe the SS gender philosophy prized. Typical, if unusually detailed, is the following appraisal of Dachau block leader Franz Josef Müller's fiancée, Anneliese F., by a neighbour:

> She is conscientious and reliable . . . she loves children . . . I know she is very house proud. In her parents' house thrift is very much the rule. Her clothing is always modest and tidy. I have never seen her spend money frivolously . . . she has a serious manner at all times . . . During the struggle for power her parents' pub hosted the first meetings of party members.[67]

We have here an apotheosis of bourgeois respectability, another discursive terrain for the SS preoccupation with decency. In addition, SS brides undertook to attend one of the 'motherhood courses' run by the German Women's Bureau, the Nazi mass organization for women. These lasted six weeks and involved tuition

---

[64] BAB, BDC RS G5309, Himmler to Eicke, 30 December 1939.
[65] In Noakes and Pridham, *Nazism 1919–1945*, Vol. 2, p. 493.
[66] Bradley F. Smith and Agnes Peterson (eds), *Heinrich Himmler: Geheimreden 1933 bis 1945* (Frankfurt, 1974), p. 55.
[67] BAB, BDC RS E109, Fragebogen, 27 January 1939.

in housekeeping, schooling, and raising children in the spirit of racial vigilance.[68] Upon marriage, SS wives were expected to give up their jobs and devote themselves to producing a family, ideally, in Himmler's view, with at least four children.[69] For brides born after 1920, the requirement to possess the Reich sports badge was added. As one SS *Gruppenführer* put it, alighting on a familiar theme, the 'javelin and the springboard are more useful than the lipstick in promoting health'.[70] The most common reasons for the rejection, or mere provisional acceptance, of proposed brides were inadequate height, excessive age, being significantly older than the SS man, and being of 'poor' racial stock.

Sometimes many factors combined to elicit rejection. Josef Kestel joined the Dachau guard units in September 1933 and applied to marry his sweetheart Elise B. in 1937.[71] But the RuSHA deemed that the proposed bride fell well short of expectations on 'moral grounds'. Her failings of character had been demonstrated in 1927 as the guilty party in a divorce due to serial infidelities. The following year she had also been convicted of several instances of petty theft. The RuSHA noted that Elise's sister, too, had fallen foul of the law, indicating eugenic pathogens in the family. This toxic prehistory made Elise an unsuitable candidate, on a financial level alone, for a marital loan. Unusually, Kestel appealed against the decision and the paperwork was sent to Himmler to review. The *Reichsführer* upheld the verdict and in May 1937 Kestel was summoned to meet Max Simon, commander of the Dachau guard units. He was invited to assure Simon that he would not pursue the marriage as a member of the SS. Instead, Kestel decided to have Simon meet Elise to get him to change his mind. The gambit was successful and Simon weighed in on their side with the RuSHA. He declared that Kestel was a 'mediocre NCO' and as such 'unlikely to be considered for promotion' in the future. The couple were duly permitted to marry and Kestel was brought onto the commandant's staff at Dachau, transferring to Sachsenhausen in 1940. He did indeed, however, fail to progress to officer rank.

Albert Breh, whose career as an officer in Dachau was dogged by scandal, fared no better in his love life.[72] Breh met his Austrian fiancée, Ingeborg R., through his work as manager of the Dachau camp canteen. In the course of a complicated dispute over tobacco contracts the two fell foul of Ingeborg's landlady, who was involved in an affair with another SS officer, *Obersturmführer* Herbert Vollmer from the nearby SS cadet school at Bad Tölz. As revenge the landlady had Vollmer pen a vicious character assassination of Ingeborg to the RuSHA.[73] In the course of this lapse of solidarity and comradeship, Vollmer presented a heinous antitype to the SS bride. He reported that Ingeborg was 'not morally beyond reproach'. He claimed that she had had numerous affairs, including two with married men, before she had met Breh. In a grave lapse of racial vigilance, one of these had

[68]  Schwarz, *Frau*, p. 35.
[69]  BAB, NS 19, Bd 3973, Himmler to SS Führer, 13 September 1936, pp. 2–3.
[70]  In Mosse, *Nazi Culture*, p. 43.     [71] The following from Riedle, *Angehörigen*, p. 127.
[72]  BAB, BDC SSO Breh, Persönlicher Bericht Albert Breh, 21 November 1938.
[73]  BAB, BDC SSO Breh, Anzeige Ingeborg R., 9 January 1939.

been with a Yugoslavian. She had even had an abortion. Moreover, Ingeborg had fled Austria not, as she had claimed, due to political persecution for her Nazi fervour, but due to embezzlement. She had arrived in Germany without clothes or money, both of which she had since secured via sexual liaisons with assorted men in Munich. She was work-shy and indolent, and stayed in bed until midday. Vollmer hinted darkly that one of her parents might not be Aryan. The adulterer's letter concluded in a flush of idealism: he had always impressed upon his own wife how proud she should be to be admitted to the SS clan community with its 'strictest principles of selection'. These tenets, Vollmer felt, would be cast into ridicule should Ingeborg R. become wife of an SS officer. Breh's marriage application was brusquely rejected; in addition to the calumnies above, Ingeborg was, at 155 cm tall, too short to be accepted into the SS elite.

## SS MASCULINITY AT DACHAU

The social capital available to successful Dachau SS marriage applicants could be significant. In all patriarchal societies, marriage and setting up a household is an unambiguous assertion of masculine social status.[74] Presiding over a household of racially pure children was also the most unequivocal signifier of masculinity in the pronatalist SS and the opportunity to do so at Dachau seems to have been another integrative phenomenon. The example of 'white raven' Hans Mursch has already been considered (Chapter 3). Karl Fritzsch took a very different attitude to his role in Dachau. Born in 1903, Fritzsch had spent a nomadic youth with his salesman father. In 1928 he married his sweetheart Fanny Stich but, lacking independent means, the two lived at her parental home in Regensburg. In 1930 Fritzsch joined the Regensburg NSDAP and SS. In 1933, when Fanny became pregnant, Fritzsch learned of an opportunity for regular work with the guard detail at Dachau. Fanny later recalled that they had been enthused at the prospect of receiving a small house near the camp where they would 'live solid lives, with regular work hours . . . both of us wanted a normal family life'.[75] Fritzsch came to Dachau as an SS NCO and commander of the 1st Guard company, where he was promoted to officer rank in April 1934. The couple thrived at Dachau—a son and daughter born there attended the SS nursery—until 1941, when Fritzsch transferred to Auschwitz. Here Fanny gave birth to their third child. Fritzsch was a notoriously cruel camp compound leader at Auschwitz and supervized the camp's first trial gassings with Zyklon B pellets; indeed, he later boasted to comrades that he was the inventor of the gas chambers.[76] Yet although the steep trajectory of Fritzsch's journey from Dachau sentry to pioneer of mass murder was atypical, the social incentives which, in part, attracted and integrated him into the SS camp system were not.

---

[74] Tosh, 'What Should Historians Do With Masculinity?', pp. 185–8.
[75] Segev, *Soldiers*, p. 179.
[76] Wachsmann, 'KL: A History of the Nazi Concentration Camps', ch. 5.

Something of a parallel world developed at Dachau for these SS families, illustrating the social capital on offer for household and fatherhood. On the 'Road of the SS' approaching the camp, SS officers enjoyed spacious houses and management suites. South-west of the camp lay Theodor Eicke Platz, with dozens of flats for married NCOs. SS families could avail of communal leisure facilities, as well as medical care from Death's Head troop doctors. Dachau prisoners recalled blonde, blue-eyed children playing in the gardens, unconcerned by passing work details.[77] An elementary school was built by the camp for the children of the 150 SS families living on the Dachau complex.[78] The former inmate Alfred Werner, visiting the site in the mid-1950s, relived painful memories when he beheld the large pink stucco houses still scattered around the area. 'Once', he recalled, 'it was a model community, with a beautiful playground for children, a fine swimming pool, and lovely gardens . . . the idyllic family life'.[79] Life was rendered still more amenable by the employment of prisoners who tended to the gardens and sundry chores. SS wives had a role to play here in maintaining the subjugation of the prisoners; with social status came ideological responsibility. A terse circular from Eicke reminded staff of some ground rules.[80] Before allocating inmates to SS families, camp commandants were to verify that the work was in the interests of the state rather than the convenience of the family, which would amount to 'corruption'. Whilst working, the prisoners were to be guarded closely. Eicke had received reports of SS wives 'forgetting who they were' (*artsvergessen*) and providing snacks and drinks for the inmates. More shameful yet, some sentries had been accepting drinks in their presence. In the future, he concluded, SS wives caught doing so would be imprisoned in the women's concentration camp at Moringen. Hans Schwarz recalled being part of a small detail of prisoners delivering bags of coal to Dachau SS families in early 1939. A small child in the household of block leader Franz Senksis grabbed a prisoner's arm, wanting to play with him. Senksis wrenched the child away and hurled him to the floor. When his wife protested, Senksis hit her and yelled that 'if he doesn't learn that he can't play with the criminals, you'll be for it . . . The son of an SS man does not speak to criminals'.[81]

It is clear that officers' wives could also have a restraining influence on aspects of prisoner treatment. Franz Hofmann ventured the following anecdote in his post-war testimony:

One day, *Reichsführer* SS Himmler paid a surprise visit to Dachau and gave me a real dressing down because the priests were working lazily in the nursery [for plants, CD]. He shouted at me that I was the compound leader, and if I didn't turn the priests into productive workers then I'd be in for it. I told him that when the priests were dealt with more severely I received outraged letters from the wives of SS officers who lived in the area.[82]

[77] Kalmar, *Zeit*, p. 67.     [78] Steinbacher, *Dachau*, p. 131.
[79] Alfred Werner, 'Return to Dachau', *Commentary*, 12 (1951), p. 542.
[80] IfZ, MA293, IKL Befehlsblatt, 1 April 1937, s. 2550219.
[81] Schwarz, 'Wir Haben es nicht Gewusst', p. 248.
[82] SAM, StA 34590, Vernehmungsprotokoll Franz Hofmann, 22 April 1959.

Such material undermines the argument put forward by the historian Claudia Koonz that the wives of SS camp officers kept their households and families protected from, even ignorant of, the masculine brutality of the camps.[83] These Dachau SS wives clearly felt able to write to a thug like Hofmann to complain about the treatment of Catholic priests, a prisoner group with whom they identified as good Bavarians. In the concentration camp environment, domesticity and criminality were not opposing poles, but frequently intertwined.[84]

This intertwining was not always harmonious. A fractured picture of domestic life for Dachau SS families emerges—not surprisingly—from the records of divorce proceedings. In 1944 the Munich State Court heard Josef Voggesberger's petition for divorce from his wife Cäzilie.[85] Long-term sweethearts, the two had wed in October 1933, some six months after Voggesberger had joined the Dachau sentry units: another reminder of the empowering function of regular paid work for guards. Life by a concentration camp, however, seems to have palled for Cäzilie and the court was presented with a detailed account of her disruptive behaviour. She was said regularly to have passed adverse comment about Voggesberger to his superiors and to have been rebuked by the camp commandant for her efforts. She had illicitly procured feed for her rabbits from camp stocks. At home, too, her housekeeping had been negligent and dishonest, and had taken the couple into the shame of debt. Worst of all, she had frequently been seen in local taverns, consorting and even kissing with men. She had had an affair with a worker from Augsburg. Voggesberger too had evinced failings of uxoriousness, however, including a long-term affair of his own, and in this case the court deemed that he bore the greater share of blame for the marital breakdown, and should pay the majority of the legal costs.[86]

The court was thoroughly appalled, however, at the social indignities suffered by the commander of the Dachau guard units, Michael Lippert. In September 1934 Lippert petitioned for divorce from his wife Marie.[87] Many grounds were presented, including the fact that she had, on being confronted by Lippert about supposed affairs, smashed his framed pictures of Hitler, Himmler, and Göring in calculated fashion, knowing that he revered them 'as a passionate devotee of the National Socialist ideal'. Predictably, there was considerable discussion of the political implications of this wanton act. Marie had also clearly been a disruptive influence on polite Dachau SS society. According to Lippert's lawyer, in May 1934 she had gone from house to house in the officers' residential area slandering her

---

[83] Claudia Koonz, *Mothers in the Fatherland: Women, the Family and Nazi Politics* (London, 1987). According to Koonz, SS wives were able to keep 'their family world apart from the masculine sphere of brutality, coercion, corruption and power . . . a haven from public horror for the men who arrested, deported, tortured and killed . . . a buffer zone from their husbands' jobs. Far from wanting to share their husband's concerns, they actively cultivated their own ignorance and facilitated his escape' (p. 419).

[84] Sybille Steinbacher, *'Musterstadt' Auschwitz: Germanisierungspolitik und Judenmord in Ostoberschlesien* (Munich, 2000), p. 187.

[85] BAB, BDC SSO Voggesberger, Urteil Landgericht Munich II, 7 June 1944.

[86] BAB, BDC SSO Voggesberger, Urteil Landgericht Munich II, 7 June 1944.

[87] BAB, BDC SSO Lippert, Urteil Landgericht Munich II, 19 September 1934.

husband. She told her interlocutors that she had deliberately drunk during her pregnancy so as to yield 'an idiot child, all he deserved'. Marie had also tried to turn Dachau sentries against Lippert, depicting him as a 'cruel and malicious' husband. She had remarked to the sentry Ludwig L., while he was on duty, that she doubted there could be any thugs or felons in the camp worse than Lippert himself. To the guard Ludwig S. she confided that Lippert had become too big for his boots since the seizure of power. All this, the court heard, had caused 'unrest' and commotion among the Dachau sentries. Marie admitted that she had occasionally let off steam when passing guards, but not to the extent reported. The court took the view, however, that the credentials of the Dachau SS personnel in question as witnesses were 'beyond reproach' and that such besmirching of Lippert's honour was beyond the pale. The petition for divorce was accepted, and Marie instructed to pay both sides' costs.[88]

These cases indicate that the intrusion of domestic and marital discontent could unsettle the gritty masculine habitus at Dachau, disturbing the psychology of domination at the camp. Contrary to Himmler's hopes, for the rank-and-file sentries harangued by Marie Lippert it was probably a rare interaction with a female. The great majority of the Dachau SS were very young, and overwhelmingly single. According to SS statistics for 1939, fully 93.5 per cent of its concentration camp personnel were bachelors, compared to 57.5 per cent in other branches.[89] For such men, the social capital enjoyed by heads of households was a distant aspiration. It was also one to which the SS restricted access in the interests of ensuring stable, fecund, and racially desirable marriages. Starting in 1935, recruits in barracks-dwelling formations such as the Dachau SS swore an oath undertaking not to set up a household before fulfilling defined coming-of-age criteria: to have attained either the age of twenty-five or the non-commissioned rank of *Oberscharführer*. Until this time they were sworn to remain in the common SS barracks and to make no undertakings other than those 'appropriate to me as a bachelor'.[90] As in the German army, the age of twenty-five was regarded in the SS as the earliest point at which a professional soldier should take on the responsibilities of marriage and fatherhood. By the time an SS man was twenty-five or an *Oberscharführer* he was deemed to have attained the requisite maturity and financial security for full masculine status. An *Oberscharführer* in the concentration camp SS brought in, as has been seen, 182 Reichsmark per month, while a married couple might also be provided with a flat.

The personnel files of SS guards at Dachau indicate that this provision was quite rigidly adhered to and caused numerous social problems. Johann E., born in 1914, joined the SS from the Hitler Youth in 1932. He was among the earliest intake of Dachau guards in April 1933, rising by 1937 to *Scharführer* on the commandant's staff. In the same year, his application to marry his pregnant fiancée Marianne was rejected as he had not quite met either of the SS criteria for this status. In some

[88] BAB, BDC SSO Lippert, Urteil Landgericht Munich II, 19 September 1934.
[89] Segev, *Soldiers*, p. 128.   [90] Schwarz, *Frau*, pp. 31–2.

desperation Marianne wrote to Himmler directly.[91] She informed the *Reichsführer* that her father had thrown her out of the parental home after furious rows over her renunciation of Catholicism; a step almost mandatory in Dachau SS circles at this time, the height of the regime's campaign against organized religion. *Scharführer* E. had found them a flat in town, and she begged permission for them to wed and live together despite his falling just short of the SS coming of age requirements. She shrewdly pointed out to Himmler that her fiancé had both the 'badge of honour' (*Ehrenzeichen*) for early NSDAP membership and a low SS number, always valuable capital in the organization. Scheingraber, as *Scharführer* E.'s commanding officer, wrote a supportive memorandum remarking that 'I have got to know E. as a perfect SS man in terms of both character and ideology and am thus convinced that he will make a success of the marriage'.[92] The allusion to 'ideology' as a prerequisite to a 'successful' marriage is interesting but not amplified; presumably Scheingraber had in mind such facets as racial vigilance, uxoriousness, and natal enthusiasm. Max Simon also recommended that the marriage certificate 'be approved urgently'. The couple were given special dispensation and married in January 1938.

Alfred E., born in 1917, joined the SS from the Hitler Youth in 1935 as a specialist 'Death's Head musician'. Underage, he got engaged with Leni L. in 1938. Even though he, like Johann E., was already a *Scharführer*, one rank below the required *Oberscharführer*, he was not deemed ready to set up a household. It was doubtless with a certain sense of emasculation that he obtained, as instructed by the SS, the following sworn statement from his future father-in-law:

> I hereby declare myself prepared to continue to provide food and housing to my daughter Leni L. until the SS *Scharführer* Alfred E. is 25.[93]

E. was eventually given permission to marry his sweetheart when on leave from the Waffen SS in 1940. It is not possible on the basis of the available source material to determine how many Dachau SS personnel were permitted to set up households around the camp: that the cases above caused so much difficulty despite the guards in question only marginally failing to meet the minima, however, suggests that it was a privilege taken seriously in the SS.

It is easy to see why some guards were eager to leave the Dachau SS barracks. The living arrangements therein are poorly documented, but surviving photographs from the early years reveal dingy huts filled with cheap makeshift beds (Figure 5.1), later improved courtesy of prisoner labour to airier wooden barracks but with the beds still closely hemmed together.[94] Among the perpetrators, Dachau as a 'total institution' was experienced at its most total by the rank-and-file guards. Every act took place in the company of others: washing, showering, eating, sleeping, even

[91] BAB, BDC RS B133, Mariane L. To Himmler, 22 November 1937.
[92] BAB, BDC RS B133, Scheingraber to Totenkopfverband Oberbayern, 11 December 1937.
[93] BAB, BDC RS B223, Bestätigung P. Langer, (n.d.).
[94] Christopher Ailsby, *The Waffen SS: The Unpublished Photographs* (Basingstoke and London, 2000), pp. 48, 52.

**Figure 5.1** Bunk beds and male togetherness in the early Dachau SS barracks, May 1933. Bundesarchiv, image 152-01-01. A postcard of Hitler hangs on the near wall, while the guard in the centre amuses his neighbours by adopting an ironic 'prayer' posture.

the latrine. This was of necessity a comradely environment with no scope for the 'loner'. The barracks were a site where large numbers of post-adolescent males were cooped up together for months on end, a situation in which individual sexual frustration could only seldom be sated even by masturbation.[95] The collective pre-occupation with sex evinced by young males in barracks is well-known, and their coarse, centripetal dynamic serves the interests of military institutions everywhere. There was no discursive space in the SS barracks for reflection or compassion: the only sentimentality acceptable, as will be seen, was for comrades. All this helped to forge group loyalties and to displace pre-existing social identities. The SS presumably recognized the value of all this, which may explain its determination to keep young personnel in barracks until a relatively advanced age or seniority. For many 18-year-old recruits, the prospect of seven years in the Dachau SS barracks cannot have been wholly enticing. The suicide rate for Death's Head personnel was three times higher than elsewhere in the SS.[96] The integrative dividend for all-male barracks life, however, was a largely untrammelled empowerment over the inmates of the Dachau prisoner compound, and it is to the gendered enactment of this power that the next section turns.

---

[95] Goldstein, *War and Gender*, p. 334.     [96] Segev, *Soldiers*, p. 128.

## THE DACHAU SCHOOL AND MASCULINITY

SS domination in the camps began with visual and physical cues. The SS guard was expected to command the abjection of inmates as a paradigm of 'Aryan' masculinity and ambassador, even, for the healthy nationalist manhood of the Third Reich.[97] The notion that a man's exterior reflected his inner qualities was a staple of right-wing German thought. Typically, something of a Prussian metaphysics had developed around the concept, starting with the eighteenth-century classical scholar Johann Joachim Winckelmann's idolizing of the classical Greek male nude.[98] Increasingly counterposed to this in the *völkisch* variant—structured, like all racist creeds, on visual stimuli and stereotypes—was the 'degenerate' male Jew. Hitler and Himmler were particularly beholden to the ideal of the neo-classical 'Aryan new man', seeing in him the path to military conquest and national redemption. One distinguished historian, with pardonable exaggeration, has gone so far as to suggest that 'the success of the Nazi ideal would manifest itself in shoulder width'.[99] For such reasons, the SS placed great value on the physical, manly qualities of recruits. Himmler was particularly proud of his elite formations:

> Until 1936 we did not accept a man in the Leibstandarte or the Verfügungstruppe if he had even one filled tooth. We were able to assemble the most magnificent manhood in that early Waffen SS.[100]

In practice, a rather lower standard of physical manhood had to be accepted for the less glamorous Death's Head units, although here too recruiters were reminded that 'only the very best human material' was up to the tasks of the concentration camp guard troops.[101] Men who wore glasses (*Brillenträger*) were not admitted in principle to the SS, the lens-sporting of its *Reichsführer* notwithstanding. Indeed, prisoners wearing glasses were targets for chicanery by camp guards since they were regarded as eugenically deficient and as potential intellectuals.

The key signifier of physical manliness in the SS universe, however, was height. As Himmler told his Wehrmacht audience in 1937, he insisted on height minima having realized that 'men whose height exceeds a given number of centimetres must somehow have valuable blood'.[102] A staple of soldierly ideals since Ancient Rome, it had particular precedents in German military culture. Frederick-William I of Prussia, the 'soldier-king' and as such on the pantheon of SS heroes, had scoured the Continent to assemble a regiment of preposterously tall guards at Potsdam known affectionately as the *lange Kerls* ('tall lads').[103] Closer to home, the Bavarian King, too, had his own *Leiber* or Guard regiment comprising men of 175 cm or

[97] On these self-conceptions in the SS, see Diehl, *Macht-Mythos-Utopie*, pp. 18–37.
[98] Mosse, *Nationalism*, esp. pp. 13–15; Wildmann, *Begehrte Körper*, esp. pp. 23–6.
[99] Paul Fussell, *Uniforms: Why We Are What We Wear* (New York, 2003), p. 12.
[100] In Stein, *SS*, p. 12.
[101] IfZ, Fa 127/1, Merkblatt für die Einstellung in die SSTV, s. 8.
[102] IMT, Vol. XXIX, 1992 (A)-PS, s. 208.
[103] Christopher Clarke, *The Iron Kingdom: The Rise and Downfall of Prussia* (London, 2007), p. 95. On SS reverence for the Prussian military tradition, see Wegner, *Waffen SS*, pp. 41–4.

taller whose daily changing had been a popular spectacle in Munich.[104] Himmler hoped that the SS would be regarded as an analogous elite guard and Nazi officials did indeed refer to his showpiece unit, the Leibstandarte, as the '*langen Kerls* of the *Führer*'.[105] The minimum height for the Leibstandarte was 178 cm, for the Verfügungstruppe 174 cm, and for the Death's Head troops initially 172 cm, reduced pragmatically in the mid-1930s to the 170 cm also used by the General SS.[106] SS recruitment posters offered consolation to shorter males: men between 165 and 170 cm tall were alerted to the opportunity to join the non-SS militia formation 'General Göring'. It seems that all this was not without success in forging a sense of a masculine select, even that pride in a tall and masculine physique may have been a motivation for seeking to join the SS in the first place. Piorkowski's wife was still proud after the Second World War that he had been accepted into the Bremen SS. As she told American investigators, 'not everybody could join the SS, it had to be an elite at that time. People had to be of a certain size'.[107]

Of the 254 pre-war Dachau personnel for whom heights are recorded, either in SS files or custody records, the average height is comfortably above the minima at 174.85 cm. For those recruited during the war, it is down slightly to 171.75 cm with 115 recordings. Riedle's study of the commandant staff in Sachsenhausen, too, finds that 88 per cent of the sample were at least 172 cm tall.[108] Yet it did not suffice, in theory at least, merely to make the height grade. Himmler also decreed that the SS man must be of

> well-proportioned build; for instance there must be no disproportion between the lower leg and the thigh, or between the legs and the upper body; otherwise an exceptional effort is required to carry out long marches.[109]

There was considerable hand-wringing in the SS about the underwhelming physical credentials of many applicants. The Frankfurt SS, for example, was appalled by the supposed effeminacy of candidates from the Hitler Youth in 1937. Pervasive 'feminine elements' noted by SS doctors included a broad pelvis, narrow shoulders, secondary female sexual characteristics, fatty tissue, thin bones, and 'feminine movements'. Some 'even had their hair cut in a feminine manner', others were apparently 'heavily perfumed'.[110] The desperation for new recruits, however, led to an easing in standards. In December 1938 the minimum SS height requirement was further dropped to 165 cm, on the basis that this generation of German males had grown up in an era of poor nutrition through food shortages in the Great War and the privations and mismanagement of the Weimar Republic.[111] And however far short the average Dachau guard fell of the physical ideal type, he no doubt drew succour from being surrounded by malnourished and enfeebled prisoners.

---

[104] Large, *Where Ghosts Walked*, p. 47.
[105] Weingartner, 'Leibstandarte SS', p. 269.
[106] IfZ, Fa 127/1, Merkblatt für die Einstellung in die SSTV, ss. 1–2.
[107] SAM, StA 34881/11, Deposition Berta Piorkowski, 16 January 1947, s. 417.
[108] Riedle, *Angehörigen*, p. 151 fn 208.    [109] IMT, Vol. XXIX, 1992 (A)-PS, s. 211.
[110] Rempel, *Hitler's Children*, p. 31.
[111] IfZ, Fa 127/1, Brief Heißmeyer, 14 December 1938, s. 417.

He was further reconciled to the SS model of soldierly masculinity in Dachau's training academy, the Death's Head units' impersonation of the venerable Prussian 'school of manliness'. Since Sparta, cultures have brought males together for drilling and 'muscular bonding', reinforcing group cohesion and combat effectiveness through the stylized repetition of military acts.[112] Military drill defines and inculcates submission to legitimate authority. It blurs individual boundaries and identities, fostering pride in the collective entity. It coordinates body and mind, transforming thought and emotion, as one author puts it, 'into movement, movements of the body'.[113] Bodily strength and dexterity become collective markers of healthy masculinity and military prowess. The German traditions of Prussian drill, politicized gymnastics, and fresh-faced youth movements lent these activities a particular resonance. At rallies and propaganda events during the Third Reich the serried columns of the SS in black parade uniforms shared front billing with Hitler himself.[114] As has been seen, by the end of the 1930s the Death's Head units drilled and exercised far more than they stood sentry at the 'front'. Yet here those on duty could still watch the bedraggled, emasculated prisoners as they were forced at roll calls to carry out their own abject, pitiful parody of drill in the main square. As the historian Hans Buchheim points out, it seems not to have concerned the SS that by forcing the so-called criminals in the camps 'to participate in the militarism which they worshipped, they were being guilty of *lèse-majesté*'.[115]

Naturally, SS training in Dachau entailed more than such positive experiences. The school of violence was calculatedly harsh, designed to foster aggression and to overcome recruits' inhibitions about using it against others. It was expected that drilled SS personnel would cascade their wounded pride onto the prisoners. Officially, Eicke forbade his instructors to use what he termed 'Himmelstoss methods'—after Corporal Himmelstoss, the brutal drill sergeant in *All Quiet on the Western Front*—as incompatible with the voluntarist, egalitarian comradeship of the SS.[116] Yet in reality hazing was the order of the day and, as in the prisoner camp itself—although with far less devastating results—those who 'stood out' attracted chicanery.[117] One sentry remembered Steinbrenner as a particularly 'ruthless' drill sergeant during his introductory training who had really 'dragged us over the coals'.[118] Recruits who failed this test of manhood

---

[112] See the ambitious monograph by William H. McNeill, *Keeping Together in Time: Dance and Drill in Human History* (Cambridge, MA, 1996), pp. 1–12. The author argues that the 'extravagant expenditure of bodily energy' in communal dance and drill evident since primordial times had an evolutionary pay-off, and that modern man, too, experiences a euphoria when carrying out group dance and drill (p. 38). 'Words are inadequate', he concludes, 'to express the emotion aroused by the prolonged movement in unison that drilling involved' (p. 2).

[113] Theweleit, *Male Fantasies*, Vol. 2, p. 153.

[114] See the excellent discussion in David Welch, *Propaganda and the German Cinema, 1933–1945* (Oxford, 1983), pp. 147–59, as well as the iconic analysis by Susan Sonntag, 'Fascinating Fascism', in Brandon Taylor and Wilfried van der Will (eds), *The Nazification of Art: Art, Design, Music, Architecture and Film in the Third Reich* (Winchester, 1990), pp. 204–18.

[115] Buchheim, 'Command and Compliance', p. 342. See also Levi, *Drowned*, pp. 92–4.

[116] IfZ, MA293, IKL Befehlsblatt, 1 Feb 1937, s. 2550220.

[117] Segev, *Soldiers*, pp. 109–12; Neurath, *Society*, pp. 74–6; Orth, *Konzentrationslager SS*, pp. 127–32.

[118] SAM, StA 34462/1, Vernehmungsniederschrift Hermann Hofmann, 28 January 1948.

were held up to scorn and feminized. One has left a particularly vivid account.[119] When, during rifle drill, a recruit accidentally dropped a cartridge from his magazine, he was expected to retrieve it with his teeth. No orders were necessary, the SS NCO simply turned down his thumb and the recruit concerned knew 'what to do'. It was bound to happen to most recruits eventually, as it did to this man. His refusal to pick up the cartridge with his mouth brought the customary drill punishment—a ten minute public 'showpiece'—and symphonic range of gendered abuse: *Schlappschwanz* (sissy), *Muttersöhnchen* (little mummy's boy), *Heulbase* (crybaby), that he was a disgrace to the fallen of the Great War. The recruit recalled that he had been unable to stop himself weeping 'although I knew that it was neither manly nor soldierly'. Detailed to latrine cleaning for a week as punishment, the next time he was ordered to retrieve a bullet with his teeth he did so reflexively. Shame is a key tool in fostering martial manhood and very young males, often insecure in their masculinity, are particularly susceptible to gendered modes of socialization.[120] The societal wisdom that 'boys' were turned into 'men' by military service, from which 'quitting' was a masculine disgrace, undoubtedly helped to draw SS recruits piecemeal into criminality in the camps. Even Höß, whose violent CV included the Eastern Front and the *Freikorps*, confides to his reader that he felt unable to request permission to leave camp service because 'I did not want to make a laughing-stock of myself'.[121] While offered in an exculpatory spirit, this probably bears an uncomfortable degree of authenticity in the wider context of concentration camp sentries.

Training and drill prepared the SS 'soldiers' concerned for sentry duty. The seemingly fragile kinship between terrorizing unarmed civilians in the camp and martial masculinity was navigated though the construction of an 'inner Front', where concentration camp guards purportedly held the line against such internal, hostile elements as effected the 'stab in the back' in 1918.[122] The participation of Death's Head units in public parades, including the annual Nuremberg rallies, likewise advertised their claimed status of 'military preparedness'. SS guard masculinity was signified and performed to inmates and observers from the earliest days of the camp. On the occasion of Hitler's birthday in April 1933, the *Daily Telegraph* journalist George Gedye was invited for a stage-managed tour of Dachau. He reported that his 'inspection' of a group of hand-picked and terrified prisoners was

> cut short by three of the guards of the outer walls hurrying up, stopping dead six paces from the commandant, and then advancing up to him with goose-step of such exaggerated rigidity that but for the horrible air of Dachau I think I should have been unable to avoid bursting out laughing.[123]

[119] The following from Buchheim, 'Command and Compliance', pp. 340–1; see also Orth, *Konzentrationslager*, pp. 129–30.

[120] John H. Farris, 'The Impact of Basic Combat Training: The Role of the Drill Sergeant', in Nancy L. Goldman and David R. Segal (eds), *The Social Psychology of Military Service* (Beverly Hills and London, 1976), pp. 13–26, here p. 15; Goldstein, *War and Gender*, pp. 264–7.

[121] Höß, *Commandant*, p. 81.

[122] The term 'Front' appears throughout SS documentation. For a discussion of the interdependence of 'inner' and 'outer' Fronts see Orth, *Konzentrationslager SS*, pp. 153–204.

[123] G. E. R. Gedye, *Fallen Bastions: The Central European Tragedy* (London, 1940), p. 169. I would like to thank Paul Moore for bringing this excerpt to my attention.

Even the inherently theatrical Prussian military *Stechschritt* was amplified to convey a disciplined military deportment to this foreign observer. The Dachau SS remained eager to demonstrate their marching prowess to local journalists throughout the 1930s (see Chapter 6). Inside the prisoner compound, too, formation marching was used to project strength and empowerment. For the administration of corporal punishment, a platoon of marching SS men in black dress uniform with drums, steel helmets, and fixed bayonets followed members of the commandant staff out to the 'block' where public lashings were administered. During the gruesome event, they stood pertly to attention on one side of the square. The whole episode, one prisoner recalled, was 'like a military parade on some state occasion'.[124]

The topos of an orderly, masculine hierarchical system was also served by the intricate system of badges, stripes, insignia, and awards which sprawled across the various uniforms of the camp SS. Encoded in these was the rank, status, and biography of every member, largely unintelligible to outsiders and as such an expression of the belonging and inclusion of the wearer. Uniforms have a complex social impact: in the obvious sense of the otherness they project and signify, but also in the way that non-wearers expect particular behaviours from individuals in uniform, above all service uniform. This cyclical dynamic goes a good deal further towards accounting for differentiated behaviour on- and off-duty than the vocabulary of 'doubling'.[125] As William Shakespeare wrote in *The Winter's Tale*, 'Sure, this robe of mine doth change my disposition'.[126]

There can be no doubt that the crisp black dress uniform helped to attract young men to the SS. So central was it to the identity of the organization, after all, that its newspaper was called *The Black Corps*. One early concentration camp guard told Henry Dicks that every time they donned their uniform the guards felt that they had 'closed their account with life . . . we wear the death's head'.[127] An SS Guidance Book (*Leitheft*) published on the fourth anniversary of the seizure of power described SS uniform as 'the expression of our comradeship, our steadfastness, our loyalty . . . bound up with the concepts of soldiering, fighting spirit, and proactivity . . . it is worn by healthy men and not by weaklings'.[128] Himmler even fretted that it was crucial that the SS avoid recruiting members simply drawn to its 'good looking' uniform.[129] And in March 1945, as the Third Reich was in its death throes, Hitler chose to punish the unauthorized retreat of four Waffen SS divisions from Hungary not with courts martial, but with the confiscation of their cherished Leibstandarte armbands.[130] Uniforms were at the heart of the collective identity of the SS but perhaps above all in the camps, where they were an expression of the permanent structured conflict with the inmates.

Another manifestation of this conflict was bearing weapons. In the concentration camps, rank-and-file sentries carried rifles, officers and NCOs pistols and bull

[124] Heilig, *Men Crucified*, p. 91.        [125] Lifton, *The Nazi Doctors*, passim.
[126] *The Winter's Tale*, Act IV, Scene 4 (see Zimbardo, *Lucifer*, p. 301).
[127] Dicks, *Licensed*, p. 85.        [128] In Diehl, *Macht*, p. 179.
[129] Smith and Peterson, *Geheimreden*, p. 27.
[130] Reitlinger, *Alibi*, p. 370–1; Messenger, *Hitler's Gladiator*, pp. 168–9.

whips. Guns have long been recognized by feminist literature as a phallic signifier, the quintessential icon of hypermasculinity and power. Jünger, typically, provides the most eloquent confirmation:

> What purpose would be served by all these iron weapons levelled against the universe, were they not intertwined with our nerves, were it not in our blood that hissed on every axis?[131]

In the pseudo-militarized environment of Dachau, bearing arms was an assertion of status, 'a proud right' as one camp training document puts it,[132] bringing to mind the old German proverb 'unarmed is unhonorable' (*Wehrlos—Ehrlos*).[133] It was also an integrative status, another expression of inclusion: once a man wields a gun he becomes part of a military unit, with disciplinary and firearms-related safety protocols coming into play.[134]

Service regulations for Dachau guards were always preoccupied with striking the right deportment with their rifles, choreographing collective guard masculinity. The first directives, issued by the State Police, enjoin sentries to stand with rifle slung over the right shoulder, right hand on the strap at chest height, and at no point to talk, smoke, sit, or lean.[135] Eicke's regulations six months later opine that the guard should be a 'model of leadership' to the prisoners, that it would look 'ridiculous and unsoldierly' to seek cover from the elements, and that 'the SS man must show pride and dignity and through his soldierly example prove to the Communists and big shots that he is the representative of the Third Reich'.[136] Later regulations would elevate the guard to an 'ambassador of a superior ideology, a flawless political outlook, and a higher moral plane'.[137] This was presumably supposed to come across in his posture; once again appearance was linked to inner worth. Similar concerns surrounded guard deportment when giving the 'Hitler Greeting'. A circular from Eicke in 1937 set out the complex, historically inflected semiotics of the Nazi salute:

> I ask everyone to be sure that on performing the Hitler greeting they should refrain from all type of bowing, even to women. We never bent our spines during the struggle for the victory of our movement, nor will we bend them today. Superiors are to be greeted stood up straight and with a properly outstretched arm. Informal greetings with a limp arm likewise represent a lapse of vigilance. I also ask that greeting without head attire be avoided. The Hitler salute need not be confused with bourgeois mores.[138]

---

[131] Cited in Theweleit, *Male Fantasies*, Vol. 2, p. 179.
[132] BAB, NS3/426, Unterricht über Aufgaben und Pflichten der Wachposten, n.d. (1943), s. 126.
[133] In Wette, *Wehrmacht*, p. 144.
[134] Jacques Sémelin, *Purify and Destroy: The Political Uses of Massacre and Genocide* (New York, 2005), p. 263.
[135] DA, A4118, Übergabe-Protokoll, 30 May 1933.
[136] DA, A3195, Dienstvorschriften für die Begleitposten und Gefangenenbewachung, 1 October 1933.
[137] BAB, NS3/426, Unterricht über Aufgaben und Pflichten der Wachposten, n.d. (1943), s. 128.
[138] IfZ, MA293, IKL Befehlsblatt, 4 May 1937, s. 2550182. More broadly on the Hitler Greeting, see the fascinating sociological analysis by Tilman Allert, *The Hitler Salute: On the Meaning of a Gesture* (London, 2009).

Every gesture of the concentration camp SS was potentially enmeshed in relations of power. Inside the prisoner compound, the sociologist Sofsky observes, 'the masters of the camp stood before the assembled mass, legs spread, knees straight, bodies bent slightly forward, tapping their whips casually against the leather of their boots'.[139] Well versed in decoding gestures of domination, and well aware of the self-regarding ideals among the SS, prisoner memoirs accordingly place great value on highlighting the unsoldierly deportment of SS men. Jewish males imprisoned in the camps after the pogrom of November 1938, many of whom had served in the Imperial army, were sometimes able to preserve their sense of pride in their military records by ridiculing the SS's pretensions to soldierliness.[140]

The theatrical aspects of guard masculinity were directed at comrades as well as prisoners. Steinbrenner recalled in his testimony that a competitive toughness between SS men had developed in the earliest days of the camp:

> Once SS men from Munich and Schwabing stood guard together the banter started, in which it was claimed that the men of the 29th *Standarte* were much better National Socialists than the men of the 1st: bolder, more dependable, and more devoted to the *Führer*. An old game, one that always broke out when men from different formations served together.[141]

Such gamesome competition between SS men and between different guard platoons would come to wreak terrible daily suffering on the inmates of the Nazi concentration camps. In Dachau the sentries stood in a dispersed cordon around prisoner work details, in open space at a prescribed distance from the prisoners and each other. This, recalled Neurath,

> gave a great deal of publicity to each act, and this publicity seemed to play a large role in the amount of mistreatment or teasing the sentries accorded the prisoners. Apparently, the individual guards wanted to show off to their friends and comrades, sometimes to their superiors, and prove what tough guys they were.[142]

Conversely, when guards were alone with prisoners or out of sight of their comrades, as frequently happened in more expansive camps such as Buchenwald, they were often disinterested or even helpful.[143] This illustrates once again the comradely capital accrued from tough and proactive handling of prisoners. Another expression of the latter was SS camp diction, a parody of that associated with a particular kind of all-male environment, as coarse rustic swear words, misogyny, and homophobic abuse vividly documented a space free of women.[144] Prisoners were 'dung flies', 'swine', 'pieces of shit'; all rendered in the brutal, hectoring SS

---

[139] Sofsky, *Order*, p. 79.

[140] Kim Wünschmann, 'Die Konzentrationslagererfahrungen deutsch-jüdischer Männer nach dem Novemberpogrom 1938: Geschlechtergeschichtliche Überlegungen zu männlichem Selbstverständnis und Rollenbild', in Susannah Heim, Beate Meyer, and Francis Nicosia (eds), *Wer bleibt, opfert seine Jahre, vielleicht sein Leben* (Göttingen, 2010), pp. 39–58.

[141] DaA, 19.862, Hans Steinbrenner, 'Hinter den Kulissen von Dachau', s. 3.

[142] Neurath, *Society*, p. 73; see also Aretin, *Krone und Ketten*, p. 292.

[143] Neurath, *Society*, p. 74; Riedle, *Angehörigen*, p. 209; Cohen, *Human Behaviour*, p. 255.

[144] Neurath, *Society*, pp. 74–5.

tone memorably captured by Primo Levi as 'that curt, barbaric barking of Germans in command which seems to give vent to a millennial anger'.[145] The human voice is an inherently gendered phenomenon, and the SS default delivery, as elsewhere, was in this sense a hypermasculine parody.

The notion that toughness was a mark of masculine character commanded a broad assent in German society much instrumentalized in the Dachau School. SS personnel were constantly exhorted to toughness, presented relative to unmasculine softness, pity, individualism, and mere obedience. The following speech from Eicke, recounted by Höß, on the occasion of the dishonourable discharge of four Dachau guards in 1935 is exemplary:

> Any show of sympathy would be regarded by the 'enemies of the state' as weakness, which they would immediately exploit. Furthermore, it was unworthy of an SS man to feel pity for the 'enemies of the state'. He had no room for weaklings in his ranks, and if any man felt that way they should withdraw to a monastery as quickly as possible. Only tough and determined men were of any use to him. It was not for nothing they wore the death's head badge and always kept their weapons loaded![146]

This conflation of toughness and soldierliness, set against feminized weakness and Christian tolerance, underpinned the SS conception of manliness. It was explicitly acknowledged as an individual duty: one of the assessment criteria in SS personnel annual review forms was 'Toughness against oneself' (*Härte gegen sich selbst*). This meant, loosely, is the SS man in question alert to his potential for weakness and irresolution, is he able to repress these unmasculine qualities and to fulfil his exacting duties?

'Toughness against oneself' was a pillar of SS hypermasculinity in Dachau. Eicke's camp regulations of October 1933 open with the maxim 'Tolerance means weakness'.[147] This applied not simply to the handling of prisoners, but also to the guard's interior life. Höß reports going 'hot and cold all over' when watching his first public flogging in Dachau but not allowing his emotions to register.[148] He claims to have remained '[o]utwardly cold and even stony . . . because I might not show weakness, I wished to appear hard'.[149] Typically of concentration camp personnel, Höß presents this toughness against himself as a very draining exercise, laudable but rarely appreciated. His resolute stoicism and lack of tolerance for his own 'weakness' is paradigmatic of the masculine 'decency' preached by the SS. Any residue of compassion was to be displaced into a sentimental comradeship with colleagues. Not all concentration camp personnel were able to strike this balance and those failing to make the grade suffered a loss of masculine reputation: they had failed as SS 'soldiers'. Some case studies of Dachau SS men will now illustrate the variable operation of these entangled attributes of toughness and comradeship.

---

[145] Primo Levi, *If This Is a Man* (London, 2006), p. 25.
[146] Höß, *Commandant*, p. 68.
[147] BAB, R3001/21167, Dienstvorschriften für die Begleitposten und Gefangenenbewachung, 1 October 1933, s. 62.
[148] Höß, *Commandant*, p. 66.      [149] Höß, *Commandant*, p. 81.

SS *Oberführer* Karl Taus was a Nazi 'old fighter' who had risen through the SS ranks in the Weimar Republic. Born in 1893, he is an example of the kind of older man deployed to senior command staff roles as a reward and sinecure. Yet in neither Dachau nor Buchenwald was he able to make the grade, as his emotional armour was deemed too slender. Dachau commandant Hans Loritz wrote that Taus was 'a good comrade, but much too weak' for concentration camp service. Buchenwald's Karl Koch concurred:

> Whereas *Oberführer* Taus tries to give the external appearance of a certain toughness, especially when his softness is brought to his attention, he will never be able to change on the inside and in my opinion will never find the proper tone to win the respect of the criminals. He lacks the toughness against himself and against the officers and men under his command ever to get tasks accomplished, or to summon the necessary will and decisiveness.[150]

Eicke intended despite this to give Taus a third and final chance; but significantly at a projected new concentration camp for women at Schleissheim. Even there, he feared, Taus' female staff would wear him down to a 'straw man'. Nevertheless, Eicke concluded, this was 'not so much of a risk', as it was 'just' a women's camp.[151] Female prisoners evidently lacked the subversive will of their male counterparts, while female camp staff were, by definition, beyond the universe of SS male comradeship.

Another superannuated street fighter, *Sturmbannführer* Hans Kreppel, fared only marginally better when transferred to Dachau as compound leader in November 1937. By June 1938, according to a report by Koegel, although Kreppel, too, was a 'good comrade', his nerves were shot through. He could no longer sleep, his health was ruined, and he had contemplated suicide. Kreppel was also unduly influenced by his wife, who did not like the flat the couple had been provided with at Dachau. She was no longer, the report continues with irony, prepared to sit by and watch him ruin his health, and wanted to go back to Nuremberg.[152] The purported abdication of responsibility to one's wife invited jibes and accusations of emasculation in such patriarchal circles.

Kreppel also failed to strike the right balance at work. The memoirs of Alfred Hübsch recall an incident of, in SS terms, shameful 'softness' when Kreppel rebuked the *Kapo* of his work detail for forcing the prisoners to run around at the customary 'Dachau trot', on the grounds that they 'were working hard enough already'.[153] Still more scandalous, the inmates concerned were part of the Dachau 'punishment battalion' where intensified chicanery was the order of the day. Hübsch, a shrewd and wry observer of camp life, notes that this outburst of compassion cost Kreppel his reputation. There were already warning signs in Kreppel's personnel file that he would be unable to find the requisite masculine equilibrium between toughness towards prisoners and comradeship with the SS. His 1937 appraisal had

[150] BAB, BDC SSO Taus, Beurteilung, 10 June 1938.
[151] BAB, BDC SSO Taus, Eicke to Schmitt, 14 June 1938.
[152] BAB, BDC SSO Kreppel, Koegel to Loritz, 30 June 1938.
[153] Hübsch, 'Insel', pp. 68–70.

warned that he was a 'know it all' lacking the right tone with officers and men.[154] Kreppel was duly released from concentration camp service in November 1938, at his own request, 'on health grounds'.

No such problems afflicted Kreppel's contemporary as compound leader, the squat and supercilious Hermann Baranowski. His comradeship was compromised instead by a lordly arrogance conspicuous even by SS standards. Eicke described him in his personnel file as being of 'the old, hard-headed naval type'.[155] Baranowski's outlook was of the traditional anti-establishment SA genre. He had also served in the famously disciplinarian Imperial navy for twenty years and was fifty-one by the time he was appointed commandant of Lichtenburg. One consequence of this prior socialization was that he was never able to evince the comradeship expected of an SS officer. Not without misgivings, Eicke transferred him to Dachau on probation as compound leader in November 1936. Predictably, Baranowski interpreted this as a demotion which besmirched his 'honour', although no duel was fought over the episode, nor over the numerous other slights which pepper his correspondence. Nevertheless, Baranowski had a certain imperious Röhm-like charisma, and was an inspiration and father figure to Höß in particular:

> He was for me the prototype of the original SS leader and National Socialist. I always regarded him as a much enlarged reflection of myself. He, too, had moments when his good nature and kind heart were in evidence, yet he was hard and mercilessly severe in all matters appertaining to the service. He was a perpetual example to me of how, in the SS, 'hard necessity' must stifle all softer emotions.[156]

There is, as we have seen, precious little evidence of Baranowski's 'good nature and kind heart' in his dealings with prisoners. His greatest joy was to ride around Dachau on his horse looking for infringements, and for opportunities to demonstrate his earthy wit to the appreciative Höß.[157] As far as the SS was concerned, however, Baranowski was re-schooled in Dachau under the disciplinarian hand of Loritz and was rewarded with appointment as commandant of Sachsenhausen in March 1938.

## THE DACHAU SS AND
## PRISONER MASCULINITIES

The Dachau School was not unique in the Third Reich in this war-minded hyper-masculine celebration of hardness and male comradeship. It was far more singular in drawing succour from the emasculation of concentration camp inmates. The homosocial environment of the concentration camp prisoner compound, the ultimate site of exclusion, left no space for heterosexual masculinity to express itself. Patriarchal structures, too, were inverted. Teenage guards had disciplinary control

---

[154] BAB, BDC SSO Kreppel, Beurteilung, 28 September 1937.
[155] BAB, BDC SSO Baranowski, Beurteilung, n.d. (1937).
[156] Höß, *Commandant*, p. 83.    [157] Hübsch, 'Insel', pp. 25–38.

over adult men of attainment and prior status, a valuable consolation for their otherwise lowly status in the SS barracks. This generational dimension was deeply discomforting for many inmates. Hübsch recalled very keenly one afternoon of persecution from a callow sentry of seventeen 'on whose upper lip not the faintest trace of bum fluff was to be seen'.[158] Schnabel found himself wondering how exciting it must have been for such youngsters to have the power to compel men 'who might have been their fathers or grandfathers, to crawl along the floor on their bellies'.[159] This pervasive sense of generational transgression—a feature of the youth-empowering Third Reich more broadly—is another reminder of the societal prevalence of patriarchal ideals.

This chapter has demonstrated that hegemonic male values were instrumentalized in the Dachau School to socialize guards into a supposedly masculine toughness offset, to an extent, by the compensations of comradeship. Toughness and comradeship, however, were the last qualities the SS wanted to develop among the prisoners. The withholding of masculine status was another gendered component to SS power in the camp.[160] The changing prisoner nomenclature is an interesting example. Initially the inmates of Dachau were framed as something like prisoners of civil war. They lived in 'companies' (*Kompanien*) under an SS 'company commander' (*Kompanieführer*) who was assisted by a prisoner 'sergeant' (*Kompaniefeldwebel*) and corporal (*Korporal*). In the early years, newspaper reportage frequently acclaimed the efficacious and rehabilitative military culture of the prisoner camp. As late as 1936, the *Illustrierten Beobachter* could hail the 'military discipline and punctuality' of the prisoners, the operation of the hallowed 'leadership principle' (*Führerprinzip*) through prisoner functionaries, even the 'comradely feeling' among rank-and-file inmates.[161] In this case it seems that the camp leadership may indeed have become troubled by the implications of militarist *lèse-majesté*. For, somewhere around this time (the observant Schecher dates it to 1937), the nomenclature was changed to 'blocks', 'block leader', 'block elder' (*Blockältester*), and 'room elder' (*Stubenältester*) respectively.[162] As will be seen, the local press was no longer invited to report on the prisoners, but instead on the gleaming new SS training base and military parades. It can scarcely be coincidental that just as the Death's Head troops' public assertion of soldierly status was becoming strident, the prisoners were discursively demilitarized: another example of the relational and acclamatory character of masculinity.

Inside the camp the prisoners were expected to treat guards with humility and deference. As Eicke wrote in 1934, '[r]egardless of origin, status, or occupation the prisoners are, without exception, in a subordinate position. Whether young or old, everyone has to get used to military discipline and order from the very first day'.[163] They had to recognize and cite SS ranks when addressed, always of course using

[158] Hübsch, 'Insel', p. 69.          [159] Schnabel, *Frommen*, pp. 46–7.
[160] Caplan, 'Gender', p. 85.          [161] *Illustrierte Beobachter*, 3 December 1936.
[162] Schecher, 'Rückblick', p. 89; see also Günther Kimmel, 'Das KZ Dachau: Eine Studie zu den nationalsozialistischen Gewaltverbrechen', *Bayern in der NZ Zeit*, Vol. 2, (Munich, 1979), p. 369.
[163] Goeschel and Wachsmann, *Nazi Concentration Camps*, p. 151.

the formal appellations *Sie* and *Ihnen*, and, as Laurence recalled, 'woe to the man who did not know the distinction between a "Herr Oberscharführer" and a "Herr Rottenführer" instantly'.[164] When a prisoner was about to pass an SS man in the camp, he was obliged to remove his cap, place his hands by his side, and walk stiffly and respectfully past. Failure to do so invited chicanery. The inmate was likewise obliged to prostrate himself when passing guard towers or the shrines to Nazi martyrs Horst Wessel and Leo Schlageter.[165] He was forbidden, however, to use anything but the informal *Du* when addressing fellow inmates, even those he had never met, a practice common usually only among children. Bettelheim believed that this was part of a deliberate strategy to infantilize the prisoners: by 'forcing the prisoners to adopt childlike behaviour' the SS was 'destroying all autonomy', filling them with a child's 'impotent rage'.[166] Bettelheim suggested, plausibly, that this philosophy was also manifested in a discursive obsession with excrement:

> curses thrown at prisoners by both the SS and prisoner foremen were almost exclusively connected with the anal sphere. 'Shit' and 'arsehole' were so standard that it was rare when a prisoner was addressed otherwise. It was as if every effort were being made to reduce prisoners to the level they were at before toilet training was achieved.[167]

Inmates were required to abject themselves before guards when seeking permission to go to the toilet during work. Afterwards 'the prisoner, having relieved himself, had to report back using the same formula, much as an infant might report on having done his "duty"'.[168] This would be met with sarcastic approval. There are also reports of torments, even murders, meted out to prisoners through the medium of excrement.[169]

At a collective level, then, Dachau's inmates were variously infantilized, demilitarized, and emasculated. But the increasing diversity of the prisoner population also complicated gender relationships in the camp. The respective masculine ideals among the prisoner group influenced social relations. These alternative conceptions of masculinity, some clearly complicit in a functional sense with the norms promoted by the Nazi regime, in turn shaped the habitus of the Dachau SS to a greater extent than the Manichean structure of most literature on the camp implies. Three inmate groups will be considered here: the political Left, Jews, and male homosexuals. The gendered interaction between these groups and the SS was in many ways a refraction of broader societal conflicts beyond the barbed wire.

The most stable, and certainly the best-documented, dissenting or competing masculinity in Dachau was that of the organized working class who formed the majority of its pre-war inmate population. Socialist conceptions of masculinity were based on relations of production; solidarity through the sweat of one's brow. They sought to reclaim the workplace as a site of redemption rather than oppression. The factory was a Communist's battleground, the cradle of a future Utopia

[164] Laurence, 'Out of the Night', p. 66.   [165] Ecker, 'Die Hölle Dachau', p. 32.
[166] Bettelheim, *Informed Heart*, pp. 130–1.   [167] Bettelheim, *Informed Heart*, p. 132.
[168] Bettelheim, *Informed Heart*, p. 133.
[169] Burkhardt, *Tanz Mal*, pp. 53–4; Klausch, *Tätergeschichten*, p. 138.

led by muscular Stakhanovite workers. German communism, one historian notes, promoted 'tough masculinity to demarcate, and idealize, workers from the "foppish" or "aesthete" middle and upper class'.[170] On the softer, Catholic, Left too, Bavarian workers in the Weimar Republic developed a masculine aesthetic—even poetic—based on glorification of labour.[171] As one young luminary of the movement put it:

> The modern worker, this man of iron, has discovered his soul. He believes in loyalty and comradeship, in brotherhood and the courage to sacrifice. He hopes in a new humanity. Yes, out of his heavy everyday existence he hammers bridges to the eternal and the divine. He turns hard slave labour into an act of worship.[172]

The topos of the muscular German worker had a powerful presence in German politics. He was a recurrent motif on the electoral posters of all the main parties in the twilight of the Weimar Republic, haughtily staring down Nazis, elbowing aside KPD paramilitaries, or crushing the top-hatted elite of international high finance.[173] Socialist industrialism's prizing of muscularity, endurance, and standing up for comrades were deeply resonant concepts in Dachau. The daily scenes of oppressed working men toiling under the armed guard of the SS seemed to provide eloquent confirmation of the Comintern's interpretation of fascism as 'the open terroristic dictatorship of the most reactionary, most chauvinistic, and most imperialistic elements of finance capital'.[174] The conflict between Nazism and the Left was refracted in concentration camp masculinity. At the points of contact between the SS ideal of the soldier patriot and the Left's muscular comradeship emerged occasional opportunities for undermining the terroristic domination of the former.

Prisoner literature from the early months of the camp offers several vivid examples. The top prisoner functionary position at this time was work sergeant (*Arbeitsfeldwebel*), held by the 43-year-old Communist Josef Zäuner. Zäuner's robust military bearing in the face of his 'welcome beating' by the SS impressed the whole camp. It was a deeply gendered episode, at the time and in prisoner memory. Walter Hornung recounts it as follows:

> As he stood there being punished, with every muscle of his bony face disciplined, watching with a cool expression the repulsive activity of the SS, he was the picture of powerful manliness, which must secretly have had a provocative effect on the SS.[175]

Erwein von Aretin recorded his admiration for another leading Communist in Dachau, Georg Groener—known among the prisoners as 'General' after the Weimar-era Reichswehr general. For Aretin, Groener's 'iron fists' cast him as 'a muscular representative of the teaching of absolute solidarity among the prisoners'.[176]

---

[170] Eric D. Weitz, *Creating German Communism, 1890–1990: From Popular Protests to Socialist State* (Princeton, 1997), pp. 188–232, here p. 191.

[171] Raymond C. Sun, '"Hammer Blows": Work, the Workplace, and the Culture of Masculinity Among Catholic Workers in the Weimar Republic', *Central European History*, Vol. 37, No. 2 (2004), pp. 245–71.

[172] Sun, 'Hammer Blows', p. 246.    [173] Evans, *Coming of the Third Reich*, p. 382f.

[174] In Kershaw, *Nazi Dictatorship*, p. 32.    [175] Hornung, *Dachau*, p. 82.

[176] Aretin, *Krone und Ketten*, pp. 288–9.

Groener is best remembered in prisoner memoirs for his holding of drill for prisoners not assigned to work details. One expert on this material, the Dachau survivor and historian Stanislav Zámečnik, argues that the experience uplifted and bound the prisoners together in their own muscular drill: for them, it was the SS who committed militarist *lèse-majesté*:

> In the spirit of the German mentality, this drill was for them a sort of escape from reality. They felt like soldiers, elevated above the SS men, who were mostly untrained boys with a non-military deportment. It was an opportunity to show them 'how it's done'.[177]

Eicke, evidently, was discomfited by this manifestation of Remarquian comradeship and cancelled Groener's drilling. He announced that he had no intention of allowing the training of another 'Red Army' in his concentration camp.[178]

In daily work too, opportunities arose to assert the endurance and skill of the working man against the artless brutality of the SS. Some of the better-documented examples come from the operation of the Moor Express, the exhausting work detail in which prisoners loaded and pushed heavy carts usually drawn elsewhere by horses or tractors. Occasionally the SS or *Kapos* would assign an inexperienced, weaker inmate to the detail if the normal incumbent was needed elsewhere. The new man would invariably 'stand out' for his comparative lack of dexterity and attract the wrath of the detail's SS block leader. On at least one occasion, along with the customary physical violence, the NCO in question grabbed his shovel to demonstrate, patronizingly, what he should be doing. This, Neurath recalls, presented the work commando with an opportunity:

> It was only an incautious act on the part of the officer. But there he would be, on the spot. Now he shovels like a fiend. And invariably the prisoners shovel ahead like two fiends, their piles rise faster and higher. Those who are not shovelling try to encourage with their eyes and with nods those who are at it. As soon as the officer realises what is going on, he tries to extricate himself from the embarrassing situation. He throws the shovel back into the weak man's hands, perhaps beats him up, barks at the rest of the crew, and leaves the scene.[179]

This episode is a reminder of the relationship between gender and shame. Another, playing again on the masculine self-conception of the sentries, was at the political *Kapo*'s instigation to make the Moor Express run so quickly as to exert them:

> the prisoners, realizing what was happening, would run like mad, and the guards, with their heavy uniforms and weapons, would be sweating and lagging behind, usually not daring to order the thing to stop, afraid that it might look like the prisoners had gotten them out of breath . . . the smallest chance to do something against the guards was worth a dear price in a situation where the men could practically never take any action of their own choosing.[180]

---

[177] Zámečnik, *Dachau*, p. 53.        [178] Richardi, *Schule*, p. 83.
[179] Neurath, *Society*, p. 217.        [180] Neurath, *Society*, p. 179.

Although the historian must be vigilant with the memoirs of prisoners from the political Left, tending as they understandably do to emphasize socialist cooperation and resistance in the camp, there is a definite ring of authenticity to these scenes, particularly in the pre-war years when German and Austrian political prisoners were dominant and camp nutrition had not yet wrought the deadly havoc on constitutions it would during the war. The camp leadership was dependent on achieving a certain output from strategic details like the Moor Express and tolerated established working groups. Moreover, even as a construct, an ideal, it was one which Nazism and the SS feared. The pseudo-socialist rhetoric of what was, after all, the National Socialist German *Workers'* Party made it a sensitive issue. And such scenes, however mythologized, embedded themselves in camp discourse and served as a consolation and challenge to the SS monopoly claim to tough masculinity.

Another prisoner group whose gender identity in Dachau very clearly reflected events outside the camp was Jewish men.[181] As a prisoner category, they were far more a manufacture of Nazism than the organized working class and it was the male Jew who pervaded the demonology of Nazi antisemitism. He was at once the germ cell of Asiatic Bolshevism, the corrupter of 'Aryan' maidens, the puppeteer of Anglo-Saxon finance capitalism, and, as a supposedly rootless and wandering parasite, the absolute countertype to nationalistic martial masculinity. Jewish men were at the base of the concentration camp hierarchy, the 'outcasts among the outcast'.[182] One of the many ways their masculinity was degraded inside and outside the camp was withholding from them the status of 'military preparedness', that key historical manifestation of manhood in Germany. In the antisemitic imagination, Jewish men were starkly unmilitary: wheezing, corpulent, manipulative, and elderly, too busy swindling blonde girls out of their virtue, and trusting, rosy-faced farmers out of their livelihoods.[183] The male Jew was the congenital outsider, irreconcilable with healthy, nationalistic masculinity and *Männerbund*. In Jünger's poisonous words, the 'knowledge and realization of the typical German figure separates off the figure of the Jew as visibly and plainly as clear and still water renders oil visible as a particular layer'.[184]

Jewish men had in fact both volunteered and been enlisted to serve in the Wars of Liberation, and had hoped that this manifest military preparedness would be recognized and rewarded with equal rights and civic integration.[185] They were to be disappointed; while the army was prepared to field Jewish soldiers in times of crisis, they were forced out in peacetime and never considered for commission. In 1916, the Imperial army, to rapturous applause from the political Right, carried

[181] For detail, see especially Wünschmann, 'Jewish Prisoners in Nazi Concentration Camps, 1933–1939'.

[182] Wünschmann, 'Jewish Prisoners', p. 579.

[183] See, for example, an RuSHA leaflet on the topic from 1936 printed in Matthäus, *Ausbildungsziel*, pp. 152–62.

[184] In Weisbrod, 'Jünger', p. 82. Remarkably, Jünger continued to garner literary awards into the 1980s.

[185] Frevert, *Nation in Barracks*, pp. 65–70.

out a survey on the participation of German Jews in the war. The findings, that German Jews were more than doing their bit, was hushed up so as not to impair a useful belligerent nationalist discourse.[186] The topos of the service-evading Jew was one of many beer-hall staples replicated in *Mein Kampf* and one of the most wounding to Jewish masculinity. Hindenburg's later haggling to exempt Jewish males with military service from Nazi legislation exemplified the Right's contortions in attempting to elide a glorification of military service with a thoroughgoing antisemitism. The 1935 Army Law eventually excluded male Jews from this 'honourable service for the German people' and hence from the kudos of military preparedness. This left, however, the problem of Jewish males who had demonstrably established their military credentials, and it was one faced repeatedly by the Dachau SS. In August 1933, a Jewish prisoner was imprisoned in the camp whose biography offered a seemingly insurmountable challenge to antisemitic wisdoms. Siegmund Hertz from the Palatinate was the possessor of no fewer than seventeen war decorations, including the cherished Iron Cross 1st Class. He was also a war invalid, and had citations for rescuing injured comrades under fire. According to *Nazi Bastille Dachau*, a procession of Dachau SS men came to look at him in his barracks 'as if he were a fantastical creature (*Wundertier*). All were of the opinion that there must be elements of German blood in his Jewish family'.[187]

The subversive threat to SS soldierly masculinity posed by Jewish men with military records became particularly apparent in the pogrom of November 1938. Many of the older 'November Jews' had fought for Germany in the war, and brought medals and military passes into the camp to demonstrate their patriotic contribution.[188] The results of the confrontation between SS stereotypes and Jewish males with military records were not uniform, but it always provoked a reaction. Several Jewish men reported being spared physical abuse in Dachau due to their military service, and one even on the basis that two of his brothers had died as volunteers in the Great War.[189] For the most part, however, protestations of military service brought sarcastic incredulity or outraged violence. Many Jewish men, in turn, sought to preserve the masculine integrity they had earned in military service by interpreting the camp experience in the models and vocabulary of the trenches.[190] Here, once again, Dachau SS conceptions of soldierly masculinity proved brittle.

Homosexual prisoners were another inmate group whose interaction with the SS was deeply gendered. The first homosexual men arrived in Dachau in 1933, followed by a sharp increase after the Röhm purge when raids in Munich

[186] For detail see Werner T. Angress, 'The German Army's "Judenzählung" of 1916: Genesis—Consequences—Significance', *Leo Baeck Institute Year Book* 23 (1978), pp. 117–37. See also the fine recent monograph on German-Jewish soldiers by Tim Grady, *The German-Jewish Soldiers of the First World War in History and Memory* (Liverpool, 2011).
[187] *Nazi Bastille Dachau*, p. 51.
[188] Wolfgang Benz, 'Mitglieder der Häftlingsgesellschaft auf Zeit: "Die Aktionsjuden" 1938/39', in Benz and Königseder, *Dachau*, pp. 214–15.
[189] Wiener Library Testimony (WL) P.II.d. No. 175, s. 1. A decree by Reinhard Heydrich on 28 November 1938 ordered that Jewish male front veterans be released from the camps.
[190] Wünschmann, 'Konzentrationslagererfahrungen', pp. 11–12.

combed the Englischer Garten, other parks, and gay bars to bring fifty-four allegedly homosexual men to Dachau in October 1934 alone.[191] It is particularly difficult to reconstruct their experience in the camp. They have left few memoirs, and
their presence in the voluminous political prisoner literature is deeply inflected
with the authors' prejudices. Anti-gay attitudes served, and serve, to consolidate
the male holder's security in his own masculinity; as such homosexual prisoners
suffer even beyond the camps from their fellow prisoners' performing gender in
their memoirs. Such attitudes were also for some inmates a means of ingratiating
themselves with an SS whose hatred of male homosexuality, as has been seen, knew
no bounds. In doing so, of course, these inmates provided a functional affirmation
of the SS world view.

Homosexual prisoners suffered conspicuous abuse from the Dachau SS. There
was a bespoke induction procedure, in which they were required to shout their
names prefaced by a homophobic adjective.[192] There is some evidence that their
pubic, as well as head, hair was shaved off. A report from the Bavarian Ministry
of the Interior noted that homosexual prisoners were kept in a separate barracks
with the lights left on at night and a sentry posted inside to prevent them engaging in sexual activity. The preoccupation of Höß's memoirs with these inmates is
characteristic of his milieu. In his view, male homosexuality was not so much congenital as the result of sexual frustration and 'a search for a stimulating or exciting
activity that promises to give the men something out of life, in surroundings where
absolutely no form of moral restraint applies'.[193] Höß congratulates himself on his
role in containing what he sees as a latent epidemic of male homosexuality among
the prisoners. In Dachau, he reports, homosexual men were initially distributed
among blocks and 'the epidemic spread' until he hit upon the notion of confining
them to one barrack and according them heavy manual work to take their minds
off sex. Some prisoners from other categories 'also afflicted with this vice' were
sent to join them. 'In this way', Höß continues, 'the epidemic was at once stopped
from spreading'.[194] This idea that homosexual desire was a situational lifestyle
choice reflected historical anxieties about the moral hazard of the *Männerbund*.
The perceived challenge presented by homosexual men to the saccharine comradeship preached by the SS suggests that with this prisoner group, too, the Dachau SS
confronted the brittleness of its masculine ideals.

Another interesting and pertinent comparator here are female concentration
camp guards, who have recently begun to attract greater attention from historians.[195] Significantly, Himmler was reluctant to deploy male SS personnel to guard
female concentration camp prisoners. Violence against women did not fit with
its masculine ideals at this stage, although such inhibitions were later overcome

[191] Albert Knoll, 'Totgeschlagen—totgeschwiegen: Die homosexuelle Häftlinge im KZ Dachau',
*Dachauer Hefte*, Vol. 14 (Nov., 1998), p. 79.
[192] Knoll, 'Totgeschlagen', p. 86.       [193] Höß, *Commandant*, p. 48.
[194] Höß, *Commandant*, p. 93.
[195] Simone Erpel (ed.), *Im Gefolge der SS: Aufseherinnen des Frauen-KZ Ravensbrück* (Berlin, 2007);
Koslov, *Gewalt*; Jutta Mühlenberg, *Das SS-Helferinnenkorps: Ausbildung, Einsatz und Entnazifizierung
der weiblichen Angehörigen der Waffen-SS 1942–1949* (Hamburg, 2011).

during the Holocaust. In 1937 the concentration camp for women was moved from Moringen to Lichtenburg and placed for the first time under the authority of Eicke's IKL. At Lichtenburg SS men remained responsible for perimeter security and held the senior roles in the camp but female wardens carried out the internal supervision of inmates. Conditions inside were tough but not as in Eicke's male camps: there was no corporal punishment, far less labour, and violent abuse was rare.[196] In May 1939 the prisoners were transferred to the newly built concentration camp for women at Ravensbrück.

Life under female overseers in Ravensbrück was harsher, though still not comparable to male concentration camps. Overseers were never part of the SS *Männerbund* but classified as a 'retinue' (*Gefolge*). There was something of a 'Ravensbrück School' for female personnel but its focus was on order, discipline, and efficiency rather than the drilling, hazing, and ideological schooling which characterized Dachau.[197] During the war, German women were deployed as guards in all the main concentration camps in Eastern Europe. By 1945 there were some 3,500 female guards in all, around 10 per cent of the overall guard contingent.[198] They were never entrusted with senior positions and reported to male SS officers. For veterans of the Dachau School like Höß, working with female guards tarnished the masculine ideals of the camp SS. He depicts his overseers as indolent, individualistic, and weak: the inversion of camp SS values. Their morale, he claims, was low and they often grumbled both to him and his wife. They lacked the discipline and resolution of male personnel and ran around at roll calls 'like a lot of flustered hens'.[199] Characteristically, he even claimed that the women's camp at Auschwitz experienced 'an epidemic of lesbianism' under their supervision, including sexual relations between inmates and guards.[200]

Such eroticism is typical of sources by male authors on female guards and it remains difficult to venture forthright comparisons between male and female personnel in the camps. For one thing, acts of violence by German women were more shocking to witnesses than those of SS men, since they represented far more of a transgression of accepted gender norms zealously promoted in the Third Reich. On balance, it seems that some overseers could be as capricious and desensitized as male personnel, but that their daily scope for personal initiative was narrower and their violence less devastating.[201] Presumably because they were regarded as lacking in the learned emotional steeliness, female personnel did not participate directly in mass gassing operations in the camps, although they were involved in preparatory 'selections'.[202] The evidence also indicates there was less esprit de corps among female staff and that they were unsentimental about their uniforms. An order

---

[196] For detail on staff at Lichtenburg, see especially Hördler, 'SS Kaderschmiede Lichtenburg'; comparison of camp cultures in Wachsmann, 'KL: A History of the Nazi Concentration Camps', ch. 2.

[197] Koslov, *Gewalt*, pp. 137–57.

[198] Eberle, 'Einführung', in Eberle (ed.), *Im Gefolge der SS*, pp. 23–4.

[199] Höß, *Commandant*, p. 137.     [200] Höß, *Commandant*, p. 139.

[201] Caplan, 'Gender', pp. 99–100; Koslov, *Gewalt*, pp. 475–81.

[202] Koslov, *Gewalt*, pp. 487–8.

from the Ravensbrück commandant in 1942 despaired that overseers had been going out in the locality in a combination of service and civilian clothing: almost unthinkable for the preening males of the Dachau School.[203] The post-war trials of notorious female personnel such as Irma Grese, a senior overseer in Ravensbrück, Bergen-Belsen, and Auschwitz attracted much prurient international attention with the defendants either hypersexualized or defeminized as 'manly'.[204] Perhaps the most that can be said is that this pathologizing, and the difficulty male SS men had working with female personnel, illustrates the resilience of the connection between violence and masculinity in the SS and beyond.

The SS continued to be fortified by its masculine ideals during the years of war and genocide. Executioners were frequently exhorted to draw on their comradeship and unflinching steeliness. In one characteristic speech, the *Reichsführer* mused that mass executions were 'frightful for a German' to behold and a 'grim duty for our men'. 'Nevertheless', he concluded, 'they must never be soft; they must grit their teeth and do their duty'.[205] In doing so, he boasted at Posen, the SS had 'remained decent, that is what has made us tough'.[206] Individual executioners lacking the requisite toughness for murder might be held up to shame and emasculated—as a *Pimpf*, for example, a Hitler Youth 'cub scout', merely playing at soldiers.[207] In the concentration camps, too, Dachau School alumni drew on their learned toughness, as deteriorating and eventually catastrophic living conditions for inmates brought ever more pitiless intolerance from the perpetrators. The murderous camps in the East in particular, notes one historian, were 'a working environment where a cold heart and an iron fist were seen as essential parts of the male anatomy'.[208]

Whatever emotional sensitivity survived focused on the perpetrator's self and its own plight. The aggrieved tone present throughout Höß's autobiography reaches its zenith when, as Auschwitz commandant:

> I had to appear cold and indifferent to events that must have wrung the heart of anyone possessed of human feelings. I might not even look away when afraid lest my natural emotions got the upper hand. I had to watch coldly, while mothers with laughing or crying children went to the gas chambers.[209]

It is unlikely that Höß experienced much pleasure during these viscerally unpleasant operations. Yet he is still unable to disguise a certain pride at his steely and professional emotional detachment. The passage has clear, perhaps intentional,

---

[203] Jeanette Touissant, 'Nach Dienstschluss', in Eberle (ed.), *Im Gefolge der SS*, pp. 89–100, here p. 94.

[204] More broadly on this, see Susannah Heschel, 'Does Atrocity Have a Gender? Feminist Interpretations of Women in the SS', in *Lessons and Legacies Volume VI: New Currents in Holocaust Research* (2004), pp. 300–21. It must be said that, like many musings on female perpetrators, the piece is rather better at raising questions than hazarding answers.

[205] Quoted in Buchheim, 'Command and Compliance', p. 338.

[206] Noakes and Pridham, *Nazism 1919–1945*, Vol. 3, p. 1199.

[207] Browning, *Ordinary Men*, p. 118.

[208] Wachsmann, *KL: A History of the Nazi Concentration Camps*, ch. 7.

[209] Höß, *Commandant*, p. 154.

linguistic echoes of his account of Eicke's lectures on toughness at the Dachau School. Höß was socialized in an era of hard and unyielding masculine norms, and constantly committed himself to groups and institutions at its vanguard. He would go to his death at the gallows in Auschwitz like a caricature of soldierly stoicism: upright, composed, silent, and emotionless.[210]

[210] Orth, *Konzentrationslager SS*, p. 283.

# 6

# The Dachau SS and the Locality

'You are to blame for these shameful deeds!' So ran the caption to harrowing photographs of Dachau's liberation in 1945 posted around Germany that summer.[1] 'You looked on and took no action. Why did you not shake the German conscience awake with some word of protest, some cry of indignation? That is your great fault—you share in the responsibility for this cruel crime!' Communities in the vicinity of concentration camps were viewed in an especially dim light. Allied liberators staged compulsory tours of the camps for local citizens whose attempts to cover their eyes against the horror met with the barked order 'Hands down!'[2] In Dachau, selected townspeople were forced to cart thousands of putrefying corpses from the camp (see Figure 6.1) to mass graves dug by captured SS men. One stinking empty cart was then left in the town centre as a final gesture of condemnation.[3] Local worthies bristled at the accusations, explicit and implicit. Dachau's mayor, Josef Schwalber, voiced the feelings of many in speaking pointedly of the camp's 'hermetic isolation' from the locality, of 'nonlocal sadists' who had descended on the town in 1933 and proceeded to tarnish its name 'in the eyes of the entire civilized world'.[4] 'For twelve long years', he lamented, 'the concentration camp weighed like a nightmare upon us'.

Characteristic of concentration camp localities throughout Germany, the apologia met with well-founded scepticism from American occupying personnel. Yet after the Dachau and Nuremberg trials, the appetite for engagement with such delicate issues receded in the circumstances of a Cold War requiring the moral rehabilitation of West German society. Mayor Schwalber's depiction of the camp as an autonomous institution whose social context was incidental—a matter of happenstance—anticipated the ensuing consciousness of the concentration camps. The imagery of their 'hermetic isolation' as 'laboratories' of domination was soon equally entrenched in scholarship, sustained above all by sociological and social psychological literature.[5] Not until the history workshop movement and

---

[1] Imperial War Museum (IWM), PST 8350.

[2] Harold Marcuse, *Legacies of Dachau: The Uses and Abuses of a Concentration Camp, 1933–2001* (Cambridge, 2001), pp. 55–6.

[3] Marcuse, *Legacies*, p. 57.     [4] Quoted in Marcuse, *Legacies*, p. 73.

[5] Hannah Arendt, *Origins of Totalitarianism* (Columbia, 1967 [1951]), pp. 437–56. Buggeln also notes the prevalence of 'laboratory' imagery in older scholarship on the camps. Buggeln, *Arbeit*, pp. 607–8. Even the most recent sociological literature sustains the trope, with Sofsky writing that '[o]nly

**Figure 6.1** American soldiers watch civilians cart corpses out from Dachau concentration camp, 1 May 1945. USHMM Photo Archives 89,157.

blossoming of interest in the 'history of everyday life' (*Alltagsgeschichte*) in the 1980s were the uncomfortable questions of the liberation period revisited.[6] Since then, an accomplished body of historical writing has begun to probe the manifold connections between concentration camps and their localities.[7] In line with broader trends, the emphasis has fallen ever more on the opportunism and complicity displayed by German citizens 'in the shadow of death', a preview in many respects of their role in the Holocaust. The very term 'bystander' has fallen into disfavour, supplanted by the idea of proximate participants in the National Socialist People's Community.[8]

after space was sealed off totally, hermetically, did the camp become that closed locus where absolute power could unfold freely, unhampered by limits'. Sofsky, *Order*, p. 55.

[6]  Caplan and Wachsmann, *Concentration Camps*, p. 5; Marcuse, *Legacies*, pp. 343–8.

[7]  Gordon J. Horwitz, *In the Shadow of Death: Living Outside the Gates of Mauthausen* (London and New York, 1991); Steinbacher, *Dachau*; Jens Schley, *Nachbar Buchenwald: Die Stadt Weimar und ihr Konzentrationslager, 1937–1945* (Cologne, 1999); Bernward Dörner, 'Ein KZ in der Mitte der Stadt: Oranienburg', in Wolfgang Benz and Barbara Distel (eds), *Terror ohne System: Die ersten Konzentrationslager im Nationalsozialismus 1933–1945* (Berlin, 2001), pp. 123–38; Anja Decker, 'Die Stadt Prettin und das Konzentrationslager Lichtenburg: Zwischen Bedrohung, Profit und Alltag', in Stefan Hördler and Sigrid Jacobeit (eds), *Lichtenburg: Ein deutsches Konzentrationslager* (Berlin, 2009), pp. 205–28; Karola Fings, 'The Public Face of the Camps', in Caplan and Wachsmann, *Concentration Camps*, pp. 108–26.

[8]  Michael Wildt, *Volksgemeinschaft als Selbstermächtigung: Gewalt gegen Juden in der deutschen Provinz 1919–1939* (Hamburg, 2007); specifically on concentration camp 'liminal zone actors' see Helen Whatmore, 'Exploring KZ "Bystanding" within a West-European Framework: Natzweiler-Struthof, Neuengamme and Vught-Herzogenbusch', in Christiane Heß, Julia Hörath, Dominique

This research also offers a fresh perspective on the perpetrators, as the prevalence of 'closed world' imagery in theoretical literature begins to look like an expression of weakness elsewhere in explanatory models.[9] Such stark distinction between camp and context is misleading. Dachau was part of an institutional web of terror and social discipline which lent concentration camp service much of its professional identity and validation. Sworn foes of the Bavarian establishment in the Weimar era, Himmler and the SS were soon among its stakeholders. On an immediate, social level, too, Dachau personnel interacted frequently with the local community. The camp was an object of local curiosity and potential custom for a whole range of businesses, while the presence of thousands of young male guards with disposable incomes transformed the local entertainment and dating scene. The varying outcomes of these institutional and social transactions indelibly marked the life and culture of the Dachau School.

## THE DACHAU LOCALITY

Located 18 km to the north-west of Munich in the midst of the picturesque Dachau moors, the market town of Dachau was renowned in the Imperial era for its excellent beer, restorative spa waters, and thriving colony of artists. In 1897 a group of local painters founded the 'New Dachau School' specializing in wistful landscape pieces.[10] Yet, as elsewhere in Bavaria, the tendrils of industrialization had begun to reach Dachau in the mid-nineteenth century. In 1862 the MD paper factory was built on the banks of the river Amper in the teeth of local protests about its environmental impact.[11] The MD was soon the largest paper concern in Germany, turning out large-scale circulations such as the satirical weekly *Simplicissimus* and driving the formation of the locality's first worker organizations. It was the advent of the Great War, however, which dragged Dachau fully into the modern age. The idealistic male artists marched off to their deaths in Flanders and in 1916 the Imperial Army, drawn by a plentiful supply of timber, chose Dachau as the site for a vast new munitions and gunpowder combine. Some 8,000 workers from across Bavaria came to work there. German defeat and the Treaty of Versailles ended

---

Schröder, and Kim Wünschmann (eds), *Kontinuitäten und Brüche: Neue Perspektiven auf die Geschichte der NS-Konzentrationslager* (Berlin, 2011), pp. 64–79.

[9] Sofsky, for example, argues that '[i]f violence is considered normal in a social collective, it gradually becomes a binding norm . . . The more isolated a group is from the surrounding social environment, the more unquestioned is the validity of its internal norms and ideals. The members of the camp SS were, for the most part, removed from the world of their former civilian social roles and relations. They had been transplanted into a milieu that was beyond external control, an ambience in which an independent world of norms could develop'. Sofsky, *Order*, p. 228. Other invocations of the 'closed world' perpetrator mentality include Arendt, *Origins*, p. 438; Lifton, *Nazi Doctors*, p. 210–11; Goffman, *Asylums*, p. 5; Milgram, *Obedience*, p. 69–71; Zimbardo, *Lucifer*, pp. 185–92; Bloxham, *Final Solution*, pp. 284–5.

[10] Richardi, *Schule*, p. 39.

[11] Norbert Goettler, *Die Sozialgeschichte des Bezirkes Dachau 1870 bis 1920: Ein Beispiel struktureller Wandlungsprozesse des ländlichen Raumes* (Munich, 1988), pp. 127–30.

production but most of its workers remained, largely unemployed, in Dachau. In June 1926, the height of the 'golden years' of the Weimar Republic, the Dachau district had the highest percentage of unemployed in Germany.[12]

All this amounted to a wholesale restructuring of the social and political character of the area. Previously conservative and agrarian, a pronounced worker consciousness emerged, consolidated by memories of 1919. The parties of the Left enjoyed strong electoral support in Dachau throughout the Weimar period. The modest enthusiasm for the NSDAP also reflected the hold of Catholicism, staunch even by Bavarian standards: compared to a state average of 70 per cent, 90 per cent of Dachau's inhabitants identified themselves as Catholic in 1933.[13] During the Nazi era, the regime's total claim often encountered difficulties among a Catholic flock which did not on the whole invest the same millenarian hopes as German Protestants in the advent of the Third Reich.[14] Dachau, as a concentration camp town, may have won a reputation as a hotbed of Nazism in the 1930s, but this was hardly anticipated in its prehistory. The story of Dachau in the Third Reich was one of manifold actors, of opportunism and coercion, of ardour and apathy, of inclusion and exclusion, of race, violence, generation, and gender: in short, a tale of the National Socialist People's Community.

## THE DACHAU SITE

Much to the chagrin of local newspapers, the 190-acre plot taken over by the SS in 1933 had lain dormant since 1918.[15] It comprised hundreds of buildings, including ten workers' barracks, a canteen, and numerous workshops, all wired and plumbed into the local infrastructure.[16] The workers' barracks became inmates' barracks and the adjoining buildings would delineate the prisoner compound until it was built anew in the winter of 1937 to 1938. Prisoners toiled at the expansion and renovation of the SS complex at Dachau throughout the 1930s, a programme which marks cumulatively the biggest economic project undertaken by the SS in the pre-war era.[17] Beyond barracks and diverse SS accommodation, they built kitchens, infirmaries, storerooms, a library, garages with petrol depots, a riding school with stables, a sports hall with tennis court, and even an open-air swimming pool.[18] The existing rail connection was extended and additional termini constructed for the prisoner and SS camps.[19] There was accommodation for cadets

---

[12] Steinbacher, *Dachau*, p. 227.     [13] Steinbacher, *Dachau*, p. 179.

[14] Eric Johnson, *The Nazi Terror: The Gestapo, Jews, and Ordinary Germans* (New York, 1999), pp. 222–50; on Protestant fervour 'from below' see Kyle Jantzen, *Faith and Fatherland: Parish Politics in Hitler's Germany* (Minneapolis, 2008). On Broszat's useful concept of *Resistenz* (limitations to the regime's societal purchase) see Kershaw, *The Nazi Dictatorship*, pp. 150–79.

[15] For an excellent discussion of its prehistory, see Steinbacher, *Dachau*, pp. 35–48. The plot was finally purchased by the NSDAP in September 1936 for 600,000 Reichsmark.

[16] BAB, R2 28330, Chronik der gesamten SS-Lageranlage in Dachau, pp. 1–2. This meticulously detailed history of the Dachau site was drawn up by the SS in March 1938.

[17] Kaienburg, *Wirtschaft*, p. 114.     [18] BAB, R2 28330, Chronik, ss. 4–8.

[19] Steinbacher, *Dachau*, pp. 130–1.

at Bad Tölz who came to Dachau for military training. For a time in 1937, the site also housed an officers' academy for the General SS.[20] According to SS accounts, the real estate value of the whole site rose from 4 million Reichsmark when the early Dachau SS arrived in 1933 to around 25.8 million by the end of 1937, an appreciation achieved largely on the backs of costless prisoner labour.[21]

In 1934 and 1935, civilians living on the road approaching the camp were forced to move out and the properties renovated for SS use.[22] Yet the demand for SS accommodation continued to outpace supply. Reich finances alone were insufficient to underwrite the new building so in 1938 the SS set up Public Flat and Housing Association Dachau, a limited liability company to attract private investment for 'the construction of healthy and practical flats for the growing and still undetermined community of SS members'.[23] According to its first annual report, Eickeplatz, the main thoroughfare in the SS living area, already had twenty-six flats and a restaurant, while a further twenty-nine flats were in construction on the Road of the SS linking the camp with the town.[24] Among the residents was Oswald Pohl, a rising star in the SS and future manager of the concentration camp system, who was instrumental in raising capital for the company. The interaction between the Dachau SS and Bavarian financial services was grounded in sound risk management rather than ideological admiration. Isar Life Assurance, for example, declined the company's application for a 400,000 Reichsmark mortgage as the projected rents from SS residents were too low.[25] Although it did secure some private finance, its resources continued to be squeezed between the low rents deducted at source from SS personnel and the commercial rates of interest charged on its debt. In 1942 the assets were sold back to the Reich, which now took over the implicit subsidy to the SS men.[26]

The net result of the frenetic development projects of the 1930s was that the Dachau complex by the end of the decade looked, in the words of an SPD exile publication, 'ever more like a small town, with the low-rise prisoner housing blocks as its centre'. Surrounded by a moat and high wall with electrified wire, the perimeters were patrolled every fifteen minutes by a detail of twelve SS men. To the east the vast plantation for cultivating herbs had been built on land reclaimed from marshes. The streets around the Dachau complex, lined with well-tended flowerbeds, gleamed with cleanliness. Signposts at crossroads pointed the way respectively to the SS training complex and concentration camp. To the rear, machine gun towers raked the camp and its surroundings with searchlights throughout the night.[27]

---

[20] Kaienburg, *Wirtschaft*, p. 119, fn. 12.      [21] Kaienburg, *Wirtschaft*, p. 122.

[22] Kaienburg, *Wirtschaft*, p. 120.

[23] BA NS3 572 Gemeinnützige Wohnungs und Heimstättengesellschaft mbH Dachau. Gesellschaftsvertrag.

[24] BA NS3 1146 Errichtung der SS-Wohnanlage in Dachau (Kreditaufnahme, Hypotheken, Rechnungsangelegenheiten).

[25] BAB, NS3 942, Hypothekengesuch für die Wohnanlage in Dachau, s. 32.

[26] Kaienburg, *Wirtschaft*, pp. 211–12.

[27] *Nazi Bastille Dachau*, pp. 14–15; Neurath, *Society*, p. 12. More broadly on camps as 'mini-towns' see Stefanie Endlich, 'Die äußere Gestalt des Terrors: Zu Städtebau und Architektur der Konzentrationslager', in Benz and Distel, *Ort des Terrors*, Vol. 1, pp. 210–29.

## THE DACHAU SS IN
## INSTITUTIONAL CONTEXT

This Dachau complex was to be the springboard and 'bastion' of Himmler's ambitions for the SS.[28] A snapshot of its early institutional context is offered by the telephone exchanges listed in the police handover documentation at the end of May 1933. They include extensions at the State Police, SS Group South, the Bavarian Ministry of the Interior, Stadelheim Prison, Brown House, the Dachau county court, the town council, Schwabing hospital, the local dentist, and the Hörhammer pub.[29] Yet the long-term prospects for the concentration camps, Dachau included, were far from assured in these early years.[30] In the wake of Wäckerle's acrimonious tenure as commandant, Himmler's key concern was to secure Dachau's future.

The first institutional threat to deal with was the Bavarian judiciary which had helped to bring Wäckerle down. Contrary to the impression given in some literature, the struggle between the Dachau SS and the judiciary should not be presented in moral terms as a conflict between enlightened officials and arbitrary SS.[31] The great majority of legal officials, not least in conservative Bavaria, had great sympathy for the nationalist Right. This was a turf war, a contest over jurisdiction: protective custody traversed institutional boundaries. Most Dachau inmates spent some time in police or judicial custody before transportation to the camp. Some spent years in judicial confinement only to be brought to Dachau on release as part of Gestapo 'corrections' of legal sentences. Indeed, the Bavarian Ministry of Justice was pioneering in demanding that state prison governors review the case of every male prisoner due for release to determine whether he should instead be taken into protective custody.[32] Strikingly, this directive was issued on 31 May 1933, at the very height of the storied judicial outrage at the SS. Throughout the 1930s, a visit to Dachau was mandatory for trainee jurists in Munich, who would learn that conditions there were 'hard but fair' and comparable to judicial confinement.[33]

In December 1933 the Bavarian cabinet assembled once again to discuss a series of suspicious deaths in Dachau. Wagner had asked for the investigations be shelved as hurtful to the public image of the Nazi paramilitary movement.[34] Yet Frank once again stood firm and at this meeting secured the backing of Reich Governor von Epp. Cornered, Himmler turned to his increasingly powerful boss, Röhm, for support. Röhm ruled that the proceedings should be suspended pending a final verdict from Hitler.[35] Himmler and the Dachau leadership were now able to

---

[28] Kaienburg, *Wirtschaft*, pp. 114–15.

[29] DaA 4118, Übergabe-Protokoll, 30 May 1933.

[30] Wachsmann, 'Dynamics', pp. 20–3.

[31] Richardi, *Schule*, pp. 88–115; 179–220. More broadly, see the historiographical discussion in Christian Goeschel, 'Suicide in Nazi Concentration Camps', *Journal of Contemporary History*, Vol. 45, No. 3, pp. 628–48, esp. pp. 628–30.

[32] See the case studies in Wachsmann, *Hitler's Prisons*, pp. 175–83.

[33] Riedel, *Ordnungshüter*, p. 168.

[34] Goeschel and Wachsmann, *Nazi Concentration Camps*, pp. 21–2.

[35] IMT, Vol. XXXVI, ND-926-PS, pp. 54–5.

stonewall attempts to revive the investigation, a strategy which bore fruit in March 1934 when Hartinger and his boss were transferred away from Munich.[36] Their successors decided to close the investigation on the basis of 'inadequate evidence' of foul play in the deaths of the inmates.[37] Himmler had won an important victory on the road to establishing an extra-judicial institution of terror at Dachau: as one historian puts it, the dismissal of Wäckerle turned out to be a 'pyrrhic defeat' for the SS.[38]

One reason for the success of the stalling tactics had been the more orderly and discreet techniques of terror and murder developed by Eicke at Dachau. His new camp regulations in October 1933 were marked by an obsession with secrecy. They vowed to hang any inmate who

> collects true or false information about the concentration camp: receives such infor-
> mation, buries it, talks about it to others, smuggles it out of the camp . . . passes it on
> in writing or by word of mouth . . . conceals it in clothing or other articles, throws
> stones or objects over the camp wall containing such information . . . climbs on bar-
> rack roofs or trees, or seeks contact with the outside world by giving light or other
> signals.[39]

This was no idle threat. Just two weeks later the camp command allegedly discovered a cache of 'atrocity propaganda' in the camp intended for smuggling to Czechoslovakia. Two prisoners accused by Eicke of involvement were murdered, and their deaths covered up as suicide. Introducing a temporary ban on releases and letters, Eicke announced that there were 'no atrocities and no Cheka cellars in Dachau'.[40]

The regulations also provided a framework for avoiding the judicial attention such crimes could attract. Although they retained illegal provisions for executing mutineers, Eicke sought to insulate guards from individual responsibility for violence. The range of potential disciplinary infractions was now so expansive that it would be impossible to establish that a particular inmate had not committed one, providing in essence a retroactive indemnity for almost all disciplinary steps by guard personnel. In the separate regulations issued for guards, care was taken to provide elastic pretexts for such measures—the innocuous-sounding 'lazy prisoners are to be made to work' (*träge Gefangene sind zur Arbeit anzuhalten*) offering, as has been pointed out, a very flexible warrant for violence.[41] The guards in turn were deindividuated, since they could claim to be acting not on personal initiative, but in line with regulations authorized by Himmler as commander of the Bavarian Political Police. The net effect, as one historian has put it, was to turn the Dachau prisoner compound into 'an unlegislated world, a "terra incognita"

---

[36] Seubert, 'Vierteljahr Haft', p. 97.
[37] IMT, Vol. XXXVI, 926-D, s. 57f.
[38] Nikolaus Wachsmann, 'KL: A History of the Nazi Concentration Camps', ch. 1.
[39] Noakes and Pridham, *Nazism*, Vol. 1, p. 171.
[40] Tuchel, *Konzentrationslager*, pp. 141–4; Ecker, 'Hölle', p. 15.
[41] Julia Hörath, 'Experimente zur Kontrolle und Repression von Devianz und Delinquenz: Die Einweisung von "Asozialen" und "Berufsverbrechern" in die Konzentrationslager 1933 bis 1937/8' (PhD Dissertation, Freie Universität Berlin, 2012), p. 149.

for the judiciary'.[42] Unsolicited judicial visitors to the camp were obstructed and intimidated in the most flagrant manner. Dachau court judge Lorenz Meyer, for example, testified to having visited the camp in October 1933 for the post-mortem of Dr Delvin Katz, murdered in the 'atrocity propaganda' incident described above. During the autopsy, Dachau SS NCOs held hand-grenade practice with live grenades just outside the hut.[43]

These informal strategies, however, were never enough to sequester the protective custody compound entirely. Civilian officials still needed access to the camp to attend inmate interrogations in the Political Department, and to ascertain the circumstances of irregularities such as prisoner deaths. The post-war testimony of Hans Brücklmayr, an employee of the Dachau county court from 1933 to 1938, reveals that he visited the camp on 'several hundred' occasions to tie up paperwork.[44] In 1935 he was given an identity pass to show at the camp gate, and on one occasion the clearly unabashed commandant, Loritz, even offered to give him a guided tour of the prisoner compound itself. Throughout the era of the Dachau School, murders continued to be disguised as attempted escapes or, increasingly, as suicides.[45] This registers the ongoing presence of external constraints. Not until the outbreak of war did the SS gain the power to execute inmates, and the SS internal court jurisdiction over all matters pertaining to its members. By 1940, SS courts also had sole competence for investigating the deaths of inmates. The SS and judiciary continued to cooperate: under a 1942 agreement between Himmler and Minister of Justice Otto-Georg Thierack, so-called 'asocials' and selected 'habitual criminals' were handed over to the SS for 'extermination through labour' in concentration camps.[46]

This murderous wartime partnership between the camp SS and the institutions of the state had origins in pre-war violence against social outsiders. Numerous stakeholders were involved in a process which served to define concentration camp imprisonment—and service—within a 'tightly-woven net of surveillance and detention'.[47] Bavaria, once again, led the way. In September 1933 a 'raid on beggars' saw charitable organizations, welfare offices, Gestapo, police, and SS work together to bring itinerants to jails, workhouses, and Dachau. A regular traffic developed between Dachau and the Rebdorf workhouse in Eichstätt, which saw some 450 workhouse inmates brought to the concentration camp between November 1933 and May 1934. The SS soon sent forty-two of them back to Rebdorf as 'unusable' due to illness and, no doubt, injuries sustained in the camp.[48] The Bavarian Ministry of the Interior came to regard Dachau as a superior disciplinary instrument in its struggle against 'begging and work-shyness', although it haggled over the 1 Reichsmark per day fee demanded by the camp

[42] Tuchel, *Konzentrationslager*, pp. 144–9; quote p. 149.
[43] SAM, StA 34462/9, Zeugenvernehmungsniederschrift Lorenz Meyer, 24 April 1951.
[44] SAM, StA 34461/4, Zeugenvernehmungsprotokoll Hans Brücklmayr, 27 June 1951.
[45] On the SS practice of 'suiciding' inmates in the pre-war Nazi camps see Goeschel, 'Suicide'.
[46] Wachsmann, *Hitler's Prisons*, pp. 284–306.    [47] Hörath, 'Terrorinstrumente', p. 514.
[48] Hörath, 'Experimente', s. 416.

leadership for the accommodation of such men.[49] Depicting Eicke's regulations as fully in line with Weimar-era guidelines for workhouses, the Ministry even envisaged a new detention category of 'work custody' (*Arbeitshaft*) in the camp.[50] Although the Dachau SS ultimately declined to accord these inmates a bespoke category, the negotiations are another example of partnership with Bavarian institutions. The local press briefed readers that 'feckless fathers and the workshy are coming to Dachau' and regional mood reports averred that the population was 'grateful' for such decisive action against outsiders.[51]

Local agencies continued to probe Dachau's potential throughout the 1930s. The Garmisch-Partenkirchen branch of the National Socialist People's Welfare organization enquired in 1936 whether the SS would accept an allegedly 'asocial' man and compel him to undergo castration. The camp leadership, overriding the reluctance of the camp physician, declared itself prepared to admit the man and to 'induce' him to undergo the operation provided that the People's Welfare pay accommodation costs of 1.20 Reichsmark per day.[52] A particularly intimate relationship developed between the Dachau SS and the Herzogsämühle hostel— the largest institution for the homeless in Bavaria. SA *Sturmbannführer* Alarich Seidler, head of the Bavarian association which owned the hostel, arranged for 'asocial' inmates who broke institutional rules to be imprisoned in Dachau for three months. This developed into an exchange programme in 1937, with elderly and infirm concentration camp inmates heading the other way to the hostel. Three Dachau guards were also seconded to Herzogsämühle to help introduce a more repressive regime, among them the notorious block leader Schöttl. Loritz periodically inspected its security measures.[53]

An eloquent and exposed outpost of Dachau in the early years was Schwabing hospital, where a special ward of fourteen beds was set up in the surgical department under the constant guard of two to four SS men. According to its head nurse, this sealed area was 'almost always fully occupied', and the medical staff were forbidden to speak to the prisoners.[54] It was from this ward that Erwin Kahn spoke to Evi and his doctors about the April shootings. Hospitals throughout Germany found themselves treating the victims of early concentration camp violence: yet another phenomenon difficult to reconcile with the hypothesis of the camps as a secret site of crime.[55] This outpost of Dachau was eventually closed down, and the SS established a much-feared prisoner infirmary of their own.[56]

---

[49] Bavarian Ministry of the Interior to the Ministry of Finance, 17 August 1934. Printed in Goeschel and Wachsmann, *Nazi Concentration Camps*, pp. 256–7.

[50] Hörath, 'Experimente', s. 206–8.

[51] Hörath, 'Experimente', pp. 213–14; Moore, 'German Popular Opinion', pp. 207–8.

[52] Dachau Concentration Camp to Garmisch-Partenkirchen District NS People's Welfare, 22 September 1936. Printed in Goeschel and Wachsmann, *Nazi Concentration Camps*, p. 258.

[53] Riedel, *Ordnungshüter*, pp. 167–8; Eberle, 'Asoziale', p. 257.

[54] SAM, StA 34462/7, Zeugenvernehmungsprotokoll Babara M., 3 October 1950.

[55] Moore, 'German Popular Opinion', pp. 129–36.

[56] It is unclear when it was closed; Schecher reports it still being in use for serious medical cases in late 1935: Schecher, 'Rückblick', p. 17.

Another public testament to the nature of the camp, and to its administrative enmeshing with the locality, lay in the files of the responsible registry offices which recorded 3,857 deaths there between 1933 and 1941.[57] These troubling statistics did not deter local politicians from trying to wring additional revenue from Dachau. The camp leadership certainly resented its financial obligations to the locality. Dachau's busy SS canteen, for example, refused to pay beer tax and the case made it to the Munich Administrative Court in 1935 before the SS authorities agreed a compromise payment, distinctly advantageous in relation to the volume of ale consumed.[58] When the camp did deign to pay taxes, the process was complicated by the fact that only a small part of the site lay in Dachau, with the rest in four other administrative tax districts, above all Prittlbach.[59]

Dachau's mayor, contrary to his successors' post-war homilies, was eager to secure the full tax yield from the camp for the town. The Dachau SS leadership was equally keen to simplify its tax arrangements. The resultant negotiations lasted for two years until spring 1939, when von Epp confirmed that municipal boundaries would be redrawn to register the whole site in Dachau. The other districts, with bitterness, surrendered significant territory to Dachau whose own area increased fivefold.[60] In 1916 the Dachau town council had rejected a similar proposal, unpersuaded by the economic benefits. Now, with a concentration camp and SS training base, the position of the town fathers was very different. Dachau annexed 1,785 hectares and 8,000 new residents, taking its population to 16,684, excluding concentration camp inmates. Loritz attended the celebrations; indeed, the Dachau commandant became something of a local dignitary, his name prominent on the list of invitees to local events.[61] The growing municipal clout of the SS was also felt by the 300 residents of a barracks settlement of unemployed workers located within sight of the camp's southern walls. The mounting impatience of Eicke and his successors to have this 'nest of Bolshevism' razed to the ground by the authorities as an eyesore and security risk, with the inhabitants brought into the camp if necessary, bore fruit in 1938 when they were rehoused in nearby Allach.[62]

## CAMP AND CITIZENRY

Throughout Germany, newly opened concentration camps were objects of public curiosity.[63] Dachau, unveiled in a blaze of publicity, particularly so. One of the many security concerns in its first months was the tendency of curious locals out for a Sunday walk to try to sneak a look into the camp. On the festive occasion of

---

[57] Steinbacher, *Dachau*, p. 127.

[58] Steinbacher, *Dachau*, p. 135. The camp helped to ensure that the Dachau area remained chronically short of business taxation: whereas the 1937 per capita business tax average in Bavaria stood at 36.25 RM, in Dachau it continued to languish at 9.95 RM. For detail see Steinbacher, *Dachau*, p. 98.

[59] BAB, R 28350, Chronik der gesamten SS-Lageranlage in Dachau, s. 7.

[60] Steinbacher, *Dachau*, pp. 117–21.     [61] Riedel, *Ordnungshüter*, p. 166.

[62] Riedel, *Ordnungshüter*, p. 168.

[63] Moore, 'German Popular Opinion', pp. 88f.

Hitler's birthday on 20 April 1933, Wäckerle commissioned an 'urgent warning' in the *Amper Bote* and *Münchner Neueste Nachrichten* warning that persons with business near the camp should not tarry about it, given the presence of his armed sentries.[64] In June a further advert was taken in both the *Dachauer Zeitung* and *Amper Bote* by the Supreme SA command. It warned that two locals spotted 'hanging around' the outer walls of the camp a few days previously had been arrested. They had apparently confessed to a curiosity to see how the inside of the camp looked and to 'satisfy this' had been detained in Dachau overnight. The notice concluded that in the future 'curious individuals' would be afforded a 'more prolonged opportunity to study the camp'.[65]

In September the *Amper Bote* reported on a party of 160 Dachau prisoners working under armed guard cutting peat from the moors near Gröbenried, around 6 kilometres to the north-west of the town. In their spare time, it commented, the prisoners were able to play sport and games and during the day could be seen 'cheerfully working'. Nevertheless, it reiterated, 'members of the public are requested not to loiter in the area'.[66] One prisoner memoir suggests that civilians were shocked by the grey, expressionless faces of the inmates, so contrasting to the demonized figures of Nazi propaganda. Contact between inmates and civilians was strictly forbidden and the sentries, rifles slung over their shoulders, were quieter and more restrained now they were in public gaze.[67] It is unclear how long the detail existed, but it appears to the be the first collaborative venture using inmate labour between the local private sector and the camp, and the only one from the (pre-war) era of the Dachau School.[68]

Yet local businesses had viewed the opening of the camp with entrepreneurial optimism. The *Dachauer Zeitung* envisaged 'a significant financial advantage' for the town, not least through the custom of its staff.[69] Adolf Wagner promised the town council that Dachau would also profit from the camp itself, which would buy locally. Town bakers were soon delivering 7,000 loaves of bread per week to the camp, the rent market was vibrant, and Dachau's many innkeepers enjoyed a sustained boost in demand. Yet the upbeat mood proved short-lived. As has been seen, under Eicke the SS developed its own workshops with a costless and terrorized labour force. Local businesses soon came to regard them as unfair competition, much as German private enterprise had always been wary of carceral labour.[70] By 1939, to pursue the bread index, the camp bakery was turning out 25,000 loaves of bread each week, while in-house camp butchers, carpenters, metalworkers, tailors, saddlers, and shoemakers ensured that local enterprises could expect little custom from the concentration camp.[71] There was one notable exception. Hans Wülfert, co-owner of a sausage-making factory in Dachau, had been a founder of the local branch of the NSDAP in 1930. Between 1937 and the camp's liberation,

---

[64] *Münchner Neueste Nachrichten*, 20 April 1933.          [65] *Dachauer Zeitung*, 2 June 1933.

[66] *Amper Bote*, 7 September 1933.          [67] Hornung, *Dachau*, pp. 175–6.

[68] Schalm, *Überleben*, pp. 69–72.          [69] In Steinbacher, *Dachau*, p. 94

[70] Kaienburg, *Wirtschaft*, p. 117; Wachsmann, *Prisons*, p. 98.

[71] Kaienburg, *Wirtschaft*, p. 128.

the factory sold almost half a million Reichsmark of meat products to the SS canteen. During the war, the Wülfert factory also earned millions from profitable contracts with the Wehrmacht and Waffen SS.[72]

The Dachau SS was not averse to opportunistic engagement with the local economy. Prisoner rations increased markedly in volume in the summer of 1938 when a serious outbreak of foot-and-mouth disease in surrounding farms necessitated the wholesale slaughter of cattle. Compound leader Max Koegel acted quickly to buy up the carcasses and recognizable chunks of meat—at other times considered a 'sensation' by ordinary prisoners—found their way into the cheerless daily broth.[73] One prisoner ascribes the occasional appearance of salted herring in the midday soup to the arrival of fresh consignments in Munich; the old stock was then cleared out and bought up by the SS.[74] These kinds of irregular arrangements guaranteed a level of petty corruption. The camp carpentry seems to have been a prime venue for black marketeering and general pilfering, while Höβ reports Eicke uncovering 'an immense racket' in the butchers which led to the dishonourable discharge of four SS guards.[75] The Dachau camp store was a site of crony capitalism known by the prisoners as 'Streicher's shop', after the venal Nuremberg *Gauleiter*. Curious goods such as ear muffs would surface for sale there from surplus inventories in Munich. In the final year of the Dachau School, merchandise extorted from emigrating Jews—from tinned meat to luxury scarves—appeared 'on special offer' in the store and prisoners were compelled to purchase useless or usually banned goods at astronomic prices.[76]

A final channel of engagement with the concentration camp was the local priest, Friedrich Pfanzfelt. An ambiguous figure, in the early months Pfanzfelt held services in the camp attended by inmates and SS alike. Initially the priest—who may have served in Wäckerle's Bavarian infantry regiment in the First World War—was welcomed into the camp to provide spiritual guidance to the errant prisoners. When, in May 1933, Pfanzfelt came into conflict with some local SS men over the production of a play about Horst Wessel, Wäckerle was moved to write to him 'deeply regretting' the incident given that the priest's 'nationalist orientation' was well known to the SS troops.[77] Under the fiercely anticlerical Eicke, however, the drive for autonomy led to periodic rows with Pfanzfelt and to a ban on him taking confession.[78] Under Loritz, after 1936, the SS took unambiguous exception to his presence and his arrival in the camp on Sundays and religious holidays met with abuse from the guards posted at the front gate. Eventually, in 1937, Pfanzfelt was denounced to the Gestapo by Baranowski—in a charge of distinctly Stalinist tenor—as 'a Jesuit conduit between Rome and Moscow'.[79] He wisely decided to forego his visits, which due to intimidation of prisoners by the SS had anyway

---

[72] Steinbacher, *Dachau*, pp. 65–7; Marcuse, *Legacies*, pp. 95–7.

[73] Hübsch, 'Insel', p. 109; Neurath, *Society*, p. 172.

[74] G. R. Kay, *Dachau* (London, 1942), p. 82.

[75] *Nazi Bastille Dachau*, pp. 40–5; Höβ, *Commandant*, pp. 67–8. See also Laurence, 'Out of the Night', p. 26.

[76] Karst, *Beasts*, pp. 70–1, 121–33.    [77] In Steinbacher, *Dachau*, p. 166

[78] Steinbacher, *Dachau*, p. 168.    [79] Steinbacher, *Dachau*, p. 171.

been finding few attendees. The guards themselves were vehemently encouraged to renounce Catholicism, a residue of traditional local power structures in rural Bavaria. The family crises this caused for sentries can only have reinforced their cognitive dependence on the SS and their work at Dachau. Yet the revolutionary anticlericalism of the SS was infelicitous public relations in such an observant locality, and it is to public responses to the perpetrators that the next section turns.

## SS GUARDS AND LOCALITY

'I know that there are people who shudder when they see the black uniform', wrote Himmler in 1936. 'We understand this and do not expect to be loved by everyone'.[80] Not 'loved', perhaps, but certainly valued and respected. As has been seen, Himmler imagined the SS to be a professional, military, and fundamentally 'decent' organization: the presentable face of Nazi paramilitarism. Sopade reports from the period suggest some success in this regard.[81] A preoccupation with public perception distinguished the SS from an SA which rejoiced in its coarse, masculinist, counter-culturalism. Both internally and externally, the SS sought to gentrify its punitive doctrines through a discursive emphasis on social 'respectability' and 'decency', bourgeois values which its purported *Freikorps* forebears would have found repellent.[82]

The SA, conversely, disported itself as a revolutionary armed mob, congenitally restless, thuggish, and arbitrary in its violence; 'the mood of the displaced, demobilised soldier' made permanent, as one historian puts it.[83] The winter of 1933/34 was the high water mark for the Brownshirts in the Third Reich. Marauding through towns throughout Germany, thumbs in buckles, disdainful and arrogant, SA men sung of a 'second revolution'. Any number of auxiliary police armbands could not dispel the impression that this was a force for lawless chaos. Brownshirts beat up suspected opponents, army personnel, and one another, and extorted protection money from businesses.[84] The spectre of brown Bolshevism resurfaced, fuelled by the widespread belief that Communists had infiltrated its ranks. By the beginning of 1934 some 4.5 million paramilitaries marched under the SA banner and the prospect of civil war was emerging once again.[85]

The public reaction to the ensuing purge of Röhm and the SA leadership was instructive in the extreme for the SS. Sopade reported a mixture of surprise, gratitude, relief, and not a little gloating.[86] The generally cheerful response refocused SS minds on the need to win respectability. The central role of the SS in the events helped to promote an image of responsible, public-spirited activism in clearing out

---

[80] Heinrich Himmler, *Die Schutzstaffel als anti-bolschewistische Kampforganisation* (Berlin, 1936), p. 29.
[81] Hein, *Elite*, p. 113.        [82] Longerich, *Himmler*, pp. 308–11.
[83] Reitlinger, *Alibi*, p. 4        [84] For detail see Longerich, *Geschichte der SA*, pp. 184–200.
[85] Longerich, *Geschichte der SA*, p. 184.
[86] For a detailed analysis of public reactions to the Röhm purge, drawing heavily on Bavarian data, see Ian Kershaw, *The Hitler Myth: Image and Reality in the Third Reich* (Oxford, 1987), pp. 84–95.

some of the moral dung from the brown stable. At Dachau, too, there are indications even before the purge of a drive by the SS to market itself as the better class
of Nazi paramilitarism. In February 1934, the *Dachauer Zeitung* reported on the
Dachau guard troops' *Fasching* ball, held in its favoured local, the Hörhammer.[87]
As well as the concentration camp guards, attendees included comrades from the
Upper Bavarian *Standarte* of the SS and 'the civilian population of Dachau'. The
paper found that it was above all the 'crisp black uniforms of the SS' which 'lit up
the scene'. Lippert, as commander of the sentry units, opened proceedings with a
heartfelt speech, welcoming the guests and expressing his hopes for an evening of
'joyful sociability'. The 'lovely hours raced by in dance and conviviality' and the
*Dachauer Zeitung* reporter, who was 'reminded very much of the garrison balls of
the past', looked forward to a repeat next year.

This was not the kind of event the beer-swilling Brownshirts put on. *Fasching*,
moreover, a kind of pre-Lent carnival in Southern Germany and Austria, was
closely associated with the Catholic Church. The gathering neo-paganism of the
SS meant that the Dachau guards would be holding no further *Fasching* balls.
The one staged in 1934 was a signifier of respectability and social participation,
a gesture towards the local community. So too were the periodic public performances of the guard troops' band led by Dachau SS officer Leander Hauck.[88] The
SS social centre on the site of the training complex held regular public concerts
and film showings from 1936.[89] And when, in 1937, the 5-kilometre stretch of
road between the train station in Dachau and the camp was awarded its own bus
line, Loritz insisted that it be available for public use. As he wrote to the Bavarian
authorities, it was unthinkable that 'school children and local workers' be forced
to walk or take taxis while SS men and their families enjoyed a bespoke bus service.[90] Two thirty-two seat public omnibuses were soon running along a route from
Etzenhausen via the camp to Dachau town hall.

Loritz had uncomfortable memories from his tenure as Esterwegen commandant, where the boorish public conduct of his SS guards had created bitterness
and hostility.[91] As Dachau commandant he introduced evening patrols in town to
check the leave permits of SS men found in pubs or roaming the streets after the SS
night curfew.[92] He declared that SS men found drunk in public would be incarcer-
ated in the camp, while any landlords who complained about the patrols were to
be reported to him. Loritz's campaign against public disorder culminated in 1937
with a ban on attendance of that year's Oktoberfest for SS men in uniform. The
concern for public opinion extended also to the staple activity of the Dachau SS,
the brutal terrorization of prisoners. In June 1938, as the sentry units continued
to bring in savagely beaten transports from Vienna, Max Simon issued a torrent
of orders regulating unloading protocol; this was to be done out of public gaze
as far as possible, weapons were not to be discharged in public, and the prisoners

---

[87] *Dachauer Zeitung*, 8 February 1934.
[88] *Dachauer Zeitung*, 9 December 1934; BDC, SSO Hauck, passim.
[89] Steinbacher, *Dachau*, p. 178.          [90] Steinbacher, *Dachau*, pp. 129–30.
[91] Riedel, *Ordnungshüter*, pp. 126–36.          [92] DaA 8644, Standortbefehl, 15 July 1937.

themselves were not to be tortured en route. Simon noted that he had received complaints from civilians about 'boxed ears' administered to the prisoners by SS men, and of fatuous boasting in town about the tough justice being meted out to the arriving outcasts from the expanded German Reich. Overall, he lamented, 'if the men under my command are unable to act discreetly, I will be forced to lock up otherwise dutiful SS men for disobeying my orders'.[93]

While all this is clearly evidence of constraining forces on the official culture of the Dachau School, individual SS personnel very often let it down. Disciplinary measures for disturbances of the civic peace pepper their personnel files and it will suffice here to recount only a few of the more dramatic examples, those most likely to have shaped local impressions of the SS beneath obsequious reportage in the local press. Violence pervaded every sphere of life for these men and became a reflex response to any kind of social challenge. In May 1934 two guards, Anton Putz and Johann Bach, were drinking with a large group of comrades in a pub in Esting near Dachau.[94] Matters soon got out of hand and culminated in the party beating up three local farmers who had remonstrated with them for rowdy behaviour. Local gendarmes who hastened to the scene were also abused and threatened, very much in the contemporary SA spirit, that Esting was overdue for a political 'cleansing'. The SS patrons were ejected from the premises only by the arrival of a police special response unit, and even then after spirited resistance. The response of the camp leadership to the ensuing investigation was one of self-righteous defiance. In a lengthy memorandum, Lippert lambasted Esting as a 'former Bavarian People's Party stronghold' and hotbed of reactionary opinion. It was a haven, he declared, for 'grumblers' and 'phoney National Socialists' (*Mussnationalsozialisten*). Lippert documented his outrage that the farmers in question had seen fit to slight his guards, fighters for the 'new Germany', as 'troublemakers'. Was an SS man, he concluded, supposed to tolerate his 'honourable black uniform' being spat on by 'concealed enemies of the national awakening'?[95]

Such incidents continued long after the 'Night of the Long Knives'. An episode at Passau train station in December 1934 illustrates how the native arrogance of Dachau personnel could quickly turn into public violence and PR disaster. *Scharführer* Johann F., a veteran of the early Dachau SS, had been purchasing a ticket in civilian attire.[96] Described by the Bavarian Political Police as a 'somewhat clumsy person', a euphemism for blind drunk, the *Scharführer* took an eternity to collect his ticket and change from the counter. Noting the mounting impatience of the queue, a member of the railway police asked him to step aside to allow the next traveller to the counter. Incensed, Johann F. threw a punch at the policeman, fell over, and was dragged towards the station exit. Further attempts at resistance saw the policeman beat him round the head with his truncheon. As the *Scharführer* fell to the ground again, his Walther automatic service pistol fell out of his pocket.

[93] DaA, A2894, Simon to Führer der I, II, III Totenkopfverbände Dachau, 3 July 1938.
[94] DaA, DA3206, Staatsanwaltschaft Munich to Oberlandesgericht Munich, 6 June 1934, n.p.
[95] DaA, DA3206, Memorandum Kommandantur des KLD, 29 June 1934, n.p.
[96] BAB, BDC SSO Deubel, Der Oberstaatsanwalt beim Landgericht Passau, 3 January 1935.

By all accounts he was about to use it against the policeman when he was over-powered. When F. got back to Dachau he informed Deubel about the fracas, and the two returned to the station a few days later. According to witnesses, Deubel announced himself as the commandant of Dachau and claimed to have authoriza-tion from the Gestapo to investigate the incident. Pointing to the railway police-man in question, Deubel remarked that 'he's coming with us to Dachau and he'll be paid back with a horse-whip, not a truncheon'. Making an undignified scene worse, the report continues, was the presence of a delegation of officials from the Austrian railways. One of the Austrians evidently made a cryptic, sarcastic allusion to the Wöllersdorf internment camp in Austria, which at this stage housed recalci-trant Austrian Nazis. This Deubel also took exception to, and he threatened to take the entire party to Dachau for a beating. His remarks apparently found their way to the Austrian press, and the commandant was severely reprimanded by Himmler for his thoughtless and negligent conduct.[97]

More detrimental still to the reputation of Dachau and its staff was an unfor-tunate public altercation near the Munich Hauptbahnhof on the evening of 11 July 1935. After an afternoon drinking in the Spatenbreuerei beer hall, two carloads of senior Dachau SS personnel were driving back through Munich to the camp.[98] One was driven by Deubel and contained Schelkshorn, head of the Dachau Political Department, and *Obersturmführer* Becker, then deputy com-mander in the guard troops. The other was driven by *Untersturmführer* Hans Dorn with three SS officers as passengers, among them camp adjutant Gerlach. Several of the party were in SS uniform. Due to road repairs, part of the Marstraße was closed and off access. The second car, finding its route blocked by the road works, lurched into reverse, straight into the path of an incoming tram. Remarkably, no one was injured. The irate tram driver made his way to the car and demanded to see Dorn's driving licence, for which impertinence he was promptly assaulted by Gerlach. By now, a group of some 400–500 Munich citizens had gathered around the scene. The occupants of the car proceeded to belabour the road workers and tram officials with such epithets as 'worker swine', 'bloody communist scum', and 'we'll soon sort you out', intermingled with threats to the crowd. Dorn began to throw punches at passers-by. Gerlach attempted to reverse out of the tram lane, almost running over several members of the public. One of the road workers tried to block his exit and Dorn now assaulted him with a 2-metre iron bar plucked from a barrier, leaving a fist-sized lesion in his head and hospitalizing him. Not yet through, Dorn next brandished his ceremonial SS dagger (*Ehrendolch*) in rage at the workman's colleagues, who fled the scene. A bank clerk who tried to intervene was beaten up: to considerable embarrassment as it later emerged that he had taken part in the 1923 Munich *Putsch*. Other members of the public were also assaulted, including two policeman and an SA man. Others still were threatened with being put in the car and taken off to Dachau. The police report concluded that all the

---

[97] BAB, BDC SSO Deubel, RFSS Förmlicher Verweis, n.d.
[98] BAB, BDC SSO Dorn, Report Dr Joel Berlin, 20 March 1936.

SS perpetrators were drunk, and that the unsavoury scenes had been witnessed by a number of foreigners. Questioned by the Bavarian Political Police, the SS men unanimously claimed to have been acting in self-defence.[99] Criminal proceedings were eventually launched against Gerlach, but quashed under a general amnesty in April 1938.

A final example of the violent and alienating culture of the SS occurred closer to the camp in 1938. *Untersturmführer* Josef Elkemann-Reusch, a 53-year-old front veteran and father of eight, had visited the Three Lions pub in Dachau after work, in full uniform.[100] After drinking four beers he joined a small group of men at a table, and the party got through a further five bottles of wine. Eventually, at four in the morning, Elkemann-Reusch paid his share of the bill and left. The details of the fracas which ensued outside the pub are difficult to reconstruct, for Elkemann-Reusch's file contains only generous reports by other SS officers based on his own testimony. He was evidently drawn into an 'exchange of words' with two 'national comrades' in front of the pub. Remarks seem to have been exchanged about his uniform, and the 'golden badge' documenting his long-term membership of the NSDAP pinned onto it. In the perpetrator's account the two civilians leapt at him unprovoked, knocked him to the ground, and tried to throttle him. In self-defence he stabbed them several times with his SS dagger. Both 'national comrades' subsequently died of their wounds. Given that Elkemann-Reusch was expelled in disgrace from the SS for the incident, it can be assumed that the sequence of events was otherwise, and that in a drunken fog he had taken exception to remarks about his uniform and resolved to defend its honour with his dagger. The use of the SS dagger, as by Dorn in the traffic incident above, captured and dramatized the 'otherness' and proclaimed eliteness of the SS. Much like the sabre of the Imperial Army, it had little military value but signified the legitimate martial identity of the bearer. Soldiers in the Imperial army had been honour bound to use their sabre if attacked by a civilian, in a ritualized defence of the honour of both soldier and army. Public complaints about soldiers' latitudinous interpretation of attacks on their honour had been legion.[101] The Elkemann-Reusch murders, unsurprisingly, similarly etched themselves into the local civilian consciousness: a semi-fictional novel by Rosel Kirchhoff, *At the Camp Gate*, published in 1972, recounts them at length.[102] In the novel, Dachau locals increasingly choose to drink at home after what was clearly a frenzied assault: one of the victims is said to have been stabbed thirteen times with the dagger, whose symbolism as a weapon is not missed.

These examples could be multiplied and illustrate some of the self-inflicted difficulties faced by the Dachau SS in its efforts to secure public acclaim as a respectable formation in its own right. From the mid-1930s it sought ever more to do so instead by riding on the coat tails of popular reverence for the German army.

---

[99] BAB, BDC SSO Dorn, Report Dr Joel Berlin, 20 March 1936.

[100] BAB, BDC SSO Elkemann-Reusch, Schwurgerichtverhandlung, 18 July 1938.

[101] Frevert, *Nation in Barracks*, p. 181.

[102] Rosel Kirchhoff, *Am Lagertor: Gesellschaftskritischer Roman aus dem zwanzigsten Jahrhundert in dreiunddreißig Bildern* (Munich, 1972), pp. 73–4.

It is also worth recalling in this context a German tradition of the army being seen as immune from civilian criticism, holding an almost 'extra-constitutional' status.[103] The stylization of the concentration camp SS as a military phenomenon, then, also promised the benefit of deflecting scrutiny of conditions in the camps. The most recent research on concentration camps in the media has found that public curiosity was increasingly directed towards their staff rather than inmates: as hard-working servants of the racial community but also a military phenomenon in their own right.[104] Local newspapers were given regular tours of the new training camp at Dachau and spent hours inspecting barracks and watching parades, which, gushed one, 'fill a soldier's heart with joy'.[105] The camp sentries, rebranded as the Death's Head units, enhanced their visibility and military credentials by staging war games, an assertion of military sovereignty over local territory. While two companies stayed behind to guard the prisoner compound, the remaining 'soldiers' marched through the Bavarian countryside exchanging blank rounds and practising with their real artillery; including, it seems, being obliged to pay compensation to local farmers for damage to fields.[106] One week-long set of manoeuvres in October 1936 allowed the entire locality to become acquainted with the Death's Head formation. The 315-kilometre round trip took them from Dachau through Landsberg, Pfaffenhausen, Memmingen, Wurzburg, Donauwörth, and Augsburg.[107]

As part of the PR campaign, local papers were invited along. The reportage is predictably appreciative of the SS men's soldierly demeanour and tactical insight, with the concluding observations of the *Günzburger National Zeitung* obsequious even by the exacting standard of the 'co-ordinated' German press:

> And what fairy tales are told overseas about the guards in concentration camps! So much talk of barbarity and cruelty. These lies would be refuted were the reader of every émigré paper able to see the fresh faces of these young men. No, this is no brutal *Landknechtshorde* [band of freebooters, CD], but a disciplined team recruited from the finest of German youth.[108]

The paper also informed its readers that the duties of the SS Death's Head personnel were 'among other things, the guarding of the concentration camps'. These 'other things' are not elaborated upon and this is because, the occasional war game notwithstanding, they did not exist. As has been seen, in 1936 guarding concentration camps is what Death's Head troops did: they had no ancillary function for quelling civilian unrest as did their peers in the Verfügungstruppe. The 'among other things', then, has no function in the text save to dilute what was evidently not perceived as a wholly prestigious task, and to lend an air of mystery and submerged import to the SS guard formations.

---

103 Frevert, *Nation in Barracks*, p. 149.
104 Moore, 'German Popular Opinion', pp. 192–202.
105 *Münchner Neueste Nachrichten*, 9 May 1936.
106 BAB, NS4, Da/30, SS-TK Oberbayern Vorbefehle, s. 11.
107 BA NS4 Da/30 SS-TK Oberbayern, Vorbefehle, s. 4
108 BAB, NS4, Da/30, *Günzburger National Zeitung* report, ss. 36–8.

## STANDING BY

'Bystanders', contends the social psychologist Erwin Staub, 'exert powerful influence. They can define the meaning of events and move others towards empathy or indifference. They can promote values and norms of caring, or by their passivity or participation in the system they can affirm the perpetrators'.[109] The remainder of this chapter will not concern itself with the moral implications of inaction: of all the localities in Germany, those around a concentration camp can scarcely be singled out for failings of political resistance (*Widerstand*). Staub's point about affirmation, however, seems salient. As has been seen, the camp's murderous work did not inhibit the municipal embrace of local politicians and administrators. Local citizens, too, had a good idea of Dachau's true character beneath the sanitized media representations. Indeed, the popular association between the camp and violent retribution became so common that some parents threatened their children with Dachau, not the bogeyman, when they misbehaved.[110] Yet were locals, as one historian has claimed, 'proud of having a camp in town'?[111]

The source base for such issues is always challenging, but particularly so for Dachau. Regime mood reports for Dachau, relatively abundant for elsewhere in Bavaria, seem to have been destroyed before the end of the war.[112] One distinguished study of popular opinion suggests that Dachau's middle classes regarded the camp as 'not an unreasonable way of dealing with "outsiders", "trouble-makers" and "revolutionaries"'.[113] What was 'reasonable' against such groups was not, however, seen thus when impeccably middle-class Catholic functionaries of the BVP were taken into protective custody.[114] Working-class opinion, conversely, was more exercised by violence against the organizations of the Left as well as better informed through releases, common in the early years of the camp. One released Dachau inmate, the joiner Martin Grünwiedl, bravely compiled and printed a powerful thirty-page pamphlet 'Dachau Prisoners Speak Out' based on inmate testimonies. This was distributed to some 650 Communist sympathizers in the Munich area, who were urged to pass it on 'as widely as possible'.[115]

Kirchhoff's novel narrates an initial fascination, even titillation, among Dachau locals at the influx of young men in uniforms with disposable income, giving way to a resigned wariness as SS anticlericalism and incidence of violent altercations mounted.[116] This would accord with the pattern of business opinion set out previously. It is also worth noting here that the camp's notoriety was soon identified as a cause of dwindling tourism, and in 1936 Dachau's new tourist office even lobbied to have the camp renamed. It met without success, and visitor numbers continued to decline.[117]

---

[109] Erwin Staub, *The Roots of Evil: The Origins of Genocide and Other Group Violence* (Cambridge, 1997), p. 87.
[110] Wachsmann, 'KL: A History of the Nazi Concentration Camps', ch. 1.
[111] Gellately, *Backing Hitler*, p. 52.          [112] Steinbacher, *Dachau*, p. 182.
[113] Kershaw, *Popular Opinion*, p. 73.          [114] Moore, 'Popular Opinion', pp. 164–5.
[115] DaA, 550, Martin Grünwiedl, 'Dachau Gefangene erzählen' (1934).
[116] Kirchhoff, *Lagertor*, pp. 26–7, 47–73.          [117] Steinbacher, *Dachau*, pp. 151–2.

SS personnel also had an alienating effect in the local housing market, pushing rents beyond the reach of ordinary Dachauers. In 1934 mayor Friedrichs wrote to Wagner warning of a 'catastrophe in the Dachau flat market' occasioned by incoming SS men with disposable incomes, particularly SS fugitives from Austria. Four years later his successor, Hans Cramer, penned a twenty-page memorandum entitled 'Dachau's poverty', blaming the SS presence in the town for the countless local families with children now living in single rooms or in tiny cellars and ad hoc barracks.[118] There are some indications of outspoken resentment towards the SS. Even the landlord of its favoured tavern, the Hörhammer, ran into trouble in 1937 for uttering 'disparaging remarks about the SS'. Loritz forbade his men from patronizing the Hörhammer, but Josef Schmid was forgiven after publishing an apology to his very profitable SS customers in the *Dachauer Volksblatt*.[119] In April 1938 Loritz prohibited SS men from purchasing milk from one Maria Trinkl of nearby Etzenhausen as she had 'repeatedly and in the vilest manner offended several SS men who were doing their duty'. Loritz claimed to have initiated steps to have Frau Trinkl placed in protective custody.[120]

The general issue of the conduct of locals towards camp personnel preoccupies a number of prisoners in their memoirs. The well-informed, if understandably optimistic, compilers of *Nazi Bastille Dachau* averred that the SS 'who in their uniforms wanted to be seen as heroes, evoked in the main only loathing and disgust'.[121] Hans Schwarz, a Dachau inmate from 1938 to 1944, concurs:

> if an SS man tried to strike up a conversation in a pub, he could be sure that the civilian would soon stand up, pay and leave. And woe betide the girl who danced or stepped out with an SS man! She could be certain that she would be shunned by all.[122]

Walter Feuerbach likewise defends the honour of the locals. Without indicating his sources, he asserts that 'when an SS man entered a pub, everyone else left; if the SS marched through the town, girls would shut their windows, and mothers would call their children inside'.[123] Other prisoners have a more negative take on the issue, particularly with regard to local girls. According to Walter Bunzengeiger:

> The black uniform, adorned with silver braiding and contrasting red, black and white armband, flattered their vanity. There were always plenty of girls prepared to drape themselves around their necks.[124]

Another memoirist writes disconsolately of women waiting eagerly for SS men in town and nearby voluntary labour camps.[125] Peter Wallner recalls the guards on outside work details whistling at blushing girls as they passed on the road, a distraction which offered welcome respite to the toiling prisoners.[126]

---

[118] Steinbacher, *Dachau*, p. 100.

[119] DaA, A4151, Standortbefehl 16/37 Dachau, 24 September 1937; Riedel, *Ordnungshüter*, p. 165.

[120] In Steinbacher, *Dachau*, p. 179.      [121] *Nazi Bastille Dachau*, p. 77.

[122] Schwarz, 'Wir haben', p. 264.

[123] Walter Feuerbach, *55 Monate Dachau* (Bremen, 1993), p. 62.

[124] DaA, Bericht Walter Buzengeiger, *Tausende Tage Dachau # 309*, p. 18.

[125] Kay, *Dachau*, p. 122.      [126] Wallner, *By Order of the Gestapo*, p. 115.

One statistical measure of the incidence of sexual relationships would be marriages registered in church records. The historian Sybille Steinbacher has identified just ten between 1938 and 1944.[127] However, this excludes SS marriages conducted beyond the church in its own pagan ceremonies, not to mention extra-marital liaisons. The historian Timothy Ryback, interviewing Dachauers of the time in the 1990s, uncovered a rich seam of positive female memories. One elderly resident was candid enough to present the years of Nazism as the most exciting of her life. Along with many local women of a certain age, she became misty eyed when Ryback mentioned the Café Bestler, a favoured hangout for officers to drink, dance, and flirt with girls: 'tall handsome SS men in those crisp uniforms with their shiny buttons'. Local youths waged an unequal competition with the SS for the chance to waltz and fox trot with girls to the Bestler's resident three-piece band. 'We were the luckiest girls in the Third Reich', beamed another former patron.[128] Courtships consummated at night on the banks of the Amper left so many local women with children but no fathers after the war that they acquired the dismissive epithet 'SS widows'. It is not, of course, surprising that young male guards, their physiques honed by barracks life and drill, offered a certain excitement to local girls. The Death's Head insignia, now associated with grotesque criminality, carried a daredevil, avant garde semiotic in the 1930s. And Dachau guards keenly sought female affirmation of their allure, even at work: one former prisoner told Ryback that sentries would become especially tough and lordly towards prisoners on external work details when girls were nearby.[129] The inmate Herbert Seligman recounts a close comrade being punished with twenty-five lashes for allegedly 'ogling' a local girl who had walked near their road construction detail.[130]

Irmgard Litten, the mother of the renowned Weimar-era Leftist lawyer Hans Litten, was granted permission by Himmler in 1937 to visit her son in Dachau. Her taxi driver on the way to the camp was not short of opinions on its personnel:

> on the first pretext the [chauffeur] had burst into a panegyric. What a fine man Commandant Loritz was, and what splendid fellows the SS men were! Some of them were friends of his. And what a pleasant life the prisoners led! Oh, one could be sure of that![131]

Alfred Laurence also provides vivid testimony on local attitudes towards the camp. He remembered school children pointing and laughing at his heavy roller work detail as it ground its way to and from the camp. Adults, conversely, tended to look away, embarrassed to witness inmates singing as they were cursed at and kicked by SS guards.[132]

---

[127] Steinbacher, *Dachau*, p. 179.
[128] Timothy W. Ryback, *The Last Survivor: In Search of Martin Zaidenstadt* (New York, 1999), pp. 51–3.
[129] Ryback, *The Last Survivor*, p. 92.
[130] WL, Herbert Seligman, 'Drei Jahre hinter Stacheldraht', s. 9.
[131] Irmgard Litten, *A Mother Fights Hitler* (London, 1941), p. 258.
[132] Laurence, 'Dachau Overcome', p. 114. More broadly on looking and looking away, see Fings, 'Public Face'.

The key issue, of course, is not so much that the communities around Dachau and other concentration camps were any more morally disengaged or enthusiastic than those elsewhere, as that their individual and collective responses *mattered* more. They mattered more to the inmates, to whom a sympathetic glance—or malicious joke—could mean a very great deal. They also mattered more to the SS perpetrators. Local communities were the 'front line' of public opinion, a social and economic resource, an audience and source of affirmation.[133] The Allied post-liberation pedagogy was heavy handed and counterproductive but justified in at least one more subtle, functional sense. For even before the mass death of the wartime period, in the formative era of the camp, the largely accommodating public and institutional responses to the SS had helped to validate its definition of concentration camp service and, in turn, of the concentration camp prisoner.

---

[133] On the 'front line' aspect see Horwitz, *Shadow*, pp. 175–6.

# Epilogue

## *WACHTRUPPE* AT WAR

On 27 May 1940 a company of the British Royal Norfolk Regiment found itself encircled on a farm on the outskirts of the French village of Le Paradis. They were out of ammunition and cut off from other British forces by the German advance.[1] After agonized discussion, facing the inevitable, they decided to surrender. A Platoon Sergeant-Major led a small group of men outside with a white towel affixed to his rifle. He had barely advanced ten paces when they were scythed down by machine-gun fire. Five minutes later a second surrender party ventured forth into the meadow, greeted this time by cheering German troops waving their rifles in triumph. The one hundred surviving members of the company, bloodied and exhausted by battle, were ordered to kneel down with their hands on their heads. A gamesome chicanery began. Cigarettes were seized from the captives and scattered across the grass. An Englishman was asked if he wanted one: when he reached down to pick it up a rifle butt crashed into his face. Private Albert Pooley, too, had four teeth smashed out with a rifle for glancing sideways at a guard. An animated discussion then began among the Germans which he could not follow. After what seemed like hours in the meadow, the British prisoners were ordered to line up in threes. As they marched down a dusty road, further soldiers assailed them with rifle butts. The captives were led into another field where two heavy machine-guns had been set up. As the final men of the column reached the field the command '*Feuer!*' rang out and the machine-guns began to rake across the prisoners from either side. Pooley, hit twice in the leg, then heard a metallic rattle as the German troops fixed bayonets. The butchery lasted for more than an hour.

This massacre, the first major war crime of the Western theatre, was perpetrated by the Death's Head Division. It only came to light due to the miraculous survival of two English soldiers who later had the greatest difficulty getting their accounts believed by the British command.[2] It was not the first crime committed by Eicke's personnel during the war. In September 1939 battalions of guards from Dachau,

---

[1] The following from Cyril Jolly, *The Vengeance of Private Pooley* (Norfolk, 1977 [1956]), pp. 35–48; see also Hugh Sebag-Montefiore, *Dunkirk: Fight to the Last Man* (London, 2007), pp. 279–302.

[2] Jolly, *Vengeance*, pp. 131–8.

Sachsenhausen, and Buchenwald had taken part in the invasion of Poland. The Dachau contingent tailed the Tenth Army and operated behind the lines south of Warsaw on 'pacification' duty, which included the torture and murder of captured soldiers, Polish intelligentsia, and Jews.[3] Eicke directed their activities from Hitler's headquarters train 'Amerika'. Whilst it was found that the distinctive uniforms of Death's Head officers made them choice targets for Polish snipers, the fact that the Dachau units were not in the spearhead of the invasion spared them serious losses.[4] The battalions were withdrawn in early October to be reinforced, reorganized, and equipped in Dachau as a single formation: the camp was emptied of inmates for four months for this purpose. The resultant Death's Head Division was a motorized infantry division based on a core of 6,500 former concentration camp guards: all but one of its divisional staff had served either in the guard units or at the IKL. Dachau's farmers and merchants enjoyed a surge of business providing food and general supplies to the Division, and the Bavarian countryside once more hosted elaborate war games by Death's Head units.[5]

After re-equipping and training over the winter of 1939 and 1940, the newly formed Division transferred west ready for the French campaign. When this finally got underway in May 1940, the shortcomings of concentration camp militarism became starkly clear. The Wehrmacht had earmarked Eicke's Division only for a reserve role in the invasion, assigned to the Second Army. This represented another sizeable snub to the Death's Head troops given that only seven of the ninety-three divisions in the invasion force were equally motorized, and that the other formations fielded by the SS were included in the first wave.[6] The stain of the camps clung to the Death's Head troops and, in a familiar dynamic, a feeling of collective slightedness contributed to the Division's obsession with proving itself in the field. Brought into play unexpectedly quickly by the lightening German advance, Eicke's hazy grasp of tactics led to reckless frontal assaults on British positions and embitterment at casualties to which Death's Head personnel were not attuned. In a report requested by the Second Army on Le Paradis, Eicke marshalled the kind of rationalizations routinely used to justify atrocities in his concentration camps, blaming the perfidy of the vicious and cunning captives. Eicke raged that he had lost 710 soldiers killed, wounded, or missing that day. He claimed that the British soldiers had been using illegal dum-dum bullets against his men and had brandished a swastika flag to trick SS men into the farmstead before ambushing them, shooting them in the back. Working himself into a self-righteous lather of lies, Eicke concluded:

> It was in our interest to take our revenge for the treacherous and villainous tactics adopted by the English by shooting the remainder of those who took part in the cowardly ambush following a court martial. Reports which give a different account of what happened are malicious and false.[7]

---

[3] Sydnor, *Soldiers*, p. 41. Sydnor's account of the Death's Head Division is much the most scholarly and reliable and will be drawn on heavily in the following discussion.

[4] Sydnor, *Soldiers*, p. 80 fn. 27.    [5] Sydnor, *Soldiers*, p. 45.

[6] Sydnor, *Soldiers*, p. 86.    [7] Quoted in Montefiore, *Dunkirk*, p. 302.

Le Paradis was almost certainly only one of several such crimes in this sector of the Front. There are, in particular, indications of the indiscriminate execution of French colonial troops from North Africa, even as their white French officers and NCOs were taken prisoner.[8] Nevertheless, the Le Paradis murders were quickly forgotten by the army in the euphoria of the French capitulation. Participation in the swift defeat of France, so contrasting to the travails of 1914–1918, prompted much triumphalism in the SS 'war youth' contingent and lavish collective and biographical myths were spun around the Death's Head contribution.[9]

The Division remained in France as an occupation force for almost a year and its conduct with the civilian population—regarded generally as racially sound by SS ideology—was indeed, for once, 'decent'. Stationed near Bordeaux its main duties were getting services up and running again and helping with the harvest. They were assigned a detachment of POWs for this purpose and there is no indication of any mistreatment. Concerned as ever with masculine deportment, Eicke did however upbraid his troops for becoming sloppy and comfortable and enjoined them to offer the 'fresh and tight' Hitler salute of 1929, rather than the more leisurely variant which had allegedly developed since. Some Death's Head soldiers had apparently even taken to not returning the salute when offered, thus risking 'the impression that they wanted nothing to do with the greatest of all Germans'. Eicke concluded by noting that 'the name of the Führer cannot be called often enough and loudly enough in the streets of France'.[10] The Division was dogged, too, by indiscipline and low-level criminal activity—including members trying to pass off 1,000 Mark notes from the hyperinflation era as legal tender in French cafes—but the overall deportment of the SS towards civilians marks a strong contrast with that a year later in Russia.[11]

It was in Operation Barbarossa that the Death's Head personnel should have come into their own. A merciless war of annihilation, boundaries between combatants and citizens erased: this truly elided the inner and outer fronts of concentration camp discourse. But the German army, unimpressed with Eicke's performance in France, once again excluded him from the first attacking wave. It is difficult to gauge the exact level of criminality in the Division's conduct in Russia. Stung by the reaction to Le Paradis, Eicke explicitly forbade any mention of the treatment of supposed irregulars or partisans in divisional reports. The evidence indicates that captured Soviet personnel were shot on the spot from the earliest days of the campaign.[12] The desperate resistance of the Red Army and ongoing lack of tactical finesse among Eicke's commanders saw the Division lose 10 per cent of its manpower in two weeks, with the losses particularly acute among the pre-war concentration camp contingent. The original Death's Head Division, clustered around

---

[8] Sydnor, *Soldiers*, p. 117; Raphael Scheck, *Hitler's African Victims: The German Army Massacres of Black French Soldiers in 1940* (Cambridge, 2006), pp. 40, 61 fn. 110.

[9] Orth, *Konzentrationslager SS*, pp. 158–60.

[10] In Sheck, *Hitler's African Victims*, pp. 123–4.      [11] Sydnor, *Soldiers*, pp. 123–7.

[12] Sydnor, *Soldiers*, p. 160.

**Figure E.1** Max Simon, Heinrich Himmler, and Theodor Eicke in Russia with the Death's Head Division, December 1941. Bundesarchiv, image 101III-Cantzler-053-14A.

these personnel, was by now closing in on the area south of Leningrad where it was to make a protracted last stand (Figure E.1).

The shockwaves across the Eastern Front from the Red Army's counteroffensive outside Moscow exposed the right wing of Army Group North and led to the encirclement of the Division in what was known as the Demjansk pocket. It remained trapped in dire conditions between January and April 1942, partially supplied from the air by the Luftwaffe. Eicke's men undeniably demonstrated a formidable defensive tenacity but at the cost of being bled almost white. A report sent by a divisional doctor to Simon likened the physical condition of some of the survivors to concentration camp prisoners: as the historian Sydnor observes, 'a most revealing comment in several respects'.[13] After the first year of Operation Barbarossa the Wehrmacht's losses stood at 40 per cent: by the time the Death's Head Division was evacuated in October 1942 only 10 per cent of its personnel remained fit for service.[14]

A couple of brief biographies will lend texture to these arid statistics and illustrate how service as a Dachau guard, was often an intermediate stage in a path from adolescence to an early unmarked grave. Hermann Reschreiter was born in Mattsee in 1920. He joined the Hitler Youth in April 1937, renounced Catholicism in November of the same year, and joined the Dachau troops in

---

[13] Sydnor, *Soldiers*, p. 230.      [14] Orth, *Konzentrationslager SS*, p. 163.

1938 just after his eighteenth birthday. In October 1939 he was assigned to the newly-formed Division and saw action in the conquest of France, before being killed in the early days of Operation Barbarossa in July 1941.[15] Johann Nusser was also born in 1920. He was a member of the Hitler Youth in St Ingbert from May 1933 to April 1938, when he joined the Dachau guards and in turn the Death's Head Division where, like many of his comrades, he perished in the Demjansk pocket.[16] Johann Riedel, born in 1916, had been a member of the Hitler Youth even before the 'seizure of power'. He signed up to serve as a Dachau guard in 1937 and followed the Death's Head Division to the front where he was killed in August 1941, even as his fiancée and the RuSHA squabbled over her hereditary health and suitability to be an SS bride.[17] Such examples could be multiplied many times, and are intended merely to illustrate some of the nuances and gradations of SS criminality.

It was in this spirit that the admirable Ludwig Schecher looked back on the fate of the pre-war Dachau sentries, the majority of whom, he reflected, were killed, captured, frozen to death, or starved in the bleak expanses of the Soviet Union. When they volunteered for the SS, he reflected

> they were barely out of short trousers and too young to see how they were being mis-used . . . for many, perhaps, their final hours were not made easier by the memory of their dubious acts of heroism. But they died at last as soldiers.[18]

Schecher, who survived in Dachau for ten terrible years, was entitled to offer abso-lution to many of the young 'soldiers' of the Dachau Death's Head personnel. Yet the close involvement of former Dachau sentry personnel in gruesome criminality is also striking. Three of the four commanders of the Death's Head Division had been leading figures in the Dachau School: Simon, Becker, and Eicke himself. Simon was condemned to death as a war criminal by the British but the sentence was commuted to life imprisonment and he was released in 1954. The Soviets also documented war crimes but the case was never formally pursued. Becker's conduct in Russia has been described as 'bad enough to embarrass even the SS'.[19] A Soviet court sentenced him to twenty-five years' penal labour for crimes stretching from rape, murder of civilians, burning villages, to the execution of captured soldiers. In 1952 he was found guilty of sabotage as leader of a brigade of mutinous German POWs and shot.[20]

Beyond this, hundreds of personnel were exchanged between the Death's Head Division in Russia and *Einsatzgruppe* A in the Baltic states.[21] Transfers of wounded personnel between the Death's Head Division and the concentration camps for convalescence were frequent. Participation in the many other wartime crimes of the SS can also be found in personnel files. Alfred E., for example, whose marriage

[15]  BAB, BDC RS E5393, Hermann Reschreiter, Summary August 1941.
[16]  BAB, BDC RS E355, Johann Nusser, Report June 1942.
[17]  BAB, BDC RS E5441, Letter RuSHA August 1941.
[18]  Schecher, 'Rückblick', p. 145.        [19]  Sydnor, *Soldiers*, p. 317.
[20]  Merkl, *General Simon*, p. 96, fn. 4; Sydnor, *Soldiers*, p. 311.
[21]  Sydnor, *Soldiers*, p. 323.

travails as a Dachau guard were addressed in the fifth chapter, rose during the war to become an NCO in the Death's Head 3rd Panzer Grenadier battalion. There, one of his superiors was Jürgen Stroop. Stationed near Warsaw, in May 1943 his battalion was assigned to 'night security detail' in the city's Jewish ghetto, at that time in the final stages of 'liquidation' under Stroop's supervision after a spirited but hopeless uprising by its remaining population. E.'s men combed the ghetto in a state of drunkenness they defended as 'essential in view of the nerve-wracking conditions and the constant stench of corpses'.[22] The depiction of the aftermath of an engagement in which a handful of SS men were killed against some 15,000 subjugated and poorly armed Jewish 'partisans', as dangerous and 'nerve wracking' strikes a familiar refrain. So too does the fact that the unit was under a cloud for alcohol abuse and the attendant damage to the professional 'reputation' of the SS. *Oberscharführer* E. himself was punished with two weeks' solitary confinement for setting a demoralizing example to his men as an SS officer, collapsing after overdoing it on schnapps.

Back in the concentration camps, sentry duty was at first taken over by General SS reservists over the age of forty-five. Höß recalled that Eicke had given a war-like address to their officers on the very first day of hostilities. They were to act with 'inflexible harshness' as the Führer's domestic shield against any repetition of the strikes and revolutionary agitation which had undermined the previous war effort.[23] This theme was also explored by *Das Schwarze Korps*, which in December 1939 characterized the concentration camps as 'island-like sites of battle on the domestic front, theatres of war in each of which a handful of men protect Germany from its internal enemies'.[24] Practical measures were devised to ensure that camp guards felt like auxiliaries to the SS combat units: private letters by camp sentries were officially categorized as 'field post'.[25] Höß found the older SS men called up for sentry service were weak as guards, lacking the learned techniques of pre-war sentries and 'physically unsuited to the arduous requirements of the service'.[26] One such reservist in Dachau apparently even confessed to a party of prisoners that he hated the job and had no wish to shoot at 'helpless and desperate people'.[27] Not all reservists felt this way. Röder recalls that Dachau prisoners had welcomed the sudden appearance of 'potbellied, stolid family fathers' in the watchtowers and at worksites. But they discerned no improvement in guard culture; on the contrary, as Great War veterans, many 'could accomplish with two shots what took the youngsters four or five'.[28] SS reservists were followed in time by so-called 'ethnic German' volunteers and the injured or elderly Wehrmacht personnel who eventually accounted for over half the guard personnel in the camp system.[29] Yet, Röder

---

[22] BAB, BDC RS B223, Vernehmungsniederschrift, Warsaw, 10 August 1943.
[23] Höß, *Commandant*, p. 83.
[24] Quoted in Fings, 'The Public Face of the Camps', p. 113.
[25] Wachsmann, 'KL: A History of the Nazi Concentration Camps', ch. 4.
[26] Höß, *Commandant*, p. 242.
[27] Cited in Wachsmann, 'KL: A History of the Nazi Concentration Camps', ch. 4.
[28] Röder, *Nachtwache*, p. 85.
[29] For detail see Bertrand Perz, 'Wehrmacht und KZ-Bewachung', *Mittelweg*, Vol. 36, No. 4 (1995), pp. 69–82.

concluded, 'nothing changed in the slightest. They had scarcely donned their SS uniforms before all our hopes were crushed'. Although something of an exaggeration, this is a powerful reminder of the strength of the concentration camp situation.[30] And there were always SS veterans from the era of Eicke's Dachau School on hand to provide toxic leadership: many of them sheltered from the privations of war on the commandant's staff.

## THE COMMANDANT STAFF AT WAR

The commandant staff personnel in the wartime concentration camps changed far less than the sentry formations. Veterans of the Dachau School remained in key positions in Dachau and, indeed, throughout the camp network. An IKL memorandum from 1940, detailing the senior personnel in all concentration camps, registers the singular legacy of Dachau as an academy of SS terror.[31] Piorkowski, Hofmann, and Zill remain at the helm in Dachau. In Flossenbürg commandant Künstler, adjutant Ludwig Baumgartner, compound leader Hans Aumeier, and administrative leader Otto Brenneis have lengthy recent spells in Dachau on their CVs. In Mauthausen we find adjutant Viktor Zoller, compound leader Georg Bachmayer, camp engineers Kantschuster and Walter Ernstberger, as well as three further sub-departmental heads. Sachsenhausen, the nerve centre of terror in Prussia, has fewer Dachau graduates but these include commandant Loritz, adjutant Emil Reichherzer, and treasurer Emil Roßner. Senior Buchenwald with Dachau exposure, excluding Koch, are 1st compound leader Athur Rödl, 2nd compound leader Max Schobert, trainee compound leader Norbert Scharf, and treasurer Alfred Driemel. In Neuengamme we find commandant Weiß, camp engineer Traugott Meyer, and administrative chief Karl Faschingbauer. In newly opened Auschwitz, commandant Höß, adjutant Kramer, and compound leader Fritzsch would shortly be joined by Hofmann, Schwarzhuber, Schöttl, Hößler, Thumann, and Baer (Höß, Kramer, and Thumann are pictured in Figure E.2). Ravensbrück is terrorized by commandant Koegel.

For these senior camp SS personnel, the Dachau School was a shared referent in their biographies, a purported 'inner' battlefield where they had proven their Nazi mettle and nurtured the spirit of the concentration camp SS 'aristocracy'.[32] The camp held symbolic resonance for other high-ranking SS men, too. Himmler repeatedly visited his first camp during the war to check up on the progress of medical experiments. Pohl, who won control of the camp system in March 1942, also had a close personal attachment to Dachau. He had lived near the camp since the mid-1930s and, according to Höß, had often spent his Sundays touring the

---

[30] For an excellent discussion of the new guard personnel, see Wachsmann, 'KL: A History of the Nazi Concentration Camps', ch. 9; also Buggeln, *Arbeit*, pp. 480–4.

[31] IfZ, Fa183/1, Führerstellenbesetzungsplan für den Stab des Inspekteurs der Konzentrationslager 1940, s. 78.

[32] Orth, *Konzentrationslager SS*, pp. 298–9.

**Figure E.2** Dachau School graduates Rudolf Höß, Josef Kramer, and Anton Thumann relax with Josef Mengele (far left) at the SS retreat by Auschwitz, July 1944. USHMM Photo Archives 34755.

complex.[33] His second wife owned a manor in the Bavarian countryside which was renovated by a commando of Dachau inmates. The Pohls also owned a flat overlooking the Dachau plantation, where Pohl was sometimes to be found idling in a deckchair being ministered to by prisoners, including a personal waiter and cook.[34]

Yet, even by the outbreak of war the centre of gravity in the concentration camp system had begun to tilt towards Sachsenhausen in Berlin. And as the focus of the war shifted eastwards in 1941, so too did the balance of inmates and SS personnel: towards Auschwitz. The relative decline of Dachau in the landscape of Nazi terror was reflected in the classification of camps issued by the RSHA in 1940. This divided the concentration camps for men into three categories: Class 1 for 'definitely reformable' prisoners, Class 2 for the 'reformable', and Class 3 for 'barely reformable'. Dachau, which lacked Mauthausen and Flossenbürg's murderous quarries, was assigned to Class 1. As Eugen Kogon wrote, 'this can only bring a grim smile to the lips of those who knew the camp'.[35] Prisoners began to return to Dachau in February 1940 following the departure of the Death's Head Division. The national, 'racial' profile of the inmate population now changed

---

[33] Höß, *Commandant*, p. 222.
[34] Wachsmann, 'KL: A History of the Nazi Concentration Camps', ch. 7.
[35] Kogon, *Theory and Practice*, p. 23; Wachsmann, 'KL: A History of the Nazi Concentration Camps', ch. 4.

rapidly, with some 13,337 Polish prisoners registered in the remaining ten months of 1940 alone.[36] In the following years inmates arrived from throughout occupied Europe. By April 1942 the camp contained 8,000 inmates, mainly Poles, Germans, and Czechs.[37] Italians began to arrive after the signing of the armistice with the Allies in July 1943. In 1944 large numbers of Jews from Eastern Europe, especially Hungary, were transported to the Dachau complex. From the summer of 1944 some 2,200 alleged resistance activists from Western Europe, so-called 'night and fog' prisoners, were registered in the camp and housed in separate barracks.[38] In the final, chaotic year of the camp system even female inmates were imprisoned in Dachau, although they never comprised more than 4 or 5 per cent of the total inmate population.[39] The final prisoner registration by the SS in April 1945 counted 67,665 inmates in Dachau, no fewer than 12,067 of them Hungarian.[40]

In the latter stages of the war the main camps developed 'satellite camps', semi-permanent external work facilities attached usually to private firms and production sites.[41] By the end of 1944 there were at least seventy-seven satellite camps in the Dachau complex, most with rudimentary versions of a commandant staff.[42] This placed additional strain on already stretched SS resources. A very small number of seconded Wehrmacht personnel were appointed to key satellite camp command positions but the preference was for experienced camp SS men. Dachau School veterans who ended their concentration camp careers in Dachau satellite camps included Weiß, Schöttl, and Aumeier.[43] Here, a handful of ardent camp SS stalwarts provided toxic leadership to an inexperienced guard contingent of ethnic Germans and army personnel. *Kapos*, too, were vectors of the Dachau spirit and had an even greater impact on conditions in sub-camps with the constraints on SS personnel resources.[44]

The satellite camps were the product of a long-standing project of the WVHA to increase the economic contribution of the SS and camps to the war effort. In the wake of the military crisis outside Moscow, Pohl was charged with increasing the productivity of concentration camp prisoner labour and made commandants personally responsible for achieving this.[45] To disrupt settled practices and

[36] For detail, see Beate Kosmala, 'Polnische Häftlinge im Konzentrationslager Dachau 1939–1945', *Dachauer Hefte* 21 (2005), pp. 94–113.

[37] IMT, Vol. 38, 129-R, Pohl to Himmler, 30 April 1942, s. 363.

[38] Barbara Distel et al. (eds), *The Dachau Concentration Camp 1933 to 1945* (Dachau, 2005), p. 158. One particularly powerful memoir by a night and fog prisoner is the Dutch Communist Nico Rost's *Goethe in Dachau* (Berlin, 1948).

[39] Sabine Schalm, 'Außenkommandos und Außenlager des KZ Dachau', in Benz and Könisgeder, *Dachau*, pp. 53–69, here p. 65.

[40] Dirk Riedel, 'Ungarische Häftlinge', p. 282.

[41] The outstanding monograph on satellite camps (Neuengamme in this case) is Buggeln, *Arbeit*. On Dachau see Schalm, *Arbeit*; Edith Raim, *Kaufering*.

[42] Sabine Schalm, 'Außenkommandos und Außenlager des KZ Dachau', in Benz and Könisgeder, *Dachau*, pp. 53–69, here p. 54.

[43] Edith Raim, 'Die KZ-Außenlagerkomplexe Kaufering und Mühldorf', in Benz and Königseder, *Dachau*, pp. 71–88, here pp. 78–9.

[44] Wachsmann, 'KL: A History of the Nazi Concentration Camps', ch. 10.

[45] Orth, *System*, pp. 162–9; Wachsmann, 'KL: A History of the Nazi Concentration Camps', ch. 8.

networks among key commandant staff personnel he replaced five of the fourteen commandants and experimented with switching block leaders between camps.[46] Piorkowski, Loritz, and Künstler were among the casualties and Pohl claimed after the war to have been seeking to remove punitive 'roughnecks' educated in 'Eicke's school'.[47] Yet despite experimentation and exhortation the violent culture and increasing deprivation in the camps stymied SS hopes for increased productivity.[48] Though 1942 and 1943 saw some decline in mortality compared to the unbound, 'euphoric' terror of 1941, Dachau mortality began to skyrocket in late 1944.[49] A meaningful shift in productivity and mortality would, as one historian notes, have required deep 'structural changes, transforming the ethos of the camps'.[50] For all its ambitious rhetoric, the SS leadership lacked the will and resources to push through such structural change. Dachau was wired to produce death, not armaments.

This was also evident in the commandant staff's contribution to Operation Barbarossa. By the end of the war at least 25,000 Soviet prisoners had been transported to Dachau, some as young as six.[51] A further 4,000 were not registered but shot, often within days, by the SS. These were alleged 'political commissars' uncovered in the miserable POW camps overseen by the Wehrmacht. On 21 July 1941, Reinhard Heydrich set out on a tour of the camps and concluded that these prisoners, who fell under the terms of the Commissar Order, should be transported back to the Reich for 'covert execution in the nearest available concentration camp'.[52] In all, at least 34,000 Red Army 'commissars', and probably nearer 45,000, were murdered in the concentration camps. Eicke, back in Germany convalescing from injuries sustained driving over a Soviet landmine, characteristically justified the executions as 'retaliation' for German soldiers murdered in Soviet captivity.

The method of murder varied from camp to camp. Some followed the procedure developed at Sachsenhausen, where the POWs were funnelled into a fake hospital and shot in the nape of the neck by block leaders. In Dachau, for reasons of overcrowding rather than military honour, the alleged commissars were shot in the open by the *Bunker* or on the nearby SS shooting range at Herbertshausen. The Dachau commandant staff murdered some 4,400 POWs in this way between September 1941 and June 1942. Prisoners working nearby report exuberant block leaders jumping with excitement around the arriving trucks, eager to play their role

[46] Wachsmann, 'KL: A History of the Nazi Concentration Camps', ch. 8.
[47] Wachsmann, 'KL: A History of the Nazi Concentration Camps', ch. 8.
[48] Wachsmann, 'KL: A History of the Nazi Concentration Camps', ch. 8.
[49] Annual estimates in Berben, *Dachau*, p. 281. For an overview including the execution of Soviet POWs and more recent data from the International Tracing Service, see Zámečnik, *Dachau*, pp. 377–9.
[50] Wachsmann, 'KL: A History of the Nazi Concentration Camps', ch. 8.
[51] Distel, *Dachau*, p. 156; Wachsmann, 'KL: A History of the Nazi Concentration Camps', ch. 8; Longerich, *Himmler*, pp. 617–25.
[52] On the murder of Soviet POWs in the camps, see Orth, System, pp. 122–31, Heydrich quote p. 123; Reinhard Otto, *Wehrmacht, Gestapo und sowjestische Kriegsgefangene im deutschen Reichsgebiet 1941/42* (Munich, 1999); Wachsmann, 'KL: A History of the Nazi Concentration Camps', ch. 5; Zámečnik, *Dachau*, pp. 185–201.

in Operation Barbarossa.[53] Inmates worked round the clock repairing the steel fetters used to fasten the soldiers to posts as they were damaged during the fusillades. The familiar factors of theatricality and boastful, competitive toughness among the SS took on a particularly macabre aspect: one SS man is said to have clubbed the genitals of a murdered POW and shouted to his comrades 'Look here, he is still standing!'[54] Inmates in the terrible crematorium work detail found Soviet coins and hammer-and-sickle buttons in the ashes and were instructed to get rid of 'that filth from Bolshevik pigs' without delay. In all the concentration camps the participating SS personnel were rewarded with schnapps, beer, a cash bonus, and a war service medal.[55] Not all Dachau SS personnel were prepared to join in. *Oberscharführer* Karl Minderlein, stationed in the camp since 1933, received a serious dressing-down from Piorkowski for disobedience and was sentenced to imprisonment by the SS court. He spent six months in the SS penal camp at Dachau before being transferred to a punishment company on the Eastern Front.[56]

Yet the most lethal era in Dachau's history was not the mass executions of 1941 and 1942 but the final months before liberation, when living conditions and deprivation in the complex were at their most appalling. Almost half the inmate deaths in Dachau occurred in its last four months. The scenes at liberation of tangled emaciated corpses and blinking, bewildered survivors still dominate the historical consciousness of Dachau. They prompted a handful of enraged American GIs to execute around forty captured guards.[57] But these were by no means the SS men primarily responsible: the commandant staff personnel had left long before the arrival of the Seventh Army. With the Third Reich shrinking daily from all sides, senior concentration camp SS officers everywhere had begun to flee. Höß headed north to Himmler in Flensburg, gallantly bringing Eicke's widow and children along to protect them from the Red Army.[58] Others trekked south towards Dachau, the pre-war bastion of the concentration camp SS. A few days before the liberation of the camp, Pohl hosted a lavish valedictory dinner there for WVHA leaders and the displaced commandants of Buchenwald and Dora.[59] Dachau's final commandant, Eduard Weiter, led a convoy out from the camp towards the Tyrol, which deluded SS leaders imagined as a final impregnable fortress for the SS. But contrary to much rousing talk of steadfast resistance and operatic last stands, almost all senior camp personnel sought to escape the abyss they had created by melting into the German population. Divested of their uniforms and captive audience, deflated

[53] Zámečnik, *Dachau*, p. 191.

[54] Wachsmann, 'KL: A History of the Nazi Concentration Camps', ch. 5.

[55] Orth, *Konzentrationslager SS*, pp. 175–6; Wachsmann, 'KL: A History of the Nazi Concentration Camps', ch. 8; Newspaper feature on trip reproduced in Riedel, *Ordnungshüter*, pp. 273–5.

[56] SAM, StA 28791/3, Vernehmung K. Minderlein, 25 July 1949. I am grateful to Nikolaus Wachsmann for bringing this document to my attention.

[57] For detail, see Jürgen Zarusky, 'Die Erschießungen gefangener SS-Leute bei der Befreiung des KZ Dachau', in Benz and Königseder, *Dachau*, pp. 103–24. As any online search will show, this isolated event greatly agitates sundry neo-Nazis and 'revisionists'.

[58] Höß, *Commandant*, p. 171.

[59] Wachsmann, 'KL: A History of the Nazi Concentration Camps', ch. 11.

from their former swaggering personae, most lay low hoping to evade the judicial reckoning which lay ahead.

## JUSTICE AND MEMORY

Unlike the lavish multimedia spectacle staged 65 miles to the north at Nuremberg, the US military trial of concentration camp personnel at Dachau was a low-budget affair.[60] With Congress and American public opinion impatient for justice, the military commission worked in haste. Forty Dachau personnel were selected, somewhat arbitrarily, by the prosecutors to answer for an institution which had killed over 40,000 prisoners (Figure E.3). The trial was unsatisfactory and incomplete in other ways, too. None of the defendants was charged with a specific crime, but with the novel legal concept of 'common design' to violate the laws of war. This meant that a Wehrmacht soldier posted as sentry to a satellite camp in early 1945 was judicially equivalent to a seasoned compound leader, that a Mursch was as culpable as a Steinbrenner. The prosecution was also restricted juridically to crimes committed against Allied nationals after America's entry into the war. This encouraged some unseemly defence strategies: the prosecutor's attempt to raise the topic of the box cars full of corpses discovered by US soldiers had to be withdrawn as he was unable to prove that they were not merely German corpses.[61]

As in every trial of camp personnel held by the military commission at Dachau, all the defendants were found guilty.[62] Fifteen had also been in the pre-war Dachau School and all but one of these were hanged at the end of May 1946, including Weiß, Schöttl, Aumeier, and Josef Seuss, brother of Wolfgang. The sentences look draconian in light of what was to follow. Public interest in the camps, particularly their comparatively prosaic pre-war history, flagged after Nuremberg. Neurath complained of his struggle to find a publisher for his memoir:

> The audience is spoiled. The fact that our people were hanged by their wrists from the trees during a snowstorm, crying for their fathers and mothers, who cares about that in the age of crematorium ovens and millions murdered?[63]

The Munich coroner Nikolaus Naaff cared. While the American military commission had put Dachau as an institution on trial, German prosecutors were concerned with specific crimes and perpetrators. In 1947 Naaff was appointed to lead the investigation into the murders by the early Dachau SS, aided by the discovery of the original case files from the 1930s in Adolf Wagner's desk.[64] Naaff threw

---

[60] On the trials, see especially Robert Sigel, *Im Interesse der Gerechtigkeit: Die Dachauer Kriegsverbrecherprozesse 1945–1948* (Frankfurt and New York, 1992); Holger Lessing, *Der Erste Dachauer Prozess* (Baden-Baden, 1993); Joshua Greene, *Justice at Dachau: The Trials of an American Prosecutor* (New York, 2003).

[61] IfZ, MB 22, United States vs. Martin Gottfried Weiß et al., Roll 1.

[62] An excellent recent monograph on the trial of Mauthausen personnel at Dachau is Thomaz Jardim, *The Mauthausen Trial: American Military Justice in Germany* (Harvard, 2012).

[63] Neurath, *Society*, p. 297.      [64] Raim, 'Westdeutsche Ermittlungen', p. 216.

**Figure E.3** Group portrait of the defendants in the Dachau war crimes trial, 1945. USHMM Photo Archives 12607.

himself into the task, reading the inmate memoir literature and personally interviewing hundreds of witnesses.[65] Nor could his successors be faulted for dogged persistence: the final document in the file on the missing Kantschuster dates from 1986, when the former *Bunker* specialist would have been only a few days short of his hundredth birthday.[66] Steinbrenner, Seefried, Unterhuber, Ehmann, Seuss, Hofmann, and Wicklmayr were among the sixteen pre-war, Dachau School personnel to receive lengthy custodial sentences for involvement in the murder of inmates.[67]

Naaff and his team were much preoccupied with the concepts of intent and agency. German criminal law generally is more concerned with the perpetrator's specific subjective motives than its Anglo-American counterpart.[68] It places unusual weight on the individual psychology and disposition of the perpetrator at the time of the criminal act. This makes it largely insensitive to the contribution of social forces and environmental factors, a shortcoming shared by recent historiography on the Third Reich. But legal judgement and historical explanation

---

[65] SAM, StA 34825/2 Brief Nikolaus Naaff an Landgerichtspraesident München II, 30 January 1954. Naaff writes that he had not taken a holiday in six years.

[66] SAM, StA 34832/5 Az.: Da 12Js 800/49, Band I und II. Kantschuster Hans.

[67] Raim, 'Westdeutsche Ermittlungen'.

[68] See the excellent discussion in David O. Pendas, *The Frankfurt Auschwitz Trial, 1963–1965: Genocide, History, and the Limits of the Law* (Cambridge, 2006), pp. 53–79.

are discrete phenomena.[69] Legal judgment is innately mechanical and reductive, seeking resolution, certitude, and retribution. The historian is not a prosecutor and trades in nuance and context. He or she is less concerned with individual guilt than with weighting environment, agency, and contingency. Goldhagen, the advocate par excellence, complains that the resultant complex of explanatory factors is a 'laundry list' but, as his book unwittingly demonstrates, this is the only plausible approach to historical causation.[70] To be sure, Dachau guards were not engulfed by irresistible social structures or 'destiny'. They acted as deliberative and creative individuals, and as volunteers, but within a group context and a particular, toxic environment. While many were clearly by no means 'ordinary' men, excessive demonization of these perpetrators is unhelpful and even hazardous. The role of universal and 'banal' factors in their schooling and conduct at Dachau warns against such complacency.

The key specific, indeed singular, historical significance of Dachau in the grim ledger of National Socialist criminality lies in the pre-war Dachau School. The prototype state-run SS concentration camp was the academy of violence for a cohort of future SS murderers. History and commemoration, however, have proven difficult to reconcile. When an academic commission was set up to review the memorial site on the fiftieth anniversary of Dachau's liberation in 1995, the participants were clear that the hitherto minimal attention to SS personnel should be increased. But prominent survivors, including Zámečnik, felt this would intrude into and tarnish the remembrance of the prisoners.[71] They wanted any material on the perpetrators to be sited outside the prisoner compound in the former SS complex. The latter is unavailable, still used today, rather unfortunately, by the Bavarian State Police. As a consequence, in the otherwise excellent new exhibition opened in 2003—visibly influenced by Zámečnik's monograph on Dachau—the SS have little presence save for some brief biographies of commandants.[72] The result is to perpetuate the disconnect between Dachau's historical uniqueness as a perpetrator location and its place in international memorial culture as a symbol of the *victims* of Nazism. Barbara Distel, the memorial site's eminent ex-director, has recently questioned whether it is its purpose to address 'how people became torturers and mass murderers'.[73] Yet the site's pedagogic potential, not to mention its historical

[69] Failure to grasp this is most obvious in Goldhagen-style interpretations, but also evident in the historiographical trend in recent years to downplay coercion in the Third Reich and prioritize ideological enthusiasm and material gain. On this 'voluntarist turn', see Neil Gregor, 'Nazism—A Political Religion?' and Evans, 'Coercion and Consent'.
[70] Daniel Goldhagen, 'A Reply to my Critics: Motives, Causes, and Alibis', *The New Republic*, 23 December 1996, pp. 37–45, here p. 38.
[71] Barbara Distel, 'Die Täter in der Erinnerung an das Konzentrationslager Dachau', in Angelika Benz and Marija Vulesica (eds), *Bewachung und Ausführung: Alltag der Täter in nationalsozialistischen Lagern* (Berlin, 2011), pp. 199–206.
[72] See the highly informative memorial site website, with links to download the panels: <http://www.kz-gedenkstaette-dachau.de/permanent-exhibition.html> (accessed 25 August 2013). On the memorial sites as exclusive 'victims' spaces' (*Orte der Opfer*), see Detlef Garbe, 'Die Täter: Kommentierende Bemerkungen', in Herbert, Orth, and Dieckmann (eds), *Die nationalsozialistischen Konzentrationslager*, Vol. 2, pp. 822–40, quote p. 824.
[73] Distel, 'Täter', p. 206.

significance, is suppressed by keeping it as a sanitized, sacred space with the perpetrators partitioned off or out of sight. This invites only reverence, and reverence alone can stifle and constrain comprehension. In a Europe where the social and political dislocations of the interwar era may yet come to feel less remote, historians and educators need more than ever to communicate the historical organization of terror and violence.

# *Appendix*

## LIST OF SS RANKS

| | |
|---|---|
| *Reichsführer* der SS | Field Marshall |
| SS-*Oberstgruppenführer* | General |
| SS-*Obergruppenführer* | Lieutenant General |
| SS-*Gruppenführer* | Major General |
| SS-*Brigadeführer* | Brigadier |
| SS-*Oberführer* | N/A |
| SS-*Standartenführer* | Colonel |
| SS-*Obersturmbannführer* | Lieutenant Colonel |
| SS-*Sturmbannführer* | Major |
| SS-*Hauptsturmführer* | Captain |
| SS-*Obersturmführer* | Lieutenant |
| SS-*Untersturmführer* | 2nd Lieutenant |
| SS-*Hauptscharführer* | Battalion Sergeant Major |
| SS-*Oberscharführer* | Company Sergeant Major |
| SS-*Scharführer* | Platoon Sergeant Major |
| SS-*Unterscharführer* | Sergeant |
| SS-*Rottenführer* | Corporal |
| SS-*Sturmmann* | Lance Corporal |
| SS-*Mann* | Private |
| SS-*Anwärter* | Candidate |

# Bibliography

## ARCHIVES

**Archiv der KZ-Gedenkstätte Dachau**
Berichte ehemaliger Häftlinge des Konzentrationslagers Dachau
Häftlingsdatenbank
Dokumentensammlung: SS im KL Dachau
Dokumentensammlung: Dachau—Die Stadt und das Lager

**Bayerisches Hauptstaatsarchiv, Munich**
Stk 5487; Stk 6300; StK 106682

**Bundesarchiv, Berlin-Lichterfelde**
NS 4/Da Konzentrationslager Dachau
NS 19 Personalstab Reichsführer SS
NS 33 Allgemeine SS
R 2 Reichsministerium der Finanzen
R 22 Reichsjustizministerium
R 58 Reichssicherheitshauptamt

**Berlin Document Center (BDC) files**
OPG Oberstes Parteigericht—Personalakten
PK Parteikorrespondenz—Personalakten
RS Rasse- und Siedlungshauptamt—Personalakten
SSO SS-Offizierspersonalakten

**Institut für Zeitgeschichte, Munich**
F/Fa Prozesse vor in- und ausländischen Gerichten
MA Records of the Reich Leader of the German Police/SS
MB21 US Military Tribunal, United States vs. Martin Gottfried Weiß et al.

**Staatsarchiv Munich**
Ermittlungsverfahren Staatsanwaltschaft München II 3498–34868

**Stadtarchiv Dachau**
Fach 96, Nr. 19

**Wiener Library, London**
P. II. D Eyewitness testimony Kristallnacht

**Imperial War Museum, London**
IWM Interviews

## PRIMARY SOURCES

Adam, W., *Nacht über Deutschland: Erinnerung an Dachau* (Vienna, 1947).

Ailsby, C., *The Waffen-SS: The Unpublished Photographs 1923–1945* (London, 1999).

Asgodom, S. (ed.), *'Halts Maul—sonst kommst nach Dachau!' Frauen und Männer aus der Arbeiterbewegung. Berichten über Widerstand und Verfolgung unter dem Nationalsozialismus* (Cologne, 1983).

*Auschwitz in den Augen der SS* (Oświęcim, 1997).

Behnken. K. (ed.), *Deutschland-Berichte der Sozialdemokratischen Partei Deutschlands (Sopade) 1934–1940*, 7 vols, (Frankfurt am Main, 1980).

Beimler, H., *Four Weeks in the Hands of Hitler's Hell-Hounds: The Nazi Murder Camp of Dachau* (London, 1933).

Bettelheim, B., *The Informed Heart: Autonomy in a Mass Age* (New York, 1960).

Bohrmann, H. (ed.), *NS-Presseanweisung der Vorkriegszeit: Edition und Dokumentation vol.4/III: 1936* (Munich, 1993).

Boulanger, J., *Eine Ziffer über dem Herz: Erlebnisbericht über zwölf Jahre Haft* (Berlin, 1957).

Burkhard, H., *Tanz Mal Jude! Von Dachau bis Shanghai: Meine Erlebnisse in den Konzentrationslagern Dachau—Buchenwald—Ghetto Shanghai, 1933–1948* (Nuremberg, 1967).

Cohen, E. A., *Human Behaviour in the Concentration Camp* (London, 1988 [1954]).

Diels, R., *Lucifer ante Portas: es spricht der erste Chef der Gestapo* (Stuttgart, 1950).

Ecker, F., 'Die Hölle Dachau', in *Konzentrationslager: Ein Appell an der Gewissen der Welt* (Karlsbad, 1934), pp. 12–55.

Eickmann, A., *Der KZ Gärtner . . . vom gesundheitspolitischen Standpunkt ein Staatsfeind* (Bremen, 2007).

Feuerbach, W., *55 Monate Dachau: Ein Tatsachenbericht* (Bremen, 1993).

Frankl, V., *Man's Search for Meaning* (Boston, 2006 [1959]).

Göhring, L., *Dachau: Flossenbürg: Neuengamme. Eine antifaschistische Biographie* (Berlin, 1999).

Grünwiedl, M., *Dachauer Gefangene erzählen* (Munich, 1934).

Geyde, G. E. R., *Fallen Bastions: The Central European Tragedy* (London, 1940).

Hausser, P., *Soldaten wie andere auch* (Osnabrück, 1966).

Heilig, B., *Men Crucified* (London, 1941).

Herker-Beimler, C., *Erinnerungen einer Münchner Antifaschistin* (Augsburg, 1999).

Himmler, H., *Die Schutzstaffel als anti-bolschewistische Kampforganisation* (Berlin, 1936).

Hitler, A., *Mein Kampf* trans. Ralph Manheim (London, 1972 [1926]).

Höß, R., *Commandant of Auschwitz* trans. Constantine FitzGibbon (London, 2000 [1947]).

Hoffmann, H., *Ein Jahr Bayrische Revolution im Bild* (Munich, 1937).

Hornung, W., *Dachau: Eine Chronik* (Zurich, 1936).

Jünger, E., *Der Kampf als inneres Erlebnis* (Berlin, 1922).

Jünger, E., *The Storm of Steel* trans. Basil Creighton (London, 1975).

Kalmar, R., *Zeit ohne Gnade* (Vienna, 1946).

Karst, G. M., *The Beasts of the Earth* (New York, 1942).

Kautsky, B., *Teufel und Verdammte: Erfahrungen und Erkenntnisse aus sieben Jahren in deutschen Konzentrationslager* (Zurich, 1946).

Kay, G. R., *Dachau* (London, 1942).

Kirchoff, R., *Am Lagertor: Gesellschaftskritischer Roman aus dem zwanzigsten Jahrhundert in dreiunddreizig Bildern* (Munich, 1972).

Kogon, E., *The Theory and Practice of Hell: The German Concentration Camps and the System Behind Them* trans. Heinz Norden (New York, 2006).

Kupfer-Koberwitz, E., *Die Mächtigen und die Hilflosen: als Häftling in Dachau* (Stuttgart, 1960).

Levi, P., *The Drowned and the Saved* (London, 1988).

Levi, P., *Survival in Auschwitz* (London, 1990).

Marx, O. and Marx, H., *Dachau, 1933–35* (New York, 1987).

Mochulsky, F. V., *Gulag Boss: A Soviet Memoir* trans. Deborah Kaple (Oxford, 2011).

*Nazi-Bastille Dachau: Schicksal und Heldentum deutscher Freiheitskämpfer* (Paris, 1939).

Neurath, P. M., *The Society of Terror: Inside the Dachau and Buchenwald Concentration Camps* (Colorado, 2005).

Pelican, F., *From Dachau to Dunkirk* (London, 1993).

Röder, R., *Nachtwache: 10 Jahre KZ Dachau und Flossenbürg* (Wien, 1985).

Schmolze, G. (ed.), *Revolution und Räterepublik in München 1918–1919 in Augenzeugenberichten* (Munich, 1969).

Schnabel, R., *Macht ohne Moral: Eine Dokumentation über die SS* (Frankfurt am Main, 1957).

Schnabel, R., *Die Frommen in der Hölle* (Berlin, 1965).

Schuler, E., *Die Bayerische Landespolizei 1919–1935* (Munich, 1964).

*The Brown Book of Hitler Terror and the Burning of the Reichstag. Prepared by the World Committee for the Victims of German Fascism* (London, 1933).

*The Trial of the Major War Criminals before the International Military Tribunal, Nuremberg 14.11.1945–1.10.1946*, 42 vols (Nuremberg, 1947–9).

Toller, E., *Eine Jugend in Deutschland* (Hamburg, 1963).

Von Aretin, K., *Krone und Ketten: Erinnerungen eines bayerischen Edelmannes* (Munich, 1954).

Von Salomon, E., *The Outlaws* (London, 1931).

Wallner, P., *By Order of the Gestapo: A Record of Life in Dachau and Buchenwald Concentration Camps* (London, 1941).

Werner, A., 'Return to Dachau', *Commentary*, 12 (1951), p. 542.

Wollenberg, E., *Als Rotarmist vor München* (Hamburg, 1972).

## SECONDARY SOURCES

Abel, T., *Why Hitler Came to Power* (Cambridge, 1986).

Ackerman, J., *Heinrich Himmler als Ideologe* (Göttingen, 1970).

Adorno, T. W. et al., *The Authoritarian Personality* (New York, 1950).

Allen, M. T., *The Business of Genocide: The SS, Slave Labour, and the Concentration Camps* (Chapel Hill, 2002).

Allen, W. S., *The Nazi Seizure of Power: The Experience of a Single German Town* (New York, 1984).

Allert, T., *The Hitler Salute: On the Meaning of a Gesture* (London, 2009).

Applebaum, A., *The Gulag: A History of the Soviet Camps* (London, 2004).

Arendt, H., 'Social Science Techniques and the Study of Concentration Camps,' *Jewish Social Studies*, Vol. 12 (1950), pp. 149–64.

Arendt, H., *The Origins of Totalitarianism* (London, 1973 [1951]).

Arendt, H., *Eichmann in Jerusalem: A Report into the Banality of Evil* (New York, 1994 [1963]).

Aronson. S, *The Beginnings of the Gestapo System: The Bavarian Model in 1933* (Jerusalem, 1969), pp. 20–1.

Aronson, S., *Reinhard Heydrich und die frühgeschichte der Gestapo und SD* (Stuttgart, 1971).

Asch, S., 'Effects of Group Pressure on the Modification and Distortion of Judgements', in H. Guetzkow (ed.), *Groups, Leadership and Men* (Pittsburg, 1951), pp. 177–90.

Aschheim, S. E. (ed.), *Hannah Arendt in Jerusalem* (Berkeley, 2001).

Ayaß, A., *'Asoziale' im Nationalsozialismus* (Stuttgart, 1995).

Baganz, C., 'Dachau als Historischer Ort im System des Nationalsozialismus', in Wolfgang Benz and Angelika Königseder (eds), *Das Konzentrationslager Dachau: Geschichte und Wirkung Nationalsozialistischer Repression* (Berlin, 2008), pp. 31–42.

Bahne, S., 'Die Kommunistische Partei Deutschlands', in Erich Matthias and Rudolf Morsley (eds), *Das Ende der Parteien 1933: Darstellungen und Dokumente* (Düsseldorf, 1960), p. 690.

Bahro, B., *Der SS-Sport: Organisation—Funktion—Bedeutung* (Paderborn, 2013).

Bandura, A., 'Moral Disengagement in the Perpetration of Inhumanities', *Personality and Social Psychology Review*, Vol. 3, No. 3 (1999), pp. 193–209

Bankier, D., *The Germans and the Final Solution: Public Opinion under Nazism* (Oxford and Cambridge, 2002).

Barta, T., 'Living in Dachau, 1900–1950' (Unpublished MS).

Barth, B., *Dolchstoßlegenden und politischen Desintegration: Das Trauma der deutschen Niederlage im Ersten Weltkrieg 1914–1933* (Düsseldorf, 2003).

Bartov, O., *Hitler's Army: Soldiers, Nazis, and War in the Third Reich* (New York, 1993).

Bartov, O., *The Eastern Front 1941–1945: German Troops and the Barbarization of Warfare* (London, 1995).

Bartov, O., *Germany's War and the Holocaust: Disputed Histories* (New York, 2003).

Bauer, Y., *Rethinking the Holocaust* (New Haven, 2001).

Bauman, Z., *Modernity and the Holocaust* (Cambridge, 2000 [1989]).

Behrenbeck, S., *Der Kult um die toten Helden: Nationalsozialistische Mythen, Riten und Symbole 1923 bis 1945* (Vierow bei Greifswald, 1996).

Benz, W., 'Mitglieder der Häftlingsgesellschaft auf Zeit: "Die Aktionsjuden" 1938/39', in Wolfgang Benz and Angelika Königseder (eds), *Das Konzentrationslager Dachau: Geschichte und Wirkung nationalsozialistischer Repression* (Berlin, 2008), pp. 207–18.

Benz, W. and Distel, B. (eds), *Terror ohne System: Die ersten Konzentrationslager im Nationalsozialismus 1933–1935* (Berlin, 2001).

Benz, W. and Distel, B. (eds), *Herrschaft und Gewalt: Frühe Konzentrationslager 1933–1939* (Berlin, 2002).

Benz, W. and Distel, B. (eds), *Der Ort des Terrors: Geschichte der nationalsozialistischen Konzentrationslager*, 8 vols (Munich, 2005–9).

Benz, W. and Distel, B (eds), *Flossenbürg: Das Konzentrationslager und seine Außenlager* (Munich, 2007).

Benz, W. and Königseder, A. (eds), *Das Konzentrationslager Dachau: Geschichte und Wirkung nationalsozialistischer Represson* (Berlin, 2008).

Berben, P., *Dachau 1933–45: The Official History* (London, 1975).

Berg, N., *Der Holocaust und die westdeutschen Historiker: Erfahrung und Erinnerung* (Göttingen, 2004).

Bessel, R., 'The Potempa Murder', *Central European History*, Vol. 10, No. 3 (Sep., 1977), pp. 241–54.

Bessel, R., *Political Violence and the Rise of Nazism: The Storm Troopers in Eastern Germany 1925–1940* (Yale, 1984).

Bessel, R., *Germany after the First World War* (Oxford, 1993).

Bessel, R., *Nazism and War* (London, 2004).

Beyer, H., *Von der Novemberrevolution zur Räterepublik in München* (Berlin, 1957).

Blasius, D., *Weimars End: Bürgerkrieg und Politik 1930–1933* (Vandenhoeck und Göttingen, 2005).

Blass, T., *Obedience to Authority: Current Perspectives on the Milgram Paradigm* (New Jersey, 1985).

Blass, T., 'Understanding Behavior in the Milgram Obedience Experiment: The Role of Personality, Situations, and their Interactions', *Journal of Personality and Social Psychology*, Vol. 60 (1991), pp. 398–413.

Blass, T. 'Psychological Perspectives on the Perpetrators of the Holocaust: The Role of Situational Pressures, Personal Dispositions, and their Interactions', *Holocaust and Genocide Studies*, Vol. 7, No. 1 (1993), pp. 30–50.

Blass, T., *The Man Who Shocked the World: The Life and Legacy of Stanley Milgram* (New York, 2009 [2004]).

Bleuel, H. P., *Strength Through Joy: Sex and Society in Nazi Germany* (London, 1973).

Bloxham, D., *The Final Solution: A Genocide* (Oxford, 2009).

Bock, G., *Zwangssterilisation im Nationalsozialismus: Studien zur Rassenpolitik und Frauenpolitik* (Opladen, 1986).

Bock, G., 'Ordinary Women in Nazi Germany: Perpetrators, Victims, Followers and Bystanders', in Dalia Ofer and Lenore J. Weitzman (eds), *Women and the Holocaust* (New York, 1998), pp. 85–100.

Boehnert, G. C., 'A Sociography of the SS Officer Corps 1925–1939' (PhD Dissertation, University of London, 1977).

Bourke, J., *An Intimate History of Killing: Face to Face Killing in Twentieth Century Warfare* (London, 1999).

Bourke, J., *Dismembering the Male: Men's Bodies, Britain and the Great War* (London, 1999).

Bracher, K. D., *Die Auflösung der Weimarer Republik: Eine Studie zum Problem des Machtverfalls in der Demokratie* (Villingen, 1960 [1955]).

Breitschneider, H., *Der Widerstand gegen den Nationalsozialismus in München 1933 bis 1945* (Munich, 1968).

Brendon, P., *The Dark Valley: A Panorama of the 1930s* (London, 2000).

Bridenthal, R. et al. (eds), *When Biology Became Destiny: Women in Weimar and Nazi Germany* (New York, 1984).

Broszat, M. (ed.), *Rudolf Höß: Kommandant in Auschwitz. Autobiografische Aufzeichnungen* (Munich, 1963 [1958]).

Broszat, M., 'The Concentration Camps 1933–45', in Helmut Krausnick, Hans Buchheim, Martin Broszat, and Hans-Adolf Jacobsen, *Anatomy of the SS State* (New York, 1965), pp. 397–504.

Broszat, M., *The Hitler State: The Foundation and Development of the Internal Structure of the Third Reich* (London and New York, 1981).

Broszat, M. et al. (eds), *Bayern in der NS-Zeit*, 6 vols (Munich, 1977–83).

Browder, G. C., *Foundations of the Nazi Police State: The Formation of Sipo and SD* (Kentucky, 1990).

Browning, C. R., *Ordinary Men: Reserve Police Battalion 101 and the Final Solution in Poland* (London, 2002 [1991]).

Browning, C. R., *Collected Memories: Holocaust History and Postwar Testimony* (Madison, 2003).

Bruns, C., *Politik des Eros: Der Männerbund in Wissenschaft, Politik und Jugendkultur (1880–1934)* (Cologne, 2008).

Bry, G., *Wages in Germany 1871–1945* (Princeton, 1960).

Bryant, M., 'Die US-amerikanischen Militärgerichtsprozesse gegen SS-Personal, Ärzte und Kapos des KZ Dachau 1945–1948', in Eiber, L. and Sigel, R. (eds.), *Dachauer Prozesse: NS-Verbrechen vor amerikanischen Militärgerichten in Dachau 1945–1948* (Göttingen, 2007), pp. 109–26.

Buchheim, H., 'Command and Compliance', in Helmut Krausnick, Hans Buchheim, Martin Broszat, and Hans-Adolf Jacobsen, *Anatomy of the SS State* (London, 1968), pp. 305–96.

Buggeln, M., *Arbeit und Gewalt: Das Außenlagersystem des KZ Neuengamme* (Göttingen, 2009).

Bull, H. (ed.), *The Challenge of the Third Reich* (Oxford, 1986).

Burleigh, M. and Wippermann, W., *The Racial State: Germany 1933–1945* (Cambridge, 1991).

Burleigh, M., *Ethics and Extermination: Reflections on Nazi Genocide* (Cambridge, 1997).

Burleigh, M., *The Third Reich: A New History* (London, 2001).

Butler, R., *Hitler's Death's Head Division: SS Totenkopf Division* (Yorkshire, 2004).

Caplan, J. (ed.), *Nazism, Fascism and the Working Class: Essays by Tim Mason* (Cambridge, 1995).

Caplan, J., 'Political Detention and the Origin of Concentration Camps in Nazi Germany, 1933–1935/6', in Neil Gregor (ed.), *Nazism, War and Genocide: Essays in Honour of Jeremy Noakes* (Exeter, 2005), pp. 22–41.

Caplan, J., 'Gender and the Concentration Camps' in Caplan and Nikolaus Wachsmann (eds), *The Concentration Camps in Nazi Germany: The New Histories* (London, 2010), pp. 82–107.

Caplan, J. and Wachsmann, N. (eds), *Concentration Camps in Nazi Germany: The New Histories* (London and New York, 2010).

Cesarani, D., *Eichmann: His Life and Crimes* (London, 2004).

Childers, T., *The Nazi Voter: The Social Foundations of Fascism in Germany* (London, 1983).

Clark, C., *Iron Kingdom: The Rise and Downfall of Prussia 1600–1947* (London, 2006).

Clendinnen, I., *Reading The Holocaust* (Cambridge, 2002).

Comité Internationale de Dachau (ed.), *Konzentrationslager Dachau 1933–1945* (Munich, 1978).

Connell, R. W., *Masculinities* (Cambridge, 1995).

Cramer-Fürtig, M. and Gotto, B. (eds), *'Machtergreifung' in Augsburg: Anfänge der NS-Diktatur* (Augsburg, 2008).

*Dachauer Hefte: Studien und Dokumente zur Geschichte der nationalsozialistischen Konzentrationslager.*

Darley, J., 'Review: Social Organization for the Production of Evil', *Psychological Inquiry*, Vol. 3, No. 2 (1992), pp. 199–218.

de Vries, H., 'Herzogenbusch (Vught)—Stammlager', in Wolfgang Benz and Barbara Distel (eds), *Der Ort des Terrors: Geschichte der nationalsozialistischen Konzentrationslager* (Munich, 2005–9), Vol. 7, pp. 136–8.

Dicks, H. V., *Licensed Mass Murder: A Socio-Psychological Study of Some SS Killers* (New York, 1972).

Diehl, J. M., *Paramilitary Politics in Weimar Germany* (Bloomington, IN, 1977).

Diehl, P., *Macht—Mythos—Utopie: Die Körperbilder der SS-Männer* (Berlin, 2005).

Dietrich, A. and Heise, L. (eds), *Männlichkeitskonstruktionen im Nationalsozialismus* (Frankfurt am Main, 2013).

Distel, B. (ed.), *Frauen im Holocaust* (Gerlingen, 2001).

Donson, A., *Youth in the Fatherless Land: War Pedagogy, Nationalism and Authority in Germany 1914–1918* (London, 2010).

Dove, R., *He Was a German: A Biography of Ernst Toller* (London, 1990), pp. 88–93.

Drobisch, K. and Wieland, G., *System der NS-Konzentrationslager 1933–1939* (Berlin, 1993).

Dudink, S., Hagemann, K., and Tosh, J. (eds), *Masculinities in Politics and War* (Manchester, 2004).

Eberle, A., 'Häftlingskategorien und Kennzeichnungen', in Benz and Distel (eds), *Ort des Terrors*, Vol. 1 (Munich, 2005), pp. 91–109.

Eberle, A., '"Asoziale" und "Berufsverbrecher": Dachau als Ort der "Vorbeugehaft"', in Benz, W. and Königseder, A. (eds), *Das Konzentrationslager Dachau: Geschichte und Wirkung nationalsozialistischer Represson* (Berlin, 2008), pp. 252–68.

Ehrt, A. and Roden, H., *Terror: Die Blutchronik des Marxismus in Deutschland* (Berlin, 1934), pp. 10–29.

Eiber, L. and Sigel, R. (eds), *Dachauer Prozesse: NS-Verbrechen vor amerikanischen Militärgerichten in Dachau 1945–1948* (Göttingen, 2007).

Eksteins, M., 'War, Memory, and Politics: The Fate of the Film *All Quiet on the Western Front*', *Central European History*, Vol. 13, No. 1 (March, 1980), pp. 60–82.

Eksteins, M., '*All Quiet on the Western Front* and the Fate of a War', *Journal of Contemporary History*, Vol. 15, No. 2 (April, 1980), pp. 345–66.

Eksteins, M., *Rites of Spring: The Great War and the Birth of the Modern Age* (Boston, 2000).

Erpel, S. (ed.), *Im Gefolge der SS: Aufseherinnen des Frauen-KZ Ravensbrück* (Berlin, 2007).

Evans, R. J., *The Coming of the Third Reich* (London, 2004).

Evans, R. J., *The Third Reich in Power* (London, 2006).

Evans, R. J., 'Coercion and Consent in Nazi Germany', *Proceedings of the British Academy*, Vol. 151 (2007), pp. 53–81.

Exenberger, H., 'Was wußte man in Österreich über das KZ Dachau?', *Dachauer Hefte*, Vol. 17 (November 2001), pp. 78–93.

Faatz, M., *Vom Staatsschutz zum Gestapo-Terror: Politische Polizei in Bayern in der Endphase der Weimarer Republik und der Anfangsphase der nationalsozialistischen Diktatur* (Würzburg, 1995).

Fackler, G., *'Des Lagers Stimme': Musik im KZ. Alltag und Häftlingskultur in den Konzentrationslagern 1933–1936* (Bremen, 2000).

Feske, H., *Konservatismus und Rechtsradikalismus in Bayern nach 1918* (Bad Homburg, 1969).

Fischer, C., *Stormtroopers: A Social, Economic and Ideological Analysis* (London, 1983).

Fischer, J. K., *Die Schreckensherrschaft in München und Spartakus im bayerischen Oberland: Tagebuchblätter und Ereignisse aus der Zeit der 'bayrischen Räterepublik' und der Münchner Kommune im Frühjahr 1919* (Munich, 1919).

Fleck, C. and Müller, A., 'Bruno Bettelheim and the Concentration Camps', *Journal of the History of the Behavioral Sciences*, Vol. 33, No. 1 (Winter, 1997), pp. 1–37.

Foucault, M., *Discipline and Punish: The Birth of the Prison* (New York, 1995).

Fränkel, E., *The Dual State: A Contribution to the Theory of Dictatorship* trans. E. Shils (New York, 1969).

Frei, N., '"Machtergreifung": Anmerkungen zu einem historischen Begriff', *Vierteljahrsheft für Zeitgeschichte*, Vol. 31 (Jan., 1983), pp. 136–45.

Frei, N., *Adenauer's Germany and the Nazi Past* (New York, 2000).

Frei, N. et al. (eds), *Standort und Kommandanturbefehl des Konzentrationslagers Auschwitz 1940–1945* (Munich, 2000).

Frevert, U., *Ehrenmänner: Das Duell in der bürgerlichen Gesellschaft* (Munich, 1991).

Frevert, U., *A Nation in Barracks: Modern Germany, Military Conscription and Civil Society* (Oxford, 2004).

Friedländer, S. (ed.), *Probing the Limits of Representation: Nazism and the 'Final Solution'* (London, 1992).

Friedländer, S., *Nazi Germany and the Jews: Volume 1: The Years of Persecution, 1933–1939* (New York, 1997).

Fritz, S. G., *Frontsoldaten: The German Soldier in World War II* (Kentucky, 1997).

Fulbrook, M., *Dissonant Lives: Generations and Violence Through the German Dictatorships* (Oxford, 2011).

Fussell, P., *The Great War and Modern Memory* (Oxford, 1977).

Fussell, P., *Uniforms: Why We Are What We Wear* (New York, 2003).

Gallé, V., 'Karl d'Angelo: Lagerleiter des Konzentrationslagers Osthofen', in Hans-Georg Meyer (ed.), *Die Zeit des Nationalsozialismus in Rheinland-Pfalz*, Vol. 2 (Mainz, 2000).

Garbe, D., 'Selbstbehauptung und Widerstand', in Wolfgang Benz and Barbara Distel (eds), *Der Ort des Terrors: Geschichte der nationalsozialistischen Konzentrationslager*, 8 vols (Munich, 2005–9), Vol. 5, pp. 315–46.

Garbe, D., 'Erst verhasst, dann geschätzt: Zeugen Jehovas als Häftlinge im KZ Dachau', in Benz and Königseder (eds), *Das Konzentrationslager Dachau: Geschichte und Wirkung nationalsozialistischer Repression* (Berlin, 2008), pp. 219–36.

Garnett, R. S., *Lion, Eagle, and Swastika: Bavarian Monarchism in Weimar Germany, 1918–1933* (New York and London, 1991).

Gay, P., *Weimar Culture: The Outsider as Insider* (New York, 1968).

Gellately, R., *Backing Hitler: Consent and Coercion in Nazi Germany* (Oxford, 2001).

Gellately, R. and Stoltzfus, N. (eds), *Social Outsiders in Nazi Germany* (Princeton, 2001).

Geyer, M., *Aufrüstung oder Sicherheit: Die Reichswehr in der Krise der Machtpolitik 1924–1936* (Wiesbaden, 1980).

Geyer, M., *Verkehrte Welt: Revolution, Inflation, und Moderne. München 1914–1924* (Göttingen, 1998).

Gilbert, M., *The Holocaust: The Jewish Tragedy* (London, 1987), pp. 32–3.

Gilbhard, H., *Die Thule Gesellschaft: vom okkulten Mummenschanz zum Hakenkreuz* (Munich, 1994).

Giles, G. J., 'The Denial of Homosexuality: Same-Sex Incidents in Himmler's SS and Police', *Journal of the History of Sexuality*, Vol. 11, No.1 (2002), pp. 256–90.

Goeschel, C., 'Suicide at the End of the Third Reich', *Journal of Contemporary History*, Vol. 41, No. 1 (Jan., 2006), pp. 153–73.

Goeschel, C., *Suicide in Nazi Germany* (Oxford, 2009).

Goeschel, C., 'Suicide in the Nazi Concentration Camps', *Journal of Contemporary History*, Vol. 45, No. 3 (Jul., 2010), pp. 628–48.

Goeschel, C. and Wachsmann, N. (eds), *The Nazi Concentration Camps, 1933–1939: A Documentary History* (Nebraska, 2011).

Goettler, N., *Die Sozialgeschichte des Bezirkes Dachau 1870 bis 1920: Ein Beispiel struktureller Wandlungsprozesse des ländlichen Raumes* (Munich, 1988).

Goffman, E., *Asylums: Essays on the Social Situation of Mental Patients and Other Inmates* (New York, 1961).

Goldhagen, D. J., *Hitler's Willing Executioners: Ordinary Germans and the Holocaust* (London, 1997).

Goldman, N. L. and Segal, D. R. (eds), *The Social Psychology of Military Service* (Beverly Hills and London, 1976).

Goldstein, J. S., *War and Gender: How Gender Shapes the War System and Vice Versa* (Cambridge, 2006).

Grady, T., *The German-Jewish Soldiers of the First World War in History and Memory* (Liverpool, 2011).

Grant, T. D., *Stormtroopers and Crisis in the Nazi Movement: Activism, Ideology and Dissolution* (London and New York, 2004).

Grau, B., *Kurt Eisner 1867–1919* (Munich, 2001).

Gregor, N. (ed.), *Nazism, War and Genocide: Essays in Honour of Jeremy Noakes* (Exeter, 2005).

Gregor, N., 'Nazism—A Political Religion? Rethinking the Voluntarist Turn', in Gregor (ed.), *Nazism, War and Genocide: Essays in Honour of Jeremy Noakes* (Exeter, 2005), pp. 1–21.

Griffin, R., *The Nature of Fascism* (London, 1991).

Gross, R., *Anständig geblieben: Nationalsozialistische Moral* (Frankfurt am Main, 2010).

Gruchmann, L., 'Die bayerische Justiz im politischen Machtkampf 1933/34: Ihr Scheitern bei der Strafverfolgung von Mordfällen in Dachau', in Martin Broszat and Elke Fröhlich (eds), *Bayern in der NS-Zeit*, Vol. 2 (Munich, 1979), pp. 416–21.

Gruchmann, L., *Justiz im Dritten Reich 1933–1940: Anpassung und Unterwerfung in der Ära Gürtner* (Munich, 1988).

Gruner, M., *Verurteilt in Dachau: Der Prozess gegen den KZ-Kommandanten Alex Piorkowski vor einem US-Militärgericht* (Augsburg, 2008).

Guetzkow, H. (ed.), *Groups, Leadership and Men* (Pittsburg, 1951).

Gutman, Y. and Berenbaum, M. (eds), *Anatomy of the Auschwitz Death Camp* (Washington, 1998).

Haffner, S, *Germany: Jekyll and Hyde. An Eyewitness Account of Nazi Germany* (London, 2005 [1940]), pp. 49–64.

Haffner, S., *Defying Hitler: A Memoir* (New York, 2002), pp. 14–18.

Hagemann, K., 'German Heroes: The Cult of the Death for the Fatherland in Nineteenth Century Germany', in Stefan Dudink, Karin Hagemann, and John Tosh (eds), *Masculinities in Politics and War* (Manchester, 2004), pp. 116–31.

Hagemann, K. and Schuler-Springorum, S., *Home/Front: The Military, War, and Gender in Twentieth Century Germany* (Oxford, 2002).

Haney, C., Banks, C., and Zimbardo, P., 'A Study of Prisoners and Guards in a Simulated Prison', *Naval Research Reviews*, Vol. 9 (1973), pp. 1–17.

Haslam, S. A. and Reicher, S., 'Rethinking the Psychology of Tyranny: The BBC Prison Study', *British Journal of Social Psychology*, Vol. 45 (2006), pp. 1–40.

Haslam, S. A. and Reicher, S., 'Response. Debating the Psychology of Tyranny: Fundamental Issues of Theory, Perspective, and Science', *British Journal of Social Psychology*, Vol. 45 (2006), pp. 55–63.

Haslam, S. A. and Reicher, S., 'Identity Entrepreneurship and the Consequences of Identity Failure: The Dynamics of Leadership in the BBC Prison Study', *Social Psychology Quarterly*, Vol. 70, No. 2 (2007), pp. 125–47.

Hein, B., *Elite für Volk und Führer? Die Allgemeine SS und ihre Mitglieder 1925–1945* (Munich, 2012).

Heinemann, I., *'Rasse, Siedlung, deutsches Blut': Das Rasse- und Siedlungshauptamt der SS und die rassenpolitische Neuordnung Europas* (Göttingen, 2003).

Hensle, M. P., 'Die Verrechtlichung des Unrechts: Der legalistische Rahmen der nationalsozialistischen Verfolgung', in Wolfgang Benz and Barbara Distel (eds), *Der Ort des Terrors*, Vol. 1 (Berlin, 2005), pp. 76–90.

Herbert, U., 'Labour and Extermination: Economic Interest and the Primacy of *Weltanschauung* in National Socialism', *Past and Present*, Vol. 138, No. 1 (Jan. 1993), pp. 144–95.

Herbert, U., *Best: Biographische Studien über Radikalismus, Weltanschauung und Vernunft, 1903–1989* (Bonn, 1996).

Herbert, U. (ed.), *National Socialist Extermination Policies: Contemporary German Perspectives and Controversies* (New York and Oxford, 2000).

Herbert, U., Orth, K., and Dieckmann, C. (eds), *Die nationalsozialistischen Konzentrations lager: Entwicklung und Struktur*, 2 vols, (Göttingen, 1998).

Herzog, D. (ed.), *Sexuality and German Fascism* (New York and Oxford, 2005).

Hess, C. et al. (eds), *Kontinuitäten und Brüche: Neue Perspektiven auf die Geschichte der NS-Konzentrationslager* (Berlin, 2011).

Hett, B. C., *Crossing Hitler: The Man Who Put the Nazis on the Witness Stand* (Oxford, 2008).

Hilberg, R., *The Destruction of the European Jews* (London, 1983).

Hilberg, R., *The Politics of Memory: The Journey of a Holocaust Historian* (Chicago, 1996).

Hillmayr, H., 'Rätezeit und Rote Armee in Dachau', *Amperland*, No. 3 (1960), pp. 74–80.

Hinz, U., *Gefangen im Grossen Krieg: Kriegsgefangenschaft in Deutschland 1914–1921* (Essen, 2006).

Hirschfeld, G. and Kettenacker, L. (eds), *Der 'Führerstaat': Mythos und Realität* (Stuttgart, 1981).

Hobsbawm, E., *Age of Extremes: The Short Twentieth Century 1914–1991* (London, 1994).

Hoegner, W., *Die verratene Republik: Geschichte der deutschen Gegenrevolution* (Munich, 1979 [1958]), pp. 109–32.

Hofmann, U. C., *'Verräter verfallen der Feme!': Fememorde in Bayern in den zwanziger Jahren* (Cologne, 2000).

Höhne, H., *The Order of the Death's Head: The Story of Hitler's SS* (London, 1980).

Holborn, H. (ed.), *Republic to Reich: The Making of the Nazi Revolution* (New York, 1972).

Holzhaider, H., '"Schwester Pia". Nutznießerin zwischen Opfern und Tätern', *Dachauer Hefte*, Vol. 10 (1994), pp. 101–14.

Hörath, J., 'Terrorinstrumente der "Volksgemeinschaft"? KZ-Haft für "Asoziale" und "Berufsverbrecher" 1933 bis 1937/38', *Zeitschrift für Geschichtswissenschaft*, Vol. 60, No. 6 (2012), pp. 513–32.

Hörath, J., 'Experimente zur Kontrolle und Repression von Devianz und Delinquenz: Die Einweisung von "Asozialen" und "Berufsverbrechern" in die Konzentrationslager 1933 bis 1937/8' (PhD Dissertation, Frei Universität Berlin, 2012).

Hördler, S. and Jacobeit, S. (eds), *Lichtenburg: Ein deutsches Konzentrationslager* (Berlin, 2009).

Hördler, S., 'SS Kaderschmiede Lichtenburg', in Hördler and Sigrid Jacobeit (eds), *Lichtenburg: Ein deutsches Konzentrationslager* (Berlin, 2009), pp. 75–129.

Horwitz, G. J., *In the Shadow of Death: Living Outside the Gates of Mauthausen* (London and New York, 1991).

Hosking, G., *A History of the Soviet Union* (London, 1985).

Hull, I. V., *Absolute Destruction: Military Culture and Practices of War in Imperial Germany* (Ithaca and London, 2005).

Jäger, H., *Verbrechen unter totalitärer Herrschaft* (Frankfurt am Main, 1982).

Jahnke, K. H. and Buddrus, M., *Deutsche Jugend 1933–1945: Eine Dokumentation* (Hamburg, 1989).

Jahnke, K. H., 'Heinz Eschen: Kapo des Judenblocks im Konzentrationslager Dachau bis 1938', *Dachauer Hefte*, Vol. 7 (1991), pp. 24–33.

Jardim, T., *The Mauthausen Trial: American Military Justice in Germany* (Harvard, 2012).

Jensen, O. and Szejnmann, C. W. (eds), *Ordinary People as Mass Murderers* (Basingstoke, 2008).

Johnson, E., *The Nazi Terror: The Gestapo, Jews and Ordinary Germans* (New York, 2000).

Jolly, C., *The Vengeance of Private Pooley* (Lavenham, 1977 [1956]).

Jureit, U. and Wildt, M. (eds), *Generationen: Zur Relevanz eines wissenschaftlichen Grundbegriffs* (Hamburg, 2005).

Kaienburg, H., *Die Wirtschaft der SS* (Berlin, 2003).

Kanzler, R., *Bayerns Kampf gegen den Bolshevismus* (Munich, 1931).

Kaplan, M., *Between Dignity and Despair: Jewish Life in Nazi Germany* (New York, 1998).

Karl, M., *Die Münchner Räterepublik: Porträts einer Revolution* (Düsseldorf, 2008).

Kárný, Miroslav, 'Waffen-SS und Konzentrationslager', in Ulrich Herbert, Karin Orth, and Christoph Dieckmann (eds), *Die nationalsozialistischen Konzentrationslager*, Vol. 2, pp. 787–99.

Kater, M. H., 'Zum gegenseitigen Verhältnis von SA und SS in der Sozialgeschichte des Nationalsozialismus von 1925 bis 1939', *Vierteljahrschrift für Sozial- und Wirtschaftsgeschichte*, Vol. 62 (1975), pp. 339–79.

Kater, M. H., *Hitler Youth* (Harvard, 2004).

Katz, F. E., 'Implementation of the Holocaust: The Behaviour of Nazi Officials', *Comparative Studies in Society and History*, Vol. 24, No. 3 (Jul. 1982), pp. 510–29.

Kelman, H.C., 'Violence Without Moral Restraint: Reflections on the Dehumanization of Victims and Victimizers', *Journal of Social Issues*, Vol. 29, No. 4 (1973), pp. 25–61.

Kershaw, I., *Popular Opinion and Political Dissent in the Third Reich: Bavaria 1933–1945* (Oxford, 1993).

Kershaw, I., *The Hitler Myth* (Oxford, 2000 [1987]).

Kershaw, I., *Hitler, 1889–1936: Hubris* (London, 1998).

Kershaw, I., *Hitler, 1936–1945: Nemesis* (London, 2000).

Kershaw, I., *The Nazi Dictatorship: Problems and Perspectives of Interpretation* 3rd edn (London, 2000).

Kessler, H., *The Diaries of a Cosmopolitan 1918–1937* (London, 2000 [1971]).

Kimmel, G., 'Das KZ Dachau: Eine Studie zu den nationalsozialistischen Gewaltverbrechen', *Bayern in der NZ Zeit*, Vol. 2 (Munich, 1979), pp. 349–413.

Klausch, H-P., *Tätergeschichten: Die SS Kommandanten der frühen Konzentrationslager im Emsland* (Bremen, 2005).

Klein, E., *Jehovas Zeugen im KZ Dachau: Geschichtliche Hintergründe und Erlebnisberichte* (Bielefeld, 2001).

Knoll, A., 'Totgeschlagen—totgeschwiegen: Die homosexuellen Häftlinge im KZ Dachau', *Dachauer Hefte*, Vol. 14 (1998), pp. 72–93.

Knox, M., *To the Threshold of Power, 1922/33: Origins and Dynamics of the Fascist and National Socialist Dictatorships*, Vol. 1 (Cambridge and New York, 2007).

Koehl, R., *The Black Corps: The Structure and Power Struggles of the Nazi SS* (Winsconsin, 1983).

Koepp, R. G., 'Conservative Radicals: The *Einwohnerwehr, Bund Bayern und Reich*, and the Limits of Paramilitary Politics in Bavaria, 1918–1928' (PhD Dissertation, University of Nebraska, submitted 2010).

Kolb, E., *Die Arbeiterräte in der deutschen Innenpolitik 1918–1919* (Düsseldorf, 1962).

Koonz, C., *Mothers in the Fatherland: Women, the Family and Nazi Politics* (London, 1987).

Koonz, C., *The Nazi Conscience* (Cambridge, MA and London, 2003).

Koslov, E. M., *Gewalt im Dienstalltag: Die SS-Aufseherinnen des Konzentrations- und Vernichtungslagers Majdanek* (Hamburg, 2009).

Kosmala, B., 'Polnische Häftlinge im Konzentrationslager Dachau 1939–1945', *Dachauer Hefte*, Vol. 21 (2005), pp. 94–113.

Krausnick, H., Buchheim, H., Broszat, M., and Jacobsen, H. A., *Anatomy of the SS State* (New York, 1965).

Kren, G. M. and Rappaport, L., *The Holocaust and the Crisis of Human Behaviour* (New York, 1980).

Krüger, G., *Kriegsbewältigung und Geschichtsbewusstsein: Realität, Deutung und Verarbeitung des deutschen Kolonialkrieges in Namibia 1904 bis 1907* (Göttingen, 1999).

Kühne, T., *Kameradschaft: Die Soldaten des nationalsozialistischen Krieges und das 20 Jahrhundert* (Göttingen, 2006).

Lang, B., *Act and Idea in the Nazi Genocide* (Chicago and London, 1990).

Lang, J., 'Questioning Dehumanization: Intersubjective Dimensions of Violence in the Nazi Concentration and Death Camps', *Holocaust and Genocide Studies*, Vol. 24, No. 2 (Fall, 2010), pp. 225–46.

Langbein, H., 'Work in the Concentration Camp', in Wolfgang Benz and Barbara Distel (eds), *Dachau and the Nazi Terror*, Vol. 1 (Dachau, 2002), pp. 64–74.

Langbein, H., *People in Auschwitz* (North Carolina, 2004).

Large, D. C., *The Politics of Law and Order: The Bavarian Einwohnerwehr 1918–1921* (Philadelphia, 1980).

Large, D. C., *Where Ghosts Walked: Munich's Road to the Third Reich* (London and New York, 1997).

Lasik, A., 'Historical-Sociological Profile of the Auschwitz SS', in Yisrael Gutmann and Michael Berenbaum (eds), *Anatomy of the Auschwitz Death Camp* (Washington, 1998), pp. 271–87.

Lifton, R. J., *The Nazi Doctors: Medical Killing and the Psychology of Genocide* (New York, 1986).

Linder, A. P., *Princes of the Trenches: Narrating the German Experience of the First World War* (Columbia, 1996).

Littell, J., *The Kindly Ones* (New York, 2009).

Loewenberg, P., 'The Psychohistorical Origins of the Nazi Youth Cohort', *American Historical Review*, Vol. 76, No. 5 (Dec., 1971), pp. 1457–502.

Lohalm, U., *Völkischer Radikalismus: Die Geschichte des Deutschvölkischen Schutz- und Trutz-Bundes, 1919–1923* (Hamburg, 1970).

Longerich, P., *Die braunen Bataillone: Geschichte der SA* (Munich, 1989).

Longerich, P., *Heinrich Himmler* (Oxford, 2010).

Lüdtke, A., *Eigen-Sinn: Fabrikalltag, Arbeitererfahrung und Politik vom Kaiserreich bis in den Faschismus* (Hamburg, 1993).

Lumsden, R., *Himmler's Black Order: A History of the SS 1923–1945* (Somerset, 1997).

MacLean, F. L., *The Camp Men: The SS Officers Who Ran the Nazi Concentration Camp System* (US, 1999).

Mann, M., 'Were the Perpetrators of Genocide "Ordinary Men" or "Real Nazis"? Results from Fifteen Hundred Biographies', *Holocaust and Genocide Studies*, Vol. 14, No. 3 (Winter, 2000), pp. 331–66.

Mann, M., *Fascists* (Cambridge, 2004).

Mantell, D. M., 'The Potential for Violence in Germany', *Journal of Social Issues*, Vol. 27, No. 4 (1971), pp. 101–12.

Marcuse, H., *Legacies of Dachau: The Uses and Abuses of a Concentration Camp, 1933–2001* (Cambridge, 2001).

Martschukat, J. and Stieglitz, O., *'Es ist ein Junge!': Einführung in die Geschichte der Männlichkeit in der Neuzeit* (Tübingen, 2005).

Mason, T., 'The Legacy of 1918 for National Socialism', in Anthony Nicholls and Erich Matthias (eds), *German Democracy and the Triumph of Hitler: Essays in Recent German History* (London, 1971), pp. 215–39.

Mason, T., 'Intention and Explanation: A Current Controversy about the Interpretation of National Socialism', in Gerhard Hirschfeld and Lothar Kettenacker (eds), *Der 'Führerstaat': Mythos und Realität* (Stuttgart, 1981), pp. 23–42.

Mason, T., *Social Policy in the Third Reich: The Working Class and the 'National Community'* (Oxford, 1993).

Matejka, V., *Widerstand ist Alles: Notizen eines Unorthodoxen* (Vienna, 1984), pp. 78–82

Matthäus, J., 'Historiography and the Perpetrators of the Holocaust', in Dan Stone (ed.), *The Historiography of the Holocaust* (Hants, 2004), pp. 197–215.

Mazower, M., *Dark Continent: Europe's Twentieth Century* (London, 1998).

McCormick, R. W., *Gender and Sexuality in Weimar Modernity: Film, Literature and the New Objectivity* (New York, 2001).

McNeill, W. H., *Keeping Together in Time: Dance and Drill in Human History* (Cambridge, MA, 1996).

Mehringer, H., 'Die KPD in Bayern 1919–1945', in Martin Broszat and Harmut Mehringer (eds), *Bayern in der NS Zeit*, Vol. 5 (Munich, 1983), pp. 110–33.

Merkl, F. J., *General Simon: Lebensgeschichte eines SS-Führers* (Augsburg, 2010).

Merkl, P. H., *The Making of a Stormtrooper* (Princeton, 1980).

Merson, A., *Communist Resistance in Nazi Germany* (London, 1985).

Messenger, C., *Hitler's Gladiator: The Life and Times of Oberstgruppenführer and Panzergeneral-Oberst der Waffen SS Sepp Dietrich* (London, 1998).

Michaelis, R., *Die Waffen SS: Mythos und Wirklichkeit* (Berlin, 2006).

Micheler, S. and Szobar, P., 'Homophobic Propaganda and the Denunciation of Same-Sex-Desiring Men under National Socialism', *Journal of the History of Sexuality*, Vol. 11, No. 1 (Jan.–Apr., 2002), pp. 95–130.

Milgram, S., *Obedience to Authority* (London, 2005 [1974]).

Mitchell, A., *Revolution in Bavaria 1918–1919: The Eisner Regime and the Soviet Republic* (Princeton, 1965).

Moeller, R., 'Dimensions of Social Conflict in the Great War: The View from the German Countryside', *Central European History*, Vol. 14 (1981), pp. 142–69.

Mommsen, H., 'The Reichstag Fire and its Political Consequences', in Hajo Holborn (ed.), *Republic to Reich: The Making of the Nazi Revolution* (New York, 1973), pp. 129–222.

Mommsen, H., 'Die Realisierung des Utopischen: Die 'Endlösung der Judenfrage' im Dritten Reich', *Geschichte und Gesellschaft*, Vol. 9 (1983), pp. 381–420.

Mommsen, H., *From Weimar to Auschwitz: Essays in German History* (Princeton, 1991).

Mommsen, H., *The Rise and Fall of Weimar Democracy* trans. Elborg Forster and Larry Eugene Jones (Chapel Hill, 1996).

Mommsen, H., 'Hannah Arendt's Interpretation of the Holocaust as a Challenge to Human Existence', in Steven E. Aschheim (ed.), *Hannah Arendt in Jerusalem* (Berkeley, 2001), pp. 224–31.

Moore, P., 'German Popular Opinion on the Nazi Concentration Camps, 1933–1939' (PhD Dissertation, University of London, 2010).

Moore, P., '"And what concentration camps those were!": Foreign Concentration Camps in Nazi Propaganda, 1933–1939', *Journal of Contemporary History*, Vol. 45, No. 3 (July 2010), pp. 649–74.

Moore, P., '"The Man Who Built the First Concentration Camp". The Anti-Brown Book of Concentration Camp Commandant Werner Schäfer: Fighting and Writing the Nazi "Revolution"' (Unpublished MS).

Morsch, G. (ed.), *Konzentrationslager Oranienburg* (Berlin, 1994).

Morsch, G., *Mord und Massenmord im Konzentrationslager Sachsenhausen* (Berlin, 2005).

Morsch, G., 'Organisations-und Verwaltungstruktur der Konzentrationslager', in Wolfgang Benz and Barbara Distel (eds), *Der Ort des Terrors: Geschichte der nationalsozialistischen Konzentrationslager*, Vol. 1 (Munich, 2005), pp. 58–75.

Morsch, G., 'Formation and Construction of Sachsenhausen Concentration Camp', in Morsch (ed.), *From Sachsenburg to Sachsenhausen* (Berlin, 2007), pp. 87–194.

Morsch, G. (ed.), *From Sachsenburg to Sachsenhausen* (Berlin, 2007).

Moses, A. D., 'Structure and Agency in the Holocaust: Daniel J. Goldhagen and his Critics', *History and Theory*, Vol. 37, No. 2 (May 1998), pp. 194–219.

Mosse, G. L., *The Crisis of German Ideology: The Intellectual Origins of the Third Reich* (New York, 1981).

Mosse, G. L., *Nationalism and Sexuality: Middle-Class Morality and Sexual Norms in Modern Europe* (Wisconsin, 1985).

Mosse, G. L., *Fallen Soldiers: Reshaping the Memory of the World Wars* (Oxford, 1990).

Mosse, G. L., *The Image of Man* (Oxford, 1996).

Mühlberger, D., *Hitler's Followers: Studies in the Sociology of the Nazi Movement* (London, 1991), p. 188.

Musiol, T., *Dachau 1933–1945* (Katowic, 1968).

Neitzel, S. and Welzer, H., *Soldaten: On Fighting, Killing, and Dying* (London, 2012).

Neuengamme Memorial Site (ed.), *Entgrenzte Gewalt: Täter und Täterinnen im Nationalsozialismus. Beiträge zur ns Verfolgung in Norddeutschland*, Vol. 7 (2003).

Neugebauer, W., 'Der erste Österreichertransport in das KZ Dachau 1938', in Wolfgang Benz and Angelika Königseder (eds), *Das Konzentrationslager Dachau: Geschichte und Wirkung Nationalsozialistischer Repression* (Berlin, 2008), pp. 193–205.

Nicholls, A., 'Hitler and the Bavarian Background to National Socialism', in Nicholls and Eric Matthias (eds), *German Democracy and the Triumph of Hitler: Essays in Recent German History* (London, 1971), pp. 99–128.

Nicholls, A. and Matthias, E. (eds), *German Democracy and the Triumph of Hitler: Essays in Recent German History* (London, 1971).

Noakes, J., 'Nazism and Eugenics: The Background to the Nazi Sterilization Law of 14 July 1933', in Roger Bullen et al. (eds), *Ideas into Politics: Aspects of European History 1880–1950* (London, 1984), pp. 75–94.

Noakes, J. and Pridham, G. (eds), *Nazism 1939–1945*, 4 vols (Exeter, 1983–1998).

Oosterhuis, H., 'Male Bonding and Homosexuality in Nazi Germany', *Journal of Contemporary History*, Vol. 32, No. 2 (Apr. 1997), pp. 187–205.

Orth, K., *Das System der nationalsozialistischen Konzentrationslager: Eine politische Organisationsgeschichte* (Hamburg, 1999).

Orth, K., *Die Konzentrationslager SS: Sozialstrukturelle Analysen und Biographische Studien* (Munich, 2004), pp. 127–52.

Orth, K., 'Egon Zill: ein typischer Vertreter der Konzentrationslager-SS', in Klaus-Michael Mallmann and Gerhard Paul (eds), *Karrieren der Gewalt* (Stuttgart, 2004).

Overy, R., *The Dictators: Hitler's Germany and Stalin's Russia* (New York, 2004).

Overy, R., 'Das Konzentrationslager: Eine internationale Perspektive', *Mittelweg*, Vol. 36, No. 4 (2011), pp. 40–5.

Parker, I., 'Obedience', *Granta*, Vol. 71 (Autumn, 2000), pp. 99–126.

Paul, G. (ed.), *Die Täter der Shoah: Fanatische Nationalsozialisten oder ganz normale Deutsche?* (Göttingen, 2002).

Paul, G., 'Von Psychopathen, Technokraten des Terrors und "ganz gewöhnlichen" Deutschen: Die Täter der Shoah im Spiegel der Forschung', in Paul (ed.), *Die Täter der Shoah: Fanatische Nationalsozialisten oder ganz normale Deutsche?* (Göttingen, 2002).

Pauley, B. F., *Hitler and the Forgotten Nazis: A History of Austrian National Socialism* (North Carolina, 1981).

Pendas, D. O., *The Frankfurt Auschwitz Trial, 1963–1965: Genocide, History, and the Limits of the Law* (Cambridge, 2006).

Peukert, D. J. K., *Inside Nazi Germany: Conformity, Opposition and Everyday Life* (London, 1982).

Phelps, R. H., '"Before Hitler Came": Thule Society and Germanen Ordnen', *Journal of Modern History*, Vol. 35 (1963), pp. 245–61.

Pingel, F., *Häftlinge unter SS-Herrschaft: Selbstbehauptung, Widerstand und Vernichtung im nationalsozialistischen Konzentrationslager* (Hamburg, 1978).

Pingel, F., 'Social Life in an Unsocial Environment: The Inmates' Struggle for Survival', in Jane Caplan and Nikolaus Wachsmann (eds), *Concentration Camps in Nazi Germany: The New Histories* (London and New York, 2010).

Plant, R., *The Pink Triangle: The Nazi War Against Homosexuals* (New York, 1986).

Pridham, G., *Hitler's Rise to Power: The Nazi Movement in Bavaria, 1923–1933* (London, 1973).

Raim, E., 'Westdeutsche Ermittlungen und Prozesse zum KZ Dachau und seinen Aussenlagern', in Eiber and Sigel, *Dachauer Prozesse: NS-Verbrechen vor amerikanischen Militärgerichten in Dachau 1945–1948* (Göttingen, 2007), p. 214.

Reich, W., *The Mass Psychology of Fascism* trans. Vincent R. Carfagno (Harmondsworth, 1983).

Reichardt, S., *Faschistische Kampfbünde: Gewalt und Gemeinschaft im italienischen Squadrismus und in der deutschen SA* (Cologne, 2002).

Reitlinger, G., *The SS: Alibi of a Nation 1922–1945* (London, 1981).

Rempel, G., *Hitler's Children: The Hitler Youth and the SS* (North Carolina, 1989).

Richardi, H. G., *Schule der Gewalt: Das Konzentrationslager Dachau 1933–1934* (Munich, 1983).

Riedel, D. A., 'Der "Wildpark" im KZ Dachau und das Außenlager St. Gilgen', *Dachauer Hefte*, Vol. 16 (2000), pp. 54–70.

Riedel, D. A., *Kerker im KZ Dachau: Die Geschichte der drei Bunkerbauten* (Dachau, 2002).

Riedel, D. A., *Ordnungshüter und Massenmorder im Dienst der Volksgemeinschaft: Der KZ-Kommandant Hans Loritz* (Berlin, 2010).

Riedle, A., *Die Angehörigen des Kommandanturstabs im KZ Sachsenhausen: Sozialstruktur, Dienstwege und biografischen Studien* (Berlin, 2011).

Rohe, K., *Das Reichsbanner Schwarz Rot Gold: Ein Beitrag zur Geschichte und Struktur der politischen Kampfverbände zur Zeit der Weimarer Republik* (Düsseldorf, 1966).

Rohrkamp, R., *'Weltanschaulich gefestigte Kämpfer': Die Soldaten der Waffen-SS 1933–1945* (Paderborn, 2010).

Roseman, M. (ed.), *Generations in Conflict: Youth Revolt and Generation Formation in Germany 1770 to 1968* (Cambridge, 1995).

Rosenfeld, G. D., 'Monuments and the Politics of Memory: Commemorating Kurt Eisner and the Bavarian Revolutions of 1918–1919 in Postwar Munich', *Central European History*, Vol. 30, No. 2 (1997), pp. 221–51.

Rosenhaft, E., *Beating the Fascists? The German Communists and Political Violence 1929–1933* (Cambridge, 1983).

Ross, L. and Nisbett, R. E., *The Person and the Situation: Perspectives of Social Psychology* (New York, 1991).

Russell, N. J. C., 'Stanley Milgram's Obedience to Authority Experiments: Towards an Understanding of their Relevance in Explaining Aspects of the Nazi Holocaust' (PhD thesis, Victoria University of Wellington, 2009).

Ryback, T. W., *The Last Survivor: In Search of Martin Zaidenstadt* (New York, 1999).

Schalm, S., *Überleben durch Arbeit? Außenkommandos und Außenlager des KZ Dachau 1933–1945* (Berlin, 2009).

Schenk, D., *Hans Frank: Hitlers Kronjurist und Generalgouverneur* (Frankfurt am Main, 2006).

Schilde, K. and Tuchel, J., *Columbia-Haus: Berliner Konzentrationslager 1933–1936* (Berlin, 1990).

Schilling, R., *'Kriegshelden': Deutungsmuster heroischer Männlichkeit in Deutschland 1913–1945* (Paderborn, 2002).

Schley, J., *Nachbar Buchenwald: Die Stadt Weimar und ihr Konzentrationslager 1937–1945* (Cologne, 1999).

Schmolze, G. (ed.), *Revolution und Räterepublik in München 1918–1919 in Augenzeugenberichten* (Munich, 1969).

Schoenbaum, D., *Hitler's Social Revolution: Class and Status in Nazi Germany 1933–1939* (New York, 1966).

Schönhoven, K., *Die Bayerische Volkspartei 1924–1932* (Düsseldorf, 1972).

Schricker, R., *Rotmord über München* (Berlin, 1934).

Schulte, J. E. (ed.), *Die SS, Himmler und die Wewelsburg* (Paderborn, 2009).

Schulze, H., *Freikorps und Republik 1918–1920* (Boppard, 1969).

Schumann, D., *Political Violence in the Weimar Republic 1918–1933: Fight for the Streets and Fear of Civil War* (New York and Oxford, 2009).

Schuster, K., *Der Rote Frontkämpferbund 1924–1929* (Düsseldorf, 1975).

Schwarz, G., *Eine Frau an seiner Seite: Ehefrauen in der 'SS-Sippengemeinschaft'* (Hamburg, 1997).

Schwarz, J., *Die bayerische Polizei und ihre historische Funktion bei der Aufrechterhaltung der öffentlichen Sicherheit in Bayern von 1919 bis 1933* (Munich, 1977).

Sebag-Montefiore, H., *Dunkirk: Fight to the Last Man* (London, 2007).

Segev, T., *Soldiers of Evil: The Commandants of the Nazi Concentration Camps* (London, 2000 [1977]).

Seligmann, M., *Aufstand der Räte* (Grafenau, 1989).

Sémelin, J., *Purify and Destroy: The Political Uses of Massacre and Genocide* (New York, 2005).

Sereny, G., *Into that Darkness: From Mercy Killing to Mass Murder* (London, 1974).

Seubert, R., '"Mein lumpiges Vierteljahr Haft . . ." Alfred Anderschs KZ-Haft und die ersten Morde von Dachau: Versuch einer historiografischen Rekonstruktion', in Jörg Dörig and Markus Joch (eds), *Alfred Andersch 'Revisited': Werkbiographische Studien im Zeichen der Sebald-Debatte* (Berlin, 2011), pp. 47–146.

Shils, E. A. and Janowitz, M., 'Cohesion and Disintegration in the Wehrmacht in World War II', *The Public Opinion Quarterly*, Vol. 12, No. 2 (Summer 1948), pp. 280–315.

Shirer, W. L., *The Rise and Fall of the Third Reich: A History of Nazi Germany* (New York, 1960).

Siemens, D., *The Making of a Nazi Hero: The Murder and Myth of Horst Wessel* (London, 2013).

Sigel, R., 'Heilkräuterkulturen im KZ: Die Plantage in Dachau', *Dachauer Hefte*, Vol. 4 (1988), pp. 164–73.

Siggemann, J., *Die kasernierte Polizei und das Problem der inneren Sicherheit in der Weimarer Republik: Eine Studie zum Auf-und Ausbau des innerstaatlichen Sicherheitssystems in Deutschland 1918/1919–1933* (Frankfurt am Main, 1980).

Smelser, R., *Die SS: Elite unter dem Totenkopf. 30 Lebensläufe* (Paderborn, 2000).

Smith, B. F. and Peterson, A. (eds), *Heinrich Himmler: Geheimreden 1933 bis 1945* (Frankfurt, 1974).

Smith, B. F., *Heinrich Himmler: A Nazi in the Making* (Stanford, 1974).

Sofsky, W., *The Order of Terror: The Concentration Camp* (Princeton, 1997).

Spalek, J. M., 'Ernst Toller: The Need for a New Estimate', *The German Quarterly*, Vol. 39, No. 4 (Nov., 1966), pp. 581–98.

Sprenger, M., *Landsknechte auf dem Weg ins Dritte Reich? Zu Genese und Wandel des Freikorpsmythos* (Paderborn, 2008).

Springmann, V., '"Sport machen": eine Praxis der Gewalt im Konzentrationslager', in Wojciech Lenarczyk et al. (eds), *KZ-Verbrechen: Beiträge zur Geschichte der nationalsozialistischen Konzentrationslager und ihrer Erinnerung* (Berlin, 2007), pp. 89–101.

Stachura, P., *Nazi Youth in the Weimar Republic* (Santa Barbara, CA, 1975).

Staub, E., 'The Psychology of Perpetrators and Bystanders', *Political Psychology*, Vol. 6, No. 1 (Mar., 1985), pp. 61–85.

Staub, E., *The Roots of Evil: The Origins of Genocide and Other Group Violence* (Cambridge, 1997).

Stein, G. H., *Waffen SS: Hitler's Elite Guard at War 1939–1945* (Bristol, 2002).

Steinbacher, S., *Dachau: Die Stadt und das Konzentrationslager in der NS-Zeit* (Frankfurt, 1993).

Steinbacher, S., *'Musterstadt' Auschwitz: Germanisierungspolitik und Judenmord in Ostoberschlesien* (Munich, 2000),

Stephenson, J., *Women in Nazi Society* (London, 1975).

Stephenson, S., *The Final Battle: Soldiers of the Western Front and the German Revolution of 1918* (Cambridge, 2009).

Stibbe, M., *Women in the Third Reich* (London, 2003).

Stone, D. (ed.), *The Historiography of the Holocaust* (Hants, 2004).

Striefler, C., *Kampf um die Macht: Kommunisten und Nationalsozialisten am Ende der Weimarer Republik* (Berlin, 1993).

Sun, R. C., '"Hammer Blows": Work, the Workplace, and the Culture of Masculinity Among Catholic Workers in the Weimar Republic', *Central European History*, Vol. 37, No. 2 (2004), pp. 245–71.

Sydnor, C. W., *Soldiers of Destruction: The SS Death's Head Division, 1933–1945* (Princeton, 1977).

Szejnmann, C. W., *Nazism in Central Germany: The Brownshirts in 'Red' Saxony* (New York, 1999).

Tennenbaum, J., 'Auschwitz in Retrospect: The Self-Portrait of Rudolf Hoess, Commander of Auschwitz', *Jewish Social Studies*, Vol. 15, No. 3/4 (Jul.–Oct., 1953), pp. 203–36.

Theweleit, K., *Male Fantasies. Vol 1: Women, Floods, Bodies, History* (Minneapolis, 1987).

Theweleit, K., *Male Fantasies. Vol 2: Male Bodies: Pyschoanalysing the White Terror* (Minneapolis, 2003).

Todorov, T., *Facing the Extreme: Moral Life in the Concentration Camps* (London, 2000).

Tooze, A., *The Wages of Destruction: The Making and Breaking of the Nazi Economy* (London, 2007).

Tosh, J., 'What Should Historians Do With Masculinity? Reflections on Nineteenth Century Britain', *History Workshop Journal*, Vol. 38, No. 1 (1994), pp. 179–202.

Tosh, J., 'Hegemonic Masculinity and the History of Gender', in Dudink et al. (eds), *Masculinities in Politics and War* (Manchester, 2004), pp. 41–58.

Treml, M., *Geschichte des modernen Bayern: Königreich und Freistaat* (Munich, 2006).

Tuchel, J., 'Selbstbehauptung und Widerstand in nationalsozialistischen Konzentra-tionslagern', in Jürgen Schmädeke and Peter Steinbach (eds), *Der Widerstand gegen den Nationalsozialismus: Die deutsche Gesellschaft und der Widerstand gegen Hitler* (Munich and Zurich, 1985), pp. 938–53.

Tuchel, J., *Konzentrationslager: Organisationsgeschichte und Funktion der 'Inspektion der Konzentrationslager' 1934–1938* (Boppard, 1991).

Tuchel, J., *Die Inspektion der Konzentrationslager 1934–1938: Das System des Terrors* (Berlin, 1994).

Tuchel, J., 'Die Kommandanten des Konzentrationslagers Flossenbürg: Eine Studie zur Personalpolitik in der SS', in Helge Grabitz, Klaus Bästlein, and Tuchel (eds), *Die Normalität des Verbrechens: Bilanz und Perspektiven der Forschung zu den nationalsozialis-tischen Gewaltverbrechen* (Berlin, 1994), pp. 201–19.

Tuchel, J., 'The Commandants of the Dachau Concentration Camp', in Wolfgang Benz and Babara Distel (eds), *Dachau and the Nazi Terror: Studies and Reports* (Dachau, 2002), pp. 223–45.

Turner, H. A., *Hitler's Thirty Days to Power: January 1933* (London, 1996).

Verhey, J., *The Spirit of 1914: Militarism, Myth, and Mobilization in Germany* (Cambridge, 2000).

Volkmann, H-E. (ed.), *Das Russlandbild im Dritten Reich* (Cologne, 1994).

Wachsmann, N., 'Marching under the Swastika? Ernst Jünger and National Socialism in the Weimar Republic', *Journal of Contemporary History*, Vol. 33, No. 4 (July, 1998), pp. 573–89.

Wachsmann, N., *Hitler's Prisons: Legal Terror in Nazi Germany* (New Haven and London, 2004).

Wachsmann, N., 'Looking into the Abyss: Historians and the Nazi Concentration Camps', *European History Quarterly*, Vol. 36, No. 2 (2006), pp. 247–78.

Wachsmann, N., 'The Dynamics of Destruction: The Development of the Concentration Camps 1933–1945', in Wachsmann and Jane Caplan (eds), *Concentration Camps in Nazi Germany: The New Histories* (London and New York, 2010), pp. 1–43.

Wachsmann, N. and Steinbacher, S. (eds), *Die Linke im Visier: Zur Errichtung der Konzentrationslager 1933* (Munich, 2014).

Wachsmann, N., 'KL: A History of the Nazi Concentration Camps' (Unpublished MS).

Wagner, P., *Volksgemeinschaft ohne Verbrecher: Konzeption und Praxis der Kriminalpolizei in der Zeit der Weimarer Republik und des Nationalsozialismus* (Hamburg, 1996).

Waite, G. L., *Vanguard of Nazism: The Free Corps Movement in Postwar Germany 1918–1923* (Cambridge, MA, 1952).

Waller, J., *Becoming Evil: How Ordinary People Commit Genocide and Mass Murder* (Oxford, 2007).

Watt, R. M., *The Kings Depart: The German Revolution and the Treaty of Versailles 1918–1919* (London, 1973 [1968]).

Weale, A., *The SS: A New History* (London, 2010).

Wegner, B., *The Waffen SS: Organisation, Ideology and Function* (Oxford, 1990).

Weingartner, J. J., 'Sepp Dietrich, Heinrich Himmler, and the Leibstandarte SS Adolf Hitler, 1933–1938', *Central European History*, Vol. 1, No. 3 (Sep., 1968), pp. 264–84.

Weingartner, J. J., *Hitler's Guard: The Story of the Leibstandarte SS Adolf Hitler 1933–1945* (London, 1974).

Weisbrod, B., 'Military Violence and Male Fundamentalism: Ernst Jünger's Contribution to the Conservative Revolution', *History Workshop Journal*, Vol. 49, No. 2 (Spring 2000), pp. 68–94.

Weisbrod, B., 'The Hidden Transcript: The Deformation of the Self in Germany's Dictatorial Regimes', *German Historical Institute London Bulletin*, Vol. 34, No. 2 (Nov., 2012), pp. 61–72.

Weitz, E. D., *Creating German Communism, 1890–1990: From Popular Protests to Socialist State* (Princeton, 1997).

Welch, D., *The Third Reich: Politics and Propaganda* (London, 2002).

Welzer, H., *Täter: Wie aus ganz normalen Menschen Massenmörder werden* (Frankfurt am Main, 2005).

Westermann, E., *Hitler's Police Battalions: Enforcing Racial War in the East* (Kansas, 2005).

Wette, W., *The Wehrmacht: History, Myth, Reality* (Cambridge, MA and London, 2006).

Whatmore, H., 'Exploring KZ "Bystanding" within a West-European Framework: Natzweiler-Struthof, Neuengamme and Vught-Herzogenbusch', in Christiane Heß, Julia Hörath, Dominique Schröder, and Kim Wünschmann (eds), *Kontinuitäten und Brüche. Neue Perspektiven auf die Geschichte der NS-Konzentrationslager* (Berlin, 2011), pp. 64–79.

Wildmann, D., *Begehrte Körper: Konstruktion und Inszenierung des 'arischen' Männerkörpers im 'Dritten Reich'* (Würzburg, 1998).

Wildt, M., *Generation des Unbedingten: Das Führungskorps des Reichssicherheitshauptamtes* (Hamburg, 2002).

Wildt, M., *Volksgemeinschaft als Selbstermächtigung: Gewalt gegen Juden in der deutschen Provinz 1919–1939* (Hamburg, 2007).

Wildt, M., *An Unconditional Generation: The Nazi Leadership of the Reich Security Main Office* (Wisconsin, 2009).

Williamson, G., *Die SS: Hitlers Instrument der Macht* (Klagenfurt, 1998).

Wirsching, A. (ed.), *Das Jahr 1933: Die nationalsozialistische Machtoberung und die deutsche Gesellschaft* (Göttingen, 2009).

Wittman, R., *Beyond Justice: The Auschwitz Trial* (Harvard, 2012).

Wootton, G., *The Official History of the British Legion* (London, 1956).

Wünschmann, K., 'Cementing the Enemy Category: Arrest and Imprisonment of German Jews in Nazi Concentration Camps, 1933–1938/39', *Journal of Contemporary History*, Vol. 45, No. 3 (July 2010), pp. 576–600.

Wünschmann, K., '"Natürlich weiß ich, wer mich ins KZ gebracht hat und warum . . ." Die Inhaftierung von Juden im Konzentrationslager Osthofen 1933/34', in Andreas Ehresmann, Philipp Neumann, Alexander Prenninger, and Régis Schlagdenhauffen (eds), *Die Erinnerung an die nationalsozialistischen Konzentrationslager: Akteure, Inhalte, Strategien* (Berlin, 2011), pp. 97–111.

Wünschmann, K., 'Jewish Prisoners in Nazi Concentration Camps, 1933–1939' (PhD Dissertation, University of London, 2012).

Wünschmann, K., 'Before Auschwitz: Jewish Prisoners in Nazi Concentration Camps 1933–1939' (Unpublished MS).

Wünschmann, K., 'Die Konzentrationslagererfahrungen deutsch-jüdischer Männer nach dem Novemberpogrom 1938: Geschlechtergeschichtliche Überlegungen zu männlichem Selbstverständnis und Rollenbild' (Unpublished MS).

Yerger, M. C., *Allgemeine SS: The Commanders, Units and Leaders of the General SS* (USA, 1997).

Zámečnik, S., *That Was Dachau 1933–1945* (Paris, 2004).

Zarusky, J., 'Die juristische Aufarbeitung der KZ-Verbrechen', in Wolfgang Benz and Barbara Distel (eds), *Der Ort des Terrors: Geschichte der nationalsozialistischen Konzentrationslager* (Munich, 2005), pp. 345–62.

Ziemann, B., 'Republikanische Kriegserinnerung in einer polarisierten Öffentlichkeit: Das Reichsbanner Schwarz-Rot-Gold als Veteranenverband der sozialistischen Arbeiterschaft', *Historische Zeitschrift*, Vol. 267, No. 2 (Oct., 1998), pp. 357–98.

Ziemann, B., *War Experiences in Rural Germany 1914–1923* (Oxford, 2007).

Zimbardo, P., 'On the Psychology of Imprisonment: Alternative Perspectives from the Laboratory and TV Studio', *British Journal of Social Psychology*, Vol. 45 (2006), pp. 47–53.

Zimbardo, P., *The Lucifer Effect: How Good People Turn Evil* (London, 2007).

# Index

Printed and bound by CPI Group (UK) Ltd, Croydon, CR0 4YY